ALSO BY ANDREW E. KERSTEN

Labor's Home Front: The American Federation of Labor During World War II

Race, Jobs, and the War: The FEPC in the Midwest, 1941–46

A. Philip Randolph: A Life in the Vanguard

Clarence Darrow

CLARENCE DARROW

American Iconoclast

ANDREW E. KERSTEN

HILL AND WANG
A division of Farrar, Straus and Giroux
New York

Hill and Wang
A division of Farrar, Straus and Giroux
18 West 18th Street, New York 10011

Copyright © 2011 by Andrew E. Kersten
All rights reserved
Distributed in Canada by D&M Publishers, Inc.
Printed in the United States of America
First edition, 2011

Library of Congress Cataloging-in-Publication Data
Kersten, Andrew Edmund, 1969–
  Clarence Darrow : American iconoclast / Andrew E. Kersten.—1st ed.
    p. cm.
  Summary: "A new biography of American legal giant Clarence Darrow"—
Provided by publisher.
  Includes bibliographical references and index.
  ISBN 978-0-8090-9486-8 (hardback)
  1. Darrow, Clarence, 1857–1938.   2. Lawyers—United States—
Biography.   I. Title.

KF213.D3K47 2011
340.092—dc22
[B]

2010054369

Designed by Abby Kagan

www.fsgbooks.com

1   3   5   7   9   10   8   6   4   2

FOR MY GRANDFATHER,

Irving W. Kersten

Contents

Preface

I imagine Clarence Darrow would have winced at the thought of yet another biography. Certainly it was not because the celebrated lawyer was afraid of the airing of his imperfections. As he once told an adoring crowd of unionists, "most lawyers only tell you about the cases they win. I can tell you about some I lose."[1] And it is not because he wanted to avoid scrutiny. He wrote two autobiographies, a few pieces of fiction, and dozens of statements of his political and philosophical beliefs. Indeed, there was a time when he worried that his life might be forgotten. "I fear that I shall die, and future generations will never know that I have lived," he wrote in 1904, "or I am quite certain that no one else will ever write my story."[2] But historians, journalists, lawyers, playwrights, filmmakers, and avid admirers have produced numerous accounts of his life and his work. What could be left to say?

Further, Darrow might have thought twice about my writing this biography. In many ways, I'm not like those who have come before. I am not directly connected to the grand tradition of writers on the left. I have no legal training, nor am I a part of any crusading lawyer's quest. I have not dedicated my life in pursuit of understanding or investigating or memorializing Darrow's life and legal career. But those deficits aside, I do share a long-standing fascination with America's greatest attorney. My first introduction to him came when I was a young boy. In 1975, my father's mother died, and my grandfather, to whom I've dedicated this book and who had suffered a massive stroke just weeks before my birth, moved into a nursing home. His and his wife's book collection ended up in my family's garage. On slow, hot summer days, I often dug through those boxes, hoping for old baseball cards and finding neat books instead. Among my first discoveries was Irving Stone's *Clarence Darrow for the Defense*, the abridged paperback edition, now held together with a rubber band. For thirty years, I have turned to Stone's Darrow for my sensibilities, for comfort, and for inspiration. Yet up to now that passion has been private. I cherish Darrow for the same reasons others do. Darrow lived life fearlessly, sometimes recklessly. But if you were in trouble, he was the lawyer you wanted, and he was the friend you needed. He was extraordinarily kind and sensitive, especially to those in need and to those less fortunate. He noted no distinction among people. This in part explains why Darrow is the subject of more than one loving biography, poem, and work of art. This biography does not share that devotion, though I admire Darrow and his life's work very much. What it does add to the literature is an emphasis on his politics. In my view, what made Darrow an American icon was his social and political activism. Although we can see his life as a compendium of cases, many of them major, groundbreaking ones, I argue that his importance to United States history is not so much as a jurist but as a politico. It was Darrow's dedication to transforming American and even world politics that explains his life, and it is through the prism of nineteenth-century and early-twentieth-century politics that Darrow can be seen and understood.

From the end of the Civil War through the era of Franklin D. Roosevelt, American politics was defined by a struggle between the haves and the have-nots. For nearly his entire life, and with a few exceptions, Clarence Darrow sided with the latter against the former. He was the attorney, representative, and spokesman for the poor, weak, and oppressed. He hated and railed against those people, organizations, and institutions that chained the less fortunate to horrible, torturous fates. He saw it as his mission to help defeat conspiracies against the lowly members of society and against liberty and freedom. Always a pessimist, Darrow never held out great hope that his battles would result in a permanent victory. Rather, it was the fight, regardless of results, that Darrow was interested in. He was a scrappy lawyer who used his brashness and brains in the courtroom, and importantly outside it too, to move his goals forward.

A lifetime of service to expand and defend freedom and liberty and on behalf of the downtrodden, unionists, radicals, condemned men, skeptics, and those individuals striving to live thoughtful, peaceful lives has earned Darrow lasting historical reverence. But Darrow was no paragon of virtue. His significant foibles, faults, and failures—personal, professional, and political—dramatically influenced his life and the lives of his clients, comrades, and colleagues in various social and political movements. In modern political parlance, Darrow was occasionally a flip-flopper. His political commitments and loyalties were not always firmly held. Further, his philosophy of life was full of contradictions. Darrow was not a systematic thinker, and at times he acted in unthoughtful, self-serving, and even unethical ways. He was always more comfortable with his inconsistencies, fickle commitments, and bad behavior than his contemporaries were. As we shall see, Darrow disappointed a lot of people by changing his mind on political and social issues, by pushing the boundaries of professional propriety, and by giving up pledges and alliances.

It's hardly surprising that Darrow was human. No more than anyone else's, Darrow's life was not neat and involved inexplicable twists and turns. However, it is clear that he adhered to several irreducible core philosophical and political principles throughout his life. Darrow was a skeptic and a pessimist. He fundamentally thought that reality was essentially evil and that happiness was just beyond reach. How one carves out an existence in this world—he cared little for thoughts of an afterlife—was a lifelong project. Darrow was squarely political left, although he never joined the Socialist Party and remained a Democrat, more or less, since he began voting in the late nineteenth century. He did not reject capitalism, but he did believe that it was the state's duty to ameliorate the sad condition of the working class. Additionally, he devoted much of his life in politics and in the courtroom to rectifying the injustices that plagued the typical American. Darrow was an iconoclast; he was dedicated to smashing the structures and systems of social control that impinged on the liberties and freedoms of average people and that caged their aspirations. To do that, he sometimes believed that the ends justified the means, that he had to give up former and very publicly expressed views, and that he had to abandon friends and allies and collaborate with politicians and political movements he normally would not have. Darrow was far from perfect or irreproachable, as his former friends, former law partners, and enemies loved to point out. Darrow was a flawed champion of freedom and liberty. Darrow's story is decidedly not the chronicle of a saint; it's the story of a legal and political genius who, despite his defects, missteps, and errors, advanced democracy in America and around the world. Darrow remained true to his core beliefs throughout his adult life. What changed were the movements and causes that he supported. As a young man he was dedicated to the labor movement and fought for it as a means to help average Americans. As he grew older, Darrow became increasingly pessimistic about mass political movements of all kinds. In time, he even abandoned his allegiance to organized labor, choosing instead to fight a handful of such social structures as the death penalty and white supremacy so that regardless of their station in life, individuals had a chance to live as they chose. Thus, over the course of his life, Darrow distilled, sifted, winnowed, and shifted through his commitments and causes while maintaining a public and political fidelity to supporting the advancement of freedom and liberty, especially civil liberties and civil rights.

This biography is largely about Darrow's political activism inside and outside court. Consequently, his early years are not as important as other biographers have purported. His parents were freethinkers and political radicals, but that inheritance was less sizable than others have made out. I grant that Darrow drew inspiration from his parents. However, most of his political and social hobbyhorses were his own. Moreover, if Amirus and Emily Darrow's influence was so overwhelming to Clarence's development, why did his siblings not take up similar political causes? Darrow's childhood was, as Henry Adams declared of his own famous family, "rather an atmosphere than an influence."[3] Darrow's early surroundings were indeed important, but they were not as predictive and as transformative as the most decisive moment in his life, his move to Chicago in 1887. When Darrow entered America's quintessential Gilded Age city, it was in the midst of an epic, bitter, and bloody struggle between capital and labor. By day Darrow worked for the capitalists, and by night he spoke out against the pillage and plunder of the robber barons. Eventually he had to make a choice, and he concluded that he could not, as he put it, "wear the collar of any corporation."[4] Backing labor over capital changed his life, his fate, and his fortune. Had he gone the other way, he probably would have become a railroad mogul himself, or a mayor, or a governor, or a U.S. senator. Instead, he became America's most famous and long-lived public crusader.

Clarence Darrow

❊ 1 ❊

A Midwestern Childhood

Clarence Darrow read autobiographies and biographies with suspicion. He disliked their self-serving nature, particularly those beginning with a list of famous ancestors. "The purpose of linking themselves by blood and birth to some well-known family or personage," he wrote, stimulated only the ego and little else.[1] Like most people's, Clarence Darrow's distant relatives had no direct connection to him other than to set in motion a series of events that eventually resulted in his birth. That said, Darrow's immediate family and his childhood, especially the relationships with his mother and father, mattered to some degree. But those youthful experiences did not create the Clarence Darrow, that transformative and towering historical figure, that we know. Darrow's story is not a slow march to greatness and influence. Rather, his initial notions about right and wrong, about fairness and equality, and about citizenship and liberty sprang from his childhood experiences and his environment, the rural Midwest.

Despite writing about his childhood himself, Darrow had misgivings about exploring the "sacred ground" of his youth.[2] We ought to heed his warning, especially since most of the information about his childhood comes from his own writings. Like others who have written about their pasts, Darrow sometimes blurred the lines between reporting his life and artfully creating it. It is best to see his two autobiographies—especially the second, which was published in 1932 and titled *The Story of My Life*—as the iconoclastic lawyer's closing statements in the defense of his reputation and legacy. Both works have truths in them, but both are also part of Darrow's project to build his own public image as a hedonistic pessimist, a skeptic, and an unerring, unstinting, and unflappable champion of freedom and liberty. But as we shall see, Darrow made mistakes, distilled his views, winnowed his causes, and changed his alliances. All this is largely absent in his own writings about his life. As he explained in *The Story of My Life*, "autobiography is never entirely true."[3] This much we know: Darrow's family was an old one and one that belonged to the working class and had at various times fought privilege. Tongue in cheek, he once wrote that some Darrow genealogists claimed a relationship with Adam and Eve, but that he "should not like to guarantee the title."[4] In fact, his pedigree went back to England, likely among the lower sorts who came to the New World seeking the fortunes that they were unable to make in the Old. "But this does not matter," Darrow wrote dismissively. "I am sure that my forbears [*sic*] run a long, long way back of that, even—but what of it anyhow?"[5] Darrow saw himself as a product of chance, not relatives. He stood at the end of a long line of historical accidents, odd twists, and freak happenings. "When I think of the chances that I was up against," he remarked, "it scares me to realize how easily I might have missed out. Of all the infinite accidents of fate farther back of that, I do not care or dare to think." And ever the pessimist, at the end of his life, he mockingly wrote that "had I known about life in advance and been given any choice in the matter, I most likely would have declined the adventure."[6] Darrow was correct: he did not have that choice. But he was not a completely self-made man. For Darrow, that familial atmosphere of which Henry Adams spoke was as much about place as about a family whose members were revolutionaries and skeptics and farmers who struggled to eke out a living.

In 1630, the first Darrow arrived in the New World. He was among a party of sixteen that held a royal land grant for the town of New London, Connecticut, along the Thames River, where they scratched out a meager existence. These Connecticut Darrows were also revolutionaries, forgetting, as Clarence put it, "the lavish gift of the King" in order to fight at Bunker Hill, Valley Forge, and Brandywine.[7] Thus Darrow once joked that he was eligible for membership in the Daughters of the American Revolution, "although

I would not exactly fit their organization, for, amongst other handicaps, I am proud of my rebel ancestry."[8]

The Connecticut Darrows prospered moderately for more than a century and a half before branching out. In 1795, the Ammiras Darrow family left Connecticut for Boonville, a small town in upstate New York. Financial success remained just beyond the family's reach, so in 1824, after Ammiras's passing, his son (and Clarence's grandfather) Jedediah led his spouse and seven children on another trek west along the Lake Trail, which ran parallel to the bluffs along Lake Erie. This arduous and long five-hundred-mile trip led them to Trumbull County, Ohio. Their reward was inexpensive but excellent farmland in Kinsman.

Clarence Darrow's maternal ancestors, the Eddys, shared a similar migration story following the same path to the Western Reserve. Darrow rightly estimated that both families were "poor and obscure, else they would have stayed where they were."[9] John and Samuel Eddy arrived in Plymouth in 1630. Later, like so many of his contemporaries, Great-grandfather Eddy drove west with purpose, moving to Connecticut, then to upstate New York, and finally to Windsor, Ohio, in the Western Reserve.[10]

The families homesteaded two dozen miles apart. Given that distance in the mid-nineteenth century, it was highly unlikely for a Darrow and an Eddy to meet, let alone marry and raise a family. But Amirus Darrow and Emily Eddy—Clarence's parents—did meet and fall in love while attending Ellsworth Academy in Amboy, Ohio, thirty-five miles from Windsor and sixty from Kinsman. The Eddys, who were quite well off, had no trouble sending Emily, but the Darrows had to scrape together the money to send Amirus. Emily Eddy and Amirus Darrow became schoolyard sweethearts with a shared passion for reading. Amirus's thirst for knowledge and his zeal for books were legendary in Clarence's hometown. Amirus had a personal library unlike any other. In his 1893 reminiscence, Kinsman native Colonel Ralph Plumb recalled that "nearly every house had a Bible and an almanac, but beyond that books were very scarce." A neighbor might have another book, like "Riley's *Narrative* [but that] was lent from house to house and did good work in cultivating a taste for reading."[11] Outside the family, Amirus's book collection must have seemed an outlandish, immoral indulgence. Even Clarence Darrow thought it odd that his parents were such bibliophiles. No one else in either extended family was. Aside from one of his mother's brothers who "seemed fairly well-informed," Darrow could not remember another relative who "cared at all for books." Furthermore, Emily's parents "were inclined to believe that a love of books was a distinct weakness, and likely to develop into a very bad habit."[12] Darrow said the same of his father's family. However, this was no mere bad habit. Amirus never had much money, yet he bought books like an aristocrat. His house was littered with them. "They were in bookcases, on tables, on chairs, and even on the floor. The house was small, the family large, the furnishings meager, but there were books whichever way one turned."[13]

Like their parents, Amirus and Emily Darrow emphasized education in their children's upbringing, even to the point of straining the family's finances. Amirus was a learned man. In 1845, after they graduated from Ellsworth Academy, Emily and Amirus married and moved to Meadville, Pennsylvania, so Amirus could attend Allegheny College, a Methodist institution. He did not finish. Likely his faith in Methodism ended after the schism in the American Methodist Church over slavery. Instead, Amirus and Emily, who had become abolitionists, joined the Unitarian congregation in Meadville. In 1849, Amirus completed his theology degree but decided not to become a minister. By that time, he and his wife both were freethinkers, who sought the answers to life's questions through investigation, reason, and rigorous debate. They were also political activists, seeking justice for the oppressed.

Perhaps the most meaningful and influential part of Clarence's childhood relates to his parents' freethinking beliefs. Amirus and Emily belonged to one of the most important intellectual, political, and cultural movements of the nineteenth and early twentieth centuries. Freethinkers influenced all aspects of American life from politics and politicians such as Abraham Lincoln (1809–1865) to social movements like abolitionism and women's rights. Both Amirus and Emily adopted free thought well before its golden age between Reconstruction and the First World War. Historian Susan Jacoby has defined American free thought as an encompassing philosophy "running the gamut from the truly antireligious—those who regarded all religion as a form of superstition and wished to reduce its influence in every aspect of society—to those who adhered to a private, unconventional faith revering some form of God or Providence but at odds with orthodox religious authority."[14] What united freethinkers was a "rationalist approach to fundamental questions of earthly existence—a conviction that the affairs of human beings should be governed not by faith in the supernatural but by a reliance on reason and evidence adduced from the natural world."[15] Both Amirus and Emily were avid readers of the great American and French skeptics, they participated in free thought–inspired movements to emancipate slaves and married women, and they were unflinching supporters of public education. And yet they celebrated Christmas, and Emily never completely broke from the church. Moreover, unlike many freethinkers, Emily was a temperance advocate. Thus, as freethinkers Darrow's parents were middle of the road.

In 1849, forgoing any idea of becoming a minister and a minister's wife, Amirus and Emily, along with their two sons, Everett and Channing, moved to Farmdale, Ohio, a short distance from Kinsman. Amirus took up the trades of his forefathers and became a furniture maker as well as an undertaker. Emily assumed the role of the rural housewife, managing the household and taking care of their children: Edward Everett (who went by Everett), born in 1846; Channing, born in 1849; Mary, in 1852; Herbert (who died in infancy), in 1854; Clarence, in 1857; Hubert, in 1860; Herman, in 1863; and, finally, Jenny, in 1869. All but Everett, Channing, and Jenny were born in Farmdale. The family had moved back to Kinsman in 1864. Both Kinsman and Farmdale were small, rural towns that owed their existence to the banking, insurance, legal, agricultural, and modest cultural services that they offered farmers. They were the places for farmers to buy implements, sell their produce, mail letters and packages, consult a lawyer, deposit money, attend holiday parades, and join local celebrations.

Darrow maintained an uneasy love affair with his childhood hometown. Kinsman was confining, stilted, intolerant, and homogeneous, but it also was as ageless as it was idyllic. Nestled in a sleepy green valley near the west bank of the Shenango River Lake, and close to Pymatuning, Stratton, and Sugar creeks, Kinsman had the indelible mark of a New England village, as the writers of Ohio's Work Progress Administration guide described it.[16] It was also a quintessential small Ohio town—much like the hometowns of other Ohio notables: Sherwood Anderson (1876–1941), Thomas Edison (1847–1931), Ulysses S. Grant (1822–1885), Rutherford B. Hayes (1822–1893), and William Dean Howells (1837–1920). Kinsman had a gristmill, a sawmill, a blacksmith, a shoemaker (in whose shop men met to argue about politics), a carriage factory, a town square, a whiskey distillery, a tavern, a

few churches—Presbyterian, Methodist, and Catholic—and houses that
denoted the class of the townspeople. The largest houses were near the center of town, with the fanciest of them prominently positioned on one end of
the town square.

Kinsman was known both for its groves of heavy timber—especially
oak, beech, maple, hickory, chestnut, elm, and white pine—and for its soil,
which was "of a superior quality," according to the *History of Trumbull and
Mahoning Counties*.[17] Most farmers grew corn and raised cows, chickens,
and pigs. They made money, however, from the wheat crop. Kinsman never
had a large population, at most a few hundred, and from a child's perspec-
tive the town seemed rather staid and uninspiring. "If I had chosen to be
born I probably should not have selected Kinsman, Ohio, for that honor,"
Darrow wrote in his second autobiography. "[I]nstead, I would have started
in a hard and noisy city where the crowds surged back and forth as if they
knew where they were going, and why." Yet Darrow could never escape the
fact that his intellectual roots were in small-town America. As he wrote in
the very next sentence of that later autobiography, "my consciousness returns to the old place. My mind goes back to Kinsman because I lived there
in childhood, and to me it was once the centre of the world."[18]

His first book, a semiautobiographical novel, *Farmington*, was a thinly
disguised reminiscence of his hometown. Looking back after he had already established himself as a crusading lawyer and a political insider of
national significance, Darrow claimed that the roots of his philosophy of life
had sprung from the homespun, sleepy confines of rural Ohio. Midwestern
farm life, he wrote, taught him some cherished basic life lessons about pessimism, fatalism, and skepticism as well as about liberty, freedom, democracy, and tolerance. In these rural areas, neighbors depended upon one
another so much as to look past and forgive what they might label as antisocial behavior—of course, within reason. Tolerance, even of town skeptics
like Clarence's father, was a valued ideal. Moreover, Darrow imbibed and
imbued midwestern sensibilities about charity, decency, fairness, and citizenship. Like his neighbors, he cherished the liberties and freedoms that
rural life afforded, from owning land to profiting from hard labor. At the
same time, he came to reject the darker sides of small-community life, particularly its tendency to promote intellectually suffocating homogeneity, especially in church and in school, and certain kinds of provincialism that

were antithetical to skepticism. He also drew other, more saturnine philosophical lessons from his childhood in Trumbull County that eventually lent themselves to his pessimistic outlook on life.

Clarence Darrow had a similarly complex relationship with his immediate family. With only a few exceptions, he claimed his siblings hardly had any significant impact upon his life, and as an adult he did not keep close tabs on most of them. "I was only one of a large family, mostly older than myself; but while I was only one, I was the chief one, and the rest were important only as they affected me," he wrote egotistically.[19] And there was a pecking order among the young Darrows. "It must have been the rule of our family that each of the children should have the right to give orders to those younger than himself." At work or at play, the children rarely got along. "We quarreled," he wrote, "simply because we liked to hurt each other."[20] Chores also brought out their ugly side. "We children were supposed to help with the chores around the house; but, as near as I can remember, each one was always afraid that he would do more than his share."[21] Of course, the exception was when someone was ill. In his first autobiography, Darrow recalled a time when his brother, most likely Everett, was quite sick. "I was wretched with fear and grief," he recounted. "I remember how I went over every circumstance of our relations with each other, and how I vowed that I would always be kind and loving to him if his life were saved."[22] The brother lived, but the young Clarence did not change; neither did anyone else in the family. Darrow blamed it on their New England roots. His parents, he surmised, "were raised in the Puritan school of life, and I fancy that they would have felt that demonstrations of affection were signs of weakness rather than of love."[23]

Although they had his respect and admiration later in his life, Darrow felt alienated from his parents. "Both my father and mother must have been kind and gentle and tender to the large family that so sorely taxed their time and strength; and yet, as I look back, I do not have the feeling of closeness that should unite the parents and the child."[24] Still, they did affect the man Darrow became. And while most biographers have focused heavily on Amirus's role as father and as a teacher, believing that he had the greatest responsibility in shaping his son, Clarence himself believed that it was his *mother*, not his father, who was more influential in his life.[25]

Sadly, we don't know much about Emily or her relationship with Clarence.

In his 1932 autobiography, he praised her maternal abilities. She was "efficient and practical" and was "the one who saved the family from dire want" as her husband spent much of the family's income on books. She also made up for Amirus's lack of business and financial acumen. Darrow felt "that it was her ability and devotion that kept us together, that made so little go so far, and did so much to give my father a chance for the study and contemplation that made up the real world in which he lived."[26] Thus, "through my mother's good sense my father was able to give his children a glimpse into the realm of ideas and ideals in which he himself really lived."[27] Little is known about Emily's outlook on life. She was a prohibitionist and women's rights advocate. She shared her husband's views on religion, slavery, prohibition, and party politics. Darrow remembered her taking him to temperance rallies. She also shared Amirus's parenting skills. "I cannot recall that my mother ever gave me a kiss or a caress," Darrow wrote. But he did remember "that when I had a fever, and lay on my bed for what seemed endless weeks, she let no one else come near me by day or night . . . she seemed ever beside me with the tenderest and gentlest touch."[28]

Why we don't know more about Emily is unclear. Her quiet, stern, and stolid parenting might have kept Clarence too far from her emotionally for him to remember more. Further, she died young after a short illness at the age of forty-eight, in 1871, when Clarence was fourteen years old. He was away from home at the time and "never could tell whether I was sorry or relieved that I was not there."[29] He did remember "the blank despair that settled over the home when we realized that her tireless energy and devoted love were lost forever."[30] The cause of death was never determined. Darrow biographer Charles Yates Harrison asserted that "years of drudgery for her visionary husband and her children at last took their toll."[31] Or she may have contracted a viral infection that devastated her body. No one knows for sure. Despite the family's status as the village freethinking outsiders, much of Kinsman turned out for the funeral and burial next to Herbert near the Presbyterian church. It was a shock that never left Clarence, and her early death may have caused him to exaggerate her influence upon him. Regardless, upon reflection years later, he marked her death as a moment that "awakened me to conscious life."[32] In other words, he grew up after his mother's death and to her "infinite kindness and sympathy" owed some substantial part of the empathy for which he would be known.

There is no denying the intellectual inheritance of Clarence's freethinking father, but it was not as large or immediate as others have surmised. Clarence and Amirus had a close, meaningful, yet difficult and contentious relationship. Later in life, Darrow was quite sympathetic to him. He praised his father's character, writing that Amirus was a "just and upright man," "kind and gentle" as well as "a visionary and dreamer," always with his nose in a book.[33] "Even when he sorely needed the money he would neglect his work to read some book."[34] Amirus stayed up late to read and write. His penchant for reading over work partly made him an outcast among his neighbors, who adhered apparently both to Puritan ideals of labor and to Ben Franklin's quips about industry and thrift. They still bought his furniture and utilized his undertaking services, but they were skeptical about his commitment to his family and to the community. To add further injury to his social repute, Amirus avoided church. In Kinsman, the Presbyterians outnumbered all other denominations, and they had the largest church on the tallest hill. Amirus came to reject Christianity, not just Presbyterianism. Because of his affinity for book learning and his rejection of congregational life, Amirus became "the village infidel."[35] His life was rather lonely, especially after Emily died. The only two neighbors who visited Amirus regularly were the old Presbyterian parson and the town doctor, both of whom came to talk about ideas and books. Likely only they comprehended the unquenchable thirst for knowledge that drove Darrow's father to stay up late at night in scholarly pursuit.[36] Darrow never found out what his father was researching. Amirus spent his adult life laboring under his lamps, hoping his reading and writing would propel him out of Kinsman. They never did. "Years of work and resignation had taught him to deny [his ambitions] even to himself, and slowly and pathetically he must have let go his hold upon that hope and ambition which alone make the thoughtful man cling fast to life."[37]

All that reading and writing did convince Amirus Darrow that there was more to life than Kinsman, and he wanted his children to experience it. As his famous son wrote, "he looked at the high hills to the east, and the high hills to the west, and up and down the narrow country road that led to the outside world. He knew that beyond the high hills was a broad inviting plain, with opportunity and plenty, with fortune and fame; but as he looked at the hills he could see no way to pass beyond." As Amirus gave up his ambitions, "he slowly looked to his children to satisfy the dreams that life once held out to him."[38] Like his parents, Darrow's father thought that the way out of Kinsman was a sound education. Clarence himself did not remember a time when he did not read. Probably under Emily's tutelage, it started with lettered blocks on the kitchen floor and gradually moved to books. Darrow learned his letters "quickly and early" but not as early as Everett, who was something of a prodigy.[39] Amirus fiercely pushed his children, telling them when they complained that his idol, the British philosopher and women's rights advocate John Stuart Mill (1806–1873), had begun studying Greek when he was only three years old. Darrow felt that Mill's father must have been a "cruel" and "unnatural" parent who made miserable not only "the life of his little boy, but thousands of other boys whose fathers could see no reason why their sons should be outdone by John Stuart Mill."[40] Regardless, Clarence pressed on with his lessons. Darrow despised his Latin studies perhaps most of all and argued with his father about their utility, telling his teacher that he did "not want to be a scholar" and that he would have no use for Latin.[41] His father weathered the storm stoically and then made his son recite the Roman word for "table" in every case. "Slowly and painfully," he learned *mensa, mensae, mensae, mensam, mensa,* and *mensa.*[42] Despite his griping, Darrow had access to the town's, probably the county's, best library. It was there that he came to share his parents' love of reading, though not necessarily what his father wanted him to read. Still, he read what they read: Thomas Jefferson (1743–1826), Thomas Paine (1737–1809), Jean-Jacques Rousseau (1712–1778), and Voltaire (1694–1778). He also encountered Charles Darwin (1809–1882), Thomas H. Huxley (1825–1895), Robert G. Ingersoll (1833–1899), and Herbert Spencer (1820–1903). As an adult he came to adore these thinkers and writers.

Radical free thought was only one element of the atmosphere in the Darrow home; there was a political charge to it too. Like his parents, Clarence became quite an active and engaged citizen but, significantly, *not* as a young man. Amirus and Emily were integrally involved in the major political and social reform movements of the antebellum period. Both were abolitionists and thus members of the most important and successful reform movement of the nineteenth century. They were not alone. Trumbull County was antislavery territory. Local abolitionist leaders met in the Darrows' distinctive octagon-shaped house, and Clarence remembered hearing about Frederick

Douglass (1818–1895), Sojourner Truth (c. 1797–1883), Wendell Phillips (1811–1884), and John Brown (1800–1859). Darrow lore maintains that the household was a stop for the Underground Railroad, but it is very unlikely that Amirus and Emily would have risked their young family even for such a noble cause. Abolitionist work was extraordinarily dangerous.[43]

Similarly implausible is Irving Stone's claim that Clarence Darrow met John Brown, who allegedly "put his hand on the boy's head and said, 'The Negro has too few friends; you and I must never desert him.'"[44] Darrow was two when Brown was hanged for his raid on the arsenal at Harpers Ferry. Nonetheless, the Darrow home was always open to agitators and reformers who wandered through, looking for a warm meal, a soft bed, and sympathetic company on their journeys.

Debunked myths do not diminish the Darrow family's commitment to ending slavery. Amirus and Emily named three of the first four sons after famous abolitionists. Everett was named after Edward Everett (1794–1865), who must have appealed to Amirus for many reasons. He was the first American to earn a Ph.D. Like Amirus, Everett was also a Unitarian minister who had put down the collar for other pursuits. Everett, who became noted for his two-hour oration at Gettysburg before President Abraham Lincoln's legendary brief closing remarks, became a Whig representative and later a senator from Massachusetts and was a moderate politician but at times outspoken on the issue of slavery. Likewise, the Darrows named their second son Channing to honor William Ellery Channing (1780–1842), the Unitarian minister, prolific writer, and early abolitionist. Clarence Seward Darrow's namesake was William Henry Seward (1801–1872), also an abolitionist, who helped found the Republican Party and became Lincoln's secretary of state. Appreciative of the political allusion of his middle name, Clarence never liked his first name, which he thought was inane.[45]

Abolitionism was only one part, albeit an important one, of Amirus's and Emily's political views. They were attracted to all sorts of progressive and radical ideas, including prohibition and nineteenth-century environmental design. For example in 1864, Amirus and Emily purchased one of the few octagonal houses in the nation. Built in the 1850s, the house owed its design to Orson Squire Fowler (1809–1887), a phrenologist and sex scientist who advocated the shape as a way to increase sunshine and ventilation in the house, reduce heating costs, and facilitate communication between rooms and thus among family members. In short, it was to make the family more comfortable and interconnected. Thus, as Fowler wrote, his "*radical* improvement of both external form and internal arrangement" was designed "to bring comfortable dwellings within the reach of the poorer classes."[46] According to Clarence, the Darrows' house as well as Amirus' and Emily's freethinking beliefs made them "strangers in a more or less hostile land."[47]

In truth, Kinsman was not all that hostile to the Darrows, who lived largely unaccosted by their neighbors. Amirus reveled in his status as the village infidel, which did not cost him much standing or business in the small town.[48] The Darrow children were always able to make many friends. As Clarence wrote, the neighbors "thought [his father was] queer but hardly dangerous." Moreover, "they didn't carry any dislike of him to his children."[49] In fact, as soon as they could, Amirus and Emily sent their children to school, which despite its advantages did not emphasize free thought in the least. Darrow later figured that "schools probably became general and popular because parents did not want their children about the house all day." They were "a place to send them to get them out of the way." And "if, perchance, they could learn something it was so much to the good."[50] For its time, Ohio's tax-supported public education system was certainly adequate. Darrow claimed that there was never "a time when I did not like to go to school."[51] However, he seemed to hate all his teachers and all his subjects.[52] His introduction to public education hardly augured well. Decades after his first day of school, he still remembered events quite clearly. He was four, and his older brothers and sister had walked him to the schoolhouse. "After being in school for hours, I must have grown weary and restless, sitting so motionless and still." And then the teacher disciplined Clarence by boxing his ears. He ran out of the classroom and all the way home, his "bitter tears" sprinkling "every foot of the way."[53] Darrow harbored his anger for years.

Darrow dismissed his early education, the cornerstone of which was the series of McGuffey's Eclectic Readers. It did not prepare him well for a life as public crusader and politico. William Holmes McGuffey (1800–1873), who had also grown up in Trumbull County, Ohio, was an ordained Presbyterian minister and an early advocate of the free, common schools. In the 1830s, he began publishing his primers as a way not only to advance literacy but also to improve the morality of America's youth. Even sixty years after reading them, Darrow recalled the religious and ethical stories. He thought them "silly." But when he was a child, "it never occurred to me that those tales were utterly impossible lies which average children should have seen through."[54] Through his readers, McGuffey sought to inculcate inhibitions to things that Darrow believed were not only enjoyable but also part of American freedom. For example, there was this ditty about avoiding tobacco: "I'll never chew tobacco / No, it is a filthy weed. I'll never put it in my mouth / Said little Robert Reed." Or this one: "He'd puff along the open streets as if he had no shame. He'd sit beside the tavern door / And there he'd do the same." He also recalled the prohibitionist lines and implied threats in this refrain spoken from a girl's point of view: "The lips that touch liquor / Shall never touch mine." Spurning McGuffey's readers, which had become obsolete by the 1930s, Darrow gleefully wrote that "from what I see and hear of the present generation I should guess that Doctor McGuffey and his ilk lived in vain."[55]

Aside from the readings from McGuffey, boys spent a considerable time practicing "pieces," or small speeches, while girls worked on perfecting their essay style. The last day of school was devoted to showcasing the pupils' talents. Darrow remembered one year when his father was able to attend. The boys had memorized pieces about patriotism, valor in battle, and temperance. Darrow especially recalled a red-haired boy with freckles and a short neck who recited "How Have the Mighty Fallen," which was about Alexander, Caesar, and Napoleon and how they all failed because of strong ambition and strong drink. Although Darrow had presented a good piece, on the way home his father praised the other boy, saying that he had "all the elements of an orator, and he predicted that some day he would make his mark in the world."[56] Either careless or intentionally cruel, Amirus had crushed Clarence.[57]

Darrow seemed to enjoy only two things during his early school years: lunch and recess. Although his mother may have sent him off to school to clear the house, she routinely packed his favorites: "a dinner-pail full of pie and cake, and now and then a piece of bread and butter."[58] The lunch hour with its recess was "the best time by far of all the day." He loved not only the food, but also the break, which gave the boys time to play baseball.[59] To say that Darrow had a passion for the game would be an incredible understatement. And his lifelong obsession began in grade school.

"At the threshold of life," Darrow wrote, he graduated to the Kinsman

Academy. Built in 1842 at the end of a nationwide economic downturn, the structure was incomplete. Hence, as Trumbull County history explains, the building was "plain" but "well proportioned, commodious, neatly and substantially built."[60] Unlike the case in district school, now his teachers were men. Regardless of the change, Darrow had no taste for the curriculum. "As I look back at my days at the district school and the academy, I cannot avoid a feeling of the appalling waste of time."[61] Indeed, that education prepared him little for what he was to discover in Chicago and did not give him the tools to battle for liberty, freedom, and justice. He hated history, which was taught "not for any special purpose, or, seemingly, with any end in view, but it was necessary that we put in the time."[62] The students learned the names of kings, presidents, and generals, "but none of it had any relation to our lives." They studied the Egyptians, Greeks, and Romans as well as the English, French, and Germans. "Caesar and Hannibal and Napoleon" might as well have "inhabited Mars, so far as we students were concerned."[63] Memorizing facts, dates, and people served no purpose. Worse, according to Darrow, it distorted and confused any understanding of the past.

Similarly, Darrow found his study of grammar and pronunciation wasted time since according to him, it was habit and environment that taught appropriate speech. His continued instruction in Latin was "absolutely devoid of practical value," and learning "Greek was even more useless and wasteful of time and effort."[64] He said the same for geometry. Apparently, all he got out of the academy were refined baseball skills. As Darrow explained, "we now were older and stronger and more fleet of foot, and took more pride in the way we played."[65] After graduation in 1872, he left for Allegheny College, the same school his father had briefly attended. He spent only a year there, and learned little, although he was exposed to zoology and geology, which he liked. But the financial panic of 1873 wiped out what little money the family had saved for Darrow. Sounding a bit like Henry Adams, he wrote, "So I abandoned further school life and began my education."[66]

Darrow returned home from college "a better ball player for my higher education."[67] Without any other prospects, he went to work with his father. He hated making furniture. It brought up only bad memories from his younger days when his dad had tried to teach him woodworking laced with instruction in Latin. Darrow had cried and fussed to no avail. Returning to the workshop only reinforced his aversion to "manual labor" and his belief that he "was made for better things."[68]

In the winter of his return to Kinsman, Darrow began teaching in a county district school in Vernon, Ohio, about seven miles south. He earned a dollar a day "and found," which meant that during the week he boarded with the local families of his pupils. Darrow loved that. Either out of genuine midwestern hospitality or an attempt to impress their child's teacher, the parents served fine meals, always making sure that he had plenty of pie and cake, which he craved. His students ranged from seven to twenty years, and they adored their teacher, who devised a curriculum around some unorthodox beliefs. Here was a budding iconoclast at work. On the first day, Darrow announced that the students had nothing to fear as he promised not to hit them. There would be no boxing of ears for any reason whatsoever. Then he lengthened the time allotted for lunch hour as well as recess, which he recalled later "made me a hit with the pupils but brought criticism from their parents."[69] Shrugging off the scorn, he joined in the students' games, especially baseball when snow had not completely covered the diamond. He taught for three winters. "Whether [his students] learned much or little, they certainly enjoyed" their time at school.[70]

It was during these years teaching in the classroom that Darrow began to read law books. Unlike some of his contemporaries and peers, such as Henry Demarest Lloyd (1847–1903), who became lawyers in order to become reformers, Darrow was never sure why or "what influenced [him] to make this choice."[71] In fact, he once wrote that he was "never quite sure why [he did] any particular thing, or why [he did] not do it."[72] As for becoming a lawyer, half jokingly, he said that he "never intended to work with my hands, and no doubt I was attracted by the show of the legal profession."[73] He had seen lawyers before, especially on the Fourth of July, and was impressed by what he had seen.

In rural America in the nineteenth century, the Fourth of July was the major summer event, and Darrow loved it. He loved it more than Thanksgiving, which President Abraham Lincoln had made a national holiday in 1863. Darrow thought that holiday was simply "stupid."[74] "No one paid much attention to New Year's, and generally the people worked that day the same as any other," he recalled. The only holiday that came close to the

Fourth was Christmas, and Darrow did like Christmas. Both holidays were "made for boys."[75] Somewhat ironically, the freethinking Amirus and Emily celebrated Christmas with their children, and all received gifts from Santa Claus. Although "Christmas was a happy day to us children," over time Darrow became more and more uncomfortable with the holiday, and not merely because he was a skeptic like his parents.[76] Rather, he realized that the gift giving must have been a drain on his money-strapped parents.[77] In his later years Darrow saw Christmas as a "duty and burden" and nothing more.[78] The Fourth, however, was another matter entirely.

For Darrow and his buddies, the holiday began before daylight. They would gather at the blacksmith's shop and help themselves to two anvils. His friend who was the tin shop man's son borrowed a long rod of iron and a charcoal stove. Somehow they also acquired a good amount of gunpowder. They would march just outside town, turn one of the anvils upside down, fill it with the powder, and put the other anvil on top. Then they would trail the powder to a safe distance and use the heated iron rod to ignite it. "A mighty roar reverberated down the valley and up the sides of the hills to their very crests."[79] After "saluting the citizens whom we especially wished to favor or annoy," they wandered down to the town square and fired the anvils again.[80] As day broke, they returned home for some sleep and breakfast. Refreshed, Darrow and his gang returned to the town square armed with firecrackers. In this, they were not alone. More daring (and less intelligent) boys demonstrated their prowess by holding in their hands the lit firecrackers until they exploded. Some even held them in their teeth. Darrow commented that "this last exploit was considered dangerous, and generally was done only on condition that we gave a certain number of firecrackers to the boy who took the risk."[81] The odor of saltpeter hung heavily over the morning, and the adults often rebuked the boys for encouraging rain.

The Independence Day celebration drew most of the county. Crowds of several thousand were not unheard of. At about nine o'clock a military procession of the local militia, fire companies, veterans, band, clergy, and the town council and mayor signaled the start of the day's events. After drills in the town square, there would be a reading of the Declaration of Independence. Townspeople listened in reverence to the sacred text. As a boy Darrow hated that. It interrupted his fun. Worse, the Declaration was read by Squire Dudley Allen, one of the richest men in town and his father's friend. Laboriously, Dr. Allen put on his "gold spectacles; then he took a drink of water from a pitcher that stood on a stand on the platform; then he came to the front of the platform and said: 'Friends and fellow-citizens: The exercises will begin by reading the Declaration of Independence.'"[82] Darrow's only thought was: When will it end? "Of course, I knew nothing about the Declaration of Independence, and neither did the other boys. We thought it was something Squire Allen wrote, because he always read it, and we did not think anyone else had a right to read the Declaration of Independence."[83]

After he finished, Dr. Allen introduced the speaker of the day. One of them made an indelible impression upon the young Darrow. He was a lawyer from Warren, the county seat some twenty miles away. What first struck Darrow was his fine horse and fancy buggy, parked at the local hotel.[84] The lawyer seemed not a "bit afraid to stand up there on the platform before the audience." He wore nice clothes—"a good deal nicer than those of the farmers and other people who came to hear him talk."[85] In a loud, impassioned voice, he spoke about the "Bridish [sic]" and "waved his hands and arms a great deal." He spoke about freedom, the war, and the Grand Army of the Republic. "We must stand by the Declaration of Independence and the flag," he said, "and be ready to fight and to die if we ever had a chance to fight and die." The farmers roared with approval, and Darrow was left beaming at this "mighty smart man," a "great man, and thoroughly patriotic."[86] Darrow went home that night—after the picnic of cold chicken (which he despised); the toasts to the flag, the nation, abolitionism, public education, and the president; and the pyrotechnics—thinking that the Fourth of July "was the best day of all the year."[87] Later, stuck in Kinsman, teaching those farmers' children, he decided that he wanted to be that lawyer, not to save the world or aid the meek. Rather, it was his ticket out of that small town in Ohio's Western Reserve and perhaps to a comfortable life.

To Darrow, becoming a lawyer was a way to become rich and famous, to make a mark, and to have some fun. Becoming the attorney for the damned was yet to be conceived and something that awaited him in Chicago. It certainly was not a product of his upbringing or his immediate surroundings. In Kinsman, lawyering was something of a sport. There the tinner (the same man who lent some of his wares to the boys for the Fourth of July) was also the justice of the peace. Darrow never missed a chance to go over to his shop when a case was on trial. He wrote: "I enjoyed the way the pettifoggers abused each other."[88] Darrow even tried the game himself. While teaching in the district school, he became active in the Saturday night debates, a weekly Kinsman event. Typically, his sister Mary, who was by then a local schoolteacher, helped him prepare. Darrow consistently took the anti position. He was a lifelong contrarian. He became invigorated after his opponent sat down following an ovation. Then, in front of the hostile crowd of four hundred, Darrow drew great pleasure from, as Irving Stone vividly put it, "flailing against minds that were as sprung and shut as an iron trap over the broken leg of an animal."[89] In his early debates, Darrow tried to imitate America's most famous polemicist, Robert G. Ingersoll, who was first known as a political orator and later as a freethinker who earned the appellation "the Great Agnostic." In the 1860s, Ingersoll had made a career as an outspoken abolitionist, stumping for Republican candidates. After the war, he vigorously defended civil rights and was a constant thorn in President Andrew Johnson's (1808–1875) side. By the 1870s, Ingersoll had begun speaking on other topics as well, most famously on Tom Paine's ideology and religious skepticism. At this early juncture, Darrow did not seem as impressed by Ingersoll's philosophy of life as he later was. Rather, it was his passionate, fluid, logical, witty, and flowery—but not extravagant—style that he wanted to capture. But the drawling, slow midwestern speech did not quite match the Ingersoll method. As Darrow wrote, "I made up my mind that I could not be Ingersoll . . . the best I could do was to be myself."[90]

When Darrow announced to the family that he intended to become a lawyer, he found his brother Everett, his sister Mary, and his father quite supportive. In fact, although Darrow did not seem to remember, his father had briefly left the family in 1864 and spent one unsuccessful academic year at the University of Michigan Law School. Both Everett, who was now teaching school in Chicago, and Mary, who was teaching grade school near Kinsman, had spent time at the University of Michigan as well. So, unsurprisingly, they urged Clarence to go there too. One of the stumbling blocks was the cost. But Amirus, Everett, and Mary helped pay the twenty-five-dollar tuition and the twenty-five-dollar fee for coming from out of state. Of his brother and sister, Darrow said: "[T]hey were both as self-sacrificing and kind as any human beings I have ever known."[91]

Darrow spent one uneventful academic year in Ann Arbor. In 1878, he moved to Youngstown, Ohio, and began working for a lawyer's office. Once he had learned the ropes, he appeared at the Tod House Bar for his examinations. The lawyers, whom Darrow described as "all good fellows" who "wanted to help us through," were happy to see him.[92] Like the freethinkers Abraham Lincoln and Robert Ingersoll, he passed without much formal training and became a member of the Ohio bar that day. Later, writing in the 1930s, he reflected on how much the bar associations had changed, arguing that the bar had become dedicated "to keep[ing] new members out of the closed circle." He continued: "The Lawyers' Union is about as anxious to encourage competition as the Plumbers' Union is, or the United States Steel Co. or the American Medical Association."[93] He maintained that this hurt only the poor, who lacked the means to attain a fancy education or to forge the political connections that propel one's legal career. Regardless, in 1878, Darrow, now twenty-one, returned to Kinsman a regular lawyer, not a crusading one, who with some luck would address approving Fourth of July crowds. He showed up at the octagonal house to tell his widowed father the good news. Amirus, now fifty-nine, "was delighted, and possibly surprised, at my good luck. . . . Poor man, he was probably thinking what he could have done had Fortune been so kind to him." Neighbors too were proud and similarly surprised: "They could not conceive that a boy whom they knew, and who was brought up in their town, could possibly have the ability and learning that they thought necessary to the practice of law."[94] They were so wrong.

·2·

A Bum Profession

In 1878, Clarence Darrow returned to the octagonal house with the intention of practicing law full-time in Kinsman. His career as a jurist got off to a slow start. Although pleased with his accomplishment, his neighbors were not quick to encourage him with any employment. His skills were raw; moreover, there simply was not much legal work to be done in Kinsman. Regardless, Darrow admitted that he "was none too industrious."[1] For the moment, Darrow was content with taking a few cases from time to time and otherwise doing whatever he liked, which included playing baseball, reading, and attending community events. Increasingly he was drawn to freethinking speeches and debates. In February 1880, Clarence traveled five hundred miles to Harvard, Illinois, to hear Eli C. Ohmart, who had been delivering lectures in northern Illinois and southern Wisconsin. Ohmart, a musical instrument maker and scientist, was a freethinker of Robert Ingersoll's ilk. Darrow reported on Ohmart's lecture for *The Truth Seeker*, the famous skeptics' periodical. Darrow claimed that he had witnessed "a rival if not an equal of the great Ingersoll." Ohmart had been "eloquent in the highest degree" in his speech about evolution and its related doctrines. "His exposition of the natural origin and duties of man," Darrow commented, was "unusually forcible and convincing," giving "religion many rude shocks."[2]

Aside from his growing interest in free thought, the young Clarence

Darrow engaged in a rather traditional pursuit: he wanted to start a family. Sometime after his return home, he reconnected with Jessie Ohl, a young woman he had been dating while he was teaching school. As with most of the women in Darrow's life, we know little about Jessie. She was the daughter of relatively wealthy parents who owned a gristmill and sawmill as well as considerable farmland in Minnesota. Jessie's mother was an accomplished farmer in her own right, and she preached at an evangelical church. After months of courting, Clarence, who had dated no one else seriously, and Jessie fell in love and married on April 15, 1880. Unlike for Clarence's parents, the main question for the newlywed Darrows was not a political or social one. Rather, they struggled to decide where to settle. At first, they thought that they would move one thousand miles away to McPherson, Kansas, a relatively new town in need of a lawyer. Instead, they played it more conservatively and chose Andover, Ohio, a town slightly larger than Kinsman, just ten miles to the north. They were on their own but still close enough to their families and friends.

After their wedding, Jessie and Clarence Darrow packed up their belongings, loaded them onto a horse-drawn cart, and drove to Andover. The trip took only four hours, including a stop for a picnic. Andover was a town of four hundred residents, with not much more need of a new lawyer than Kinsman. Jessie and Clarence rented an apartment over a shoe store and turned its back room into a law office. Jessie used her dowry to help Clarence purchase a set of lawbooks and his first ream of letterhead.[3] This investment did not pay immediate dividends. Again, Clarence found little work and less respect. In his first court case the opposing attorney, who was known as the "terror of the community," hardly took notice of the young upstart, referring to him only as "bub."[4] As a result, the Darrows had to take in boarders. One was a lawyer, James Roberts, who became Darrow's first partner. After a few weeks of loafing, the partner ran up some poker debts, stole and likely hocked Darrow's lawbooks, and left town in the middle of the night. Slowly, Darrow's practice did pick up, but not enough for it to be his sole income. By 1883, lawyer Darrow was also a real estate agent, an insurance agent, and a collections agent.[5] In Andover, Darrow's cases centered on horse trades gone bad; infractions of farmland boundary lines; defense of local bootleggers and farmers who watered their milk; a criminal complaint or two; and, as he elaborated, "private quarrels and grudges, with which the world everywhere is rife."[6] In other words, he was a small-town lawyer, dealing largely in the trivial and quotidian matters of rural life. For three years, the couple lived quietly and happily in Andover. Having been selected as the main speaker at a country picnic, in 1881 Darrow had even fulfilled his dream. Speaking at the Third Annual Wayne Harvest Home in Jamestown, Pennsylvania, he told the farmers and their families that "the man who lives in the home of his fathers was beautiful and worthy of consideration."[7] At that moment in his life, he was.

Darrow's law practice was sustained on a steady diet of relatively minor infractions of the law. Yet these were formative years for his career as a jurist. Basic traits and tendencies, which were to blossom later in life and which Darrow, the iconoclast politico, put to use in Chicago and elsewhere, were established here. One was his typical courtroom demeanor. Unlike many of his rural colleagues, some of whom were also featured July Fourth speakers, Darrow did not shout people down. He was emotional when he had to be, but he mastered a keen, calm rhetorical style, sharpened in many a Saturday evening debate, to unhinge his opponent's case. Rarely did Darrow assert a positive argument of his own. Instead, he took the debate position of the negative, successfully poking holes in the prosecution's arguments. In Andover, Darrow learned to love courtroom drama. Even in rural Trumbull County, Ohio, there were plenty of thrills. Old-time country lawyers might not have been urbane, but they were "clever, and sometimes as learned, as lawyers now whose cases involve millions of dollars, or human lives." Attorneys tilting over the title to a cow drew spectators from the town and surrounding hinterlands. Darrow likened these lawsuits to the great medieval tournaments memorialized by Walter Scott (1771–1832). "The combatants on both sides," he opined, "were always seeking the weakest spots in the enemy's armor, and doing their utmost to unhorse him or to draw blood."[8] Darrow did the latter but was especially skilled at the former.

Darrow also developed his sympathies for "the weak, the suffering, and the poor."[9] A famous case in point involved a poor boy, James W. Brockway, and a horse harness with gilt trimmings. The case centered on Glove E. Clark, a Kinsman native, who had inherited a large fortune. Clark was prone to excess, especially in drinking and games of chance. In early 1885, Clark's extended family discovered that he had frittered away most of his inheritance and was borrowing heavily to cover his gambling debts. To make matters worse, in February 1885, Clark took ill and moved into Kinsman's Sawdy Hotel to recuperate. He hired a nurse, Brockway, to wash him, his clothes, and the bed. Clark had no money to pay the boy, so he offered to buy him a new harness as soon as he was well.

As Clark slowly recovered, his family appointed a guardian, a man by the name of Jewell (history has lost his first name), to take control of Clark's remaining inheritance. It is unclear if Clark realized that he was no longer in control of his affairs when he left the Sawdy Hotel in March 1885. Feeling better, he and Brockway went to the local harness maker and ordered a gilt harness. The family guardian objected to the purchase and sued. Perhaps on the recommendation of friends of the Darrow family, Brockway sought out Clarence in Andover. Darrow took the case for $5 ($120 in today's dollars), likely all the money the boy had. After a brief jury trial, the boy lost the harness. Unwilling to let the rich take advantage of the poor, Darrow pursued an appeal at his own expense all the way to the Ohio Supreme Court. When the justices ruled in favor of Brockway nine years after the initial suit, Darrow was already living in Chicago.[10] He received no compensation other than the original $5. The case, which became known as *Brockway v. Jewell*, was not only precedent-setting but also a prime example of how Darrow internalized his legal cases and later his political causes. "There was no money involved, and not much principle," he wrote, "but then it seemed as if my life depended upon the result."[11]

Andover was also where Darrow fully developed his habit of going against popular sentiments. "I had little respect for the opinion of the crowd. My instinct was to doubt the majority view."[12] In this, he was finally becoming much like his freethinking parents. It also corresponded to Clarence Darrow's growing disillusionment with rural and small-town Ohio. Akin to his father, the more his thoughts ranged beyond the sleepy confines of the Western Reserve, the more he wanted to follow them. But the more immediate cause of his and Jessie's desire to leave Andover was the birth of their only son, Paul Edward Darrow, on December 10, 1883. His given name reflected the Ohl family, and his middle name was in honor of Clarence's favorite brother. The family now needed more money, and Darrow himself needed someplace with wider horizons. Ashtabula, whose name purportedly came from the Algonquin Indian word for river of many fish, was a logical choice. Although it was thirty miles north, Darrow frequently traveled to the port city of five thousand, a former Underground Railroad station, for litigation, lectures, and leisure. He already had plenty of personal, legal, and political contacts. In terms of his career, the move was an easy one.

At the end of the nineteenth century, Ashtabula, which had been founded in 1803, was a lively urban center with designs to rival Cleveland and Chicago. Ashtabula had both passenger and freight railroad service, connecting the Western Reserve's grain and dairy farmers to larger midwestern markets. It had also become a political and cultural center of eastern Ohio.[13] Given its growing importance as a commercial and political center, it was a perfect setting for the Darrow family. Clarence's legal mentor in the city was Republican Judge Laban S. Sherman, who took a liking to the young lawyer despite his freethinking beliefs and his immutable allegiance to the Democratic Party. Sherman introduced Darrow to his Republican friends in the city government and the Ohio bar. Holding their noses at Darrow's politics, they quickly sized him up as a very capable, moldable, and smart addition to their group. In the spring of 1885, about a year after he, Jessie, and Paul had arrived, Judge Sherman arranged for Darrow to run for the vacant office of Ashtabula city solicitor. There was no opposition, and Darrow won without trying.

This was Darrow's formal introduction in the world of American electoral politics, and he seemed quite contented with this sinecure, granted under the guise of democracy. He was no iconoclast, not yet anyway. The position paid seventy-five dollars a month and allowed him to take private cases on the side. At long last, he was able to shuck the other parts of his professional career. He dropped all interest in insurance, real estate, and the dreaded collections. Life seemed to be looking up for the Darrows, as money was no longer such an immediate concern. Although later in life he claimed to have avoided a political career at all costs, in truth, he desired it, sought it, and milked it for all it was worth. His post as Ashtabula's city solicitor was the first political move in a long political career. As he later said nonchalantly, "lawyers take naturally to politics."[14]

The Darrows prospered in Ashtabula, but after only a few years Darrow again grew weary and bored. It was all so provincial. Darrow broke up the mundanity with poker games, debates, an occasional baseball game, and sleep. To mark time (and make his name better known), he also took to the public lecture circuit. As he had been in Andover, Darrow was largely a picnic and banquet speaker who traded in platitudes about sacrifice, veterans, and national unity.[15] These dinner talks were probably challenging for neither him nor his audience.

Jessie and Paul were quite comfortable in Ashtabula, and for the moment Clarence was content to put their happiness above his own. In 1886, Clarence attempted to purchase a home. He had five hundred dollars in the bank and a steady income. He and Jessie had found something that they liked. Already an old hand at real estate deals, Darrow drew up the papers. Upon receipt, the owner of the house promised to deliver them to Clarence's law office the following day. What happened next is repeated time and again in Darrow lore. The owner dutifully appeared the next day "at the appointed time only to tell me that his wife refused to sign the document, so he could not sell the house."[16] Peeved, Darrow recalled responding bluntly: "All right, I don't believe I want your house, because I'm going to move away from here."[17] Darrow's comment begs questions. Why would someone want to buy a house and then claim to be moving out of the town? Whatever the true impetus, Darrow left his wife and son on an impromptu trip to Chicago to visit Everett. Clarence always looked to his older brother for solace, support, and advice. Everett suggested to him that the cure to his discontent and ennui was to move the family to Chicago, where excitement, adventure, and profits were uncontainable. Most Darrow biographers suggest that Clarence stayed in Chicago and made "arrangements" for Jessie and Paul to follow.[18] That's not what happened.

Darrow was a rather insensitive, self-absorbed husband, but he knew that relocating the family was not his decision alone. Furthermore, he had open cases and a law partner, Charles Lawyer, Jr. He was still the city solicitor and could not just abandon his post. Moreover, Darrow had become involved in Ohio politics. He had made quite a name for himself as the unapologetic and ambitious Democrat amid Republicans. In 1885, he had run for a seat in the General Assembly but lost to the Republican candidate. The next year, he ran for Ashtabula prosecuting attorney, and again the GOP trounced him. The political infidel refused to switch parties, even though it might have improved his chances for higher office.[19] All of which provided further reasons to explore a town with a more favoring political environment, but also demanded he not just abandon the contacts and affiliations he had built in Ashtabula.

Darrow had to return home after his trip to see Everett. Although he now wanted to move to Chicago, he needed to convince Jessie, and he needed to tie up loose ends. There is no record of the discussion Clarence had with Jessie. Indeed, Darrow forgot a lot about his first marriage. He did not remember that it was Jessie who had purchased his lawbooks and whatever else he needed to start his career. And if one reads his autobiography literally, it was only Clarence Darrow who moved from Ashtabula to Chicago. As he wrote, "I came to Chicago in 1888."[20] Actually it was 1887, and the entire family moved, Jessie and Paul included. But this move was not about the family at all. It was about Clarence Darrow and *his* aspirations, particularly his political dreams. And there is no question that the move to Chicago was the most important decision in his life. In Chicago, Darrow finally found a public stage to match his ego and ambitions. For more than fifty years it was his base of operations in law and in politics. It was there that he became the dynamic, transformative force in United States history. To put it simply: no Chicago, no attorney for the damned.

The question remains: Why Chicago? Certainly, having Everett close was appealing. And the "hard and noisy city" with its "crowds [surging] back and forth as if they knew where they were going, and why"[21] was a draw; for years he had read his brother's letters from Chicago with utter fascination. But city living is more than a spectator sport, and re-creating his success in Ashtabula was not a given. While Darrow figured that there would be plenty of room for a smart, enterprising, politically savvy lawyer, he had other reasons to believe that he would find like-minded friends and mentors. Much more than Ashtabula, Chicago was awash in political and social movements. Just the thought of participating in heady political debates was exhilarating. Darrow's move to Chicago coincided with his intellectual awakening to political radicalism and reformism; it was that iconoclastic side of Darrow that urged him to move to the big city. More immediately, two books had a profound impact upon his young mind: Henry George's *Progress and Poverty* (1879) and John Peter Altgeld's *Our Penal Machinery and Its Victims* (1884). More than the urgings of his favorite brother, these two works convinced Darrow that his fortune and happiness were to be found in Chicago.

It is difficult to recapture the euphoria and acclaim surrounding the publication of George's *Progress and Poverty: An Inquiry into the Causes of*

Industrial Depressions and of Increase of Want with Increase of Wealth. The book made George (1839–1897) an overnight national and international star. His ideas became a touchstone to many other reform movements during the Gilded Age. So much so, the great American philosopher and educator John Dewey (1859–1952) ranked George with Plato for his influence on social thought. George struggled most of his life to eke out a bare existence. Several times he found himself flat broke amid spectacular wealth and abundance. In an attempt to understand his condition, in 1871 he wrote a pamphlet, *Our Land and Land Policy*, that struck a nerve. In it, he argued that land should not be treated as private property and that government had an obligation to ensure that all citizens had equal access to land. For the next eight years, George worked feverishly to elaborate on this principle.

Progress and Poverty was an investigation into the great "enigma of our times": "this association of poverty with progress."[22] How could it be that poverty was growing in the midst of economic opulence? George discovered the answers in the "dismal science," political economy.[23] In long, analytical discussions of wages, capital, labor, and rent, he attacked the laissez-faire theories of Thomas Malthus (1766–1834) and Herbert Spencer and expounded those of David Ricardo (1772–1823) and Adam Smith (1723–1790) to argue that the only clear path for progress was to eliminate all taxes but a single tax on land rent so as to discourage the unwarranted accumulation of real estate. Government could then assure that all workers had access to land, thus solving the problem of poverty. Explicitly but without much analysis, George dismissed any other explanations on the causes of poverty and any other solutions, including trade unionism, land redistribution, and social uplift "from the better education of the working classes and improved habits of industry and thrift."[24] Rather, the single tax was the sole remedy that would "open the way to advances" and usher in the "reign of the Prince of Peace." Without the tax, George predicted civilization and Christianity would die and "carry us back toward barbarism."[25]

Upon the publication of *Progress and Poverty*, Henry George became a celebrity in the United States and Europe. The public release of his criticisms of industrialism and imperialism coincided with rent boycotts in Ireland and the formation of the Irish National Land League, which stridently fought to end landlordism and which had a strong following in Chicago.[26]

George became an ally of the league and its leaders and made frequent trips to Great Britain. In the United States, reformers of all political stripes became captivated by George's critique and especially with his advocacy of a single tax on land. Darrow was one of them. A friend in Ashtabula, Amos Hubbard, had read *Progress and Poverty* and encouraged Darrow to read it. The impact was immediate: "I felt that I had found a new political gospel that bade fair to bring about the social equality and opportunity that has [sic] always been the dream of the idealist."[27] Other disciples pooled their faith together and formed single tax clubs, which sprang up across the nation in the 1880s. Ohio had its share of organizations in honor of George, but none was as vibrant as the one in the nation's second-largest city, Chicago.

The other book that encouraged Darrow to seek out Chicago was John Altgeld's *Our Penal Machinery and Its Victims*. Both "this book and the author came to have a marked influence upon me and my future," Darrow observed.[28] This is an understatement. Altgeld (1847–1902) became as important a figure in Darrow's life as his parents, perhaps even more important. Altgeld was Darrow's mentor in politics. An Ashtabula police judge named Richards had given a copy of the book to Darrow. Richards had received his copy for free. Altgeld had paid for the publication of ten thousand copies of his book and had sent them to every public official, community leader, reformer, and clergyman that he could find in the Midwest. Far from the monotonous tome that George had launched, Altgeld's short book was a succinct summary of a major problem in the United States: the entire legal and justice system had run amok and was in fact destroying the social fabric of the nation. Altgeld estimated that more than 2.5 million arrests happened every year, with roughly 1.5 million of them involving first-time offenders.[29] In all, about 5 percent of the nation's population found itself in jail or prison every year. In Altgeld's hometown of Chicago, in 1884, a similar pattern appeared. That year the city police arrested nearly 39,500 people, more than 100 per day. This figure was nearly double that of 1871. Altgeld argued that the costs associated with these incarcerations were far too expensive in terms of dollars and wrecked lives. To run America's penal system, cities, counties, and states employed 50,000 constables, 10,000 deputy sheriffs, and 2,200 sheriffs. There were also armies of judges, clerks, and jailers staffing large penitentiaries, local jails, and police prisons. Altgeld estimated that the nation spent $400 million ($9.5 billion in today's dollars) on the penal system.

"This is all dead capital," he charged. In Illinois alone the state spent about $27 per prisoner and thus over $4 million a year ($95 million in today's dollars). Chicago itself spent over $800,000 ($19 million in today's dollars).

These investments in the penal machinery, however, paled in comparison to the costs borne by the families of those arrested. Altgeld believed that for every one incarceration there were at least five dependents who suffered. "Then take the 1,500,000 persons arrested for the first time each year, and remember that there are annually 7,500,000 different human beings, and these of the poorer and weaker classes, who are shoved downward instead of helped by our penal machinery."[30] Here, then, was the crux of Altgeld's book. The penal system hurt those who were most vulnerable. Worse, imprisonment hardened the hearts and minds of those who were arrested, encouraging further antisocial behavior. Altgeld quoted prison investigator Dr. William Greenleaf Eliot (1811–1887), who sarcastically wrote: "What school-houses of crime are these!" Considering all the harm that befell these prisoners, most of whom had only violated laws about public drunkenness or vagrancy, Altgeld agreed with another prison investigator, Enoch Cobb Wines (1806–1879), who maintained that "brutal treatment brutalizes the wrong-doer and prepares him for worse offenses."[31]

Moreover, the homeless boy and the hardened criminal received exactly the same treatment. Altgeld asked rhetorically: "Does clubbing a man reform him? Does brutal treatment elevate his thoughts? Does handcuffing fill him with good resolves?" To him and a host of prison reformers, the entire enterprise served only to perpetuate crime and misery. He offered four remedies. First, the system of paying police and sheriffs on the basis of their arrest records should be abolished. Second, arrests and imprisonment for breaking the law would be permitted only in cases of dangerous criminals. Third, those guilty of minor offenses should be given treatment rather than prison sentences. And fourth, criminals who engaged in "graver offenses" should be tried quickly and sent to a penitentiary where they would be allowed to learn skills and earn money so that upon their release they could reenter civil society.[32]

The reform movements that Altgeld and George sparked drew Darrow like a moth to a flame; he remained there for the rest of his life. Both Altgeld and George revealed the social, political, and economic structures in America that walled in average people's aspirations and abilities and condemned them to short, difficult lives. Like both, Darrow wanted to smash those structures, and also like them, he wanted to do that in Chicago. What exactly Darrow thought of Chicago we shall never know. Unlike his future law partner (and the extraordinary American poet) Edgar Lee Masters (1869–1950), Darrow left no homage to the city.[33] Darrow's feelings on Chicago are beyond simple explanation. By the Gilded Age, Chicago was known as the Windy City for its blowhard politicians as well as for the frequency of its winter blizzards; the Empire City and the Queen City of the West for its dominance of the Midwest's hinterlands and because it was the central hub of railroad transportation in the United States; the Second City because it had been completely rebuilt in 1872 and because it ranked second in size and influence only to New York City; and finally the Black City because dirt, disease, death, and disillusionment reigned supreme. At the end of the nineteenth century, Chicago represented at once America's greatest promise as well as its wellspring of despair and discontent. To some, opportunities for career and social advance were abundant. To others, the city was the backdrop to their brutal and short lives. Likely, Darrow chose Chicago for its reputation for both.[34] In 1887, the city's population hovered around one million. It had not merely been rebuilt after the fire of 1871; it was expanding rapidly, both horizontally and vertically. The new city had drawn America's greatest architects: Louis H. Sullivan (1856–1924), John W. Root (1850–1891), and Daniel H. Burnham (1846–1912). Although New York City had the first skyscraper, Chicago's building designers perfected the form. In the words of historian Donald L. Miller, Chicago was "spectacular." But it was also "awful."[35] Or as Max Weber wrote, Chicago was like a "human being with his skin removed": fascinating and repulsive.[36] It was this Chicago that Darrow entered.

Darrow's Chicago was a decidedly working-class city. By the time he arrived, it had the largest industrial workforce west of the Appalachian Mountains. It was also the most unionized city. By the turn of the twentieth century one out of every six union workers in the United States lived in Chicago. Unless one had money, living and working conditions were horrible. After the 1871 fire, Chicago's working-class families moved from their pine hovels into new brick tenements, or double-deckers. These apartments were overcrowded and had little access to running water. Residents were forced to use the few municipal baths to wash their clothes and themselves. And although Chicago's government sponsored the construction of a new water and sewer system, the pipes still failed to provide clean drinking water, free of the detritus of the slaughterhouses and the unpurified, rancid coastal waters of Lake Michigan. Some mothers preferred giving their children pasteurized beer from the local saloon.[37] Even so, infant mortality in the working-class "patches" along the banks of the Chicago River was outrageously high. The unsanitary conditions were perfect for diseases of all sorts: cholera, tuberculosis, and smallpox. There were other, more discreet epidemics as well. Chicago vice districts were notorious. In 1911, the city's Vice Commission estimated conservatively that there were more than five hundred brothels and nearly five thousand women engaged in the business. Even with the related enterprises in liquor not counted, the sex business alone generated over $15 million annually ($150 million in today's dollars).[38] Much of the debauchery was segregated into the Nineteenth Precinct of the First Ward, home to an area known as Hell's Half Acre, which had forty-six saloons, thirty-seven brothels, and eleven pawnbrokers.[39]

The streets were mean, dirty, and dangerous. Just walking was a life-threatening event. The railroads, which crisscrossed the city, were set at grade level. Six hundred people a year, an average of nearly two a day, were killed by moving trains. Even more—an estimated eight hundred in the first six months of 1892 alone—died violent deaths. As Erik Larson so chillingly recounts in *The Devil in the White City*, murderers stalked the working-class districts of Chicago. Many young, unaccompanied women simply disappeared "amid the stench of dung, anthracite, and putrefaction."[40]

The city's factories and industries were not much safer. In 1906, the nation learned of the perils of the stockyards after reading Upton Sinclair's realistic novel *The Jungle*. Of course, the workers who labored inside the grandiose stone gate of the Union Stock Yard, designed by Daniel H. Burnham and John W. Root, had known for decades of the horrors of the disassembly lines. Frequently death came as easily for the stunners and butchers as it did for the cattle, hogs, and sheep. Conditions were little better in the city's tenement house factories. Nestled alongside the brothels and apartments, these small manufacturing businesses, many in the Nineteenth Ward, made the same clothes that the larger factories produced in the First Ward but at far lower costs. Unlike the bigger factories, where there was decent sanitation, lighting, and ventilation, the sweatshops in the working-class neighborhoods hired newly arrived Russian Jews or Italians or Bohemians, who labored long hours for meager wages in dreadful working conditions. Overexertion led to disease and death, especially among the children employed in these mills. The largest employer of children in Chicago was a caramel factory in the Nineteenth Ward. Young boys and girls worked fourteen-hour days, wrapping and packing the candies, even longer during the rush season weeks before Christmas.

The pressure that employers put on their workers was met equally by pressure from the workers themselves. In the Gilded Age, Chicago was the nation's center for working-class activism and rebellion. It was also the center for what one radical called "the supreme question now claiming the attention of the civilized world."[41] He meant the movement to establish eight hours for work, eight hours for sleep, and eight hours for what one willed. At its most basic, the eight-hour movement represented the desire of workers to control and improve their lives and those of their family members. But the movement was more than a mere call for an ameliorative reform. It was an expression of the democratic ideals of Chicago's workers. They believed that an eight-hour day was the first step in creating a politics that served their needs, not just those of the wealthy who owned the factories and the land.

For decades the city's working class had simmered and seethed, as employers, their political stooges, and their police lackeys frustrated efforts to improve life.[42] By 1886, Chicago's workers had organized themselves into an effective political movement. Despite police invasions of their meeting places, they continued to meet in German Vereins and such venues as the Henry George Hall. Workers also began striking for an eight-hour day and, in so doing, striking for democracy. For instance, in early 1886, Honoré Joseph Jaxon (1861–1952), a Canadian labor agitator, arrived in Chicago to help six thousand striking carpenters. They wanted an eight-hour day. They had walked out on their jobs at construction sites and in furniture factories. Employers had shown resolve and hired strikebreakers. Jaxon counseled patience and told the strike leaders to invite the strikebreakers "to quit for the brotherhood of man." Union leaders returned with word that none had joined the strike. Upon hearing the news, Jaxon handed out clubs and wagon spokes, saying, "Now, try this persuasion."[43] There was little chance the eight-hour movement was going to be bloodless.

In the spring of 1886, workers under the leadership of Albert R. Parsons (1848–1887), Lucy Parsons (1852–1942), George Schilling (1850–1936), August Spies (1855–1887), and two labor federations—the Knights of Labor and the Federation of Organized Trades and Labor Unions—organized a May 1 eight-hour-day protest and strike. Although tensions were high, May 1 and May 2 passed without incident. Then, on May 3, police attacked strikers at the McCormick works, killing four. The next night there was a rally in Haymarket Square. Only fifteen hundred people showed up to listen to speeches by Parsons, Spies, and others. By 11:00 p.m. all but five hundred had headed home in the cold, drizzling rain. As Samuel Fielden (1847–1922) was speaking, a phalanx of policemen began marching double-time into the square. Despite the fact that Chicago Mayor Carter Harrison (1825–1893) had personally visited the rally earlier that evening and instructed Police Inspector John Bonfield (1836–1898) that those gathered posed no threat to the city, Bonfield had sent his troops in. The police encircled the remnants of the meeting and ordered the men to disperse peaceably. Fielden argued with Bonfield but agreed to leave without incident. As Fielden climbed down from his wagon, a bomb flew out of the air from a dark alley and whizzed down into the center of the police line. The explosion killed seven policemen, and the ensuing police melee, in which officers fired their weapons wildly, killed three civilians and wounded thirty more.

In the months that followed, police rounded up dozens of working-class leaders. Eight—Albert Parsons, Spies, Fielden, Michael Schwab (1853–1898), George Engel (1836–1887), Louis Lingg (1864–1887), Oscar Neebe (1850–1916), and Adolph Fischer (1858–1887)—were charged with conspiracy, since the bomber was never identified. Although the trial was hardly fair, given the aroused passions, the jury voted to convict, and Judge Joseph E. Gary (1821–1906) handed down the death sentence to seven, giving Neebe fifteen years. On November 11, 1887, four of the convicted—Parsons, Spies, Fischer, and Engel—were hanged; Lingg took his own life while awaiting execution. Governor Richard J. Oglesby (1824–1899) did commute the sentences of two men, Schwab and Fielden, to life in prison. These men's crime was essentially guilt by association to an idea and membership in a movement to make America more democratic.[44] Summing up Chicago, its bard, Carl Sandburg (1878–1967), wrote: "Here's the difference between us and Dante: He wrote a lot about Hell and never saw the place. We're writing about Chicago after looking the town over."[45]

In 1887—only a year after the May 1 protest and in the midst of the Haymarket Square trial—Darrow and his family arrived in hell and sublet a small apartment. Clarence found a desk to rent in an office building on La Salle Street. At first, it seemed that the young lawyer and America's most dynamic city were a total mismatch. Homesick, he made few friends and wished his old ones would somehow appear. "Sometimes I would stand on the corner of Madison and State Street," he wrote, "watching the passers-by for some familiar face."[46] None appeared. Darrow scared up few clients. There were simply too many lawyers. "We have seven thousand lawyers in Chicago," Darrow complained to a friend. "One thousand could do all the work, and probably the world would be better off without" the rest.[47] In his first year he earned only three hundred dollars, not enough to feed his family, and he had to borrow from Everett to make ends meet. Had he had the money for the trip back to Ohio, they might have left. Instead, the Darrows stayed. Clarence was determined and "dreaded to confess defeat."[48]

If clients would not come to him, he'd go to them. In 1888, Darrow began joining social clubs, trying to meet influential Chicagoans. Chicago had dozens of clubs for all interests, social classes, professions, politics, and pursuits: the Calumet Club, the Chicago Club, the North Shore Club, the Press Club, and so forth. Two organizations proved most useful to Darrow: the Henry George Club and the Sunset Club.

George's analysis of wealth and poverty and his simple single tax solution stirred Darrow's intellect, and he met weekly with other club members to discuss how to put George's theories into practice. The club, he wrote, "furnished a forum for ambitious young lawyers to win a hearing in."[49] He honed his speaking and debating skills there and soon directed his oratory toward meetings and public gatherings. Darrow tried hard to make a name for himself—especially in the newspapers—but without much luck. Front-page coverage, he hoped, would bring clients, money, and prestige. In 1888, he actively campaigned for the Democratic Party and Grover Cleveland (1837–1908). Always put at the end of the bill, he found few staying to listen to his speeches. Darrow blamed his pedestrian, politically conservative education in Ohio and his father, who had insisted that he be trained in political economy and speak only "if I had something worth saying."[50] No

McGuffey's reader or Ohio classroom offered any radical much of an inkling on how to tackle the world of injustice. Chicago audiences, however, wanted inspiration and political claptrap; no one wanted serious explications of the theory of rent or land taxation policy. Slowly Darrow began to learn how to address and sway the general public.

Darrow's triumphal moment came in early 1889 at a free trade convention in Chicago, which *The New York Times* called "one of the most important economic gatherings ever held in this country."[51] Americans no longer have any sense of the historical importance of tariff reform and the free trade movement at the end of the nineteenth century, but from the Civil War to the end of the Progressive Era, it was a dominant political issue that divided parties, elected politicians, and drove public policy. It was in part what Henry George railed against in his call for the abolition of all taxes save the one on land. Like many contemporaries, George recognized that the tariff was essentially a tax on the working and middle classes and a transfer of wealth to the rich. When duties were applied to imports, domestic prices increased, disproportionately hurting those who could least afford it and moving their money to those who had more than enough. Until free trade became a common global outlook, politicians, activists, and voters struggled mightily over it. Anyone who mattered had an opinion. At that February 1889 convention, Henry George was the featured speaker, and Darrow, the most articulate member of Chicago's single tax club, shared the stage.

The event was held at the Central Music Hall, the only place large enough to house the city's large throng of single tax adherents. Both men and women reformers were present, as Darrow had convinced his male colleagues to support his motion to recognize female delegates at the convention. The event's main attraction was the speech of Henry George. He was his brilliant self, and the audience erupted in thunderous applause as he finished his call for free trade and a suspension of all tariffs. "Every one but me," Darrow recalled, "was carried away with his able address." He was disappointed that it was so good.[52] Satisfied, the audience began to stand, stretch, and leave the hall. Quickly Darrow yelled over to the master of ceremonies, demanding his introduction. The man obliged moments before it would have been too late. Dressed in a fancy gray cutaway suit coat with matching pants and a stiff white shirt with a low white collar from which hung a droopy black string tie, Darrow took center stage and "began with the most striking phrases that I could conjure."[53] His exact extemporaneous introductory remarks were not recorded. It must have been good; the audience's interest was piqued, and everyone sat down to listen.

Darrow launched into his prepared speech. He gave a brilliantly simple— albeit cerebral—critique of the deleterious effects of the tariff on working men and women.[54] The crowd loved it, and Darrow was met with his own standing ovation. Even Henry George "warmly grasped [his] hand." The next morning the papers cheered his name. Finally, he had "made a hit" in Chicago.[55] The problem was that he still had no clients. The next day his friends who were single taxers as well as socialists showed up at his office to congratulate him and to use his telephone. "This was pleasing," he wrote, "but not profitable."[56]

Although consorting with the single taxers had brought some public attention to him, Darrow tired of their single-mindedness. He was equally frustrated with socialists. He always felt a close kinship with socialists and even called himself a "considerable socialist" from time to time, yet he was suspicious of their philosophy for the same reasons he rejected the single tax movement.[57] Darrow acknowledged that socialists believed in no God, but their faith in a "cooperative commonwealth" with its redistribution of wealth and property served the same function.[58] Socialists were living according to a "religious dogma." Darrow was not afraid of dumping his property into "the common mass" and taking out his "per capita share," even though he'd likely lose some of his wealth. But he seriously doubted that this system would create happiness.[59] For Darrow, this was the rub: allowing an individual the freedom to pursue happiness was central. A socialist government, no matter how supportive of the working class, could solve only the "bread and butter question" and not bring smiles to the faces of average citizens.[60] Socialism couldn't cure "the miseries and troubles inherent in life."[61]

Finding the cures to unhappiness and fighting for the freedom to pursue them became a lifelong journey for Darrow. He did not go alone. His quest became a very public venture. He knew there was no political panacea and therefore tried to find fellow travelers who wished to debate, experiment, and deploy reforms to create a more enlightened, tolerant, and pleasant society. In that spirit, in March 1889, he helped found a new club. The Sunset

Club of Chicago was styled on the Twilight Club of New York City, whose membership included Andrew Carnegie (1835–1919), Oliver Wendell Holmes (1841–1935), Herbert Spencer, Mark Twain (1835–1910), and Walt Whitman (1819–1892). Like its more famous cousin, the Sunset Club catered to the rich and influential. It had no regulations, bylaws, or constitution. Rather, there was a code that enjoined the members together: no clubhouse, no defalcations, no bores, no long speeches, no late hours, no dudes, no preaching, and no vituperation. The Sunset Club was created simply for "tolerant discussion and rational recreation."[62] The club's mission was to bring together anarchists, socialists, and other radicals into direct contact with "their more conservative brethren" in order to engender "a certain respect in their hearts that in no other way could have been attained." It claimed a membership of eleven hundred, mainly reformers and activists—"anarchists, socialists, single-tax men, democrats, republicans, mugwumps . . . agnostics, athetics, Christians, and free-thinkers"—with a smattering of the rich: railroad magnates and financial potentates.[63] The group had no president and no political affiliation, though a majority of its members were mugwumps, middle- and upper-class reform-minded politicos especially concerned about labor issues, free trade, and the rising power of corporations.[64] About one hundred members, who included such luminaries as Henry Demarest Lloyd, radicals like George Schilling, and up-and-coming politicians like Lloyd W. Bowers (1859–1910), a future solicitor general of the United States, convened every other Thursday evening at six-fifteen for dinner, followed by "talks" and debate on important topics of the day. They debated each other, but at times guests came to stir the pot. On November 7, 1891, Darrow had the chance of a lifetime when Robert Ingersoll visited Chicago and met with the Sunset Club. Normally, the formal meeting had disbanded by nine-thirty, and the informal session that followed at some bar generally went three more hours, especially if dignitaries like Ingersoll were in town.[65]

Of all the people Darrow engaged at the club meetings, no one had more of an effect upon him than Henry D. Lloyd, who was knighted as the first muckraker and the forerunner of the progressive movement. Like Darrow, Lloyd had been born into a relatively poor and obscure family. But after being graduated from Columbia College and passing the New York State bar exam, Lloyd rose quickly and became deeply engaged in national party politics. He helped lead the movement in 1871 and 1872 to oust President Ulysses S. Grant and elect a reform-minded and honest politician who could deliver tariff, civil service, and labor reform. Failing in his quest, in late 1872, Lloyd moved to the Windy City to become the literary editor for the *Chicago Tribune*. Soon he fell in love with Jessie Louise Bross, the daughter of William Bross (1813–1890), one of the newspaper's owners. With their marriage, Lloyd became both wealthy and powerful. The bliss was short-lived. By the early 1880s Lloyd had become a political radical. In 1885 he fell out with the newspaper's conservative boss, Joseph Medill (1823–1899), and resigned from his post. Hoping to regain some inner peace, he went to Europe but suffered an emotional breakdown. Upon his return to Chicago, he became even more devoted to antimonopoly and prolabor causes, including the amnesty movement for the Haymarket anarchists sentenced to hang.

In January 1888, reaching out to people he wished to meet and who could help him get established as a jurist as well as a politico, Darrow wrote Lloyd a fawning letter. "The cause of organized labor," Darrow declared, "is fortunate in having such a champion."[66] Shortly thereafter, Darrow regularly talked with Lloyd at the Sunset Club, and it was there that he first expressed publicly the core beliefs for which he was to become famous. It is significant to note that at no time in his life did Clarence Darrow subscribe to any clearly defined grand philosophical tradition. He remained dogmatically antidogmatic throughout his life. But he held dear a constellation of ideas and political commitments. Darrow was concerned about the lives of average American workers as well as the growing power of the wealthy and their corporations. He was angered at the attacks on freedom and liberty by various powerful organizations and institutions and believed like Altgeld, Lloyd, George, and others that something had to be done before the trend toward oligarchy and rigid class and caste control became permanently entrenched. In the 1880s and early 1890s, as his nascent freethinking sensibility and radical inclinations grew, he felt more confident to express his ideas. He had not put them into action but was seeking the company of like-minded friends. As a result, shortly after he, Jessie, and Paul had settled in, Darrow went to meet the man whose book had spurred his concern for the working class, transformed his view of criminology, and encouraged his move to Chicago, John Peter Altgeld.

Altgeld was curious to behold. The short, sinewy, strong-featured man with a harelip and monstrous cowlick spoke with an accent revealing his German birth. Darrow and Altgeld instantly liked each other. Perhaps it was their similar backgrounds. Like Darrow, Altgeld, who had been born in 1847 in Nassau, Germany, and whose family moved to Mansfield, Ohio, had grown up in the Western Reserve. Yet their childhoods were quite different. Altgeld's father saw no value in education, and his son spent only a few terms in public school. John escaped by joining the Ohio Home Guards at the end of the Civil War. During his time with the guards, he contracted malaria (aka Chickahominy fever), a disease that he never quite conquered.

In 1877, seeking fame and fortune as a lawyer, Altgeld moved to Chicago. But unlike Darrow, Altgeld quickly made a name for himself as an attorney and real estate magnate. His successes and growing wealth created opportunities in city politics. Given his criticisms of the legal system in Illinois and elsewhere, it is not surprising that Altgeld represented working-class interests. Under the wing of labor radical George Schilling, Altgeld donned the political trappings of a common man, and when Darrow met him in 1887, he had recently been elected on the Democratic Party–United Labor Party ticket to the Superior Court of Cook County. There he not only put into practice his theories about criminology but also began financing and supporting other Democratic, labor, and reform-minded candidates. Soon Altgeld stood at the epicenter of Chicago's political life. He was popular and powerful, wheeling and dealing with the so-called Gray Wolves, who ran the city, aldermen like Michael "Hinky Dink" Kenna (1858–1946) and "Bathhouse" John Coughlin (1860–1938). All of them drew their political power from their neighborhoods, which were segregated by ethnicity, race, and class. They provided patronage; social and political services, including protection from the police; and assistance when needed. In return all they asked was a cut of profits and, of course, votes on election day. At the same time, Altgeld appealed greatly to a growing number of reformers and radicals, such as settlement house workers Jane Addams (1860–1935) and Florence Kelley (1859–1932), and eight-hour-day movement leader Schilling. As historian Ray Ginger wrote, by the late 1880s Altgeld had organized an "anti-machine" in Chicago politics.

Altgeld's first major accomplishment came in 1889 with the election of De Witt C. Cregier (1829–1898), a Democrat with the strong backing of organized labor, as the thirty-first mayor of the city. Although Mayor Cregier failed to satisfy all reformers, he supported unionists and was an advocate of working-class issues. In June 1889, he signed an eight-hour-day ordinance with a time-and-a-half provision for all city employees—save firefighters and police officers. He also supported various unions in their bid to establish arbitration and favorable wage and hour rules in the building of the world's fair.[67]

Mayor Cregier repaid his political debts with patronage. Shortly after his election, in 1889, he sent a note to Clarence Darrow, who had campaigned for him as well as for all Altgeld candidates that year. The letter asked Darrow to stop by City Hall when he had the time. "The latter part of the sentence sounded like a joke," Darrow wrote.[68] He had no clients and all the time in the world. Darrow ran over to see the mayor, who offered him a job as special assessment attorney with the salary of three thousand dollars per year, a 1,000 percent increase in his yearly income.

In his autobiography, Darrow explained, feigning naïveté, that it was only some time after his appointment that he "discovered" Altgeld's assistance.[69] Surely Darrow was smart enough to see what had happened, and as in Ashtabula, he had no qualms about accepting the post. After three months on the job, Darrow was promoted to assistant corporation counsel, providing legal advice to the city's bureaucrats and politicians and representing them in court on official business. He had not been in that post a year when the corporation counsel, Judge Jonas Hutchinson (1840–1903), fell ill, and Darrow moved into that office.[70]

Darrow had become a central cog in the Chicago political machine. He was the city's lawyer, meaning he was Cregier's and Altgeld's lawyer. And he loved it. His office was as much for entertainment as for work. Darrow's Sunset Club friends were frequent visitors. One of them, Morris St. Palais Thomas, later even became a law partner. In no way was Darrow repulsed by the sordid side of politics, and he formed alliances and partnerships with all the city's power brokers, including those like Bathhouse Coughlin and Johnny Powers (1852–1930), whose support rested upon brothel owners and saloonkeepers.[71] Did Darrow follow his political peers down to the First Ward to partake in the pleasures it offered? There's no evidence suggesting that he did, but he would have been odd among his peers if he did not. Darrow loved to joke that madams and their employees did nothing immoral. "They're serving a good purpose and giving value for value received. What's so wrong about that?"[72] What we do know is that Darrow's office at City Hall, Room 41, was a hub of political business. Darrow kept his nose clean; he did not have sticky fingers, as so many Chicago politicos did. The bulk of his legal work revolved around patronage and property. Darrow led the city's campaign to pave the streets and clear rights-of-way for the streetcar traction lines. During his tenure as corporation counsel, the city added nearly six hundred miles of road, so that by 1893 visitors to the Columbian Exposition did not have to wade through the muck of old Chicago streets. Rather, Chicago finally had a modern street system.[73]

Additionally, Darrow was Mayor Cregier's labor troubleshooter. In 1890, for instance, he helped the miners in Spring Valley, Illinois, who were locked in a death embrace with their employer, the Spring Valley Coal Company. Although Spring Valley was one hundred miles to the west of Chicago, the town's labor conflagration, which began in 1888, quickly drew the attention of Chicago's left-wing activists and Mayor Cregier, who helped organize relief for the miners.

There was nothing special about the town, its mines, or the labor dispute. Established in 1884, Spring Valley was a boomtown whose founding fathers were closely tied to big mining and railroad interests. Pennsylvania's coal and rail magnate as well as Democratic congressman William L. Scott (1828–1891) was president of the Spring Valley Coal Company, whose principal owners included the Northwest Fuel Company of St. Louis and the Chicago North Western Railroad.[74] A downturn in the coal mining industry provided Scott with the excuse to lay off a third of the miners and reduce the wages of the rest shortly before Christmas 1888. When local union officials from the National Progressive Union of Miners and Mine Laborers and the rank and file rejected Scott's actions, he simply locked them out of the mines. As the months dragged on, the worry of concerned citizens turned to anger. Henry Lloyd led the charge.[75] In regional and national newspapers, Lloyd railed against "the robbery of monopolies, the jobbery of politics, and the snobbery of social life."[76] But no bad publicity changed Scott's mind. He was recalcitrant, and when the miners could no longer pay their rents, he began eviction proceedings. At this juncture, Lloyd needed a lawyer with good connections. Darrow was more than willing to help, using his legal acumen to delay the evictions and his relationship with Mayor Cregier to organize relief for the workers. Darrow's and Lloyd's efforts, however, were not enough, and eventually the Spring Valley miners, broken and defeated, crawled back to their jobs.[77]

Despite the trouncing, Darrow's reputation as organized labor's friend only grew. In February 1891, nonunion workers employed by the Chicago firm McArthur Brothers began digging a ditch in Jackson Park on the site of the world's fair. When union workers caught wind of this, five hundred of them chased the McArthur employees away. A few days later thousands of union workers, armed with homemade spears, attacked the ditchdiggers again. This time the police intervened before anyone was killed. Upon the request of the business owners, Mayor Cregier asked Darrow, who had probably helped arbitrate the original world's fair union work rules and was known to all as sympathetic to labor, to investigate. He worked out a deal that sent everyone back to work, although union officials were not completely satisfied. They had wanted the fair's administrators to hire union workers first, pay union wages regardless, and institute an eight-hour day. The unions got only the latter, but given the historic resistance to the eight-hour day in Chicago, it was an advance. Moreover, Darrow's honest brokering earned him respect, a reputation for fairness, and gratitude among Chicago's laborers.[78]

In 1891, Darrow's work at City Hall came to an abrupt end. The political winds of Chicago changed, and Cregier was voted out of office. Cregier laid the blame squarely on the shoulders of his bitter rival Carter Harrison, who had come back to reclaim his old office. The Democratic Party in Chicago split, as did the labor vote, which then allowed a Republican, Hempstead Washburne (1852–1919), to win by a very slim margin, replacing Cregier.[79] Unsurprisingly Darrow lost his plum job. He was unconcerned. By the early 1890s, he had become John Altgeld's closest political adviser, and his friend took care of him. In 1892, after another letter of introduction from Altgeld, Darrow went to work as a lawyer for the Chicago North Western Railroad (CNW). He did so with quite a bit of trepidation. The managers of the railroad did not share one iota of his sympathies for workers or equality or humanity or liberty. But a friend, colleague, and Altgeld confidant, William C. Goudy (1824–1893), the CNW's high-powered lawyer, encouraged Darrow to come work with him.[80] Moreover, Jessie, Paul, and he had moved into a comfortable flat while he was the city's lawyer, and there were bills to pay. In other words, Clarence Darrow had become a great sympathizer of the common man and woman, but he was not yet their champion. At that moment, he was content to practice law as a corporate lawyer, a "bum profession . . . utterly devoid of idealism and almost poverty stricken as to any real ideas."[81] That was about to change. Within two years he was to emerge as organized labor's greatest champion and a strident defender of American liberty and freedom.

⊰·3·⊱

Becoming the "Attorney for the Damned"

The first day of any new job is always rough, but doubtless Darrow spent a sleepless night before his first day at the Chicago North Western Railroad. He knew full well that his "opinions and attitudes" and actions—especially with the Spring Valley lockout—preceded his arrival and might well be a source of cold stares, troublemaking by colleagues, and ugly arguments near the water closet. But his fears were unfounded. To a man, they all treated him "with respect and all were most friendly."[1] His patron and protector at the company, William Goudy, had cleared the way for him.[2] Darrow's mentor, John Altgeld, who had arranged the job, and Goudy had a long personal, financial, and political past together. They also shared future plans of political glory, and Darrow fitted into them nicely.

Darrow's corporate office was essentially a local campaign headquarters for Altgeld's 1892 gubernatorial run. Goudy provided the introductions, and Darrow closed the deals. Altgeld needed money and the backing of Illinois's—not to mention Chicago's—elite, who were all tied in some way or another to the railroads. Darrow also worked closely with George Schilling, another key Altgeld lieutenant. It was Schilling's job to swing the working-class voters his way, and it was Darrow's task to mobilize the wealthy and stump for both Altgeld and Democratic presidential candidate Grover Cleveland.[3] Both men were quite effective. In the late summer of 1892,

Schilling organized "Altgeld's Labor Legion," which created momentum among workers and opened opportunities for Altgeld to speak on labor issues without being too specific. This helped Darrow raise funds among the rich who managed the monopolies as well as among upper-middle-class reformers like Henry Lloyd, who wholeheartedly endorsed candidate Altgeld in the hope that he would be an unabashed reformer once in office. Funds also came in through Mike "The King" McDonald (1839–1907), a legendary saloonkeeper and ringleader of one of Chicago's first crime syndicates. By November 1892, Altgeld was known as the million-dollar candidate. Republican candidate Joseph W. Fifer (1840–1938) did not stand a chance. In the election season that sent Democrat Grover Cleveland back to the White House, Illinois elected its first foreign-born governor and its first from the city of Chicago.

Although largely unspoken during the campaign, a central issue of the Altgeld administration was the fate of the three remaining anarchists from the Haymarket Massacre. Altgeld's supporters, particularly Darrow and Schilling, expected their friend to come through and pardon Sam Fielden, Oscar Neebe, and Michael Schwab. Darrow thought it should be the governor's first public act in office. Altgeld saw it differently. His first action was to appoint his friends to high office. Among other appointments, he made Schilling the secretary of the state Board of Labor Statistics. And on the recommendation of Henry Lloyd and Jane Addams, he made settlement house activist Florence Kelley the chief factory inspector for Illinois. Governor Altgeld made it decisively clear where his sympathies were. In 1893, he signed a bill that provided an eight-hour workday for women, sought the elimination of sweatshops, and restricted child labor in factories. Given these early deeds, Altgeld's supporters expected a quick pardon of the anarchists. That did not happen.

The inaction troubled Darrow greatly. He had long been concerned about the anarchists. Shortly after arriving in Chicago in 1887, he had gone to see them in jail. Getting to the condemned men was easy. It took only a few moments to convince the jailers that he was a lawyer who wanted to help. Darrow worked much harder to win over the prisoners. But in his typical jovial style, he eased into a conversation and got them smiling, telling them at one point that he was "something of a crank myself, although I knew nothing about dynamite."[4] He found all of them "good looking, intelligent" men and left the prison with even more sympathy for the condemned radicals than before. Hanging them, he declared to the *Democratic Standard*, Ashtabula, Ohio's main newspaper, "would be a sad mistake" and "far more dangerous to liberty and happiness than all the foolish speeches ever made in America." Darrow assured his former hometown's readers that he was no anarchist. Rather, he explained that he retained his "unfortunate habit of looking at many questions in a different light from the majority."[5]

Darrow became a strident advocate for the Haymarket anarchists, speaking on their behalf while they lived and after they died.[6] He was dumbfounded at Altgeld's hesitance. Hadn't his friend written a book about the evils of the penal system in America? Didn't he share Darrow's reverence for justice and freedom? As the days turned into weeks, Darrow grew more impatient and angry. Nothing in the historical record indicates that Altgeld had promised Darrow or even Schilling or Lloyd that he would pardon the anarchists. But we can imagine that there was an understanding sealed with an explicit but whispered statement or a telling nod or a knowing wink. Publicly Altgeld had said nothing on the subject. If he had, he would have jeopardized the election. As it was, his opponents and Republican newspapers called him a "millionaire fraud" with "socialist tendencies" while others labeled him an anarchist.[7] Candidate Altgeld had feared playing into their hands, and so did Governor Altgeld.

By the spring of 1893, Darrow was deeply frustrated. In his mind, Altgeld's decision was not a difficult one; the path to the pardons had been blazed years before. Immediately after the 1886 convictions and sentencing of the anarchists, progressives of all stripes in the United States and Europe had formed an Amnesty Association. The group had significant support in the business community. The association was led by Lyman J. Gage (1836–1927), president of the First National Bank in Chicago, and it had the backing of the influential William Goudy and his boss, Marvin Hughitt (1837–1928), president of the Chicago North Western Railroad. The public seemed to support the idea as well. The association collected more than one hundred thousand signatures for clemency. But the association fell short of its goal. Many of Chicago's rich and influential conservatives, such as Phillip Armour (1832–1901), Marshall Field (1834–1906), and George Pullman (1831–1897), won the day.[8] Nevertheless, after much soul-searching, Governor Richard J. Oglesby had commuted the death sentences of Fielden and Schwab to life in prison. They served their time with Neebe in Joliet. The rest were executed on November 11, 1887. The Amnesty Association— particularly Darrow, Schilling, and Lloyd—never gave up, and Altgeld had been their greatest hope for victory. Now Darrow resolved to make a direct plea. In late April 1893, as warmer weather began to make travel more enjoyable, he boarded a train and headed for Springfield to press Altgeld to do the right thing.

Altgeld received Darrow promptly, but with little enthusiasm. Darrow got to the matter at hand and told the governor that there was "no excuse for waiting." Altgeld replied curtly but not angrily: "Go tell your friends that when I am ready I will act." He added, "[I]f I conclude to pardon those men it will not meet with the approval that you expect; let me tell you that from that day I will be a dead man."[9]

A month and a half went by with no word from Altgeld. Then, on Monday, June 26, 1893, one day after eight thousand people had gathered at Waldheim Cemetery in Chicago to dedicate a monument to the Haymarket martyrs, Governor Altgeld issued the pardons for Fielden, Neebe, and Schwab. Accompanying the order was his eighteen-thousand-word *Reasons for Pardoning*. It was a thorough, harsh, but fair assessment of the Haymarket trials. Altgeld argued that the jury was packed in favor of the prosecution, that the evidence did not prove a crime had been committed by the defendants, that there was no case against Neebe whatsoever, and that the presiding judge, Joseph Gary, was biased and incompetent. Immediately, a rain of hatred poured down upon the governor. The vitriol came from every direction. Newspapers like the conservative standard-bearer *Chicago Tribune* used the pardons to prove that Altgeld was a crazed radical. But there was popular outrage as well. Two days after the pardon, in Naperville, thirty miles west of Chicago, Altgeld was hanged in effigy.[10]

For different reasons, Darrow too was annoyed by Altgeld's actions. He had got his wish—the remaining anarchists were freed—but he thought that Altgeld had brought outrage on himself with his "caustic and severe" criticism of Judge Gary. Darrow surprisingly let Gary off the hook. "Undoubtedly his rulings were biased and unfair," Darrow stated, but he had acted "under the lashing of the crowd." In Darrow's mind, Gary's pusillanimity paled in comparison with that of the justices of the U.S. Supreme Court, who in the clear light of day said that the highest court in the country lacked the jurisdiction to rule on the merits of the anarchists' case and that in any event the men had not been denied a trial by "a fair and impartial jury and had not been denied due process of law."[11] Gary was a coward and a tool of the privileged class, but the seven justices were traitors to liberty and justice. In a backhanded comment, Darrow concluded that "the great mass of the criticism directed against [Altgeld] would have been spared . . . if only Governor Altgeld had consulted some one."[12] *Someone*, indeed.

Not long after the pardon, Darrow and Altgeld patched up their partnership. Darrow felt for his friend, who had solemnly and stoically borne the public's "wrath of malice" during those "appallingly lonely days after the pardoning."[13] He had done the right thing, and it had cost him politically and personally. At a time when Altgeld was isolated on both accounts, Darrow remained an important ally, willing to do his bidding and to follow his orders.

On April 27, 1893, Goudy died suddenly of a massive heart attack. Without this connection to the establishment, Darrow left the company, and on the advice of Altgeld, he returned in May 1893 to the city's law department, which was still a nexus of political power and patronage. The extraordinarily popular mayor Carter Harrison was back in office, and Altgeld and Darrow thought it important to be on the inside of their Democratic rival's administration, rather than the outside. Moreover, putting Darrow inside his administration was a typically Harrisonian thing to do. The old mayor— now the world's fair mayor—had long blunted his opponents, especially those to the political left, by co-opting them through the spoils of office.[14] Harrison had offered Darrow the job of assistant corporation counsel, the post he had held before, and apparently promised to make him corporation counsel again. But when that did not happen, Darrow and Altgeld reversed course. Rather than be pigeonholed in the city's legal department, on September 13, 1893, Darrow tendered his resignation to corporation counsel Adolf Kraus (1852–1928), the millionaire corporate lawyer who had helped put Harrison in office. At the same time, Darrow issued a statement for the press: he had left because it was "time to begin establishing a practice of my own."[15] He promptly set about forming a partnership with three former judges: Lorin C. Collins (1848–1940), a former circuit court judge as well as former speaker of the Illinois House of Representatives; Adams A. Goodrich, a former state judge; and William A. Vincent (d. 1919), a former chief justice of the Supreme Court of the Territory of New Mexico. The firm's partners pledged to take on lucrative cases representing railroads and banks. But anyone paying attention to Chicago politics knew that Darrow's departure signaled a break with Mayor Harrison and that the establishment of a new firm was an attempt to maintain Darrow's legal as well as political connections among the city's wealthy in order to keep Altgeld in office and challenge Harrison in the next mayoral election. As the *Chicago Evening Post* reported, "Darrow resigned assistant corporation counsel to go into private practice but everyone understands that he did so because city administration failed to fulfill its promise and make him corporation counsel."[16] In other words, Darrow remained as politically active as ever. Within a month he had made his next political move. After discussions with Altgeld and likely Schilling and Lloyd as well, he did indeed go back to the Chicago North Western Railroad in October 1893. There was still work to be done there: Governor Altgeld had decided to run for a second term.

Darrow did his duty to Altgeld's inevitable reelection campaign, but deep down he knew the job at the Chicago North Western Railroad wasn't what he wanted.[17] Most of his day was spent dealing with lost freight and baggage claims as well as liability and accident cases. Additionally, Darrow's counsel was sought on the construction of laws and ordinances designed to help the railroad's bottom line. Darrow was especially squeamish about his work on injury and death cases, of which there were dozens every year. The CNW was not alone. In the nineteenth century, the entire American railroad industry functioned like the Grim Reaper. From the mines and forests to the rails, everyone was at grave risk. But in particular, railroad employees— yard workers, engineers, firemen, brakemen, conductors, and porters—as well as passengers were constantly getting hurt and killed.[18] Darrow assessed death and dismemberment claims, which he was expected to deny or delay. He hated this part of the job.

Luckily, the railroad's claims agent, Ralph C. Richards (later the president of the National Safety Council), shared Darrow's sympathies. Together they were able "to help a great many people *without serious cost to the road* [emphasis added]."[19] One would imagine that if the latter weren't true, their efforts would have been impeded or stopped altogether. Further, one could imagine that if Darrow developed a desire to do more for social justice than authorize payments to claimants, his career with the railroad would end. Of course, that is exactly what happened. Ultimately, those desires emerged from two dramatic and violent episodes that transformed Chicago at the very pinnacle of its fin de siècle development.

The first came during the 1893 Chicago world's fair, billed as the World's Columbian Exposition to commemorate Christopher Columbus's "discovery" of the New World four hundred years earlier. The grandeur and spectacle of this fair are beyond description.[20] In 1890, Chicago's lobbying team had won its prize, beating out its rivals in Philadelphia, New York City, and St. Louis. As soon as the city's famous architectural firm of Burnham and Root received the contract, work started on a square-mile area, carved from the Midway Plaisance and Jackson Park. For months, however, it seemed as though nothing much was happening aside from the digging of lagoons and ditches. Then, in the winter of 1892 and spring of 1893, a city began to emerge from the old prairie like crocuses. By May, the improbable White City was ready for its grand opening.

From May 1 to October 30, 1893, more than twenty-seven million exposition visitors were treated to a carnival of dazzling lights, exotic sounds and tastes, and wild experiences. It was a celebration of world cultures—or their rough approximations—on grand and small scales. No one left unaffected, and some, like Henry Adams (1838–1918), Elias Disney (1859–1941; father of Walt), Theodore Roosevelt (1858–1919), Frederick Jackson Turner (1861–1932), and Ida B. Wells (1862–1931), were forever transformed. Aside from the stunning, architecturally magnificent buildings, visitors witnessed spectacular shows and crowd-pleasing speeches, including one from Darrow himself, who spoke on the fair's Labor Day. They also saw plenty of Americana: a twenty-two-thousand-pound cheese from Wisconsin; a giant map of the United States made entirely of Heinz pickles; an enormous thirty-five-foot tower made of fourteen thousand oranges; the uncanny merman; the new folding Kodak camera; the world's first facsimile machine; Thomas Edison's kinetoscope; and demonstrations of the telephone. Visitors saw the (allegedly) cannibalistic Dahomeyans, North African women who performed the infamous belly dance, and "real" Vikings, who regularly sailed across the lagoons in menacing warships. Buffalo Bill had his own section of the exposition for his Wild West Show. Those with more daring (and a little more money) could ride on the world's first Ferris wheel, built by George Washington Gale Ferris (1859–1896). The contraption, which stood over

250 feet tall, had thirty-six gondolas, each one larger and only slightly less fancy than a Pullman passenger car.[21]

All the jocularity, frivolity, and wonder ended abruptly on American Cities Day, Saturday, October 28, which marked the penultimate celebration at the Columbian Exposition. Mayor Harrison led the festivities, which lasted all morning and all afternoon, ending with a rousing speech that some labeled "the best effort of his life."[22] The mayor celebrated the accomplishments of the world's fair, lauded the hard work of Chicago's citizens, boasted that the city itself would rival any in the world, and then bade the crowd a farewell, inviting them to attend the last festival of the exposition, October 29, 1893, the appropriately tagged Columbus Day.[23] By five o'clock he was back home, 231 Ashland Boulevard, a noble house in a very regal residential district. Dinner was at 6:00 p.m. He ate with his children. It is doubtful that anyone at the table noticed the knock at the door. A servant answered. It was a short man with a slight build who gave his name as Patrick Eugene Joseph Prendergast (1868–1894). Sweating profusely, Prendergast asked to see the mayor but was refused, as no one interrupted his dinners. He was told to come back around eight o'clock. Meanwhile, Mayor Harrison had finished his coffee and gone to the library to rest. Shortly before eight there was another knock at the door. The queer little man had returned.

The servant did her duty. Like his office at City Hall, the mayor's home was welcome to all sorts of visitors, day or night. Letting Prendergast in was not unusual, but she asked him to wait in the hall. However, the man with high rosy cheeks, a crooked nose, shifty eyes, and a pasty and sweaty face ran down the hall.[24] The mayor met him in the library's doorway. Harsh, muffled words were exchanged. Prendergast demanded to be appointed the city's corporation counsel. Even if he weren't exhausted, Harrison rarely had patience for the ridiculous. And he was as tactless as he was impatient.[25] He scoffed at this deranged office seeker and told him to go home. Prendergast drew a five-chambered .38 caliber revolver and fired point-blank at Harrison's abdomen. A second shot grazed the mayor's ear. Harrison vainly tried to slam shut the library door that might have separated him from his assailant. Prendergast fired one final shot, shattering Harrison's hand. Slumping to the floor, the mayor cried out for help. Prendergast ran out of the house and down the boulevard.[26]

At first, it was not clear to the Harrison children and the house servants what had happened. Harrison, however, knew he was fatally wounded. Upon hearing the shots, a neighbor, W. J. Chalmers, rushed in and cradled the mayor's head in his overcoat. Chalmers told Harrison that he was going to be OK and not to talk. Instead, Harrison called out for Annie, his fiancée, and barked at his dense friend that he was going to die. Sadly, the mayor won his last debate. The family gathered in the parlor and watched the old man slip away.[27]

Preston Harrison, the mayor's youngest son, immediately called for the police. They arrived quickly and in force. A hastily assembled manhunt ensued, but no police work turned up Prendergast.[28] Rather, he turned himself in at the Desplaines Street Police Station. The station's chief, Sergeant Frank McDonald, had just heard over the telephone that the mayor had been killed when Prendergast walked in and announced, "I killed Mayor Harrison!"[29] McDonald disarmed the man and walked him into the jail. After rumors of roving mobs reached him, the sergeant had Prendergast secretly moved to the Central Station downtown for his protection.

The next day Darrow as well as most of Chicago and the world learned of the murder of Mayor Harrison and the arrest of Patrick Eugene Joseph "Gene" Prendergast, a deeply disturbed twenty-two-year-old. Born in 1868, he had moved with his family from Ireland to America in 1871. Quiet as a child, Prendergast lurched further into withdrawal after his father, likely his only friend, died suddenly when Gene was only thirteen. Shortly after, he moved away from his family and began living in the basement of a house they owned on the impoverished June Street. There Prendergast's personality began to change. He took up reading the great works of the day. In particular, he was enthralled by Henry George. To his mother's and his brother's pleasant surprise, the single tax became a kind of hobby for Gene. He broke out of the basement regularly to join his "friends" at the Single Tax Club and to listen to lectures in the city about taxation, tariffs, and monetary policy.[30]

It may have been the description of Prendergast's politics that caught Darrow's attention. Indeed, he might have remembered him from some single tax meetings, since Prendergast was the kind of opinionated egocentric who always had something to offer in every debate or lecture. Almost certainly Prendergast would have remembered Darrow. As he read further down the newspaper column, chills might have gone down Darrow's back. When McDonald asked his prisoner why he had killed Harrison, Prendergast responded: "I worked hard for him during his campaign for the Mayoralty, and he promised to make me Corporation Counsel. He was elected, but he failed to keep his promise and I have shot him because he didn't do as he said he would."[31] Of course, it had been Darrow who had been promised that post, and it was Darrow whom Harrison had failed. The irony of that moment changed Darrow's life.

Over the next few days, Darrow and the rest of the country learned much more about Prendergast and his apparent motivations. He had no legal training and no understanding of how the law worked. But Prendergast believed quite rightly that the job of corporation counsel was more political than legal. As such, he thought, it would be a perfect platform for his big idea, the elevation of the city's trains. Whatever his mental illness, Prendergast was aghast at the daily carnage on Chicago's streets. From the city's legal offices, he hoped to put the thumbscrews to the railroad moguls and move the city's lethargic bureaucracy to protect the average citizen.[32]

During his arrest and in his initial interview with Inspector John Shea of the Chicago Police Department, Prendergast mentioned that candidate Harrison had promised him the job. It is not at all clear what he meant by that. Harrison and Prendergast had never met. It is more likely that Prendergast dreamed this or simply expected it after writing Harrison a postcard with political advice as Prendergast did with so many people, maybe even Darrow. After Harrison's election, Prendergast was elated. But on April 17, 1893, Harrison's cabinet was announced, and a stranger, Adolf Kraus, was listed as corporation counsel—in Prendergast's mind, a definite mistake.[33] While Prendergast waited for a retraction, weeks turned into months, and he grew only more impatient. Taking the initiative, he went down to City Hall and confronted Kraus, that cowbird. Marching into his office, Prendergast announced that he was Kraus's successor. Kraus paused and smiled and then meanly began to introduce him to his assistants and the office staff, maybe even to Darrow himself, who by then was back at City Hall. Prendergast felt a moment's relief. He had been right all along, and Harrison had been true to his word. But then Prendergast realized that everyone in the office was standing quietly, staring at him. Laughter and waves of embarrassment and shame followed, as well as a rough exit from the building.[34] For days he could not get that laughter out of his head. His malice toward Harrison became overwhelming. He had convinced himself that Harrison's betrayal was not merely a personal rebuke but one that threatened the entire city. For if he was not going to save the city from the trains, who was? The current corporation counsel or his bright new assistant? It was then he hatched the plan to confront Harrison and if necessary kill him.

Little that was mentioned in the press created any sympathy for Prendergast. Newspapers likened the killing of Harrison to the assassination of President James A. Garfield (1831–1881) by Charles J. Guiteau (1841–1882) and the more recent assassination attempt on capitalist Henry C. Frick (1849–1919) by the Soviet-born anarchist Alexander Berkman (1870–1936) in 1892. Panic swept through the city. With its chief magistrate gone, who would take control? Was this part of a larger anarchist plot? *The New York Times* reported that in churches, in saloons, and on street corners, Chicagoans blamed Governor Altgeld for their troubles. By pardoning the Haymarket anarchists, it was said, the governor had encouraged such crimes. The day after the murder, the *Chicago Tribune* ran an editorial calling for Altgeld's impeachment.[35]

Darrow was angered by this baseless personal attack on his friend. He was also irked, but probably unsurprised, that the newspapers were essentially trying the case. No sooner had a grand jury indicted Prendergast than the newspapers began debating whether he was insane—that is, not legally and morally responsible for the crime to which he had already admitted. The so-called insanity defense had been in the Western legal tradition since at least the ancient Greeks, and in the United States, insanity had always been an accepted part of criminal law doctrine.[36] By 1893, Illinois state statutes provided that a person who was insane before or during a crime was not to be held criminally responsible and, if found guilty by reason of insanity, was to be farmed out to a secure hospital or asylum. Writing days and weeks after the assassination, journalists seemed to want it both ways: Prendergast was insane yet responsible for his crime and destined for the hangman's noose. When asked, Prendergast's family stated that they thought him sane. But perhaps hoping to mount some sort of insanity defense, his mother quickly recanted the next day, telling reporters that her son's insanity was inherited from his father and grandfather.[37] Editorial remarks still sought to hold Prendergast responsible.

The debate about criminal insanity in the press likely deterred Chicago's lawyers from rushing to Prendergast's aid. Also, Prendergast and his family had no money. A week after the murder, he still had no lawyer though the state had already hired Alfred S. Trude (1847–1933), perhaps the brightest and most respected criminal lawyer in Chicago, to assist the state's attorney. Darrow may have wanted to defend Prendergast at his murder trial, but defending a man who had murdered an extraordinarily popular mayor was no way to start a corporate law firm.[38] Further, allying himself with a crazed assassin, rumored to be part of an anarchist vanguard, might short-circuit his political aspirations. Thus, although he sympathized with the deranged man trapped in an unfair legal system, Darrow initially watched from the gallery and learned what he could from the papers.

By December 1893, Prendergast had assembled a pro bono defense team of local attorneys: R. A. Wade, Robert Essex, John P. McGoorty, and John Heron. On December 6, a shackled Prendergast walked over the so-called Bridge of Sighs, which connected the jail and courtroom, as his trial began. He was happy to leave his cell. As the jailer told a reporter, "the prisoners in this jail would kill that fellow in a minute if they could get hold of him."[39] Additional bailiffs were in the courtroom too. The charge was murder in the first degree, the defense was insanity, and the prosecution followed exactly the tack suggested by the newspapers. "The line of inquiry on behalf of the State," explained a *New York Times* reporter, "showed that the intention was to get a jury which could believe Prendergast to have been a crank at the time he fired the fatal bullets into Mayor Harrison's body and yet be responsible for his deed, knowing the difference between right and wrong."[40] It took a week to impanel a jury. The trial lasted for two weeks. The defense tried hard to demonstrate, on the one hand, that Prendergast was mentally ill and, on the other hand, that his complaints about the city government had some merit. In other words, he was not simply a crank. Wade went so far as to subpoena Henry George, then living in New York, as a witness for the defense. The previous year George and Prendergast had exchanged letters, and during the summer of 1892 they had met briefly in Chicago for a conversation about taxation policy and, of course, the elevation of the city's trains.[41] George failed to respond to the subpoena, as did several doctors who Wade thought could have helped Prendergast's defense.[42] Those blows to the defense were followed by several days of testimony that, as the prosecution hoped, indicated Prendergast to be erratic but not necessarily insane. Feeling that he was about to lose his case, Wade announced to the press that he would accept only a verdict of not guilty by reason of insanity and that the family would not object to a sentence of life in the penitentiary or confinement in a mental institution.[43] Prendergast himself knew his trial was not going well and even jumped out of his chair at closing arguments to implore the court: "I was not actuated by malice. I swear before high heaven that I was not. You are my murderer if I die!"[44]

Closing arguments ended on December 28. The jurors deliberated for less than an hour. The bailiff read the jury's decision: "We, the jury, find the defendant, Patrick Eugene Prendergast, guilty of murder in the manner and form as charged in the indictment, and we fix his punishment at death."[45] Prendergast was stunned. He sank deep into his chair and made the "Catholic sign over his breast with his right hand." Prison guards stood him up and took the trembling man back to the jail to his new cell in "murderer's row" to await his sentencing. As he shuffled out of the courtroom, his brother, John, shouted: "Don't lose hope, Gene, we'll do all we can for you." Gene paused for a few seconds, put his head down, and walked on.

Given his interest in the case, Darrow might have sat in the courtroom close to the Prendergast family. After overhearing John's promise to help, he decided to meet the family and offered to help the defense team in a last-ditch effort to save Harrison's murderer. For the time being, however, the family kept their faith in Wade, who was committed to doing all he could. As he told reporters after the verdict, "I will bank my life that this boy will never hang."[46] He immediately petitioned for a new trial on the basis of one juror's having lied when he said that he was not an intimate friend of Mayor Harrison's as well as on the faulty testimony of the doctors who testified for the prosecution.[47] On February 17, 1894, all the lawyers found themselves back in Judge Theodore Brentano's courtroom to give oral arguments for and against a new trial. Trude contended that there was no reason for a new trial because the assassin was "clear, active, and healthy enough for him to fully understand" the trial, verdict, and sentencing. In other words, Prendergast was faking his mental illness. Brentano denied the motion and set Prendergast to hang on Friday, March 23. He stuck to that date despite some criticism that he was making a statement by hanging this Irish Catholic immigrant on Good Friday.[48]

At this point, Darrow decided he had to help a man caught in an overbearing legal system bent more on destruction than on justice and redemption. He could not stand by and watch a poor insane man die at the hands of those running the legal system. Someone had to help Prendergast fight against the might of the state, which desired to take his life. Darrow again approached the Prendergast family, suggesting that they dump their lawyers and hire Darrow and his friends, who were already quite well known: Stephen S. Gregory (1849–1920), future president of the American Bar Association, and James S. Harlan (1861–1927), a son of Supreme Court Justice John Marshall Harlan (1833–1911), a future city alderman, and a successful lawyer in his own right. The three offered their services without commission and had a smart plan. Darrow had in mind a little-noticed part of Illinois criminal code, which stated that if someone became insane between the period of the sentencing and the execution, the state had to stay the killing. Moreover, even if Prendergast had been insane on the night of October 28, his subsequent actions strongly suggested a significant mental illness. During the postverdict motions for another trial, Prendergast made fitful outbursts in the courtroom and in jail. The family agreed, and Darrow took over the case.

Bolstering Darrow's plan, Prendergast acted quite inappropriately when Darrow went to see his new client in jail. Darrow had brought with him seven local doctors to examine the condemned man. The jailer unlocked the door. As Darrow stepped into the cell, Prendergast stood up, embraced his lawyer, and planted a long, hearty kiss on his lips.[49] To the wide-eyed Darrow and the doctors, it was clear that something was not right with Prendergast. In addition to his experts, Darrow needed an affidavit from someone close to Prendergast. His brother John volunteered immediately, signing a statement that Gene had lost any sense of rational thought after his sentencing. Not wanting to put all his eggs in one basket, Darrow and his colleagues pursued two other strategies to prevent the hanging. First, they appealed to the U.S. circuit court for a full review of the case, fishing for a retrial on technical error. Second, Darrow went to Springfield to press his old friend the governor for clemency. Having been burned in effigy for pardoning the Haymarket anarchists, Altgeld sent his pal back to Chicago empty-handed. On March 22, the circuit court justices handed down their ruling: they refused to interfere with the execution. Prendergast's life now depended on Darrow's ability to convince a judge and jury that since the first trial the murderer had lost his mind.[50]

Darrow and his colleagues had very little time to waste. Their client was set to die less than twenty-four hours after federal judges had refused to stop the death sentence. Prendergast's lawyers rushed into court, and shortly before midnight on March 22, just ten hours before the execution, Judge Arthur Chetlain granted a stay until Prendergast's mental state could be determined. The law required that a jury decide if Prendergast was fit to be killed. However, legal maneuvering delayed the impaneling of the jurors until mid-June. By that time Chetlain's term on the bench had expired, and a new judge, John Barton Payne, had inherited the case. The second trial lasted three weeks, and it was quite similar to the first. The prosecution and the defense paraded a long line of doctors before the jurors to prove their respective points. Closing arguments came on July 2, 1894. The state's attorney, James Todd, argued that the issue was quite simple: Prendergast was "shamming" and was as sane now as he had been when originally convicted. "This man's reasoning," Todd continued, "is no more illogical, is no more incoherent than was the reasoning of the assassin who struck down the President of the French Republic."[51] He cautioned the jury to ignore "Mr. Darrow[, who] will refer to the widowed mother, and the brother of this prisoner, and tug at your heart-strings that your sympathies may be aroused and overwhelm your judgment."[52] Todd claimed to take the high road. "I'm not permitted," he explained, "to picture before you the murdered Mayor . . . shot down like a dog by a man [who] knew full well the nature of the act, and had the power at that time to refrain from doing it."[53] He admonished the jurors to do their duty, for "if Patrick Prendergast escapes the gallows at this time, we may say farewell in this case, to the proper administration of justice."[54]

Todd's closing made Darrow's blood boil. Comparing Prendergast with Sante Geronimo Caserio (1873–1894), the Italian anarchist who had slain French president Marie-François-Sadi Carnot (1837–1894), was a dirty trick, as was Todd's bogus refusal to paint a picture of the murder. He was amazed; he had never "believed that the State was so interested in taking the blood of any human being" that its lawyers would traduce the truth just to give justice a victim.[55] The facts were clear: Prendergast had been insane during the commission of the crime and ever since. He had not been "ably defended" the first time, and this was the jury's last chance to prevent the noose from being put around Prendergast's neck.[56] Further, the state's attorney had "gone up and down through the sewers of the medical profession" to find men "willing to tie the rope around this boy's neck."[57] This was not merely a case of when Prendergast had become insane. Rather, it was about what to do with an insane murderer. Channeling the ghost of Mayor Harrison, Darrow said that "he would ask [the jurors] to save the city that he loved and the State in which he lived from the infamous disgrace of sending a lunatic to the scaffold."[58] Then Darrow pulled as hard as he could on the jury's heartstrings by placing "this poor, weak, misshapen vessel . . . in your protection and in your hands." He concluded: "I beg of you, gentlemen, take it gently, tenderly, carefully. Do not, I beseech you, do not break the clay, for though weak and cracked and useless it is the handiwork of the infinite God."[59]

The jury needed only twenty minutes to return its verdict: Prendergast was shamming and was sane. Judge Payne reinstated the death order for July 12. Darrow tried one last time to get a reprieve. He telegrammed Governor Altgeld, again asking for clemency. No such luck.[60] Darrow and two hundred others made their way to the jail on the morning of the twelfth. Prendergast appeared about 11:30 a.m. His face was ashen. Mounting the scaffold, he made the sign of the cross on his forehead and on his heart. He drew a deep breath as if to start a soliloquy. Instead, he stepped forward into the noose. The floor dropped. Thus ended Prendergast's life and Darrow's first capital case.

A week after the state of Illinois had hanged Gene Prendergast, Darrow left his career as a full-time corporate lawyer. He and the Chicago North Western Railroad had parted ways not over the defense of the mayor's assassin. It was the massive labor upheaval of 1894—the second transformative event of that year—that caused Darrow to abandon his legal career with corporate America and become a lawyer for the working class and a politico for freedom and liberty. The decision was wrenching, and he tried hard to avoid making it. In the end, his conscience compelled him to walk into the limelight as a counselor for the poor and hopeless and dedicate his life to fighting for liberty and freedom. Whereas before he had taken some halting steps toward a public life as a crusading jurist, after the Pullman strike of 1894 he jumped in headfirst regardless of consequences.

Amid the economic pallor of the 1893 depression and shortly before the melancholy that followed the murder of Mayor Harrison and the unceremonious closing of the world's fair, George Pullman (1831–1897), the palace car prince who ruled over an empire of luxury passenger cars, decided that it was the time to rationalize car production operations in Pullman, Illinois, his utopian eponymous town, by cutting wages and laying off employees. To Pullman—and to almost every capitalist then and now—the bottom line and stockholders ruled business decisions. Along with men like Jay Gould (1836–1892), John D. Rockefeller (1839–1937), James J. Hill (1838–1916), Andrew Carnegie, and Tom Scott (1823–1881), Pullman belonged to an economic, social, and political elite. They set the rules, and they enforced them. Workers served their interests, not the other way around. The extent of corporate control over America, and the quickness with which it had happened following the Civil War, were almost indescribable. Later Henry Lloyd labeled these men plutocrats, or plutes.[61] The plutes structured everyday life, and their desires could not be ignored.

When Pullman's workers had tried to oppose him in the past, he had crushed their revolts. These battles were not unusual. From 1881 to 1894, railroad laborers averaged one major strike nearly every week. Not all these job actions were defensive, with workers seeking to maintain old wages and work rules. In fact, offensive strikes over such noneconomic issues as union recognition and bargaining rights were more prevalent.[62] Frequently, collective action resulted in failure, as happened time and again with fights against Pullman.[63] The leaders of the Knights of Labor, who at one time directed the largest labor organization in the United States, came to see George Pullman as their most "persistent and malignant enemy."[64] Still, there were occasional victories against the railroad barons. For instance, in 1894 the fledgling American Railway Union, the first large industrial union in the United States, waged a strike against the seemingly invincible Great Northern Railroad and won. Veteran railroad unionist Eugene Victor Debs (1855–1926) commanded the strike, which had broad implications for the future of the labor movement in the United States.

Debs's rise to prominence and power was similar to Darrow's. Like the lawyer who defended him after the Pullman strike, Debs was born in the Midwest, in Terre Haute, Indiana. Both had endured pedestrian public educations and had broken free from the intellectual binds placed upon them by their provincial communities. Like Darrow's, Debs's parents had encouraged nontraditional thoughts and ideas mainly by way of the family library. Debs's heroes were Darrow's too: Henry George, John Altgeld, and the Haymarket martyrs. Finally, Debs had also rejected the life that his parents had set out for him. Rather than take the reins of the family business, a grocery store, Debs sought his fortune and fame elsewhere. But whereas Darrow went to Chicago and enmeshed himself in corporate politics and power, Debs took another path, one that led into the labor movement. He believed resolutely that the only way to challenge, to repel, and to defeat the machinations of corporate elites was to organize workers and to engage in direct action in order to improve economic democracy in the United States.

Debs found his early years in the movement disappointing and frustrating. Labor organizations were fractured along political, racial, and craft lines. At the end of the nineteenth century only a handful of unions—in particular four large railroad brotherhoods (the Brotherhood of Locomotive Engineers, the Brotherhood of Locomotive Firemen, the Brotherhood of Railway Trainmen, and the Order of Railway Conductors)—spoke for workers in that industry. Generally, these brotherhoods rarely cooperated, handicapping any chance of success. Debs saw firsthand how damaging these cleavages could be. In late February 1888, the Knights of Labor, the Brotherhood of Locomotive Engineers, and the Brotherhood of Locomotive Firemen—Debs was a member of the latter—struck the Chicago, Burlington, and Quincy Railroad. Optimism quickly gave way to pessimism as the various unions bickered among themselves and against one another. Crumbling from within, the strike was lost.[65]

In the ashes of the Burlington strike, Debs called for a new umbrella labor organization, a federation of railroad brotherhoods designed to coordinate interunion alliances and actions. Debs's federation limped along for several years. In 1893, he gave up hope of finding peace and solidarity among the railroad brotherhoods and established a new railroad union, the American Railway Union (ARU), to replace all the brotherhoods and organize all workers regardless of their crafts. Tens of thousands flocked to the ARU, especially after its unprecedented victory over the Great Northern Railroad. Among the workers who became converts to Debs's one big union gospel were those who labored for George Pullman in his model town.

The workers in Pullman had plenty to complain about. Atop their list were basic bread-and-butter issues. It was not merely that Pullman had cut wages for workers, but not supervisors, at the exact moment that the American economy began to teeter. It was not merely that the cut in wages did not coincide with a commensurate decrease in rents and other fees associated with living in Pullman. The discontent ran much deeper. The story of Jennie Curtiss will stand for the thousands of stories of frustrated Pullman employees. Curtiss had worked for four years in Pullman as a seamstress when the trouble began. Until Pullman slashed wages, she made $2.25 every day, the same wage as her supervisor's. But after August 1893, Curtiss's wages averaged 80 cents per day, a cut far deeper than that of other workers. But it was not just the lost wages that galled her. Rather, it was "the tyrannical and abusive treatment" by her forewoman that made "daily cares so much harder to bear." This woman, whose wages had not been reduced, ruled the shop with an abrasive cruelty that made all but her favorites quit. Curtiss hung on, but not because she was in the woman's good graces. Her father, a ten-year Pullman employee, had recently passed away. At his death in his Pullman house, he owed $60 rent. Pullman managers demanded that Curtiss pay her father's debt out of her paycheck. So every week her paycheck went to her rent and his. There were weeks when it cost her more to work for Pullman than she received in wages.[66]

Curtiss surely resented her low wages, but even more, she hated the total control that Pullman exercised over her life. She was not alone. As another Pullman worker put it, "We are born in a Pullman house, fed from a Pullman shop, taught in the Pullman school, catechized in the Pullman church, and when we die we shall be buried in the Pullman cemetery and go to a Pullman hell."[67] In reporting this fundamental cause of the 1894 Pullman strike, the U.S. Strike Commission, which President Cleveland appointed to investigate the conflagration after the fires had died and the smoke had cleared, expressed a similar sentiment in more academic prose. "Men as a rule, even when employees," wrote the commissioners, "prefer independence to paternalism."[68] To get that independence, the members of the American Railway Union in Pullman were prepared to fight.

In early May 1894, a workers' grievance committee met with George Pullman. Both sides maintained that there was nothing that they could do. Wages had to be cut because of the economic slowdown, and rents and other town fees had nothing to do with wages. Finding no common ground, the grievance committee, whose members were fired before they arrived back at the union hall (which was just across the Pullman town line), recommended a strike. The ARU members agreed, and on May 11, twenty-five hundred workers laid down their tools. Their demand was simple: a return to the previous 1893 pay scale. The strikers were confident and hopeful, almost euphoric. On May 12, the union boldly staged a rally at the Pullman baseball park. The crowd was ecstatic and cheered wildly when the eighty "laundry girls" who had initially resisted the strike came down and joined their comrades.[69] As P. M. Bender, a member of the strike committee, told a reporter, "We can not help but win this strike."[70]

George Pullman thought otherwise, and even Eugene Debs harbored serious doubts. Debs knew that the union had several weaknesses. First, the ARU was not as strong as it appeared. It had won a battle over the Great Northern, but ongoing problems with GN diverted strength and resources away from the Pullman conflict. Also, the labor movement was still significantly divided. Debs could not count on the support of the American Federation of Labor, the railroad brotherhoods, or the Knights of Labor. Moreover, he feared that some labor organizations, like the Brotherhood of Locomotive Engineers, might not view the Pullman strike with benign neglect and might actively cooperate with the company. Additionally, because of the economic depression of the 1890s, there was an enormous pool of desperate unemployed workers willing to scab for Pullman. Finally, the local ARU seriously underestimated Pullman's desire to crush unionism once and for all. Thus, the margin for victory and for error was slim. Upon hearing of the strike, Debs rushed to Chicago to show solidarity and offer any resources needed.[71]

In the beginning, the ARU staged a "model strike" in the "model town." There were few disturbances. The workers themselves had issued a prohibition against drinking during the strike, and union sentinels guarded the shops to ensure that no damage was done. The guards also made it difficult for Pullman to hire nonunion replacements, as, of course, was also the point. But as the days turned to weeks and the weeks into a month, optimism began to fade. The ARU sent out feelers that it desired arbitration. The Great Northern Railroad had agreed to it; perhaps so would Pullman. But Pullman was adamantly against this. As he famously said, "We have nothing to arbitrate."[72] He waved off the pleas of such local reformers as Jane Addams and of reform organizations like the Chicago Civic Federation. In fact, few elite Chicagoans backed the ARU. The Civic Federation itself was divided. Its president, Lyman Gage, heretofore a good friend of Darrow's, refused to offer any relief to the strikers, either personally or through his First National Bank. As the union treasury began to dwindle, the strike leaders called for "radical action."[73] After one final plea for negotiations, which Debs knew would fail, the ARU held its annual convention, which was conveniently in Chicago. There the delegates voted to boycott all Pullman passenger cars. The results were spectacular and played right into the hands of Pullman.[74]

The ARU's leaders thought the boycott would lead to a smashing victory. The union vice president George W. Howard predicted: "We are going to bankrupt George M. Pullman and we are going to do it in a short space of time."[75] Indeed, there seemed a chance of success. Within days more than 100,000 workers across the nation had not only joined the boycott but also gone out on strike. When the strikers uncoupled trains and in some cases threw themselves on the rails, the entire interstate rail system west of Chicago came to a virtual halt. The strikers also halted boxcars carrying grain, fruits, and meat and, significantly, the U.S. mail. Dauntlessly and fatefully, C. H. Chappell of the Chicago and Alton Railroad, who spoke for the Chicago-based General Managers' Association (GMA), a cartel of two dozen railroad barons, told newspaper reporters that his organization was solidly behind Pullman and that "we have organized to resist this strike to the bitter end."[76] The GMA responded to the boycott quickly and decisively by organizing two subcommittees, one to recruit strikebreakers and the other to draw in the federal government on the side of the managers. Of the two, the first subcommittee had it easier. After the closing of the world's fair and the economic downturn, there was a limitless supply of unemployed workers hungry enough for scabbing. The second subcommittee's work involved more logistics, but it certainly was not worried about convincing President Cleveland to help them. That Pullman would come to depend on Cleveland for winning the strike was somewhat ironic. A lifelong Republican, Pullman had supported the president's election opponent, Benjamin Harrison (1833–1901); indeed, Pullman's workers had voted for Cleveland out of a misguided belief that the rotund Democrat was a man of the people. But Pullman and the GMA had a man in the administration's inner circle, Attorney General Richard Olney (1835–1917), who worked tirelessly to use the power of the federal government to smash the strike and destroy the working-class movement that had brought about a social convulsion.

Olney possessed a singularly brilliant legal mind, harbored an enormous ego, and had a political appetite to match. He was also arguably the most acerbic, cruel, vindictive, and unpleasant politician in U.S. history. Olney hated nearly everyone and everything but money and the law. The GMA could have had no better partner. Olney used all his legal acumen, all his malice, and all his cold, ruthless anger to destroy the ARU and its leaders. His work hinged on the simple fact that the strike had disrupted some—but certainly not all—U.S. mail shipments. In early July, President Cleveland met with his cabinet about the nationwide rail crisis. Rather than encourage arbitration, the cabinet, at Olney's instigation, assented to a plan to use the military to end the strike. As the president explained at the time, "if it takes every dollar in the Treasury and every soldier in the United States Army to deliver a postal card in Chicago, that postal card shall be delivered."[77] On July 2, Cleveland put the troops at Fort Sheridan, outside Chicago, on high alert. The next day two things happened. First, under the direction of Attorney General Olney, a team of two U.S. federal judges issued an injunction against the ARU and the strike on the grounds that the union had violated the 1890 Sherman Antitrust Act, which outlawed economic combinations and contracts that restrained trade, and that it interfered with the mails and interstate commerce. Second, blue-coated regulars marched into the city and took strategic positions. Governor Altgeld cried foul but was powerless to stop the president and to prevent what happened over the next few days. After nearly four months of a strike without any pronounced violence, clashes broke out between strikers and troops. During the night of July 5, someone set fire to the world's fair buildings in Jackson Park while others ransacked the Rock Island Railroad yards, destroying property and setting fires. The next night security guards shot two strikers outside the Illinois Central yards. In the ensuing riot, nearly the entire yard was set ablaze, destroying more than seven hundred boxcars. The next day General Nelson A. Miles (1839–1925) ordered additional troops from Kansas City and St. Louis. On July 8, the army marched on Chicago, where it declared martial law and dispersed all strikers.[78] Two days later officers arrested the ARU's leaders, including Eugene Debs, for contempt of court. The greatest labor upheaval since 1877 was over.

For Debs, although he had lost the strike, the battle was not over. On July 17, 1894, he and his ARU associates appeared in court. They were represented by William W. Erwin, the veteran labor lawyer from St. Paul who had defended the Amalgamated Association of Iron and Steel Workers after the Homestead steel strike of 1892; Erwin's understudy, W. A. Shoemaker; and Chicago's leading labor lawyer, Stephen Gregory. Noticeably absent was Gregory's legal compadre Clarence Darrow. Up to this point, Darrow had been content to watch from the sidelines. His sympathies were of course with the ARU and Debs, who he believed was "an intelligent, alert and fearless man." But his first inclination was to be neutral, taking no public stand for one side or the other. When the strike had begun in May, Darrow's boss, Marvin Hughitt, president of the Chicago North Western Railroad, had offered Darrow up to the General Managers' Association to serve as its lawyer. Darrow immediately rejected the offer. He began to realize his "anomalous position": he wanted the union "to win, and believed that they should," but he also wanted to stay at the CNW.[79] Darrow clung to his neutrality even after that terrible Friday, July 6, when rioters burned the Illinois Central yard. Upon seeing the flames on the horizon that night, Darrow had gone to see the destruction firsthand. Watching the bonfires from a safe distance in a green prairie, Darrow felt "no feeling of enmity toward either side." Rather, the scene made him "sad to realize how little pressure man could stand before he reverted to the primitive."[80] For Darrow, the strike's end stirred no more sentiment than its beginning.

This changed after Edwin Walker, the specially appointed federal government attorney, initiated the contempt proceedings against Debs and the ARU for violating the injunction. Darrow "did not regard this as fair." First, Walker was no objective jurist. He had also accepted the position that Darrow had rebuffed and was the GMA's lawyer; this was a textbook case of conflict of interest. "The government might with as good grace," Darrow snidely commented in his autobiography, have "appointed the attorney for the American Railway Union to represent the United States."[81] Second, the more Darrow thought about Debs's arrest and impending trial, the more he came to see that much more than one union leader's fate hung in the balance.

The use of federal troops against Governor Altgeld's wishes had revealed the true nature of the strike. The entire labor upheaval amounted to, in Darrow's words, an "unfriendly" political move "against the Constitution and the laws and the liberties of the people."[82]

Yet even with this realization, Darrow delayed. As Gregory began to prepare to fight the conspiracy cases, of which there were two, he begged Darrow to join him. He did not. It is not clear why. He was still depressed from the Prendergast execution just a few days prior. Additionally, Darrow feared taking on a new big public trial "with no compensation."[83] But after reading in the newspapers about the first day in court, he could no longer resist. Compelled to join the fight against the conspiracy of the corporate rich against democracy, liberty, justice, and freedom, he walked into CNW president Hughitt's office and announced his resignation. He expected a fight. Instead, Hughitt listened cordially and attentively to Darrow, praised his work for the CNW, suggested that he must do what he thought was right; Hughitt and Darrow remained lifelong friends. And so Darrow left his job at the CNW and his life among Chicago's elite and went to defend a lowly man of the working class whose strike and whose union it was said had done more damage "in a week as the Confederate Armies did in months."[84]

Darrow knew he had to act quickly. "Do you know," he wrote his friend Henry Lloyd in late 1894, "that they are making history very fast in America, and all the history is against freedom? . . . Can anything be done to [stop] them before liberty is dead?" he continued. "I am very much discouraged at the prospect . . . what can be done?"[85] During the Prendergast trial, in the midst of an economic depression, and after the fire of the 1894 labor upheaval, Darrow finally realized that he had to fight to preserve American democracy. At thirty-seven years, already quite middle-aged for his generation, he leaped into the breach to take on the rich and politically powerful for the chance to defend liberty, freedom, and fairness. Darrow was going to defend Debs and the American Railway Union's top brass, who were again in jail for their part in the great Chicago strike of 1894. He had become, as Lincoln Steffens (1866–1936) later called him, the "attorney for the damned."[86]

⊰· 4 ·⊱

Fighting for the People in and out of Court

On July 17, 1894, Eugene V. Debs and the other officials of the American Railway Union (ARU) found themselves back in jail. Federal marshals had arrested them for conspiring against the court injunction against the boycott of the Pullman Company, which had sparked a national railroad strike. There in Cell No. 5 of the local jail in Woodstock, Illinois, with his bunkmate, ARU vice president George Howard, Debs had time to contemplate what had gone so terribly wrong and so quickly. On July 10, federal marshals had arrested him and his compatriots for the first time on contempt charges. Then the cadre members had each posted a ten-thousand-dollar bail and vowed to fight on. One reporter noticed that they seemed nonplussed while strutting away from the courthouse, feeling that victory over Pullman and the entire General Managers' Association (GMA) was imminent—surely only days away.[1] In retrospect, the signs were clear that their strike, the boycott, and the ARU were doomed. A week later, head in hands, Debs tried to figure this out, map a path out of jail, and plot some rearguard action to defeat Pullman while his defense team, which soon featured Clarence Darrow, researched his case and strategized.

There were two Debs trials stemming from the Pullman strike, one civil for the contempt citation and one criminal for the conspiracy charge. Darrow was eventually instrumental to both, but at first, Debs's original attorneys, Stephen S. Gregory and William W. Erwin, took the lead. The civil case, which began on July 17, was the longer and had the clearest resolution. It began in Chicago and ended before the U.S. Supreme Court in Washington, D.C. The prosecution, led by railroad lawyer Edwin Walker and U.S. district attorney Thomas Milchrist, contended that Debs and his colleagues had intentionally violated the injunction. Walker and Milchrist had obtained scores of telegrams ostensibly signed by E. V. Debs and sent to unions around the country, telling them to stand by the Pullman boycott. Two of them, the government lawyers asserted, promoted violence. To strikers in Butte, Montana, Debs allegedly wrote: "The general managers are weakening. If the strike is not settled in forty-eight hours, complete paralysis will follow. Potatoes and ice are out of sight. Save your money and buy a gun."[2] In another, he was charged with cryptically stating: "Say nothing, but saw wood"; the latter, in "Middle State parlance," meant "arm yourself."[3] In the rest, Debs pleaded with workers to "resist the plutocracy and arrogant monopoly."[4] Debs's lawyers objected strenuously to the introduction of the telegrams while Edwin M. Mulford, manager of the Western Union Company, resisted turning over the telegrams to the prosecution. Echoing a later and larger twenty-first-century debate, Mulford believed that it was improper for the private company to provide the government with private communiqués without a court order.

When the civil trial resumed in September 1894 after a two-month hiatus, the prosecution had secured its court order, and for two days Western Union's Mulford painstakingly read the stack of telegrams into evidence. Prosecutors argued they demonstrated that all the thousands of strikers were following Debs's orders, and thus, he and the ARU had violated the court injunction. Although Darrow was present, Gregory led the counterattack, maintaining that while he was "not an apologist for riot and arson," workers had an inalienable right to strike and to quit. Judge William A. Woods conceded the point. "Well, then"—Gregory smiled and continued—"I hold that if a man has the right to strike, he has a right also to advise others to strike." Judge Woods agreed: "I do not even deny the right of laborers to conspire to strike, if it is for a legal purpose." Surprised at the friendly reception from the bench, Gregory got to the heart of his defense: "If this injunction was issued without jurisdiction by the court, my clients had a right to violate it." Woods interrupted: "I will admit to that also." Gregory then stated that the Sherman Antitrust Act, upon which the injunction rested, was never intended to deal with labor organizations, but rather with corporations. Further: "I do not think that this law was ever intended to stop mob violence."[5]

The civil trial closed on September 28, 1894. Erwin delivered the closing statement for the defense. He echoed Gregory: "[T]he act of a strike was one consistent with civil and religious liberty." And it was self-defense. "I say there was no redress from the Pullman horror. . . . What could they do?" he asked Judge Woods. "Declare war? No. Break the public peace? No. Then what might they do [to defend their rights]?" The strike and boycott were the only answers, and pointing to the courtroom's U.S. flag, he rhapsodized and said, "[T]hat is the liberty of this flag."[6] Federal attorney Walker closed for the government. He charged that the injunction was lawful and that the American Railway Union "with its 150,000 members is the worst trust that has ever been organized within my knowledge." He called on Judge Woods to punish Debs and the rest of the ARU leaders for contempt in violating the injunction.[7]

Judge Woods handed down his decision nearly three months later. ARU president Eugene V. Debs, vice president George Howard, secretary Sylvester Keliher, and newsletter editor Lewis W. Rogers were found in contempt. In his ruling, Woods refused to comment on Gregory's argument that the injunction had no legal basis. He maintained that the workers had a right to strike and a right to encourage others to strike. But those rights did not trump the injunction. Rather, "the original conspiracy [to circumvent the court order] . . . became a conspiracy against transportation and travel by railroad." Judge Woods sentenced the defendants to six months in prison. *The New York Times* remarked that the sentence was "generally considered a light one."[8] The *Times* noted one more thing about Debs's sentencing: His defense team, now led by Clarence S. Darrow, planned an appeal to the Supreme Court. It was the first time that Darrow's name had been mentioned in connection with the Pullman strikers. It was also the last time that Darrow would take a second chair in a courtroom.

While waiting for their day before the Supreme Court, Darrow and Gregory mounted their defense for Debs and his comrades in Judge Peter S. Grosscup's (1852–1921) court against the charge of criminal conspiracy. Darrow led the defense. Perhaps he felt more in his element, as this was now the second time in about a year that he had participated in a major criminal trial. While Debs's life did not hang in the balance, a loss in this courtroom could result in a lengthy jail sentence and a significant blow to the labor movement. Certainly that was the result aimed for by the lawyers for the federal government, which also explained their legal pincers movement, opening two legal fronts to stretch the defense's resources and crush Debs from two sides. Thus, Darrow had to mind two legal trains running along parallel tracks, both potentially leading toward jail. The train leaving from Judge Grosscup's courtoom got sidetracked on a branch line and was eventually abandoned.

The trial for criminal conspiracy began on January 24, 1895, almost two weeks after Debs and the other ARU leaders had begun serving their sentences for contempt of court. As had happened in Judge Woods's courtroom, Judge Grosscup found his packed with spectators and newspaper reporters. They got more than they bargained for. Darrow was charismatic and smart; he successfully turned the case on its head.

From his opening statement, Darrow put the prosecution, led by Assistant Attorney General Thomas Milchrist, on the defensive. Darrow charged that the federal government had no evidence of a conspiracy by the American Railway Union. Rather, he argued, "the evidence will show that all the defendants did was in behalf of the employees of that man whose name is odious wherever men have a drop of blood, Mr. Pullman." The General Managers' Association, in its defense of Pullman, had schemed "to use the inconvenience of the public and the feeling of sanctity for the mails as a club to defeat the effort that was being made to better the condition of the workingmen and women."[9] That was the true conspiracy and crime.

Unlike the civil proceedings, the criminal trial had many witnesses and a jury, and Darrow scored key points with the jurors as former Pullman workers took the stand and entered evidence into the record. The prosecution believed that they had produced *the* principal witness who would prove their case. O. W. Myron, a switchman for the Illinois Central (IC) Railroad and a member of the ARU at the time of the strike, testified that he had received a telegram from Debs urging him to call out his fellow IC workers in support of the boycott.[10] The damage that this evidence might have caused was quickly mitigated by Darrow's cross-examination. He coaxed the witness into admitting that he "had acted on his own responsibility and did not report to the Directors" of the American Railway Union. Thus, Debs "could in no way be held responsible for the witness's actions."[11] Debs's appearance on the witness stand was also a victory for the defense. Darrow led him calmly through the history of the boycott and strike. The jury did not see a haggard, bearded, radical zealot but a thoughtful, appealing, kind, and dedicated unionist dressed in a new suit. Looking at the jury with his soft but steely blue eyes, the ARU's president explained that the union did what was lawful in order to attain what was fair and just. Judge Grosscup consented to Darrow's request that Debs read several of his manifestos, in which he counseled his readers to abstain from violence and obey the law. Milchrist tried to shake Debs on cross-examination to no avail. Both the prosecution and the defense were eager for George Pullman to testify, but Pullman had conveniently disappeared, refusing to answer a subpoena.

Finally, Darrow presented his smoking gun evidence that he had been quietly sitting on. Through means known only to him, he had obtained the minute books of the General Managers' Association and introduced them into the record. They showed exactly what Darrow had said: a concerted and consistent effort by the railroad executives to corner the ARU into calling for some sort of union action against Pullman and then a systematic use of the federal government to crush the boycott and strike. But at the moment of Darrow's triumph, the situation changed. One juror, J. C. Coe, who was sixty-nine, came down with a strange illness and asked to be excused. Darrow consented but asked that another juror be added. Judge Grosscup refused, preferring to wait for Coe to recover. It never happened. The criminal trial was suspended—at first temporarily and later permanently—without a jury vote, without a verdict.[12] This was not exactly a defeat for Darrow and Debs; nor was it, however, a triumphant victory for the union.

When the criminal trial stalled, Darrow turned back to the civil case. Before he sent his appeal to the U.S. Supreme Court, he reshuffled the defense team. William W. Erwin went back to St. Paul, Minnesota. To take his place, Darrow recruited eighty-one-year-old Lyman Trumbull (1813–1896), the grayed abolitionist and supporter of less successful radical causes, who had first suggested to Debs that he hire both Gregory and Darrow. In 1895, Trumbull's legal and political days were almost over. To Darrow, he was a legendary hero, an icon, whose picture hung above his desk.[13] Trumbull's presence brought political weight to bear on the Court. Aside from the gravitas of the author of the revolutionary Thirteenth Amendment, Darrow hoped that Trumbull would influence Chief Justice Melville W. Fuller (1833–1910), a former Chicagoan and a probusiness jurist, who was known to bend laws and legal definitions so that American statutes and legal precedent did not restrain capitalism.[14] In 1888, Trumbull had helped secure Fuller's confirmation as chief justice. The other ace that Darrow brought was his and Gregory's tenuous relationship with Justice John Marshall Harlan, who had earned the moniker The Great Dissenter for his opinions that went against the grain of American political culture. Darrow and Gregory were also close friends with Harlan's son, James, Gregory's law partner and cocounsel on the Prendergast murder trial in 1893. These personal connections seemed to pay off, at least initially. The Supreme Court agreed to hear Darrow's motions, a writ of error and a writ of habeas corpus, the former intended to provide relief from the Court's decision and the latter designed to release his clients from an unlawful incarceration.[15]

In early January 1895, Darrow boarded a train bound for Washington, D.C. The trip took a few days, but ironically the accommodations aboard the Pullman sleeping car made life pleasant. After lunch, on January 16, 1895, Darrow walked up the steps of the Capitol Building in Washington, made his way over to the Old Senate Chamber, and presented himself to the justices of the Supreme Court. The country lawyer who had made a name for himself in Chicago was now before the highest court in the land. Staring at him on a marble and wood dais two feet above the ground ringed with Ionic columns were the seven justices, all older than Darrow. The two senior members were the products of a bygone age. Justice Howell Edmunds Jackson (1832–1895) was sixty-three and did not live to see the end of the Debs case. Justice Horace Gray (1828–1902) was sixty-seven. The youngest, Edward D. White (1845–1921), was only fifty. The room, the atmosphere, and the moment energized Darrow, and he quietly but forcefully made his case that both writs should be granted. Assistant Attorney General Edward B. Whitney appeared on Olney's behalf to oppose Darrow. The next day the justices returned a partial victory for the defense. They denied the writ of error but agreed unanimously to grant the writ of habeas corpus and to hear arguments. Moreover, they instructed that the prisoners be released on bail pending the outcome of the final decision. Darrow returned home a conquering hero.[16]

On March 25, the lawyers for the federal government and for Debs convened again inside the Old Senate Chamber. The room was full. Spectators ringed the benches up front. By agreement beforehand, the lawyers and justices had consented to a round robin of oral arguments. The main event came on March 26, when Attorney General Olney battled Darrow. It was unusual for the attorney general to make any statement before the Court. The federal government had a full-time solicitor general who did this work. But Olney believed that his reputation and perhaps his political career were on the line. As one of his biographers described him, Olney was "a hard-thinking, accomplishing, ruthless being like one of those modern war-tanks which proceeds across the roughest ground, heedless of opposition, deaf alike to messages from friends and cries from the foe."[17] That day Olney had cleaned and greased his tank's caterpillar tracks and loaded his weapons with armor-piercing rounds. To the surprise of close observers, he argued that the Sherman Antitrust Act did not matter at all. Rather, the authority to stop the ARU stemmed from the "absolute" authority the government had over interstate commerce. Thus, the Sherman Antitrust Act enhanced, but did not create, the government's jurisdiction. Further, Olney demanded that the conspirators, whose mobs under their control "terrorized communities" across the nation, be brought to justice.[18]

Darrow stood up and fired back. He provided a three-part argument. First, he went after the foundation of the injunction, the Sherman Antitrust Act. The statute was not designed to harm labor organizations. Rather, it was intended "to apply to combinations in the shape of trusts and pools, these modern devices that are controlling the necessities of life and the welfare of the people."[19] The second part of Darrow's argument concerned the alleged conspiracy. To put it simply, the ARU had engaged in none. Cleverly, he quoted a decision Chief Justice Fuller had rendered just three months earlier that economic conspiracy related to wages or prices or interfering with the natural law of supply and demand.[20] Darrow noted that the union had engaged in a boycott and strike, which were entirely legal. Third, Darrow addressed the "evidence" for the "conspiracy," the telegrams. In all of the telegrams—nearly all sent before the injunction—only one "could be tortured into any instruction or counsel to do an unlawful act"—namely, the suggestion that its recipient buy a gun. The telegram was "evidently and plainly meant without any intention of violence, but as a playful statement or a joke." To think otherwise "would be doing violence to reason and common sense."[21] Finally, Darrow made an impassioned plea on behalf of workers who had the right to organize to defend themselves at work and in their communities. Debs and his comrades were "justified not because men love social strike and industrial war, but because in the present social system of industrial evolution to deprive workingmen of this power would be to strip and bind them and leave them helpless as the prey of the great and strong."[22]

Darrow sat down. The justices thanked the lawyers, picked up their papers, and left the chambers. The decision was out of his hands now. As Trumbull, Gregory, and Darrow began to pack their briefcases, Olney appeared in front of them. The old battle tank invited them over to his house for dinner that night. The Chicago trio was too astonished, and too famished, to decline. The meal was exquisite, and the company was a cut above the rest. Darrow dined with Chief Justice Fuller and his wife and Secretary of War Daniel S. Lamont (1851–1905) and his wife.[23]

Almost three months later, on May 27, 1895, the justices presented their decision in what became known as *In re Debs*. It was unanimous; the petition for a writ of habeas corpus was denied.[24] Writing for the Court, Justice David J. Brewer (1837–1910) wrote that "we hold it to be an incontrovertible principle that the government of the United States may, by means of physical force, exercised through its official agents, execute on every foot of American soil the powers and functions that belong to it."[25] That was that. The Debs trial ended in another very public defeat for Darrow. He was in Chicago when the ruling was rendered. There was no courtesy telegram before the news hit the presses. Darrow learned the result from a United Press reporter. The defeat was a bitter pill to swallow. Worse, the opinion, he knew, "strengthened the arm of arbitrary power."[26] He was indignant. The entire case had put a nearly unquenchable fire in his stomach. It tempered his intellect and hardened his resolve to fight for working-class Americans, to fight for liberty and freedom for all regardless of accident of birth. Like Darrow, all the major actors in the 1894 upheaval—except Olney, who became more progressive and liberal on issues of labor and the working class[27]— became ossified in their positions; they include former President Cleveland, who in 1908 wrote an unrepentant history of the "Chicago Strike" for *McClure's Magazine*.[28]

The Pullman strike and boycott, one of the greatest convulsions of the nineteenth century, were but a wave of discontent in a much larger, tempestuous, churning sea of misery, anger, impatience, and protest. Now, as the political and legal fires of the ARU strike were being stomped out, only one group held out the hope for change for average Americans: the Populists. In the Populist mind, the world was divided between the people (those who labored in the mills, mines, and farms) and the rich (those who benefited from the people's hard work); between the producers of value and wealth and the syndicates that ran monopolies; and between equality and special interests. The Populists engaged in a struggle to take power away from the few who ran the factories, who had enclosed the open ranges, who ran the railroads, who controlled the banks, and who held the reins of political power.

Initially, the Populist reformers had limited appeal. Their revolt began in the country, and agrarian radicals had a hard time reaching out to urban workers. But the political leaders of the movement—Jay Burrows, a Nebraskan farmer; Iowa politician August Post; Ignatius Donnelly, editor of the highly influential magazine *The Anti-Monopolist*; and Alson J. Streeter of Illinois, who had run for president in 1888 on the Union Labor Party ticket—made solid alliances with unionists, reformers, and radicals in advance of a massive convention of labor and farm organizations in St. Louis in December 1889. Like a bright porch light at dusk, the meeting attracted farmers, stockmen, unionists, feminists, prohibitionists, single taxers, and unionists. Although the St. Louis meeting revealed many schisms, it also provided a blueprint for creating a national political platform for a new People's Party.[29]

Among those who found the historic St. Louis meeting significant was Henry Demarest Lloyd, Clarence Darrow's close friend. Lloyd was a relative latecomer to Populism, having initially rejected the movement as nothing "of any value for the workingmen's movement."[30] But he saw promise in the People's Party after the 1892 election. Although Grover Cleveland handily dispatched the Populist presidential candidate, James B. Weaver (1833–1912), handfuls of Populist politicians won at the local, state, and national levels. This piqued Lloyd's interest, and he took it as his job to weld together the industrial and agrarian wings of the movement. The flux was a new party platform, the center of which was Plank 10, which called for "the collective ownership by the people of all means of production and distribution."[31] Lloyd believed that he needed just one major convention of the People's Party to adopt it, and then the rest of the party conventions, including the inevitable national one, would fall into line. Thus the stage would be set for a People's Party electoral landslide. Logically, he looked first to his home state. In July 1894, the Illinois People's Party planned to hold its convention in Springfield. To win in Springfield meant bringing on board Governor Altgeld. That was easy. All Lloyd needed was his friend and Altgeld's alter ego Clarence Darrow, who had written him repeatedly that he was growing anxious to engage in the Populist movement. Darrow's new zeal for equality meshed nicely with the Populists' worldview. Lloyd had big plans for his thirty-seven-year-old comrade.

The July 4 Illinois People's Party convention in Springfield did not go as planned. Weeks before, Darrow had helped Lloyd put the finishing touches on the party's state platform, which was an amalgam of Populism, socialism, and patriotism. "We, the undersigned delegates of the assembled in convention in Springfield, Illinois, on the one hundred and eighteenth anniversary of the Declaration of Independence," the preamble proclaimed, "renew the mutual pledge of our lives, our fortunes and our sacred honor, in support of the rights of all to equality, life, liberty and the pursuit of happiness." A five-point program, which linked—or so Lloyd and Darrow thought—the political and economic desires of urban and rural workers, followed: (1) to recall all public franchises given to private individuals or corporations for private profit; (2) to declare all such grants of public powers for private use void; (3) to acquire all means of production and distribution, including land, for the people to operate collectively; (4) to establish a true civil service by providing public schools and colleges; and (5) to institute the referendum and initiative.[32]

Instead of being a triumph, the convention fell apart. The state People's Party's meeting coincided with the arrival of federal regulars in Chicago and the brutal end of the Pullman strike. Rather than become energized by the invasion of bluecoats, the party members became disillusioned and devolved into factional strife, especially over the modified version of Plank 10. The defection of single taxers was expected, as Henry George himself had criticized socialism, but to Lloyd's and Darrow's great disappointment, AFL president Samuel Gompers (1850–1924) backed off from his support, urging trade unionists to eschew party politics.

Hoping to recapture the momentum, Darrow and Lloyd decided to hold an October 1894 People's Party rally in their backyard. On the twenty-fourth,

Darrow, Lloyd, and other leading Chicago radicals, including the Reverend William H. Carwardine, a militant supporter of the Pullman strikers, paraded ten thousand torch-bearing People's Party supporters through the streets of Chicago.[33] The crowd hooted and hollered and sauntered its way from the business district to the city's amphitheater. The leaders of the city's People's Party did not disappoint. Lloyd laid the theoretical foundation, Carwardine gave the moral imperative, and Darrow sold the politics. Fresh off his work with Debs and the ARU, Darrow was an instant hit. "It is never easy for any of us to change our political and social relations," he began, "and it is with much reluctance and hesitation that I come here this evening to state in as plain a way as I can, why from my standpoint those who entertain opinions and views such as I hold should no longer affiliate themselves with either of the two great political parties." He placed the blame for the nation's troubles squarely on the shoulders of the country's political leadership. He castigated President Cleveland. At every turn the Democratic president had shown himself an enemy of the working class. He had inexplicably done nothing in the face of the economic depression of 1893–1894. Protests had fallen on Cleveland's large deaf ears. Then there was the Pullman strike. As he had done in July, Darrow harkened back to America's revolutionary founding, likening the president's actions to the British government in 1770. Darrow called on the crowd to adopt "another sort of patriotism" and dedicate themselves to the People's Party. Dramatically, he concluded that "today the privileged institutions of America, fattened by unjust laws and conditions, boastfully proclaim that monopoly is king, but"—he paused for dramatic effect—"I think I hear a voice rising loud, and louder from the common people"—he paused again as the crowd began to cheer—"a voice which says in thunder tones, not monopoly but the People are king, and that these people, emancipated and aroused, will one day claim their own." Wild and prolonged cheers rocked the amphitheater as Darrow stepped back.[34]

Lloyd's and Darrow's high hopes were smashed on election day. In 1894's off-year elections, every People's Party candidate for local, state, and national office went down in defeat. And worse, it was Lloyd's coalition that had failed him. As his friendly biographer Chester McArthur Destler wrote, "Lloyd had attempted to make bricks without straw with the usual result."[35] In the aftermath Darrow and Lloyd quarreled about the proper path ahead. Three weeks after the election day fiasco, in a letter, Darrow bluntly rebuked

Lloyd's Plank 10 efforts. "I might be willing to join a Socialist Party, but I am not willing to help run another socialist movement under the guise of the People's Party." Darrow believed that socialism was incompatible with Populism and that he and Lloyd "must take some stand" with one or the other.[36] Lloyd immediately penned a thousand-word response. He encouraged his younger colleague to stay the course. He argued that the effort of "the Socialists in Chicago deserve[s] sympathetic attention." By lending their Plank 10 to the Populists, the socialists had made "a greater sacrifice than any other element of the party." To repute Plank 10 and the socialists would be "to repeat the blunder Henry George made." For "if we begin to read each other out of the ranks for differences of opinion," Lloyd warned, "we are lost."[37]

Darrow wasted no time in replying. "I never did and never will believe in barring any one out of any thing," he wrote, "least of all the Socialists of whom I am one." Thinking back to their October rally, he had come to believe that they had pushed the party farther than the partisans wanted to go. He was willing to support a strong "Socialist movement," but he did not want to commit the People's Party to "any thing [the members] do not wish to indorse." In short, although Darrow pledged always to "support and defend" socialists, Plank 10 had to go.[38] Lloyd, however, stuck to his guns, and as Darrow predicted, the People's Party moved steadily away from any socialist impulses toward something else, something upon which many Populists could agree, the need for silver currency.

The Gilded Age fascination, bordering on a fetish, with bimetallism is something difficult to explain to modern readers. For most of U.S. history, there had been two forms of money, silver and gold. Paper money, often issued by private banks, was viewed with deep suspicion. A case in point was the Civil War–era greenback. In 1862, Congress authorized the issuance of treasury notes for legal tender. These bills, the reverse of which was printed with green ink, made the North's economy more fluid during the war, but it also led to inflation and therefore to the devaluation of the currency. Following the Civil War, a great debate ensued about the future of paper money. Elites hated it. They preferred having a gold standard for currency. The shiny yellow metal with peculiar physical properties kept loan rates stable, international trading simple, and wages down. Many workers preferred paper money precisely because cheap money sparked inflation or the devaluation of currency. For farmers, cheap money like greenbacks tended to cause higher prices, which meant larger profits on their crops, and for all workers generally, paying debts back in cheap money was easier than paying back in gold, which all Americans regardless of class tended to hoard. In the late 1860s and throughout the 1870s, elites tried to eliminate cheap money, first by getting rid of greenbacks. In 1873, they managed another coup, the demonetarization of silver. The Crime of '73, as critics termed it, removed silver from coinage. Like paper, silver was cheap money. Although shiny, it was never considered the equal of gold. In terms of purchasing and debt payment, a gold dollar always went farther than a silver one. Inflationists and their supporters, who included farmers, silver miners, and some workers, wanted immediate redress. Silverites never formed their own political party as the greenbackers did. Instead, they joined the Populists.

At first, the silverites were just another faction jockeying for supremacy within the People's Party. They were opposed by laborites like Henry Lloyd, who believed that currency problems were just a symptom of a much larger economic disease, the overpowering influence of the rich. This economic royalism, not the absence of bimetallism, was the root of the problem. The silverites had other ideas and their own powerful ally in the People's Party—namely, John Altgeld.

Altgeld had a relatively late conversion to the gospel of silver. As late as October 1894, he proclaimed that he had "nothing to say for silver or for any other kind of money."[39] But after the Pullman crisis, Governor Altgeld widened his criticism to include President Cleveland's other perceived failings, including his penchant for the gold standard. Such attacks were vitally important if Altgeld was going to help dump the Cleveland faction, by then known as the Gold Bug faction, at the next Democratic Party presidential convention. The silver issue provided Altgeld with the wedge he was looking for. Additionally, silver was a simple political idea and made sense to farmers, miners, and stockmen.

Altgeld first made his presence felt on February 18, 1895, at the Chicago People's Party convention, held at Uhlich Hall. With both Altgeld's and Lloyd's blessing, Darrow presided over the rowdy affair. Union leader, Populist, and close Darrow friend Thomas I. Kidd (1860–1941) called the convention to order and announced the meeting's purpose, the selection of a People's Party ticket for the upcoming city elections. Darrow welcomed the overflowing crowd, declaring, in part, "If the spirit is good, if the aim is not selfish, victory will surely come, though it may be far away." When he finished, the assembled members of the People's Party erupted in sustained cheers. Then they all got down to the business at hand, putting together a slate of candidates. On cue, Kidd nominated for mayor his friend Dr. Bayard Holmes, a successful physician who was also the chairman of the Chicago Civic Federation's Public Health Commission. Another Populist made a rival nomination and put octogenarian Lyman Trumbull's name before the group. Then, out of the blue, still another delegate put forth Darrow. Uhlich Hall erupted as Darrow's nomination was seconded with an enthusiastic and approving wild roar. "When at last the applause subsided," the *Chicago Herald* reported, Darrow said, "I consider it a great honor to have you treat me in this way. I would rather have the respect of the working people and their honest representatives than that of any other class," but he demurred: "I cannot make the sacrifice that the acceptance of this nomination would entail."[40] Put on the spot, Darrow had to choose alliances: Lloyd and the straight People's Party ticket or Altgeld and the fusion Populist/Democratic Party ticket. Or put another way, the choice was between socialism and silver.

As in all political arenas, the time came to choose partners and allies. Perhaps Lloyd and his colleagues believed that he could seduce Darrow by appealing to his political ambitions. Darrow had them, but to take this new opportunity presented by Lloyd meant to betray Altgeld, his mentor. Darrow remained loyal to the man who had been responsible for his successes and career in Chicago. He gave it only a second of thought, walked into the spotlight, and disappointed the cheering crowd. The party regulars strained to hear through the hue and cry as Darrow retreated from the People's Party. Lloyd and the party chiefs then renominated Dr. Holmes. The rest of the slate followed quickly. Afterward the Chicago People's Party convention broke down as the remaining socialists battled the few single taxers who had not bolted over "the re-enactment of 'plank 10.'"[41]

Leaving the People's Party in the lurch did not harm Darrow's political dreams. In reward for his loyalty, Governor Altgeld placed his name on the Democratic Party ticket for Congress in a safe district of Chicago.[42] Darrow and his mentor, who was seeking a second term in the governor's mansion, finally ran together. The thought appealed to both of them. During the spring of 1895, Darrow stumped for bimetallism, or, in the parlance of the day, the free and unlimited coinage of silver at the ratio of sixteen ounces of silver for one ounce of gold. He held a deep suspicion of panaceas and likely held his nose as he did Altgeld's bidding. In May, he gave a speech in favor of silver. He criticized the idea of adopting the gold standard for the sake of mirroring the English. Joking, but with a grain of truth, Darrow charged that "if we are bound to follow England in dropping silver and taking gold she might equally compel us to drop gold and take diamonds." Then the argument's dagger: "For America to wait for England to consent to bimetallism could only have been paralleled by the slaves in the south waiting for the masters to consent to freedom."[43] Throughout the summer Darrow continued to be Altgeld's silver bulldog.

It was never Altgeld's intent to take over the People's Party. His goals were larger than that. He wanted to use silver to take over the Democratic Party. He hoped to infuse his party with Populists and thereby kick out the conservative backers of Cleveland. Although improbable, his plan worked. When the Democrats met in Chicago in July, they adopted a platform largely written by Altgeld himself. The preamble embodied not only the high ideals of the party but also a jab at Cleveland:

> We, the Democrats of the United States in national convention assembled, do reaffirm our allegiance to those great essential principles of justice and liberty, upon which our institutions are founded, and which the Democratic party has advocated from Jefferson's time to our own—freedom of speech, freedom of press, freedom of conscience, the preservation of personal rights, the equality of all citizens before the law, and the faithful observance of constitutional limitations.

The last part was a direct attack upon Cleveland's role in the Pullman strike. Then the silver plank: "We demand the free and unlimited coinage of both silver and gold at the present legal ratio of 16 to 1."[44] Once nailed onto the Democratic Party's platform, the free silver plank did its political trick and sparked a Populist merger. The resulting fusion caused the gold Democrats to bolt from the party and nominate their own presidential candidate, John M. Palmer (1817–1900) of Illinois. All that remained was for the German-born Altgeld to crown a presidential candidate. He wanted the convention to select Missouri senator Richard P. Bland (1835–1899), a leading voice for currency reform. Frankly, Silver Dick Bland, as he was called, lived up to his surname and during the convention was overshadowed by a great American orator and politician, William Jennings Bryan (1860–1925).[45]

Born in Salem, Illinois, Bryan had an early life that mirrored Darrow's in many ways. Both grew up in the rural Midwest, both inherited their Democratic Party politics from their parents, and both sought escape from their boring yet comfortable small-town lives. Here their biographies begin to diverge. Bryan attended Illinois College in Jacksonville, Illinois, and was graduated as valedictorian. He excelled at rhetoric, consciously seeking to match the era's master, Robert Ingersoll. And although Bryan learned about biology, geology, and religious skepticism, his encounter with those fields failed to shake his Protestant intellectual foundation. In 1881, Bryan moved to Chicago to attend the Union College of Law. He did well, obtaining his degree in 1883, and even clerked for the preeminent Lyman Trumbull. But like Darrow, he found Chicago a very lonely place. Unlike Darrow, Bryan and his wife, Mary Baird Bryan (1861–1930), left the city in 1883 to return to Jacksonville. Four years later, they moved again, west to Lincoln, Nebraska.

On the plains of the last American frontier, Bryan became a Populist and a silverite and entered politics. His tremendous gift of rhetoric revived Nebraska's dormant Democratic Party and infused it with a new ideology. He was elected twice to the U.S. House of Representatives. After an unsuccessful and abortive U.S. Senate run in 1894, Bryan traveled the country on a prosilver speaking tour. By 1896, "the boy orator of the Platte" was the cause's leading advocate, far better known and polished than anyone else. He attended the Democratic Party convention in Chicago as a delegate from Nebraska and stole the show with a speech that earned him the Democratic Party's nomination for president.

Days into the meeting, no presidential front-runner had emerged. On July 9, after hours of speeches and mindless debate, the crowd called out for Bryan to run up the steps to the platform. The audience, which included Darrow and Altgeld, quieted as their darling began: "I come to speak to you in defense of a cause as holy as the cause of liberty—the cause of humanity."[46] He then slowly and methodically and with a great crescendo made the case for silver, the case for Populism, and the case for fusion, concluding famously: "Having behind us the producing masses of this nation and the world, supported by the commercial interests, the laboring interests, and the toilers everywhere, we will answer their demand for the gold standard by saying to them: You shall not press down upon the brow of labor this crown of thorns, you shall not crucify mankind upon a cross of gold."[47] As "gold" echoed from the far wall of the auditorium and back, Bryan moved back, pulled his hands away from the invisible crown of thorns on his head, stretched out his arms, and posed for several seconds as the crucified Christ.[48] The Democrats went wild. "The floor of the convention seemed to heave up," one reporter wrote. "Everybody seemed to go mad at once."[49] The "Cross of Gold" won Bryan the fused Democratic / People's Party nomination for president.

After the wild "stampede" for Bryan—as the generally antisilver *New York Times* reported—died down, Darrow and Altgeld went outside to smoke, clear their heads, and soothe their ringing ears.[50] Minutes of silence went by before they went their separate ways for the night. The next day they met to discuss the convention and Altgeld's disappointment that Bland's nomination had been defeated. He then turned to Darrow and opined that it took more than speeches to win real political victories. "Applause lasts but a little while. The road to justice is not a path of glory; it is stony and long and lonely, filled with pain and martyrdom." Finally, after a few moments in which his younger friend could digest the wisdom, he added much less philosophically, "I have been thinking over Bryan's speech. What did he say, anyhow?"[51]

It was Darrow, not Altgeld, who remembered that remark, and it was likely Darrow who harbored more doubts about Bryan than he let on. By 1896, Darrow had rejected Christianity completely and found Bryan's mimetic performance of Christ on the cross irksome, wondering just whom and what the convention had nominated. Regardless, Darrow campaigned for Bryan, so forcefully that he neglected his own campaign and that of Altgeld. He was not alone. Nearly all radicals, including Eugene Debs, worked on Bryan's behalf. Despite those efforts, Bryan was trounced by the Republican William McKinley (1843–1901).[52]

Bryan's electoral defeat had long coattails and broad implications. Both Altgeld and Darrow lost their election bids too. The former's defeat (Altgeld was still known as the pardoner of the Haymarket anarchists) to Republican John R. Tanner (1844–1901) is easier to explain than Darrow's. Darrow ran in the traditionally Democratic Third Congressional District; he should have won with ease. But the working people of Chicago voted for the Republican, a relatively unknown party regular, Hugh R. Belknap (1860–1901), who edged out a victory by one hundred votes. Darrow initially blamed moneyed interests. "In the last days of the campaign an enormous fund was raised and spent in the centres of population, including Chicago."[53]

Though in his autobiography Darrow claimed he "felt relief when [he] learned of [his] defeat," in truth, he was livid. The more he thought about it, the more he felt that he had been betrayed by the very people to whom he had pledged his legal and political career. He was still smarting nearly a year later when he wrote a newspaper editorial titled "People Deserve What They Get." In it, he argued that judges, plutocrats, and even presidents had "entirely subverted the liberties of the people." But he condemned the working class for its inaction. The working people simply hadn't sense or courage enough to support their friends instead of their enemies. And with that, Darrow made a brief exit from electoral politics. As he later wrote, covering up his political activities and commitments, "So I turned my attention exclusively to law."[54] Even as he did so, however, he was a crusading lawyer for the people; what's more, he *never* gave up politics.

Upon hearing the news that her husband was going to continue to devote his life to causes, legal or electoral, for people, Jessie, who in 1895 had already moved out of their Chicago home, accepted that her marriage with Clarence was at an end. It had not been the marriage that she had wanted or been promised. Suffice it to say, while Clarence was able to shuck his rural midwestern traditions, Jessie could not and did not. In typical turn-of-the-century fashion, Darrow never talked publicly about his failed marriage. But in 1927, in an article about divorce that he published in *Vanity Fair*, he wrote perhaps self-reflectively that a "marriage that does not bring companionship brings practically nothing, and sometimes less."[55] Jessie could have written much the same thing. Her husband's long hours at City Hall; those long weeks in court; the horrible press coverage of his thoughts and deeds; and those rumors of other women were too much to bear. Jessie was essentially a single parent raising a small boy in a lonely, wild, and dirty city. Moreover, Clarence's nastier side, which at first showed up only in the courtroom, made appearances at home. Perhaps he resented Jessie for who she was, the only connection left from that pedestrian, provincial life that he had abandoned in Ashtabula. He wanted to be completely free from it. Without many friends and no family of her own to support her, Jessie made a decision to bring herself and her son happiness and moved back to Ohio's Western Reserve, where she later married James Brownlee, an Ashtabula judge. Clarence took his newfound bachelorhood in stride and set about preparing for his next big case for organized labor and for freedom and liberty, which came in the summer of 1898 in the moderately sized midwestern town of Oshkosh, Wisconsin.

Oshkosh is an ancient place. Nestled between Lake Butte des Morts and Lake Winnebago, it had been inhabited by native peoples for countless centuries before Wisconsin became a state in 1848. Quickly, Oshkosh went from a sleepy outpost to a major manufacturing center for sashes, doors, and wooden blinds. There were seven such factories, all fed by Oshkosh's two dozen sawmills. "Sawdust City," which had survived two Chicago-like fires in 1874 and 1875, was known for something else, starvation wages. The corporate elite that ran the mills had organized themselves into something akin to Chicago's General Managers' Association and worked together to keep their labor costs down. Their ringleader, George M. Paine (d. 1917), ruled his factory, which was the largest sash, door, and blind mill in the country, with an iron hand, busting union-organizing drives without mercy. At the end of the nineteenth century, wages were so low that families regularly sent not only the father but also the mother and sons and daughters into the mills. This family wage formula, which made the managers doubly rich because women and children were paid a fraction of what men earned, produced enormous profits and mind-numbing poverty.

In 1898, the Sawdust City workers had had enough. They formed a local branch of the Amalgamated Wood Workers' International Union of America, affiliated with the American Federation of Labor (AFL). On Saturday, May 7, 1898, the union held a mass meeting at Turner Hall on the south side of Oshkosh. Darrow's friend and political colleague Thomas Kidd, the union's general secretary, took the train up from Chicago in order to attend and help his colleagues forge a strategy to handle George Paine and his friends. First, union leaders sent Paine a respectful letter, which was also published in the newspapers, requesting a meeting to discuss their demands, which were a wage increase of twenty-five cents; an end to female and child labor in the factories; recognition of the union; and payment of wages on a weekly, not monthly, basis. Upon receipt of his letter, Paine "referred [it] to the waste basket."[56] As days passed, union leaders realized that a strike was the only option. The union sponsored another meeting at Turner Hall, filled, as one reporter for the local business newspaper described it, "with ominous mutterings of an oncoming storm."[57] Woodworkers threw up their picket lines on May 16, 1898.

Oshkosh Mayor Allison B. Ideson, who was also the secretary of the Paine Lumber Company, ordered that the city's police force be doubled and sent to the mills to "check disorder."[58] The officers made their way to all seven factories and found that they had been shut down and that the picketers were demonstrating peacefully. Perhaps with a twinge of disappointment, they left a small complement and went back to their stations. Kidd and the other strike leaders knew that violence meant defeat.

Managers had no interest in settling with their workers and declared that they would listen to workers' grievances only on an individual basis. Such talk emboldened one Paine company worker, Andrew Ryan, to ask his foreman, Abe Getchius, for a raise. Getchius told Ryan to turn around so that he could give him a "raise in the pants."[59] No one received a pay increase.[60] For managers, the goal was nothing less than to crush the union. Paine and his friends looked to the example of the Pullman strike. They established their own strikebreaking organization, the Union Club, named after the building in which they held their meetings. Then they set about doing exactly what Pullman and his partners had done: hiring scabs and agents provocateurs.

As soon as the "nonunion" men arrived in Oshkosh in early June, the strike began to change. The *Milwaukee Sentinel* reported that an "uneasiness" had begun to spread. And the workers began to listen to the agents provocateurs such as Frank Wend, a Pinkerton secret agent who counseled violence and intimidation. At the instigation of management's spies, unionists began harassing and fighting the scabs. Trying to get ahead of the impending riot, Kidd raced to the picket lines and pleaded with the union members to stop and exhorted the nonunionists to join the union.[61] He was unsuccessful, and the strikers became more and more "pugnacious," as one reporter styled it, as the strike went on.[62] This was the slow burn to a riot, which came three weeks later.

In late June, all the major door, sash, and blind mill owners had brought in enough replacement workers to restart their operations. Encouraged by the agents provocateurs, the strikers and their relatives planned massive demonstrations to keep the city's factories shut down. On June 22, the Radford Company factory ran an entire day, using strikebreakers who had been escorted inside by local police. When the six o'clock whistle blew, workers began filing out and were met at the Ohio Street Bridge by a crowd of angry union men, their wives, and children. In fact, the women, who had suffered as much as anyone, were in the front lines, pelting the scabs with rotten eggs and cursing and chasing them all the way to their homes. The police were powerless. The commotion was repeated at the other mills over the next few days. Each time the crowd grew a bit more violent.

On June 23, a prounion force of more than a thousand met strikebreakers leaving the McMillen Mill. As one crowd of angry workers surged toward another, the police, their numbers reinforced with deputized strikebreakers, moved in, billy clubs raised. Again women were in the lead, and the ensuing fracas was a bloody mess. To disperse the crowd, Edward Casey, the plant's engineer, turned the company's fire hose on the unionists. Jimmy Morris, a sixteen-year-old striker, who was standing nearby, turned to Casey and supposedly observed, "Look at them. The women are fighting harder than [police and strikebreakers]." This mild affront to manhood seemingly caused Casey to snap. Inexplicably, the crazed man grabbed an industrial wrench and split Morris's head in two. Everyone saw the murder. For a moment the strikers stopped their fight and cried out for Casey to be arrested, and the police did so for Casey's protection. The battle of the McMillen Mill was over, and peace was restored citywide the next day when Governor Edward Scofield (1842–1925) sent in the National Guard from their station in Milwaukee, ninety miles away.

Although Oshkosh's riot alarm rang a few more times during the summer, the strike was over. Beaten and broke, the unionists limped back to the mill owners, who made temporary concessions to hold the peace.[63] Many unionists, including Thomas Kidd, were arrested on civil and criminal conspiracy charges. The factory owners had won. All that remained was the pleasure of destroying the union in court, as Pullman and the GMA had done to Debs and the American Railway Union. When Kidd called on his old Chicago friend to come to Oshkosh and defend him, Paine and his colleagues must have chuckled. Clarence Darrow was coming for the defense. It was another chance to show up labor's lawyer. Or so they thought.[64]

The comparisons with the Pullman strike and the Debs cases were misleading.[65] Darrow had several advantages in the woodworkers' conspiracy cases. The first and perhaps the most important was that he had the ability to select what he believed to be a favorable jury.[66] He also had experience. He needed only to rehearse and refresh and not to memorize his role. Finally, the Union Club and the thugs that it had hired had been sloppy. Whereas Darrow had not been able to prove that GMA agents had sparked the July 1894 riots in Chicago, Paine and his colleagues had left more than enough evidence.

After all the preliminaries, which included several agonizing days of jury selection, the trial of Thomas Kidd and two "accomplices"—unionists George Zentner and Michael Troiber, who had done nothing but go on strike—began on October 18. The trio was indicted on four counts of criminal conspiracy, violating the Wisconsin State Code, Section 4,466a, which prohibited combinations that injured another's business, and Section 4,466c, which forbade the use of violence and intimidation to hinder a person from engaging and continuing in lawful work.[67] District Attorney Walter W. Quartermass led the prosecution, though on the orders of George Paine, local attorney Frank W. Houghton was added to the team. Clarence Darrow stridently objected. Just as in 1894, he thought it grossly unfair for the corporate elite to stack the prosecution's deck with its own men. Judge Arthur Goss tossed aside Darrow's objections. Yet when Houghton and Quartermass returned the favor, objecting to Darrow's presence on the ground that he was not a member of the Wisconsin bar and hence not entitled to practice in the state, Judge Goss overruled without comment.[68]

The prosecution sought to prove that Kidd was the strike's mastermind and the person who incited the riots, that Troiber was the genius behind the pickets, and that Zentner was a lead picketer. Quartermass and Houghton paraded handfuls of witnesses claiming that the actions of the three men constituted the root of the conspiracy. Police officer James Casey took the stand to testify that another striker, Eugene Stahey, told him that Kidd had personally sent people to the picket lines. Another worker, J. E. Jones, swore that Kidd had given speeches urging violence and vandalism. But the prosecution's strategy backfired on cross-examination. Darrow and his defense team, Oshkosh lawyers Gabe Bouck and Earl P. Finch, were able to show that Paine and his son Nathan, who had organized a vigilante group to harass the strikers, had paid disgruntled unionists to appear for the prosecution.[69] Sensing their case weakening, Quartermass and Houghton decided to put George Paine on the stand. He claimed to have firsthand knowledge of the conspiracy. Picketers, he asserted, had told him about Kidd's plans but were afraid to appear in court.[70] Then came Darrow's cross-examination. For nearly two hours Darrow made King Paine look like a court jester. Paine failed to identify one striker by name. On Darrow's objection, Judge Goss had no other choice but to strike from the record Paine's testimony about conversations with picketers. It was hearsay at best, lies at worst. Darrow also got Paine to admit to hiring Pinkerton detectives as labor spies. The damage to the prosecution's case was irreparable.

Once the prosecution rested, Darrow began a mighty defense. He returned to the issue of bribery with witness Andrew Ryan, who testified that Nathan Paine had offered him twenty-five hundred dollars (sixty thousand in today's dollars) to provide documents that would guarantee a guilty verdict. Immediately Houghton jumped up to object: Darrow was trying to enter evidence already ruled immaterial. Darrow countercharged that Houghton "was conspiring and acting in a manner unbecoming a man who professed such ethics as he did."[71] Judge Goss ruled against Darrow, but a suspicion had been raised in the minds of the jurors. This suspicion about the motivation and actions of Paine and the Union Club only grew when Darrow put Kidd on the stand. Together the two friends effectively turned the tables on the prosecution, showing a conspiracy of mill owners against the workers to keep wages low and to incite violence with agents provocateurs in the employ of the Pinkerton Detective Agency. Kidd's testimony also painted a picture of Sawdust City in which boys and girls labored for pennies an hour in the most dangerous parts of the factories. Moreover, Kidd told the jury that he had advised against the strike and that once the Oshkosh woodworkers' union voted to do so anyway, he had "asked them so to conduct the affair as to violate no law and to win and keep the respect of the community."[72]

Kidd's testimony was powerful, but Darrow's closing statement was even more persuasive. "This is really not a criminal case," Darrow stated frankly. "A conspiracy for what?" he questioned. For workers organizing into a lawful body? For writing a letter to George Paine? For requesting increased wages? All this constituted a "terrible crime"? Darrow sarcastically quipped. "No," he said seriously, these actions never created a conspiracy. Then what was the trial about? Precedent, he declared. Paine, his collaborators, and his lawyer were hoping to throw Kidd, Troiber, and Zentner in jail and thereby make striking and unions illegal in the United States. "It is," he explained, "but an episode in the great battle for human liberty, a battle which was commenced when the tyranny and oppression of man first caused him to impose upon his fellows and which will not end so long as the children of one father shall be compelled to toil to support the children of another in luxury and ease." If these three men, Darrow declared, "or any one of them, can go to jail in this case, then there never can be a strike again in this country where men cannot be sent to jail as well."[73]

The trial was nothing less than the malicious prosecution of three innocent men by those who had united for an "unholy purpose." Darrow let District Attorney Quartermass off the hook; he was "a good lawyer and a good fellow" who had allowed himself to become "simply the tool that is used." Darrow had much harsher words for Houghton. Paine's hired gun was a sycophant who "would have been glad to have licked the dust from Paine's boots had he been given the opportunity." As for George Paine—"the ancient patriarch"—he was behind the entire thing, including the bribes and the hiring of the "leprous detectives" who had infiltrated the union's ranks and encouraged violence and mayhem. More like the "king of Persia," and less like an industrial statesman, Paine had colluded with the state's attorneys, Quartermass and Houghton, to crush Oshkosh's workers simply because "if there is anything that the Paines hate, it is a labor agitator."[74]

Why had a labor agitator come to Oshkosh? He came to save civilization. "If all that Oshkosh can show is these stunted, starved children," then, Darrow declared, the town should be razed and the land given back to the Indians. Time and again, Darrow referred to the city's workers as industrial slaves. The rules of work were oppressive. Workers could be fired for not being in front of their machines when the "bell rings and whistle blows for starting." By rule, "no unnecessary talking will be allowed during working hours," which, Darrow noted, violated "several constitutional guarantees." Worse, workers who quit without their employers' consent were subject to damages. Paine was less a king, more a warden. "Why, gentlemen, the difference that I can see between the state's prison and G. M. Paine's factory is that Paine's men are not allowed to sleep on the premises."[75]

It was bad enough that men were treated like this, but the misery Paine created extended to women and children. "I believe a woman should have every opportunity in this world that she wants and needs," Darrow stated, "but it is only necessity that drives these girls into Paine's sweat shop for ten hours a day." The use of child labor was inexcusable. He asked the jury if it thought it could correct this horrid situation by sending Kidd, Troiber, and Zentner to jail. "Do it, and crush out the last spark of manhood that remains in the employes of George M. Paine. Do it, and obliterate the last ray of hope from the lives of these little children of Oshkosh who are forced into their premature graves."[76]

"Gentlemen," Darrow began his final appeal to the jury, "the world is dark, but it is not hopeless." Darrow understood that all the jurymen were devout Christians. So, for the first recorded time, but not the last, he submerged his own philosophical commitments and his own religious skepticism for the sake of his clients, and he spoke as a preacher would. "Here and there through the past some man has ever risen, some man like Kidd, willing to give the devotion of his great soul to humanity's holy cause." He exhorted the twelve men not to do to Kidd and the other defendants what others had done to Christ. "It has fallen to your lot, gentlemen," he declared, "to be leading actors in one of the great dramas of human life. For some mysterious reason Providence has placed in your charge for today, aye for ages, the helpless toilers, the hopeless men, the despondent women and suffering children of the world; it is a great, a tremendous trust, and I know you will do your duty bravely, wisely, humanely and well; that you will render a verdict in this case which will be a milestone in the history of the world, and an inspiration and hope to the dumb, despairing millions whose fate is in your hands."[77]

At that, court ended for the day; Darrow had spoken for eight hours. The next morning Houghton tried to revive the prosecution's case. He spoke for five hours, rehashing the charges of conspiracy. He also derided Darrow, "the man from Chicago" who used "slum methods" in court. Both Kidd and Darrow were not to be trusted, as they were "the rankest anarchists," who plotted "the most wretched desolation and ruin." Thus, a vote to acquit was a vote in favor of "upholding such doctrines as the gentlemen advocated."[78] After five hours Houghton sat down, and Judge Goss handed the case to the jury, which needed only fifty minutes to return a not guilty verdict.

The triumph was Darrow's more than anyone else's. After years of losing big cases and elections, he had won and now was the undisputed champion of labor's causes. As his stature grew in the eyes of average workers, so did his political importance. A few months later his closing argument was transcribed and released as a booklet. Sales were strong, and it went through two editions.[79] His defendants went on with their lives, especially after 1899, when Darrow worked rather quietly to get all the remaining civil conspiracy charges dropped. The woodworkers' union did not fare well. The murder trial of Edward Casey was moved out of Oshkosh and ended in an acquittal. The moderate wage gains that the union secured in August 1898 had been lost by the next year.[80] Darrow too emerged from labor's battles of the 1890s with a mixed record. On the one hand, he had been bested by such corporate leaders as Pullman and their politicians. Worse, perhaps, was the stinging defeat of the Populists and Democrats as well as his own congressional candidacy. Seeds of doubt were sown here about the power and promise of mass movements in America. The labor movement and the Populists seemed at times to be their own worst enemies. On the other hand, the victory in Oshkosh convinced this pessimistic iconoclast that the courtroom remained a place where he could effect change, even if on a small scale. As the new century edged closer, Darrow had grand plans both in and out of court to challenge the powers that hemmed in democracy and freedom.

❊· 5 ·❊

Labor's Lyrical Lawyer

After his divorce, Clarence Darrow, the newly reminted bachelor, stayed with friends and relatives until settling in a brand-new apartment building called the Langdon Co-operative Living Club, located close to Jane Addams's Hull House. He moved in with Francis S. Wilson, a lawyer who was to become a law partner and who just happened to be his ex-wife's cousin. There was no awkwardness at all. Wilson and Darrow were two of a kind. Both lawyers were unattached members of the intellectual avant-garde in Chicago. And both desired to establish a bohemian enclave where Darrow would lead a group of culturally modern Americans in explorations of hedonism, radical politics, arts and letters, and of course sexuality, all the while making his living from the law and advancing his left-wing political causes in the courtroom and occasionally at the ballot box too.

Darrow's "plunge into the *demimonde* of Chicago," as biographer Kevin Tierney put it, was not some form of escapism after a painful divorce.[1] Darrow was serious in his intent to change the world by participating in, if not leading, a vanguard of modernism and thereby transforming culture. In the late 1890s, Chicago's bohemian movement was ill defined intellectually and geographically. In time the city's bohemians, led by such notables as Floyd Dell (1887–1969), Sherwood Anderson, and Tennessee Mitchell (1874–1929), clustered around Jackson Park and forged what critics later labeled the "Chicago Renaissance."[2] But at the end of the Gilded Age, they were spread out. On Calumet Avenue there was a free love colony, headed by Parker H. Sercombe, a banker who helped establish the American Surety Bank in Mexico City. An artist colony was centered on the Fine Arts Building, which was a converted office building on Michigan Avenue. Like that of Mabel Dodge (1879–1962) in Greenwich Village, Darrow's flat, on the corner of Bunker and Desplaines, became a common meeting place where all kinds of bohemians congregated to discuss writers and artists, debate various isms (feminism, socialism, fatalism, pessimism, and anarchism), foster tolerance, encourage freedom, and experiment in new relationships for the age's New Women and New Men.

In the 1890s, Darrow was an advocate of free love. Breaking the chains of matrimony was not an expression of misogamy. There was much more to it. Bohemians saw traditional marriage as a form of oppression. In an 1890 article, Darrow accused men of trampling on the liberty of women and making each one "little but a slave."[3] Darrow argued that the future of human evolution depended upon the rights available to women. To move ahead, out of the "injustice in which the world is wrapped," men and women must move along "the path of progress and of liberty."[4] In practical terms, Darrow advocated both women's suffrage and reform of the law to allow women equal access to divorce.

Expanding the limits of marriage and divorce was essential to the ideology of free love. Moreover, free love was as important to bohemians as suffrage was. Indeed, Darrow viewed it as a vital part of the breaking of Victorian norms and traditions as well as the reshaping of politics. It also appealed to Darrow's ego. The unattached forty-year-old was free to do as he pleased with whomever he pleased as long as the other party was willing, which was probably not as often as he would have liked. Darrow loved to engage his guests in debate about literature, radical politics, and the advance of liberty and freedom. He also did not mind if some of the female guests decided to stay over. Few did. As settlement worker and future labor organizer Gertrude Barnum (1866–1948) explained, Darrow's mind appealed to all, but he was physically repellent "because of his dirty fingernails and rather greasy hair."[5] But not everyone was repulsed. Often Darrow was seen with Ruby Hammerstrom (1869–1957), a bookkeeper and Chicago journalist who wrote under the pen name of Ruby Stanleigh.[6] Hammerstrom was born in Galesburg, Illinois, and educated at the town's Knox College. She first met Darrow at the White City Club, where he gave a lecture on Omar Khayyám (1048–1122). Their friends believed the relationship to be rather casual and had no idea how serious it actually was. Likely, Ruby and Clarence kept things under wraps, not wanting to publicly forfeit their bohemian credentials. But their deep love for each other was not secret for long.

Darrow's interests in his bohemian colleagues ranged far beyond sexual intimacy and women's rights. Above all else, at this point in his life, like so many bohemians, Darrow desired to become a writer and a philosopher whose books and articles would transform world politics and Western culture.[7] Surprising as it may seem, although being a lawyer provided him with the means to be a political iconoclast, he dreamed of another way of accomplishing his political goals. From the time he encountered the works of Paine, Voltaire, George, and Altgeld, he had thought of doing the same as they: moving the world with his pen. By the time he lived in Chicago, his idols were writers such as Walt Whitman and Leo Tolstoy (1828–1910), and now securely ensconced as labor's lawyer and a politico, he longed for his turn. Darrow was first a literary critic, and then he moved into the realms of social commentary and fiction writing. In 1899, he published his first book, *A Persian Pearl and Other Essays*. It was an anthology of philosophical tracts and tributes to his literary heroes, such as Whitman, Robert Burns (1759–1796), and Omar Khayyám, all of whom challenged social and political convention.[8]

Darrow believed he was carrying on in their tradition and thus leveled his criticism at Victorian literature, society, and politics in order to put himself squarely on the side of the working class. He despised Romantic art and literature. Its ornamental style, he wrote, befogged truth in order to serve the idle rich. Additionally, Darrow was a keen observer of and commentator on the international socialist movement. For example, he penned a lengthy and positive review of William English Walling's (1877–1936) important but largely ignored *Russia's Message: The True World Import of the Revolution* (1908) in *Arena* magazine. That said, the wellspring for Darrow's political and literary radicalism did not flow from Karl Marx (1818–1883), but rather from Tolstoy. In Tolstoy, he found a kindred spirit who hated the "idle class of parasites, a class of men and women who have managed to separate themselves from work and their fellow men, and who must therefore be amused."[9]

Like Darrow, in middle age Tolstoy had abandoned luxury to fight for the poor and oppressed. Like the socialists, Tolstoy looked around him and was disgusted at the sea of human misery. His *What to Do* (1887) had a profound impact upon Darrow. Whereas socialists in the United States and in Europe criticized Tolstoy for identifying the problem but not applying a "scientific" (that is, Marxist) solution,[10] Darrow did not care. Darrow agreed with Tolstoy that the solution to the human condition was not class conflict but class solidarity. In the future envisioned by realist writers like Tolstoy, Darrow wrote, "no man will compel the service of his fellow man, but each will gladly labor for the whole, moved by the righteous power of love."[11]

As for socialism, Darrow came to view it as nothing but unadulterated "dope." Yet in the final analysis, he concluded that he had "always been more or less a Socialist. . . . The capitalists say I have been more," he mused; "the Socialists say I have been less."[12] But at least until the coming of the Great War in 1914, or before many socialists became rigidly dogmatic, they continued to embrace Darrow as their champion—as a radical lawyer, politico, and writer—however critical of them he became.

In 1902, the socialist publisher Charles H. Kerr (1860–1944) of Chicago published Darrow's first major work of social criticism, *Resist Not Evil*. Drawing inspiration from Tolstoy and Peter Kropotkin (1842–1921), the nonviolent Russian anarchist whom Darrow had met in 1901, he made a lengthy critique of the penal system that echoed the ideas of his mentor, John Altgeld, and he made a case for the total and peaceful transformation of society.[13] Interestingly, Darrow took his title from the Bible: "Ye have heard that it hath been said: An eye for an eye, and a tooth for a tooth. But I say unto you, That ye resist not evil: but whosoever shall smite thee on thy right cheek, turn to him the other also" (Matthew 5:38–39).[14] As in the courtroom, Darrow always turned his listeners' (and readers') values and philosophical commitments toward his arguments. And he argued passionately that the world could survive only by following the principles of nonresistance and nonviolence. In "this heroic age, given to war and conquest and violence, the precepts of peace and good will seem to have been almost submerged."[15] Who was to blame for this? Government, whose authority solely rested on its ability to commit violence, was ultimately responsible for the problem and the solution.

In 1904, at forty-seven, he published *Farmington*, his first serious work of fiction and purportedly a fictionalized account of his childhood. Even more than his more famous and more widely read autobiography, published toward the end of his life, we must treat *Farmington* with care. Since we have so few historical documents from this early period of Darrow's life, there is no way of knowing what is fiction and what is fact. At best, we can say that *Farmington* is an artful retelling of Darrow's childhood and his attempt to make sense of it as an adult and to shape his reputation and legacy. *Farmington* emphasizes four themes that were essential to his grown-up freethinking bohemian philosophy of life: skepticism, pessimism, fatalism, and hedonism. All were ideas central to his political project of changing the world and increasing liberty and freedom through the printed word.

Darrow laced this remembrance of childhood with the roots of skepticism about organized religion. But his objections to religion as captured in *Farmington* were unsophisticated. Rather, typical of the young Darrow, the church was largely a bother that hindered his fun. It was, however, typical of life in Farmington, which is essentially bad, with happiness just beyond reach. Further, not only are the townspeople doomed to their fate, but also there is little anyone can do about it. Offsetting this pessimism was Darrow's hedonism. When he wrote about his childhood, he focused on life's pleasures, from eating pie to tobogganing to playing baseball. The game was no mere youthful amusement. It was in fact a living and sporting embodiment of "Nature's fatal equation."[16] By that he meant that the "joys" of playing the sport were "balanced" by the inscrutable fact that at some point even the greatest ballplayers regretfully have to give it up. Also, baseball maintains the metaphor for life because it is a game "for individual merit, for skill, for blunders, and mistakes, for chance and luck."[17] In other words, it is a game in which a wiry, tall, skinny midwesterner could excel by chance.

Farmington was reviewed time and again for nearly thirty years, as Darrow had it republished regularly in the hope that it would make money. It was neither critically nor financially successful. In the last edition, published by Charles Scribner's Sons in 1932, he wrote in the preface: "Now, Charles Scribner's Sons have undertaken to bring out another edition, and if it does not fare better than heretofore I shall be driven to the conclusion that its limited and casual sale was my fault after all."[18] Critics did not know what to make of the book, casting it as a bildungsroman and ignoring its political implications. Most were kind, comparing it with the works of Heinrich Heine (1797–1856) and William Dean Howells (1837–1920); one found *Farmington* a worthy companion to Mark Twain's *Tom Sawyer*.[19] They saw in Darrow the antithesis of Booth Tarkington (1869–1946) and a forerunner to Edgar Lee Masters (1868–1950) and Sherwood Anderson.[20] No one, however, picked up on Darrow's pessimism, fatalism, or hedonism inspired by Tolstoy and Khayyám. No one mentioned his religious skepticism either, though it further alienated him from his kith and kin in Kinsman.[21]

An Eye for an Eye, Darrow's second and last novel (it was really a no-vella of eight-six pages), appeared in 1905. Based on the real murder case of Chris Merry, a Chicago street tough who bludgeoned his wife to death in 1897, the book had all of Darrow's hallmarks: autobiographical and realist in style, it drew its political philosophy from Khayyám, Kropotkin, and Tol-stoy. It told of the last day in the life of convicted murderer Jim Jackson. His friend, Hank Clery, had come on an "errand of mercy" to visit him before his execution.[22] Jackson told him his story, one filled with fatalism and pes-simism. The book was as much a call for a transformation of class relations as for penal reform. Like Clery, Jackson had been a reasonably good citizen, at least before he murdered his wife. Though "awfully wicked," he was also a "perfect gentleman" who was "very kind and obliging."[23] What happened had not been Jackson's fault. Events, happenstances, accidents, pressures, and influences beyond his control had driven him to commit the crime. The judge acted in the only way he knew how, and instead of justice the state sanctioned the murder of a pitiful man. During that long evening of confes-sion, he kept asking Hank and the guards if the governor had telegraphed. Jackson was the only one holding out hope. Everyone else knew he was doomed.

Although reviewers largely ignored or mischaracterized the work's phil-osophical and political meanings about individuals caught in an inhumane system of retribution, they found it engrossing, if not a bit "rambling," as Darrow's prose could be.[24] One critic called it "the most powerful and truth-ful piece of realism yet done by an American writer."[25] His peers were dou-bly impressed. Literary scholars have argued that Darrow set the mold other writers, such as Upton Sinclair (1878–1968), Theodore Dreiser (1871–1945), and Frank Norris (1870–1902), were to use to cast their characters, set-tings, and stories.[26] According to Abe C. Ravitz, Theodore Dreiser's Clyde Griffiths in *An American Tragedy* (1925) is a modified version of Jackson.

And the novel's lawyer, Hindenburg, is none other than Darrow himself.[27] Dreiser was not the only one to include Darrow in a novel. In Sinclair Lewis's *Babbitt* (1922), Darrow appears as the radical jurist Seneca Doane. The writer who was most profoundly affected was Brand Whitlock (1869–1934). He and Darrow became close friends, and Darrow used his literary connections, especially with William Dean Howells, to help launch Whitlock's career.[28]

All this said, there's no denying the fact that Darrow's literary career was a failure. Had he not been the most important lawyer in modern American history, no one would remember his writings. Further, no matter how much he wanted to retire and write, his books never paid the bills. Nor did they have the political influence that Whitman's or Tolstoy's or Kropotkin's had. To eat, Darrow relied on what he knew he did well: the law and politics. This was not a betrayal of his bohemian bone fides. On the contrary, Darrow's big cases and his battles in politics were part and parcel of the avantgarde cultural rebellion; he became the lyrical left's lawyer and remained so for several decades.[29] In terms of law, he further established himself as the labor movement's counselor, at the local and at the national levels. In terms of politics, Darrow remained a central figure in Chicago and Illinois, the people's advocate fighting for the public interest. And for him, at the dawn of the twentieth century, there was no greater issue than municipal control of street railways.

For Chicagoans, urban streetcars were more than conveyances; they were supposed to be democracy in motion. Convenient and inexpensive metropolitan streetcars provided the city's poor and upwardly mobile a chance to improve their lives by offering rides to and from the clean and new suburbs and to areas of the city where factories paid better wages. They were "the workingman's ticket for escape from the slum," the means for moving to better homes with clean water, clean air, and access to shops the store owners of which did not prey upon the poor.[30]

Rather than vehicles of social uplift, the Windy City's streetcars were dangerous railed machines of oppression and inequity. In 1903, the Chicago Bureau of Statistics released accident rates for the previous year. Each day, on average, six people had been seriously injured on streetcars. Two years later the number had risen to nearly seven. Mortality rates for the period are harder to come by, but for 1905 there were more than two deaths a day, and in the spring of 1906, during a two-month period, twenty-one people were killed and eighty-six were injured on the city's streetcar system.[31] Streetcars, with their infrequent stops but frequent transfers, were filled over capacity and ran too fast. In addition, fares were expensive and beyond the means of many working-class travelers. Those who worked on the cars suffered as well. Long hours, little pay, and rabidly antiunion employers made work difficult, draining, and dangerous.

Everyone knew who was to blame. It was the streetcar barons like Charles T. Yerkes (1837–1905). Like other members of the Gilded Age generation, such as Jay Gould, John D. Rockefeller, and J. P. Morgan (1837–1913), Yerkes and his streetcar ilk had bilked millions of dollars by feasting at the public trough and by watering down their companies' stock.[32] To them, streetcars were not a means to improve society; they were a means to a financial end. Although there were such transit boosters and grafters in many cities, Yerkes was the archetype. Born into poverty in a suburb of Philadelphia, he had made his money through a host of illegal banking and stock schemes in the City of Brotherly Love. By the early 1870s, the "Little Napoleon of Third Street" had been arrested, indicted, convicted, and jailed for embezzlement and larceny. Upon his release, he moved to Chicago to rebuild his fortune, and he did so in mass transit, first with cable cars and later with streetcars and elevated trains. Yerkes's empire, built atop Chicago's already corrupt transit system, was a boondoggle, an abomination to the public good.

In 1858, Chicagoans built their first streetcar line. The city council had granted the Chicago City Railway Company the franchise to build and operate the railway for twenty-five years. By 1865, most of the city's main thoroughfares had tracks, run now by several corporations. Management and councilmen found the electric traction system profitable, and the city's streetcar companies began to pressure the state legislature for ninety-nine-year charters for their monopolies. In 1865, the Illinois legislature passed such a law, but Governor Richard J. Oglesby vetoed it. The streetcar grafters were also expert bribers; the law was passed over the governor's veto.[33] Though the corporate charters had been extended, the city council still controlled franchises of the streetcar companies, which were fixed to a twenty-year limit. Yerkes, who had obtained control of the North and West streetcar lines in 1886, led the charge to get the council to extend that franchise limit for seventy-nine more years. The extraordinarily wealthy and powerful city railroad baron wanted to make certain that his control over local transit would last far beyond his death. The only people standing in his way were Chicago's unionists, the incorruptible Illinois governor John P. Altgeld, and his sidekick Clarence Darrow.[34]

Yerkes's goal was to own and operate all transit rail lines in the city, reaping as much profit as possible. To do that, he believed that he had to dominate his workforce, which meant of course crushing any unions. Working for Yerkes was awful. As was common practice, myriad work rules governed employees, and any infringement meant loss of pay, demotion, or termination. Although working on the traction lines was better than some jobs, the wages were not high, and accidents and deaths were frequent. In 1888, the Knights of Labor, under the leadership of George Schilling, tried to negotiate better compensation and conditions for cable car operators. Yerkes bitterly told his men: "Sooner than allow my company to be dictated to by a crowd of men under the leadership of Socialists and Anarchists, I will discharge every one on the road."[35] A strike was inevitable.

Yerkes played hardball. He brought in strikebreakers from Kansas City and Philadelphia, and city police attacked strikers on several occasions. The strike ended after eight days. A group of unionists signed an agreement without Schilling's direct help or knowledge that gave union workers a 6 percent wage increase. But they also agreed that the 250 strikebreakers could stay on the job. This rump bargaining committee did not realize that these new workers had signed yellow-dog contracts, prohibiting them from joining the Knights or any other labor organization.[36]

Besting the union was just part of Yerkes's plan. In 1895, the pirate of public transportation planned to pillage the public trust. His goal was the passage of a new state law that would extend streetcar railway franchises for fifty years as well as help him consolidate under his control even more of the city's traction lines. By then, much of the statehouse was under Yerkes's control. Governor Altgeld, however, refused to be bribed. Although he desperately needed the money—his finances had been ruined since his pardoning of the anarchists—Altgeld was a man of principle; he turned down the one million dollars Yerkes personally offered him for his signature on the bill. On May 14, Altgeld sent his veto to the legislature. Yerkes viewed this as a minor setback. The nice thing about a democracy was that one just had to wait for new leadership to appear. In 1896, Republican John Tanner defeated Governor Altgeld's reelection bid, and promptly signed a modified traction bill that gave the Chicago City Council the power to grant a fifty-year franchise. The battle went back to Chicago.

Darrow and Altgeld planned to fight. When Altgeld lost the 1896 election, he fell into a dark depression, but Darrow rehabilitated the ex-governor, convincing his friend to run in 1899 as an independent for mayor of Chicago on a pro–municipal ownership platform. The idea was that the city would own and operate the street railways, which were a natural monopoly—akin to the water department—in need of tight government oversight and regulation to ensure the public good. Altgeld had strong backing among unionists, socialists, Populists, various middle-class reformers like Jane Addams, and the Municipal Voters' League, a nonpartisan good-government organization that sought to elect "honest and capable" men who would clean up the city, including the traction issue.[37] Darrow managed an efficient campaign, but once again the people let him down. On election day, the masses voted for Democrat Carter Harrison II (1860–1953), the son of the slain mayor.[38] It was no contest. Harrison received 146,914 votes to Altgeld's 45,401. The Republican candidate, Zina R. Carter (1847–1922), garnered 107,304.[39]

The New York Times predicted that Altgeld's election debacle spelled his political doom.[40] It was only partially correct. His electoral career was at an end, but Darrow offered him another lifeline, convincing him to join his law firm. Altgeld had been a lawyer and a judge after all, and again his depression passed, allowing him to join Darrow on various cases. Together the duo also poked fun at the new Mayor Harrison, giving him grief in the press over the traction system, crime, corruption, and public services. The fun ended in March 1902. On the twelfth, Altgeld traveled to Joliet to deliver a speech against the Boer War. In the middle of his talk he was stricken with a violent and acute intestinal problem. He collapsed and died. Darrow rushed to collect his friend's body and bring him home.

Darrow tried in vain to arrange a proper funeral, but the city's "liberal-minded" clergy refused to bury John "Pardon" Altgeld. "So," Darrow reported, "Miss Jane Addams, of Hull House, a woman of rare ideals and intelligence," George Schilling, and he interred the incorruptible champion of the people.[41] Darrow's eulogy praised his "dear, dead friend" as "one of the rarest souls who ever lived and died." Altgeld was "a soldier in the everlasting struggle of the human race for liberty and justice on the earth." Three days after the burial there was another tragic shock. Mary Darrow Olson, Clarence's beloved favorite sister, passed away. He attended to that funeral as well, but with no fanfare.[42]

Darrow saw it as his mission to continue Altgeld's holy cause for liberty, freedom, and justice. For him, the central antagonist in that battle was the cadre of millionaires, like Pullman, Paine, and Yerkes, who used their vast ill-gotten fortunes to rob, steal, and cheat their way to even larger fortunes. To stop them, Darrow initially sought to replace Altgeld politically. After Altgeld's death, radicals "had lost their leader," Darrow wrote.[43] So he took it upon himself to pick up the banner. In May 1902, he decided to run for the Illinois Statehouse. He wanted the Democrats to support him, but when he asked the party chiefs for their blessing, they turned him away. Darrow suspected that his potential candidacy had already raised the ire of the corporate elites. As a result, he and George Schilling formed an independent party, the Public Ownership League; Schilling was the group's president, and Darrow was its chairman. The party was built around a four-point platform: the initiative and referendum; an equitable system of taxation; the direct nomination of candidates at the primaries; and significantly, public ownership of public utilities, including street railways.[44] The platform and the league's principles resonated with voters in Darrow's district, the Seventeenth (which consisted of the Ninth, Tenth, and Nineteenth wards). Working-class citizens—with a few upper-class allies such as Darrow's new friend William Randolph Hearst (1863–1951)—were especially excited about the emphasis put on municipal ownership of the city's transit system.[45]

Darrow won easily. But as he was packing for Springfield to take his oath of office, he was sidetracked by a telegram from his old friend Henry Lloyd asking him to help the United Mine Workers in what Lloyd labeled "the greatest strike in history."[46] Of course, Darrow had been following the pitched battle between the United Mine Workers (UMW), led by Darrow's acquaintance John Mitchell (1870–1919), and the coal operators of Pennsylvania. Since the Spring Valley strike of 1890, Darrow had been a keen observer of the coal syndicates and their oppressed workers. During his closing summary in the Thomas I. Kidd case, Darrow had made an analogy between the Oshkosh sash and door factories and the infernal conditions in the anthracite regions of Pennsylvania, "where those human moles burrow in the earth for the benefit of great, monstrous, greedy corporations that are corrupting the lifeblood of the nation."[47] When the call came, he put his plans for municipal ownership of Chicago's street railways on hold. Springfield could wait; the legislature was not yet even in session. Moreover, the United Mine Workers case provided a rare and potent opportunity to transform American life—not just the lives of Chicagoans—and American politics by means of the courtroom, the place where he was most effective. Furthermore, whereas in Springfield he was just one of many, in court he was the center of all attention. Thus, his defense and advocacy in a coal strike involving nearly 150,000 miners had broad implications not only for him and his crusade for justice and liberty but for all American workers. He may not have realized that as he packed his bags for the East Coast, but by the time he returned from the Pennsylvania coal region to Chicago he knew it.

Mining had long been one of the most dangerous professions in America. A certain amount of the misfortune—the deaths and the injuries—was a product of the hazardous and capricious nature of the work. Gases, water, and weaknesses in the seams could kill regardless of all other conditions. But what made matters so much worse was that the coal operators in the United States were notoriously stingy, callous, and coldhearted. The mine owners and their minions had created work rules, extraction systems, and living and working conditions that gave those that controlled the resources the most profit no matter what the cost in human lives and misery. Only the labor movement, in its various guises and organizations, defended the interests of the workers. And there had been a long history of bloody battles between the capitalists and the coal miners.

For a time, at the end of the nineteenth century, there were signs that industrial cooperation would replace strife. In 1898, after a protracted strike, the United Mine Workers inked a historic agreement with the bituminous coal mine operators that created a system of joint conferences at which operators and union leaders would cooperate in setting and stabilizing costs, wages, and production.[48] On the heels of that victory, the UMW's president, John Mitchell, had to make a choice: to advance the union by organizing West Virginia or by organizing Pennsylvania. Significant risks came with either decision, but in the end, Mitchell and his colleagues chose the anthracite region of eastern Pennsylvania, which had been mined since the late 1700s. The region also had a traditional of working-class radicalism for almost as long.[49]

Anthracite coal miners in Pennsylvania may not have been worse off than their counterparts elsewhere, but they certainly were no better off. Supervisors worked miners for a minimum of ten hours. Those who complained were summarily fired. The shafts frequently lacked fresh air, were filled with foul and sometimes deadly gases, and were often partially flooded. The collieries were in a constant state of disrepair, yet repairs were rarely done until something disastrous happened. The dust, the danger, the cold, the water, the collapses might have been tolerable if the jobs had been remunerative. They were not. Aside from all the inequities of irregular pay schedules, the company store, and company housing, workers were paid by the loaded car, despite differences in the sizes of the cars. Miners quipped that the gondolas were made of "*live* oak, for they are always growing."[50] Other miners were paid by the ton, but it was a "miner's ton," a heavier standard that allowed supervisors to account for impurities. Either way, company officials penalized workers for slate, dirt, and waste rock when they docked their load cars outside the seams. And workers had no faith that company officials were treating them fairly; they worked for people who had a different set of ethics. After all, they hired children to work in the mines.

Union organizers had tried to help the anthracite miners with varying degrees of success. It was not until the United Mine Workers began to focus its energies there in the late 1890s, however, that the situation began to change. Of course, it was not all the UMW's doing. The workers themselves had developed solidarity and militancy. They needed that resolve, for the owners were a tight-knit lot who behaved like God-ordained feudal kings. As the president of the Central Railroad of New Jersey, of the Reading Railroad, and of the Philadelphia and Reading Coal and Iron Company, George F. Baer (1842–1914)—Darrow derisively called him "George the Last"—put it, "The rights and interests of the laboring man will be protected and cared for—not by the labor agitators, but by the Christian men to whom God in his infinite wisdom has given the control of the property interests of the country."[51] Unimpressed, union organizers and miners kept battling for a better life and industrial democracy, especially after the 1897 Lattimer Massacre, in which sheriff deputies shot into a crowd of striking miners, killing nineteen and wounding at least fifty. The UMW's first major gain came in 1900, when Mitchell led a successful strike of the workers in the Wyoming, Lehigh, and Schuylkill fields of Pennsylvania. The victory suggested to the workers and their leaders that through solidarity more was possible. The coal operators, fearing the same thing, vowed to crush the miners' organization once and for all.

The struggle came to a head in 1902. In the early spring, UMW president Mitchell sought to negotiate with the anthracite coal operators for a new contract that would bring the anthracite mining district into line with the bituminous district with joint conferences and stabilizing wage and cost measures. Mitchell did not expect trouble. He also offered four basic demands: a wage increase of 20 percent, the establishment of an eight-hour day, a new system of weighing coal and paying miners accordingly, and new grievance machinery so that the United Mine Workers and the operators could settle problems without strikes or lockouts.[52]

Speaking for the Anthracite Operators' Association, Baer rejected the proposal and the negotiations, curtly replying to Mitchell: "There can not be two masters in the management of the business."[53] If the operators expected the union to fold, they were sadly mistaken. In May 1902, 150,000 miners went on strike, and stayed on strike for five months.

President Mitchell knew that the union had to hold together, win over public opinion, and raise a lot of money. The miners did all three. As such, public and political pressure began to mount for the coal operators to settle. Mark Hanna (1837–1904), the former political adviser to President McKinley turned Republican senator from Ohio as well as a leading official of the National Civic Federation, urged a peaceable and quick resolution. Surprisingly many other establishment politicians agreed. Even sixty-five-year-old former president Cleveland, who had called out the troops on more than one occasion to crush strikes, backed a negotiated settlement.[54] Although President Theodore Roosevelt (1858–1919) had ordered his labor commissioner, Carroll D. Wright (1840–1909), to investigate the situation and report back, he did not take action until October 1902, when a coal panic and fears of a coal "famine" had set in on the East Coast. Not wanting to call out the army to take over the mines but wanting to settle the dispute fairly and squarely, TR called both sides to the White House. After a tense meeting, everyone agreed to arbitration by a blue-ribbon commission appointed by the president.[55] It was then that John Mitchell asked Henry Lloyd to bring in Darrow, who rushed to Wilkes-Barre, Pennsylvania, to represent the union in front of the commission. In the weeks before the arbitration hearing, Mitchell,

Lloyd, and others gave Darrow a crash course in the life of an anthracite miner, even taking him into the black seams.[56]

For three and a half months in Scranton's City Hall, the commission, led by Carroll Wright, collected testimony about, as Darrow remembered, "every imaginable question . . . working conditions, living conditions, education, accidents, cost of food and clothing, rents, in fact, everything that enters into living and toiling."[57] Each side had its days in the sun, but Darrow and his team, which included Louis Brandeis (1856–1941), who worked for free, had the advantage. Whereas the miners and their lawyers were united, the operators and their lawyers were less cohesive, and the owners were, as Darrow wrote, "handicapped by too many lawyers."[58] Darrow led the charge for the union, calling 241 miners—injured and not—widows, and child workers to testify. The climax came in February 1903, when Baer and Darrow made their final appeals to the commission. Darrow had been here before. But unlike George Pullman, who was a no-show in 1895, and George Paine, who made a bumbling ass of himself in 1898, Baer was more than up for the task.

As *The North American* (Philadelphia) opined, in this clash of titans, "sabre cut answered lash of whip." Both performances were tours de force. Baer strutted before the commissioners with "polished sarcasm and powerful rhetoric." He was passionate and energetic. "At times," the *North American* reporter noted, Baer "fairly shook from head to foot with the vehemence of his passion, and his voice rang high and clear as a bugle note," receiving applause from the audience.[59] Only the pessimist, Baer charged, "will not see that the masses of men have advanced, and are continuing to advance under the powerful stimulus which individual liberty gives to individual initiative." Further, there was no justification for the strike. "The lawlessness in the coal regions," Baer asserted, "was the direct result of mistaken theories as to the rights of the Mine Workers." The union was a "monster monopoly," much unlike the combination of coal operators, which "produce[s] only those things which are desirable." Baer continued to refute and reject each of the union's demands, from wage increases to the eight-hour day. "Ten hours," he commented, "is not an unreasonable length of time for a man to work in the breakers of the anthracite coal fields." So as not to sound completely unreasonable, Baer closed with a promise to the commissioners to raise wages 5 percent.[60]

Baer was slick, fearless, kinetic, and bold. But Darrow was better. Darrow matched and surpassed Baer's verve, his energy, his anger, his cleverness, his facts and figures, and his arguments word for word. He forcefully deposed King Baer. Darrow started by attacking Baer's closing lines. If the operators had been willing to give a 5 percent raise, "why did not Mr. Baer go to Mr. John Mitchell nine months ago, as he came to this commission today?" Darrow answered his own question. The owners refused to concede anything until they crushed the union. But the UMW was "dearer to [the miners] than their bread." He also lampooned Baer's accusation that the miners labored under some false political ideology. The operators' sad attempt to connect the UMW to some anarchist or socialist movement only revealed what little they knew about socialism or anarchism. Waiting for the applause and laughter to die down, Darrow got serious: this case was not about ideas or political theories. "We are all accused of being dreamers on our side," he said, but this matter was not about dreams. It was about an unfortunate reality.[61]

Darrow then painstakingly reviewed the miners' claims and demands with statistics and testimony. Even through wage scales and systems of weight measurement, he sparkled, demonstrating time and again that the owners stretched and bent the truth. The miners who had come to watch were enthralled, and several times the commission had to quiet the "outbursts of applause." They cheered Darrow's charge that Baer and his colleagues cared not for the miners but for money. "When I think of the cripples, of the orphans, of the widows, of the maimed who are dragging their lives out on account of this business, who, if they were mules or horses would be cared for, but who are left and neglected, it seems to me this is the greatest indictment of this business that can possibly be made." The practice of hiring children was, in his words, an "abominably disgraceful evil." Miners had no choice but to strike to destroy it and challenge the rapaciousness of their employers.[62]

After listening to 558 witnesses and recording over ten thousand pages of testimony, the commissioners closed the hearings, promising a quick and deliberative decision, which came on March 18, 1903. Among its eleven points, the commissioners awarded a 10 percent raise, created a Board of Conciliation to settle future issues between the employers and miners, and established a fairer means of weighing and paying wages. The commissioners maintained the open shop whereby no miner would have to join a union—namely, the United Mine Workers. Finally, they made a series of nonbinding recommendations, such as the abolition of child laborers, an end to company police, and a complete investigation into the issues behind the 1902 coal strike.[63]

Despite the limits of the decision, especially in regard to union recognition, Mitchell claimed victory.[64] For his part, Baer was clearly displeased. "I'm dumb as an oyster, or, rather as a clam, regarding the finding of the Coal Strike Commission," he told reporters. "Why, I wouldn't even discuss it with my daughter."[65] Darrow and others on the left wondered why Baer was mad. Darrow thought the decision a "cowardly document."[66] In particular, he thought that the commission was out of bounds for scolding the unionists for any acts of violence during the strike. "People cannot live at the point of want," he wrote later, "without some acts of violence."[67] Mary Harris Jones (1843?–1930)—aka Mother Jones—was Mitchell's most strident critic. She maintained that he should have held out for union recognition. Further, he let all the national attention go to his head; Mitchell was becoming a union boss, not a leader. He was getting on Darrow's nerves as well. While Darrow was preparing his final summation, he and Mitchell had a heated argument. Mitchell claimed that Darrow was working for the socialists. He told his lawyer point-blank to drop his "private theories." To some degree, Darrow heeded his client's wishes, but their relationship remained strained.[68]

Even before the Anthracite Coal Strike Commission hearings were over, Darrow's thoughts drifted back to Chicago. While he was in Scranton, he had been approached "by emissaries, friends and newspaper representatives from Chicago regarding the coming mayoralty campaign there."[69] They wanted him to run; he hesitated, asking for time. Chicago newspapers ignored the request and began to create momentum for Darrow's mayoral campaign. *The Chicago Record* published articles linking Darrow to the working-class vote. He was to inherit Altgeld's political mantle, if he dared.[70] His backers, who likely included Schilling, even organized a Darrow Club, a political association reminiscent of Altgeld's Labor Legion.

Darrow still had not made his decision when he arrived in Chicago with Mitchell and Lloyd in tow. All three were the guests of honor at a monstrous rally of six thousand on February 16, 1903. It rivaled the celebration given for Debs upon his release from the Woodstock prison in 1896. Lloyd introduced Darrow to the throng as the "steadfast champion of rights of the people . . . that rare bird, a lawyer whose first love is love of justice and who remains true to his first love."[71] Darrow congratulated Mitchell and "his associates and ourselves upon the great victory." He said the lesson was that "labor must learn that no one will stand for them unless they stand for themselves." Spontaneously members of the crowd, many of whom wore "Darrow for Mayor" buttons, began shouting, "[o]ur next mayor!"[72] Darrow did not take the bait. Sticking to the matter at hand, he only heaped further praise on John Mitchell and the miners and reflected upon "the greatest industrial struggle the world has known."[73]

Shortly after the public party, Darrow traveled to Springfield, formally joined the Illinois General Assembly, and began working toward his goals of expanding the public good and establishing public ownership of Chicago's transit system.[74] On February 23, he announced publicly that he would not run for mayor. The masses that had supported the now-aborted candidacy were disappointed, but many of Darrow's friends were satisfied. Sam Gompers congratulated him for the decision. The American Federation of Labor's chief worried that Darrow, hemmed in by the trappings of high office, would become a mere bureaucrat enforcing laws that he did not support. Additionally, with the exception of Brand Whitlock, Darrow's closest friends and colleagues—Henry Lloyd, William Randolph Hearst, and John Mitchell—discouraged him from running. Algie M. Simons (1870–1950), editor of *The International Socialist Review*, sent Darrow a letter urging him to decline, fearing that the Independent Labor Party would "wreck the Socialist movement." Although Simons's and Gompers's urgings clearly influenced Darrow's decision, William Hearst may have cast the deciding vote on the matter.[75]

Darrow wanted Hearst to run for president in 1904, and both may have concluded that they needed Mayor Harrison to remain in control of the city's Democratic Party machine in order to launch that campaign.[76] Whatever the reason, for a second time Darrow had dashed the hopes of his supporters, who then threw their weight behind Daniel L. Cruice, a young lawyer who headed the city's Independent Labor Party ticket. At first, Darrow pledged his support for Cruice. Together they had helped build the Public Ownership League, and Darrow promised to stump for him. But quickly he thought better of it.[77] Instead, he shocked many by publicly backing Democrat Carter Harrison, the politico he had been lambasting for years. Darrow ordered the leaders of the Darrow Club to distribute a leaflet in English and in German "to the friends of municipal ownership and referendum," calling on them to support "the only trustworthy candidate," Mayor Carter Harrison.[78]

Chicago's working class felt betrayed, and for good reason. At a meeting at North Turner Hall that drew twenty-five hundred men, the leaders of the Independent Labor Party held an anti-Darrow rally. Joseph S. Martin, a leader among the old Altgeld forces, claimed that Darrow had been bought. At the suggestion of this corruption, one workingman with particularly strong lungs shouted: "Send Darrow out here, and we will take care of him." Apparently, the call for blood was repeated by hundreds, and "the hissing and shouting lasted fully three minutes," a reporter noted.[79] A speaker at the rally promised a riot if Darrow appeared in Chicago to speak for Mayor Harrison.

Undeterred, Darrow went to Chicago to campaign for Harrison and to explain himself. Speaking onstage with Harrison, Darrow charged that the Independent Labor Party was a "fraud" and Cruice its patsy. The Labor Party's purpose was to defeat Harrison, after which it would disappear "like a mushroom growth." Looking at Harrison standing next to him, Darrow coldly but truthfully stated: "I am not speaking for Mr. Harrison because of any great admiration, close acquaintance, or personal enthusiasm."[80] He was, to put it simply, the only reasonable choice. The next day local papers carried an open letter to Cruice. In it, Darrow tried again to explain his position. "At the time you accepted the nomination," Darrow conceded, "I did tell you that I would support you, but I feel now that I cannot do this." It was a matter of backing the strongest horse in the race toward municipal ownership. Friendship and loyalty had nothing to do with it, or so Darrow thought. For him, it was better to ignore the wishes of his working-class allies and do what he thought best for the greater good, which in this instance was municipal control of the street railways. This was the first but certainly not the last time that Darrow made this kind of political calculus and showed a willingness to abandon people and ideas for the sake of some larger goal in the name of freedom and liberty.[81]

The rationalizations did not matter. Darrow now had fewer friends. Cruice declared "in no uncertain tones that Clarence S. Darrow is guilty of a breach of confidence with the labor party and myself."[82] Others questioned Darrow's thinking. In his six years in office, Harrison had done nothing to secure municipal ownership. Why would he start now? Regardless, that evening Darrow spoke again at a Harrison rally. As a city reporter noted, in front of that "large and enthusiastic audience, and after he had finished defending himself, he spoke on the traction issue as he had spoken the night before, and urged all laboring men to vote for Harrison."[83] The election went as Darrow wanted in one respect: Harrison was reelected with 146,323 votes, besting the Republican Graeme Stewart (139,375) and crushing Cruice (9,999).[84] Darrow was right: Cruice never stood a chance. Darrow probably had significant influence upon the electorate and the future of municipal ownership, but it came at a steep personal price.

Darrow then set about fulfilling his campaign promises in Springfield. His crowning achievement was the passage of the Mueller Act.[85] That law authorized cities in Illinois to own and operate public utilities, including street railways. Darrow also advanced other pieces of legislation to abolish imprisonment for debt, to end capital punishment, to limit the number of expert witnesses in court proceedings, and to abolish criminal conspiracy. None of them passed.[86] What connected all his work in Springfield was his sense of the public good. In his view, government should crack down on barbarity and corruption. Only initiatives that rose to that standard had Darrow's support.

Darrow's political stand also meant that at times he had to ignore his personal sympathies and uphold the public trust. In 1903, he voted against a private bill that would have provided relief for Mrs. John P. Altgeld. He had known Emma Altgeld for a long time, and she was in dire need. Her husband's financial fortune had evaporated with his political one, and she did not have the money to cover her mortgage. Moreover, she had recently fallen and broken her arm, limiting her ability to earn money. Altgeld's friends had proposed a five-thousand-dollar grant to spare the homestead. Although the Illinois legislature approved the bill by a two-thirds margin, Darrow voted against it, taking the floor to explain himself. "There are appropriations which must be met and which should be made liberally, but I do not see that we have the right to vote the money that must be paid by the property holders of this state, great and small, to any individual, no matter how much I respect him or her, no matter how well they stand in the common esteem."[87] Darrow had clung to his principles. It did not, however, win him friends or influence or appreciation.

In fact, save for the Mueller Act, the entire Springfield adventure was a bust. Darrow made no new connections there and spent more than one lonely evening in Lincoln's hometown. Worse, there was little to keep him entertained. As such, his mind wandered, as did his emotions. He was frequently "blue" and even begged friends to visit. "Come down *please*," he wrote to Henry Lloyd. "I am very lonesome."[88] Lloyd apparently never made the trip. Darrow had no desire for a second term and went back to Chicago as soon as he could.

When he got back, the first order of business was to find a law partner to replace Altgeld. Darrow's choice was Brand Whitlock, his literary and legal protégé. But Whitlock had already moved to Toledo, and that city's future mayor was already embroiled in matters there. Darrow then approached Edgar Lee Masters, then a competent lawyer but an unknown poet. They had known each other for years, at least since 1897. Both came from stifling rural midwestern childhoods and had gone to the Windy City for fame and fortune. They were similarly drawn to the cutting edge of culture and had collaborated from time to time. In 1898, Masters had arranged for Darrow to be appointed the attorney for the receiver of a bankrupt building and loan association. But when time came to settle the fees, Darrow had "grabbed the largest share of the money" while Masters had claimed he had done most of the work.[89] Darrow had then offered Masters a position in his firm. Still angry with Darrow, Masters had turned him down. In 1903, Darrow approached Masters again. Though there were vague rumors in Chicago that Darrow was not the squeaky clean lawyer for the public good that he purported to be, Masters ignored this "odor" and this time consented.[90] "The man was charming," Masters recalled. Darrow had also offered him a fair percentage of the partnership's earnings. And "his firm was busy and quite prosperous at this time."[91]

The forged partnership was never a happy one. For one thing, Darrow dumped work on him, or at least Masters thought so. When Masters joined the firm in the spring of 1903, Darrow surprised everyone and announced that he was marrying Ruby Hammerstrom and sailing off for Europe, where he planned to honeymoon, relax, and finish his magnum opus, *Farmington*. This came as a total shock, especially to his partners, who had to pick up the slack, and to those who thought Darrow's free love stance was immutable. Then there was the age difference. Ruby was sixteen years his junior. But the May-December courtship had lasted almost four years. So why did Darrow abandon his bohemian views about marriage? We can only surmise. Maybe it was middle-age angst, maybe it was loneliness, or maybe he no longer agreed with feminists (this seems partly to have been the case).[92] Regardless, free love was no longer central to his philosophical view. Darrow remained dedicated as ever to individual rights, liberties, and freedoms. As he neared fifty years of age, the great American iconoclast was becoming more selective about his battles; he could not take them all, nor did he want to. This was the first major example of the sifting, winnowing, and shifting of his political commitments. For him, breaking the bonds of marriage was not vital to the cause of challenging the robber barons, their corporate monopolies, and their political lackeys. Moreover, although he would not admit it publicly yet, Darrow harbored grave doubts about mass movements. Feminists, bohemians, and unionists had let him down before in various settings, especially political ones, and they would let him down again. Plus, aside from everything else, marrying Ruby seemed like a path to happiness, and in many ways it was.

Darrow's second European vacation—his first had been in 1895, after the Debs case—was entertaining and relaxing. He visited with such various radicals as George Bernard Shaw (1856–1950) and Henry Mayers Hyndman (1842–1921) and came home rested and ready for more legal wrangling and political fighting. He also came home to loss and disappointment. While he had been in Europe, his comrade Henry Lloyd had passed away. He heard the news the morning he arrived back in Chicago. Quickly he dispatched a letter to Lloyd's wife, Jessie, offering his condolences: "I can not tell you how sorry I am for you . . . I only wish there was something that I can do, but what can one do in the presence of death?"[93] A few months later Darrow lost his father too. Amirus, who had moved to Chicago so that his famous son could take care of him, died quickly and quietly and, as family legend has it, with a book in hand.[94]

Making matters more depressing, the political situation in Chicago had not improved at all. Mayor Harrison had turned out to be no better than his Republican rival, Graeme Stewart. Rather, he was as slick a politician as his old man, forging political alliances and staving off any reforms that might have altered the systems of boodle and bribe. Having spent his political capital in the 1903 election, Darrow could do little. Chicago's streetcar workers, however, had one last card to play.

On November 12, 1903, twenty-five hundred motormen and conductors went on strike against the Chicago Railway Company (CRC), demanding a shorter workday, higher wages, and the ability to control the scheduling of cars. They also demanded that the city work toward municipal ownership. The strikers had citywide support. The teamsters boycotted deliveries to the CRC, and within a few days the company's blacksmiths, firemen, horseshoers, linemen, machinists, and stationary engineers had also walked out. The company's executives were ready for a fight. They had hired James Farley, an expert strikebreaker who had smashed workers in similar disputes in Cleveland, St. Louis, and other midwestern cities. But the people of Chicago would not let the CRC win. On November 13, fifteen thousand Chicagoans paraded through the city's streets, blocking scab streetcars. Stockyard workers even released flocks of sheep onto the tracks. The crowd wound its way to a central location on the South Side, where they listened to impassioned speeches. After the last, a chant went out for Darrow, who had not been scheduled to speak.

He waited until the crowd's demand became irresistible. Having risen to the platform, he told them that "this strike was brought about by those persons who believe the class which holds property has all the rights, and that which does not has none; by those who believe that a business belongs absolutely to the employer and not to the employees who give their lives to it."[95] Darrow wanted to change that and give control of this business to the people and the employees. The crowd agreed by acclamation, but the city government still saw otherwise.

Ostensibly to keep the peace, Mayor Harrison called out the police, who cleared the streets and rode the streetcars to protect the strikebreakers. Eventually, after various altercations between the police and strikers and after several days of empty cars, the mayor and the CRC officials relented and agreed to arbitration. All striking workers were hired back, and the company agreed to enter talks about wages and hours, though recognition of the union was off the table. The situation was akin to the anthracite coal dispute. The difference was the call for municipal ownership, but Harrison had consented to arbitration on that as well. Darrow represented the union at City Hall. Hopes were high. Not only had Darrow delivered in the anthracite coal arbitration, but he had also won a pay increase for the union representing the employees of Chicago's other major traction line, the Union Traction Company, in October 1902.[96] This time, however, Harrison and the city council dragged their feet, brushed aside Darrow's exhortations at the arbitration hearings, and ignored a citywide referendum in support of the Mueller Act, which had passed in April 1904.

For Darrow, there was only one solution: new city leadership. In fact, he also believed the time was ripe for new national leadership. A new president could put vast amounts of political pressure on city governments and make municipal ownership a reality. In 1904, two Democratic hopefuls put a municipal ownership plank at the center of their platforms: William Jennings Bryan and William Randolph Hearst. Darrow backed the latter.

They had become fast friends in 1901, after Hearst had asked Darrow to help him incorporate his new newspaper the *Evening American* (later renamed the *Chicago American*), which in part served Hearst's political ambitions. Both men shared a similar political view. As historian David Nasaw has written, "Forced to choose between men who, like his father, worked with their hands to eke out a living, and those who sat back at leisure and profited from the labor of others, Hearst had no difficulty in siding with the former against the latter."[97] Much the same could have been said of Darrow, who not only stumped for Hearst in the primaries but also represented him at the Democratic National Convention in St. Louis in July 1904.

The pair did not stand a chance. The Democratic Party bosses like Carter Harrison did not want to elect a radical or a reformer. On the evening of July 8, Darrow addressed the convention, pleading for his candidate. Although the delegates cheered and laughed at the appropriate spots, the conservative Alton B. Parker (1852–1926) was nominated. Hearst and Darrow were left empty-handed. After Darrow's speech, Moses Koenigsberg (1878–1945), editor of Hearst's *Chicago American*, went to find Darrow to get a copy. He found him hiding in a dark corner of the auditorium "in a grouch too thick to talk."[98] Darrow abandoned the Democratic Party that election to vote for Debs, who lost—as did Parker—to Teddy Roosevelt.[99]

Weary from the St. Louis debacle, Darrow returned to Chicago to continue the fight for municipal ownership without national support. Again, he placed his hopes on a new mayor. The 1905 election pitted Democrat

Edward F. Dunne (1853–1937) against Republican John Maynard Harlan, who aped Theodore Roosevelt's pledge for a "square deal for all," as the two major party candidates.[100] Dunne and Darrow had a long political collaboration in the Democratic Party. In 1898, they had helped form the Monticello Club as a pro–William Jennings Bryan rival to the Iroquois Club, an association closely allied with the city's Democratic Party bosses. Dunne was also the judge in Darrow's celebrated 1901 "free speech" case, in which Darrow and Altgeld defended Hearst's *Chicago American* against libel charges. Darrow actively campaigned for Dunne, who defeated Harlan 161,659 to 137,411. The Socialist and Prohibition candidates garnered 20,323 and 2980 respectively.[101] MUNICIPAL OWNERSHIP WINS IN CHICAGO, *The New York Times* heralded. But how was it to be done? Dunne did not have the answer, so he decided to hire Darrow as a special corporation lawyer in charge of all traction litigation relating to the incorporation of 720 miles of streetcar track.

Dunne's plan fell apart quickly.[102] Darrow proved incapable of dealing with the traction companies. In fact, these corporate executives wanted nothing to do with him. Yerkes was gone. He had left Chicago in 1899 and died in 1905. But his friends and allies, such as Marshall Field and Phillip D. Armour, had no patience for Darrow. Their goal was either full retention of their power or some compromise that allowed them to retain as much as possible. Furthermore, in 1905 Darrow was vulnerable. A major client of his law firm, the local teamsters' union, had just lost a nasty strike. The wealthy had defeated the teamsters by building an underground railway system that bypassed cartage aboveground. The unionists were doomed despite the heroic efforts of their lawyer. Not only did the strike's defeat throw the momentum back toward the rich and powerful, but Darrow suddenly appeared weak. Under these conditions, the municipal ownership mayor equivocated, waffling between public regulation and ownership. Fed up with yet another mayor's playing the political field, Darrow bitterly tendered his resignation.

Darrow's animosity was directed toward the aldermen, not toward Dunne himself. When asked by reporters if he and the mayor had had a falling-out, Darrow replied, "Rubbish."[103] His letter to the mayor resigning his post had affirmed "that there is not the slightest personal feeling in this resignation, and I want you to know that no man believes more than I in your high purpose and your devotion to the public good."[104] Perhaps it was that last part that spurred Dunne to beg Darrow to stay. He did, albeit for five more frustrating months. In the end, Chicago's street railway barons won. The streetcar system remained in the hands of the privileged, although they consented to profit sharing and some regulation.[105]

It was not a complete debacle. There was some public control and oversight, but Darrow had been outfoxed. He was used to it. His defeats were rarely total; nor, for that matter, were his victories. Still, at each turn, as the nineteenth century gave way to the twentieth, this lyrical lawyer who wanted to be an avant-garde writer increasingly turned away from electoral politics and toward the one American institution that he thought had a chance to advance liberty, humanity, and the public good: the labor movement. His work on behalf of Chicago's unionists, such as the streetcar workers and the teamsters, and especially on behalf of the anthracite miners had propelled him beyond the confines of Chicago onto a national stage. An audience of the poor, the oppressed, and the resolute fighters for freedom called for him to deliver legal performances in order to transform American politics and society, and for the next seven years he did just that. It almost killed him.

⊰· 6 ·⊱

In Defense of Dynamiters

Clarence Darrow's experiences in Chicago and in Pennsylvania had taught him one basic lesson: America was engulfed in a titanic and violent struggle between the rich and powerful and the poor and lowly. Moreover, Darrow had little faith in electoral politics to change conditions; the vote, he once opined, was "a nice little toy to keep people satisfied."[1] No one needed to tell that to labor movement activists. They knew. Some were content to fight peacefully in court or on the picket lines, while others used violence. Although Darrow abhorred the latter, he understood that "the progress of the human race is one long bloody story of force and violence."[2] It was going to take, he declared, "a universal, world-wide conspiracy by the intelligent working people and by their friends the world over to get back the earth that has been stolen by direct action." Thus, Darrow knew that conspiracy was going to involve violence, but it was justifiable since these class conflagrations were destined to make "the world juster and fairer than it has ever been before."[3]

While Darrow was content to wage war in court, others were decidedly not. In the early 1870s a secret society appeared just south of Wilkes-Barre, Pennsylvania. Founded in Ireland as a militant organization opposed to English landlords and their agents, the Molly Maguires transplanted themselves to the United States and terrorized coal operators and their lieutenants, providing the muscle to challenge bosses during strikes. To stop the killing and to crush the miners' rebellion, operators hired a private detective agency run by former Secret Service officer Allan Pinkerton (1819–1884), whose legal career had begun in Chicago. In turn, Pinkerton had hired another Chicagoan, James McParlan (1843–1919), who also went by the name James McParlen and later by McParland, to infiltrate the Molly Maguires and gather intelligence that could be used to prosecute them. Owing to McParland's efforts, in 1875, more than twenty Mollys were convicted of various crimes. Ten were hanged, and the others were given long prison sentences. The organization was destroyed, and McParland emerged a hero, but only for some. Eugene Debs was not so sanguine. "The men who perished upon the scaffold as felons were labor leaders," he wrote in the socialist magazine *Appeal to Reason*. They were "the first martyrs to the class struggle in the United States."[4] There would be others.

Perhaps it was something about miners or mining or mine operators, but there was a similarly massive struggle in the West over gold and silver. Dreams of finding the mother lode drew thousands of miners from beyond the continental divide. A few got lucky, including an improbable pair: a hardscrabble union leader, Edward Boyce (1862–1941), and a ne'er-do-well drifter who was going by the name of Harry Orchard (1867–1954). They struck it rich when they discovered Idaho's largest vein of silver-lead rock, known afterward as the Hercules Mine. With some embarrassment, Boyce became a millionaire union president. Orchard took a much different path, becoming one of the most notorious American terrorists. His life and deeds shaped not only the nation's history but Darrow's as well.

For most miners, excavating was the devil's work. In the summer it was beastly hot; in the winter it was satanically cold. And it smelled like brimstone. The miners' reward for the sweat and the blood was not wealth. As the writer J. Anthony Lukas so memorably pointed out, the mines of Idaho, especially those in the northern Coeur d'Alene region, "produced the polar opposite: a wage-earning proletariat at the mercy of absentee mine owners and their managers, helpless in gut-wrenching cycles of boom and bust, never sinking roots in permanent communities, destined to drift from one ramshackle mining camp to another in a futile quest for their lost dream of western autonomy."[5]

There was only one solution: union. In 1891, with the assistance of the

Butte (Montana) Miners' Union, four Idaho miners' organizations merged to form the Miners' Union of the Coeur d'Alenes. Soon thereafter the region's mine operators established the Mine Owners' Association (MOA), and they began plotting the union's demise. First, the MOA hired a cadre of Pinkerton spies to infiltrate the union's leadership; then it arranged lockouts at a handful of mines to goad a strike in order to crush the miners back into submission, with force if necessary. Instead of folding, the miners' union expanded and in 1893 formed a broader organization, known as the Western Federation of Miners (WFM). This scared the hell out of the mine owners and their politicians, who feared that the western states would soon fall under the influence of the "Molly Maguires of the West."[6] Indeed, the WFM quickly became a tough, powerful social and political force, not merely an economic one.

In 1896, the union miners backed the fusion Populist candidate Frank Steunenberg (1861–1905), whose newspaper, the *Caldwell Tribune*, had supported the union miners in their war against the operators. The amalgam of radical unionists and Populists was partially successful.[7] They elected their man as governor in a landslide, but their presidential candidate, William Jennings Bryan, lost. Nonetheless, the WFM pressed its advantage. By 1898, most Coeur d'Alene operators had agreed to terms with the union, consenting to a union shop and paying the union scale. One company, however, refused: the Bunker Hill Mining Company. In April 1899, WFM president Ed Boyce decided it was time to act. WFM unionists attacked the company's collieries, blowing up its concentrator and causing more than $300,000 ($7.6 million in today's dollars) in damages. The miners thought that Governor Steunenberg would support them. They were dead wrong. Steunenberg wired President McKinley, who dispatched a famed unit of the African American Buffalo Soldiers, the Twenty-fourth Infantry Regiment, to Idaho to reestablish law and order. Under the command of Brigadier General Henry Clay Merriam (1837–1912), they arrived on the thirteenth anniversary of the Haymarket Massacre, quickly rounded up the miners, and put them into a gigantic bullpen. Those not snagged in the dragnet, like Harry Orchard, fled. A tentative peace was restored.

Steunenberg knew this was the end of his political career and did not seek reelection. In his own defense, he claimed that as governor he had acted "for the benefit" of organized labor and out of a concern to promote "mutual and cooperative" relations between labor and capital. Neither side of that divide was impressed. He was fine with that, but once out of office he had a lingering fear that his call for federal help would, as he told his wife, Belle, "cost him his life."[8]

Their defeat at Bunker Hill did nothing to crush the spirits of these revolutionary miners. Rather, they became more radical and more powerful as the years went on, expanding their undeclared war through several western states. At the turn of the twentieth century, the hopes of the WFM rested on the shoulders of two new leaders: president Charles Moyer (1866–1929) and secretary-treasurer William "Big Bill" Haywood (1869–1928). Moyer was the more conservative of the two. An Iowan by birth, he was a roughneck and an ex-con who made his way out west to restart his life. While working as a miner in South Dakota in the 1890s, he joined the WFM and jetted to the top of the organization. He was a capable union leader who favored negotiation and arbitration.[9] Haywood was the polar opposite. Whereas Moyer was a wallflower, Haywood was larger than life. People either loved him or hated him. For a time, he was the most feared unionist in America. A burly, bulky, concrete-jawed Cyclops who was, in the words of his biographer Peter Carlson, "the very personification of proletarian rage, a capitalist's nightmare come to life."[10] In part out of the owners' fear of Haywood and the Western Federation of Miners, by the middle of 1903 an ominous peace—with some notable exceptions—had descended in many of the western mining districts, especially in Colorado, as the WFM established an eight-hour day and minimum wages. It was at this moment that an old score was settled.

Although the fear never quite had left him, Frank Steunenberg no longer walked with one eye over his shoulder. Little did he know, however, that an assassin stalked him. On Saturday, December 30, 1905, while he was returning home from a wintry early-evening walk in his beloved Caldwell, Idaho, Steunenberg's would-be murderer caught up with him. As the former governor turned toward his house and put his hand on the gate that guarded the walkway to his family, he tripped a wire and a bomb exploded, shredding most of his lower body. The bomb was far bigger than necessary, and the explosion was heard throughout the town. The ex-governor's wife and neighbors came running. After a few moments, they lifted what was left of him into the house. Doctors arrived quickly, but there was nothing to do. After an agonizing twenty minutes, Steunenberg died.[11]

He was laid to rest on a bitterly cold January 3, 1906. Even before Steunenberg was in the ground, fingers were pointing to the Western Federation of Miners. Wrote a *New York Times* reporter a day after the murder, "[T]here is no known reason for the outrage, but it is charged to some members of the famous inner circle of the Coeur d'Alenes dynamiters whom he prosecuted relentlessly in 1899 while he was Governor."[12] Indeed, few union miners shed tears at Steunenberg's untimely and ghastly end. The editors of *Miners' Magazine* published an editorial the week after the funeral. "Your sole ambition was money, which in your estimation was superior to honor," the bitter unionist wrote, "but you are gone and upon your political tombstone shall be inscribed in indelible words, 'Here lies a hireling and a traitor!' "[13]

Only after the funeral did the public find out that the police had their main suspect already in custody. On December 30, just two hours after the bombing, Republican Governor Frank Gooding (1859–1928) had called the Thiel Detective Agency, renowned for its work in western states. Within a few hours after his arrival, W. S. Swain, Thiel's best investigator, had arrested a drifter, Thomas Hogan, who later gave his name as Harry Orchard. A search of his room yielded bomb-making equipment and weapons. Swain, a hard-nosed detective, made little headway in extracting a confession. Governor Gooding called in reinforcements, the aged but legendary James McParland, who arrived a week after the funeral. Thirty years after he had fought his way into the Molly Maguires and destroyed them from the inside, McParland had grown gray-haired, paunchy, and rickety, walking with a bone-handled blackthorn cane. Make no mistake about it, though. He was as sharp as ever.[14]

As soon as he relieved his rival detective, McParland immediately worked to gain Orchard's trust with treats, privileges, and pleasant visits. On January 22, he met with Orchard with the "view of breaking him down and getting a confession from him."[15] With the help of the Reverend Edwin S. Hinks, dean of St. Michael's Cathedral in Boise, he got Orchard to repent, literally. They all sat quietly without much emotion as Orchard, whom McParland described as having "as determined a countenance as I have seen on a human being," confessed to a campaign of terror and murder that stretched back to

Bunker Hill and ended with Steunenberg's assassination. Orchard revealed that he had been trying to kill him for days and had almost got him on Christmas Eve. Finally, he planted a bomb allegedly designed by George Pettibone (d. 1908). The so-called Pettibone dope, otherwise known as Greek fire, used a sulfuric acid trigger and more than one hundred giant blasting caps. McParland bought Orchard's testimony in its entirety, believing him when he named his other accomplices: WFM president Moyer, secretary-treasurer Haywood, and union troubleshooter Stephen W. "Steve" Adams.[16]

McParland moved quickly to apprehend Moyer, Haywood, Pettibone, and Adams. He picked up the latter first. Then, on February 15, 1906, his marshals swooped in and arrested the rest. Moyer and Pettibone were easily nabbed, but it took a little work to find Haywood, who was found still celebrating Valentine's Day with his mistress, Winnie Minor. The trio were shuttled onto a fast, heavily guarded Union Pacific express train to Boise, where Viper, Copperhead, and Rattler—McParland's code names for Haywood, Moyer, and Pettibone—were met at the station by a smiling McParland, who believed he was on the verge of chopping off the serpentine heads of the "inner circle" of the Molly Maguires of the West.[17]

If Haywood, Moyer, and Pettibone did not want to meet the same fate as the Mollies, they and their union had to act quickly. The prosecution—led by Steunenberg's friend William Borah (1865–1940), District Attorney Owen M. Van Duyn (1882–1948), and James Hawley (1847–1929), a former union lawyer who had switched sides—seemingly had all the cards. The prosecution held three aces. First, McParland had extracted a confession from Steve Adams that corroborated Orchard's statement exactly.[18] Second, his other prisoners were unable to contain their animosity toward one another. By December, the three were no longer talking to one another, and McParland believed it was only a mere matter of time before one would turn on the others. If all this weren't bad enough, the defense was also losing the public relations battle. Press coverage consistently weighed in on the side of the prosecution.[19] Desperate that time was running out, WFM leaders put out the call for Clarence Darrow, the great defender of miners, unionists, liberty, justice, and freedom.

In late February, a WFM official contacted Darrow. Labor's lawyer dropped everything to meet with the defense team of Edmund F. Richardson (1862–1911) and Fred W. Miller, both of whom had worked for the federation for some time; John Nugent (1868–1931), future U.S. senator from Idaho; and Edgar Wilson (1861–1915), Idaho's first U.S. congressional representative. Two obstacles were immediate. One was the money needed to mount a defense. The second concerned egos. Richardson insisted that Darrow assume the title of associate counsel. Although Darrow initially worried much more about the defense fund than the order of the chairs, in the end it was the latter that caused him the most consternation.

Darrow charged the WFM fifty thousand dollars (five times the amount he had received from the United Mine Workers in the 1902 coal commission case and more than one million dollars in today's dollars). Unions and various left-wing organizations raised more than what was needed. Darrow himself engaged in the fund-raising, lobbying his labor friends, including UMW president John Mitchell, an adversary of Haywood's who had worked against the WFM. "This is a matter which I would rather avoid if I could on account of the hard fight and the serious odds," Darrow wrote Mitchell. "However, I do not see how I can get out of it."[20] Though Haywood had labeled him a "jackass," the UMW president came through with a few thousand dollars, as did many unions big and small.[21] The Butte, Montana, Mill and Smeltermen's Union sent five thousand dollars, not an insignificant sum in 1906.[22] The stodgy American Federation of Labor executive council members held their noses and gave a few thousand too.

Darrow put the resources to excellent use. His first action was to try to get his clients sprung. The longer they languished in jail, the more likely it was that one might turn on another or make a confession or taint the jury pool by appearing guilty. Further, if their habeas corpus motion was granted, the cases might be dismissed, since the original extradition orders were unwarranted. After the habeas corpus petition was denied by the Idaho Supreme Court, Darrow and the other defense lawyers appealed to a U.S. circuit court and then took the case before the U.S. Supreme Court. The justices rendered a decision on December 3, 1906. Writing for the majority, Justice John Marshall Harlan conceded that Haywood, Pettibone, and Moyer had been arrested and deported "by fraud and connivance," but that those acts did not trump the indictment or provide grounds for their release. Justice Harlan argued further that the justices presumed the arresting officers had no evil purpose and no other motive than to enforce the law.[23]

Upon hearing this, Darrow probably laughed: the prosecution was considered innocent unless proved otherwise!

The decision came as no surprise, and throughout the fall of 1906, Darrow had kept working as if he had already lost the appeal. While Harlan was parsing the words of his ruling, Darrow was endeavoring to weaken the prosecution's case by getting Steve Adams to recant. That was no easy task; Borah and McParland prevented Darrow from seeing Adams. Darrow thus had to do the next best thing: work through Adams's family. Adams's uncle James Lillard saw his nephew in prison regularly. Somehow Darrow convinced Lillard to work on the defense's behalf and get Adams to switch sides, which he did. Why he did is unknown. Darrow suggested that Adams had originally confessed only because he had no money for a lawyer and feared the hangman's noose.[24] Others have asserted Darrow paid off his family.[25] Whatever the truth, by robbing the court of Adams's testimony, Darrow effectively turned the tables on the prosecution.

The next step was to change the news coverage of the case. When Darrow arrived in Idaho, he was already losing in the court of public opinion. Several major newspapers and magazines—the *Idaho Statesman*, the *Emporia Gazette*, *The New York Times*, and *Collier's*—were dead set against Haywood, Pettibone, and Moyer.[26] The prosecution was leaking pieces of the case, particularly Orchard's confession, and those news articles were "lurid enough," Darrow wrote, "to satisfy the cravings of any reader" and of course any prospective juror. Working with the socialist presses, Darrow and the defense team were able to push back a little. For instance, *Wilshire's Magazine*, edited by the socialist Gaylord Wilshire (1861–1927), carried the lyrical words of Edmund Richardson, who described Haywood's, Pettibone's, and Moyer's rendition as something from the tales of "Dick Turpin or of Robin Hood."[27] Such efforts were halting and ineffective. Then fate handed Darrow the best of all opportunities.

In April 1907, shortly before the trial of Big Bill Haywood, who was going first, newspapers across the nation dropped a political bombshell, accusing President Theodore Roosevelt of extorting campaign contributions from corporate elites. Key to the story was an exchange of October 1906 letters between TR and railroad baron Edward H. Harriman (1848–1909). Normally such games of the rich and well connected had little to do with the events that shaped the lives of working Americans, but in this case TR's alleged misdoings directly impacted Darrow's clients. In one of his letters to Harriman, the president had condemned Haywood, Pettibone, and Moyer as "undesirable citizens." It is not exactly clear what had prompted Roosevelt to comment. Some have speculated he meant to influence the justices of the Supreme Court, who were set to decide on the legality of the unwarranted incarceration of the three men. In any event, it provided Darrow with an ideal platform from which to change public sentiment about his clients. Now every paper in the nation would listen as he railed that "the most powerful interests of the country" were conspiring to "take the lives" of his clients, who had been kidnapped from their homes and were being railroaded by the justice system. Darrow also used this opportunity to recast his clients from bickering murderers at the end of their rope to optimistic, reassuring friends who knew that justice and fairness would prevail. Pettibone was not a mad dynamiter but a kind, gentle soul always willing to lend a hand and cheer up his bunkmates. He was the "Happy Hooligan" and the "funmaker of the trio."[28] And Haywood was not the bruiser bent on anarchistic destruction but rather a family man whose only desire was to see his invalid wife and their beautiful daughters.

The president's letter did one more thing: as the controversy dragged on through the spring and early summer, it became something of a national conversation, and as such it gave Darrow the first question for his voir dire.[29] "Do you agree with the president?" became the litmus test for selecting the jury. On June 4, 1907—seventeen months after Steunenberg's murder—Judge Fremont Wood (1856–1940), who had prosecuted George Pettibone following the Bunker Hill bombing, brought his courtroom to order in front of a jury of mostly local farmers. The room was packed with journalists and onlookers. Bankers, mine owners, and local politicians were pressed shoulder to shoulder with miners, day laborers, and lumbermen. Mrs. Steunenberg was there in her black mourning dress. Darrow easily countered that courtroom ploy. Haywood's wheelchair-bound wife, Nevada Jane, was seated next to the defense table, as were his children, who were glued to Daddy's side. Tensions ran high. There had been death threats against Borah, Hawley, and Wood. Darrow, fearing for his life, purchased a handgun and carried it everywhere he went.[30]

Right from the start, Darrow locked horns with James Hawley, not even allowing the latter to finish the prosecution's opening statement without ob-jection. Darrow's complaint was that Hawley had droned on for twenty min-utes about the so-called facts of the case without revealing any evidence. Certainly Darrow was bored by Hawley's unemotional recitation and wanted him to get to the point, but his premeditated attack was part of a larger de-fense strategy. From the first day to the last, Darrow ridiculed, teased, and taunted Hawley in order to generate some hostility toward the prosecution and some sympathy for the defense. He also hoped to goad the lead counsel into making a rash mistake and to break Hawley's ego, thus stripping the prosecution of a capable lawyer. The plan worked to a degree, and Darrow did his job well, perhaps too well. Hawley's son, Jess, threatened Darrow to cut it out or else. Maybe it was a good idea he was packing a gun after all.

The centerpiece of the prosecution's case, Harry Orchard, was called to the stand on June 5. The man who sat in the witness chair did not look like the ruffian newspapermen had previously described. He was well coiffed and tailored, looking like a younger McParland. His appearance gave no indication of his diabolical career. "Far from being the furtive weasel of a man," Haywood wrote in his autobiography, "Orchard was well-set-up, fluff, with an apparently open manner."[31] Under heavy guard, Orchard sauntered down the aisle and was sworn in. Hawley began his questioning with the basics. After Orchard had stated his name and residence (which was the Boise penitentiary), the prosecutor asked if Harry Orchard was his real name. As a hush descended over the courtroom, the witness admitted that it was not. His real name? The seconds slowed as the man leaned forward and whispered, "Albert E. Horsley." It was satisfying and terrifying at the same time, as if the miller's daughter had finally learned the name of Rumpel-stiltskin. Hawley then led him through the key testimony, marshaled so as to send first Haywood and then his colleagues to the gallows.

That night Darrow and Richardson engaged in a heated argument about the cross-examination. Each thought that he was the smartest lawyer in the room. In the end Darrow conceded. Richardson's cross-examination of Or-chard was vigorous, confrontational, and long. It lasted several days. He succeeded in scoring some points and laying the foundation for the defense's case, but he failed to make Orchard crack. According to Darrow, the cross-examination lacked "subtlety." Richardson telegraphed his swings, missing the mark several times.[32] While Richardson was able to rattle his cage,

Orchard refused to bark. Haywood later credited McParland for coaching Orchard's unflappable performance. It was as good as those of the witnesses who had sent the Molly Maguires to their deaths.[33]

This then was the trouble. The prosecution's only credible evidence against Haywood and the other would-be conspirators was the testimony of a murderer. Borah and Hawley had produced no corroboration but instead had thrown in extraneous and irrelevant fluff, such as copies of the anarchist newspaper *Alarm*, which had been published by Albert Parsons, who had been executed in 1887 after the Haymarket Massacre, and copies of the *Miner's Magazine* to demonstrate the animus that the WFM had for Steunenberg. Titillating, yes; suggestive, perhaps; evidence, no. Regardless, Darrow and Richardson thought that the prosecution had scored major points, and they needed to mobilize the defense. They were going to have to take some risks. This time it was Darrow who was going to lead. Perhaps this had been the deal all along: Richardson could cross-examine Orchard if Darrow opened the defense, as he did on June 24.

In one morning, Darrow swung the defense's fortunes completely around. His opening of the defense's case was—in the words of *New York Times* reporter Oscar King Davis (1866–1932)—a "clever, striking performance, interesting from first to last, and a shrewd forceful presentation." He quickly built a rapport with the jurors, standing close to the box, speaking to them with a friendly jocularity, often with his right foot upon the iron rail on which the jurors in the front row put their feet. He made fun of Hawley, called Orchard a "monumental liar," reintroduced Bill Haywood, "the plain, blunt, courageous fighting man," and announced that the defendant would take the witness stand in his own defense.[34]

Haywood's testimony was rather anticlimactic. He admitted knowing Orchard, but vehemently denied ordering him to murder Steunenberg. In fact, none of the defense's witnesses—not Haywood, not Moyer, not Ed Boyce—made much of an impact. Darrow, however, had an ace up his sleeve. On June 30, he put Morris Friedman on the stand. Friedman was a former Pinkerton agent whose tell-all book *The Pinkerton Labor Spy*, which had been published by the socialist Wilshire Book Company in early 1907, revealed the depths of corporate depravity and the vast upper-class conspiracy against labor unions in the West. Friedman's testimony established an alternative theory for the crime. Darrow charged that his clients had done nothing. Rather, the corporate elite with its Pinkerton hellhounds had sacrificed one of its own for the greater good of eradicating the Western Federation of Miners. Darrow had Friedman essentially summarize the penultimate chapter of his book, which concerned the "monstrous spectacle" of the Moyer-Haywood-Pettibone case. Under Darrow's direct examination and in front of a rapt audience, Friedman repeated his charge that the prosecution had "prostituted itself most shamefully in behalf of gigantic moneyed interests to intimidate and crush a great labor organization, by accepting as gospel truth the awful charges of conspiracy and murder which the Pinkerton Agency has heaped mountain-high upon the Western Federation of Miners in general, and under which they hope, particularly, to bury and entomb Messrs. Moyer, Haywood and Pettibone."[35] The union leaders were not guilty, Friedman contended. Rather, the mine owners and railroad executive's own operatives were to blame. Darrow's witness fingered others, including railroad detective K. C. Sterling, as the agents provocateurs. After Friedman's damning testimony, Darrow had all the pieces in place for his closing argument.

By all accounts, Darrow's eleven-hour summation, which began on July 24 and went well into July 25, was his best to date and an instant classic of American rhetoric. Haywood labeled it "one of Clarence Darrow's greatest."[36] Begging the jurors' indulgence and patience, Darrow self-effacingly acknowledged that he was a stranger in a strange land. He was an alien, perhaps an unwelcome one. All he asked was for an "honest" hearing and for Haywood a fair trial. "If he is guilty," Darrow told the jury, "then for God's sake, gentlemen, hang him by the neck until dead."[37] But, he implored them, do not rely on either Orchard's testimony or Hawley's line of reasoning. Both were "crazy." Moreover, continuing the months-long attack on the opposing counsel, Darrow asserted that Hawley probably thought the jurors "daffy" to buy the arguments that he was selling.[38] Pointing to Orchard, Darrow accused Hawley of having been seduced by the lies of "this monster." Also, there was no evidence beyond the dubious yarn spun by the accuser. "Was there anything in [this trial] but Orchard—Orchard—Orchard?" Hawley "has Orcharditis."[39]

While the prosecution fumed, Darrow laid out his case. It was true: Orchard was a mass murderer. But who had paid his bills? It was not the leaders of the Western Federation of Miners. Darrow reminded the jurors that testimony implicated a railroad detective, K. C. Sterling, a known associate of Orchard's. And Sterling was seemingly connected to various other crimes. Why was Orchard such a willing instrument of destruction? Darrow maintained that it all related to that Hercules Mine. Orchard believed both the Western Federation of Miners and Governor Steunenberg had conspired to rob him of his stake in the mine and his fortune. He should have been rich like Ed Boyce but had ended up poor. By killing the former governor and by fingering the WFM, Orchard had his cold revenge on both with just one bomb.

Foot on that iron railing and finger in the air, Darrow stated that Orchard "is unique in history. . . . If he is not the biggest murderer who ever lived, he is the biggest liar." Leveling his eyes with the jurors', Darrow admitted that he was "not a professed Christian." And yet he was indignant at "those sickly slobbering idiots who talk about Harry Orchard's religion."[40] The prosecution sought to sell Orchard's conversion, midwifed by "Father McParland," to give some semblance of credibility. Darrow begged the jurors to see through the ploy. The case was not about Orchard or his lies. It was not even about Haywood. It was about destroying a union. "Mr. Haywood is not my greatest concern," Darrow whispered to the jurors. "Other men have died before him. Other men have been martyrs to a holy cause since the world began. Wherever men have looked upward and onward, forgotten their selfishness, struggled for humanity, worked for the poor and the weak, they have been sacrificed." His voice rising, he exhorted: "But gentlemen, you short-sighted men of the prosecution, you men of the Mine Owners' Association, you people who would cure hatred with hate, you who think you can crush out the feelings and the hopes and the aspirations of men by tying a noose around his neck, you who are seeking to kill him, not because it is Haywood, but because he represents a class, don't be so blind, don't be so foolish as to believe you can strangle the Western Federation of Miners when you tie a rope around his neck. Don't be so blind in your madness as to believe that when you make three fresh new graves you will kill the labor movement of the world!"[41] Finally, handkerchief in hand, he blotted the sweat from his brow and the tears in his eyes and concluded: "My mind is not unbiased in this great struggle. I am a partisan, and a strong partisan at that. For nearly thirty years I have been working to the best of my ability in the cause in which these men have given their toil and risked their lives . . . I have given my time, my reputation, my chances—all this in the cause of the poor . . . You are jurors in a historical case. You are here with your verdict to make history here that shall affect the nation for weal or woe, here to make history that will affect every man that toils, that will influence the liberties of mankind and bring weal or woe to the poor and the weak, who have been striving through the centuries for some measure of that freedom which the world has ever denied to them." Fixing the jurors with his own eyes, Darrow brought his summation to a close. "The eyes of the world are upon you—upon you twelve men of Idaho tonight."[42]

The next day Borah delivered the closing statement for the prosecution. He failed to match Darrow. Like his opponent, he began in a self-effacing manner. Borah even conceded to the jury that the defense counsel was "very able and very eloquent."[43] He also apologized for Hawley, who was "more irritable at times than he should have been with Mr. Darrow."[44] Then, for eight hours, he revisited the charges and the evidence. He claimed that the trial was not "a fight on organized labor—it is simply a trial for murder."[45] Idaho's police had captured the culprit. But they also had exposed a wider conspiracy involving Haywood, Pettibone, and Moyer. They were as guilty for this "cold-blooded, deliberate murder, the malicious and premeditated killing of one who stood unchallenged in his actions before the world."[46] Orchard was not mad, but a mere hired gun! And Borah implored the jury to believe him because Orchard had turned to God in his "night of despair."[47] But then Borah completely undercut his case, claiming that "the strongest kind of corroborative evidence" was the "silence of Mr. Pettibone." Pettibone, the alleged master incendiary, had refused to testify during the Haywood trial. Borah disingenuously claimed that the lack of supportive testimony was in itself damning testimony.[48] He begged the jurors to find Haywood guilty of murder not because he was a member of a criminal organization—the Western Federation of Miners—but to keep assassins from the homestead gate. "I only want what you want," he said, "human life made safe—assassination put out of business. I only want what you want— the gate which leads to our homes, the yard gate whose inward swing tells of the returning husband and father, shielded and guarded by the courage and manhood of Idaho juries."[49]

After receiving their instructions, the jurors went into their room. It was already evening. Haywood went back to jail, and the defense team headed for Edgar Wilson's law office to wait it out. Richardson did not follow, announcing he would rather go to bed. Just as well. Darrow had grown to despise the "ass" anyway.[50] After a few hours Darrow left to walk the streets. Shortly after daybreak, the defense team heard that the jury was in. A disheveled, red-eyed, ashen-skinned Darrow sat close to Haywood. Not guilty! There were tears of joy, hugs, and handshakes. As soon as they had rested and packed, Clarence and Ruby boarded a train for Chicago.

Darrow returned home to a hero's welcome. For the second time in five years, he had fought the moneyed interests and emerged victorious. But the warm sunshine of adulation did not last. He was not in Chicago long before he began hearing whispers that something sinister had happened during the Boise trial. Rumors surfaced that the jurors had not been won over by Darrow's golden oratory but by gold itself.[51] Others mused that Darrow had saved the lives of guilty men. Darrow got little sympathy from his partners. Edgar Lee Masters resented his senior colleague's superstardom and accused him of pocketing the nine thousand dollars due him for his work on the Haywood case. Darrow denied that he had lined his pockets with Masters's money; his reputation in Chicago had been built upon the fact that he did *not* have sticky fingers. Masters did not believe him and carried that festering grudge with him for decades.[52]

More disturbing than Masters's indignation and the rumors of professional impropriety was the fact that Darrow was not bouncing back from his trip west. At first, he and Ruby attributed it to exhaustion from the Haywood case. But within weeks they realized that something more serious was wrong. His general malaise and headaches gave way to horrific pains behind his left ear. Despite the discomfort, Darrow maintained his commitment to the miners in Idaho and returned later in 1907. State prosecutors had decided to go after Steve Adams once again in the hope of facilitating some sort of plea deal in return for testimony against Pettibone and Moyer. With the help of a local doctor, Charles Hudgel, who quickly became a family friend, and Ruby, Darrow was patched up enough to carry on. His defense of Adams succeeded, and all charges against Pettibone and Moyer were dropped.

The cost to Darrow's health was substantial. On several days the blanched, slack-jawed Darrow could barely stand in the courtroom. Once Adams's trial was over, Darrow was taken to Boise's St. Alphonsus Hospital, and from there he was sent to Los Angeles for emergency surgery to cure his mastoiditis, an infection of the bone behind the ear. A Chicago newspaper reported that Darrow was in fact dying and sent a telegram to L.A. reporters asking them to gather his "famous last words."[53] Darrow lived. As he put it later, he was granted a "continuance."[54]

Drugs made the recuperation in the hospital pain-free, if not forgettable. Ruby was at his side constantly, taking care of all the details, even managing his Chicago affairs from L.A. By early January 1908, Darrow was feeling well enough to begin catching up himself, asking for mail and for newspapers. It was then that Ruby, with Darrow's doctors behind her, told him the news: although the stock market had improved after the 1907 panic, Darrow's particular holdings, including those in the Black Mountain gold mine in Mexico, were gone. Ruby had waited too long to sell. Darrow's momentary incredulity faded to red-hot anger. He leaped from the bed, threw up his hands, and, turning his bloodshot steel blue eyes on Ruby, bellowed: "Do you realize what you've done to me? You've thrown away my life savings, my dream of retiring. Now I'll have to begin all over again—be a slave to that irksome law work—we'll never be able to travel the world, write all those books!" His voice then dropped. "I'll never forgive you for this—never, never!"[55]

The train ride back to Chicago was excruciatingly uneventful. Ruby and Clarence spent little time together. She could not bear to see him like this, and he wanted no part of her company. In time he did forgive her, but their marriage was not the same. Darrow's financial ruin, which was neither his first nor his last, had put a hole in the pit of his chest, and it ached. He knew it was not Ruby's fault. In fact, he had made bad investments before. In 1906, when the Bank of America failed, Darrow lost much of his eleven-thousand-dollar stock investment, as did his son, Paul, and law partner Edgar Lee Masters.[56] Back then Darrow had kept his cool and even announced publicly that he would pay in full all small depositors who brought their saving books to his law office.[57] What's more, he knew that the markets were volatile and highly dependent on unforgiving and nearly fickle variables, such as consumer spending. How could anyone invest with confidence in the United States, let alone in Mexico? Maybe this was the source of his rage. Losing his fortune to the false promises of brokers showed that he was gullible. Given the size of his ego, he found it easier to be angry at Ruby.

As his marriage hit a rough patch, Darrow sought out a new companion.

He and the settlement house worker and budding journalist Mary Field (1878–1969) had first met in 1908 at a rally for Christian Rudovitz, a revolutionary émigré, who was fighting extradition back to Russia, where he would certainly have met an untimely end in front of a firing squad. Darrow, who was handling his legal work, had given a rousing oration, exciting the crowd to demand that Rudovitz stay in the United States. Darrow was sincere about speaking out on Rudovitz's behalf, but he had resumed public speaking also as a way to make money, which he now desperately needed. Increasingly, he would lecture and debate only when he was paid. As Darrow reminded Victor Berger (1860–1929), leader of the sewer socialists in Milwaukee, who had invited him to the city to give a talk, "if there are not enough people to pay twenty-five or fifty cents a head to look at me and hear me talk, they aren't yet ready for Socialism."[58]

After the rally, Field, whom Darrow called Molly, became smitten with this charismatic man twenty-one years her senior. His middle-age spread well hidden underneath his frumpy suits, Darrow's tall frame still struck a commanding pose. His eyes remained that piercing blue, and his penetrating gaze and engaging smile made up for his unruly hair, increasingly deeply furrowed brow, and stooped gait.

For his part, Darrow was captivated by Field. In some ways, she resembled Ruby, though a younger version. Dark hair, slim figure, cute, and smart, she reminded him of an earlier time when engaging women sought him out regularly. Molly's other attraction was that she was not Ruby. Darrow complained of Ruby's churlish nature; one memorable night at Molly's apartment he raged at length about "the little piss ant wife whose pettiness and jealousies have galled him for years."[59] By contrast, Field worshiped Darrow, even after she was married to Lemuel Parton (d. 1943). She never tired of Darrow's stories, jokes, and pontifications. For his part, Darrow was flattered by the coquettish attention and came to crave the intimacy that Molly offered. Field and Darrow were lovers, but quickly the relationship deepened beyond sexual attraction. Darrow saw his Molly as a protégée, and indeed, she looked to him to establish herself as a labor journalist. Part of her attraction to Darrow was his relationships with radicals, reformers, writers, and publishers. These connections paid great dividends. He introduced her to all sorts of people, from Mother Jones to Frank P. Walsh (1864–1939) to Joel Spingarn (1875–1939) to Theodore Dreiser. Field wound up editing Mother Jones's diminutive autobiography, with Darrow writing the introduction.[60]

Ruby knew about Molly. Darrow's other infidelities were one thing; his attraction to Molly was something else, something that despite her youthful dabbling in free love, she could not tolerate. Ruby thought Molly an impetuous, self-centered sycophant. Molly thought Ruby insane, mean, and uncouth. No one could have expected that the two women could get along. Although there is no evidence of a confrontation, at some point Clarence and Ruby must have discussed a divorce. They decided to stay together. Perhaps at fifty-one Darrow understood that he needed someone to take care of him and help manage his public career more than he did a fling with a devotee. Darrow sent Molly away, arranging for her to move to New York City and work with Dreiser on his magazine *The Delineator*. He missed her terribly, and there were frequent letters and infrequent trips to Greenwich Village.[61] There was little time for romance, however. Darrow had a fortune to rebuild.

Darrow knew how to get rich. Staying wealthy was the problem. To make money as a lawyer, one needs to defend clients with money. Some of his colleagues whispered that Darrow had become a hypocrite, but what other options did he have? He had more or less promised Ruby that he would concentrate on moneymakers and retire from lawyering for those poor unionists who often failed to pay their bills. So in the spring of 1911, he agreed to defend the board of directors of the Kankakee Manufacturing Company, which printed glossy advertising brochures luring the unsuspecting and gullible with the promise of huge profits in exchange for a modest investment. When the stock market crashed in 1907 and all sorts of investors, including Darrow himself, lost their shirts, Charles Myerhoff, a Civil War veteran, sued, claiming that he had been duped by the company's roseate forecasts. The company board hired Darrow, who put aside his great disdain for corporations as well as his sympathy for the average American to argue in court that it was the investor's responsibility to investigate the validity of investment claims. Myerhoff's purchase of Kankakee's stock represented his belief that the company's publicity was believable. Darrow's caveat emptor defense did not impress the judge, who ruled for the claimant. Darrow was paid in any event, and as he was finishing up the paperwork, the call came to defend another group of union men. They stood accused of committing the crime of the century.

Moments after 1:00 a.m. on October 1, 1910, a loud explosion broke the somnolent calm of a balmy evening in Los Angeles, California. Within five minutes a fireball had engulfed the six-story building that housed the rabidly antiunion *Los Angeles Times*. Of the 115 men working that night, 21 were consumed by the fire, crushed by the falling rubble, or suffocated by the smoke. By morning most of the fire was out; the $500,000 ($11 million in today's dollars) building was a total loss. Fire inspectors concluded that the cause was an explosion that had occurred in an alleyway at the building's center where canisters of ink were stored. As the *Los Angeles Times*, whose operations moved to an adjunct facility, began printing the lists of missing and dead, headlines revealed to a scared city that two additional unexploded bombs had been discovered, targeting the homes of the owner of the newspaper, Harrison Gray Otis (1837–1917), and Felix J. Zeehandelaar (1852–1924), secretary of the business-oriented Merchants and Manufacturers' Association. Suspicions that disgruntled unionists were behind this only sharpened.

Managing editor Harry E. Andrews the next day issued a statement declaring that the "Times building had been destroyed by dynamite by the enemies of industrial freedom." In a concurrence, Otis's assistant Harry Chandler (1864–1944) announced that "there is no doubt that this outrage can be laid at the door of labor unions."[62] Labor leaders rejected the notion. In an article that appeared in the socialist monthly *Appeal to Reason*, Eugene Debs placed the blame on Otis and his "crowd of union-haters."[63] The AFL's chief Samuel Gompers issued a blanket denial of any involvement by anyone in the labor movement. "I regret the loss of life and destruction of property," Gompers stated, "but I see no reason for thinking that union members had anything to do with it."[64] The next day at an AFL Executive Council meeting in St. Louis, Gompers reiterated his stance, with a caveat: "I will never believe any of the boys placed or exploded that dynamite until it is proven beyond doubt and if they did they should suffer for it."[65] Gompers was either out of touch or naive or trying to cover his colleagues' tracks. For it eventually became public knowledge that Otis and his lieutenants were right: it had been a union job. Los Angeles was a crucial front in the capitalist war on the labor movement, and the fighting had been quite intense especially since 1905. The bombing was yet another tragic act of violence in a two-decade struggle.

When the *Times* building exploded, Los Angeles was in the midst of a citywide strike of construction trade unions. Led by Local 51 of the International Association of Bridge, Structural, and Iron Workers (IABSIW), the city's labor movement was gaining ground.[66] Several large building contractors had adopted union contracts, perhaps out of fear of violence or perhaps out of a realization that wages and hours did indeed need to reflect the standards established in cities like San Francisco. Because of their recent successes, the L.A. Strike Committee doubted any unionist would have done the nefarious job and declared unequivocally that no "union man had anything to do with any violence against the Times employees or property."[67] They were wrong, and Otis, his colleagues, and Mayor George Alexander (1839–1923) knew it. After the bombing, they hired William J. Burns (1861–1932), who had long surpassed James McParland as the most famous detective in America. The forty-nine-year-old headed his eponymous national detective agency and had already racked up an impressive array of accomplishments. He had defeated a nasty network of land swindlers in Oregon and nearly single-handedly cleaned up the city of San Francisco of mobsters and their politicians. In September 1910, when his agency was only half a year old, executives at the McClintic-Marshall Construction Company had hired him to investigate over a dozen bombings of their structures, all made with nonunion labor and nonunion steel. He was already hot on the trail of the IABSIW's dynamiters when city leaders tapped him to find the perpetrators who had blown up the *Times*. Regardless of the money, Burns jumped at the chance. In his mind only he could stop the "hidden forces" fomenting hate and class war.[68]

Burns's initial investigation uncovered the fact that the unexploded bombs discovered at the Otis and Zeehandelaar residences were similar in design to those he had found while working for McClintic-Marshall. All signs pointed to the IABSIW. But corroboration was needed. After months of careful police work, Burns was closing in. His major break came when officials at the National Erectors' Association (NEA) turned over for interrogation Herbert S. Hocking, the NEA's mole within the ironworkers' union. The NEA's leaders, who were in the midst of a strike with the IABSIW that was already five years old, were more than happy to aid Burns. Hocking, the union's secretary-treasurer, spilled the beans; his union was responsible for the destruction of the *Times* and for several dozen other bombings.

Burns quickly tracked down the ringleaders: Ortie McManigal, James B. McNamara (1882–1941), and John J. McNamara (1876–1941). McManigal and J. B. McNamara were arrested on April 12, 1911, in Detroit. Ten days later Burns nabbed J. J. McNamara in the IABSIW headquarters in Indianapolis, seizing a large cache of documents and bomb-making materials. All three were quickly extradited to Los Angeles.

As soon as he heard of the arrests, Sam Gompers telegrammed the one lawyer he thought could free his union brothers, Clarence Darrow. "There is no other advocate in the whole United States who holds such a commanding post before the people and in whom labor has such entire confidence," he wired.[69] Darrow, in the midst of his defense of the Kankakee Manufacturing Company, did not answer Gompers, who then telephoned him long-distance. Darrow explained that he had retired from these kinds of cases, at least until he regained his constitution and rebuilt his bank account. Plus, he figured that the men were guilty. He had had guilty clients before and knew that defending them was always more difficult than defending the innocent. Living in Chicago, Darrow knew all about union violence, witnessing firsthand the work of sluggers, vandals, and dynamiters.[70] Worse, he knew that union violence had grown in intensity since the turn of the century. No city, no matter how large or small, was immune. Even his old hometown of Ashtabula, Ohio (which Darrow derisively referred to as Asstabula), was the scene of a riot of unionists and their supporters against the nonunion workers building a bridge for the Pennsylvania Railroad.[71] To Darrow, the *Times* bombing was just another skirmish in America's class war.

Never taking no for an answer, Gompers traveled to Kankakee to see the people's defender himself and followed him back to Chicago.[72] Inside Darrow's home library, Gompers minced no words. The AFL needed Darrow, and if he refused, he would "go down in history as a traitor to the great cause of labor."[73] What could he do? He was damned if he rebuffed Gompers. He of course was damned if he agreed and lost. At least if he took the case, he would get paid. Further, though he suspected his clients were guilty, there was a chance that he might win. He had seen this once before: unionists accused of using dynamite in their battle with the capitalists and their lackeys; the use of private detectives to apprehend the suspects, who were illegally kidnapped to the venue of the trial; and a turncoat star witness (in this instance Ortie McManigal) who agreed to testify against the others in exchange for leniency.[74] He had saved the condemned in Boise, and Los Angeles promised better weather.

Darrow finally agreed. Before Gompers stopped smiling, he told him his fee: fifty thousand dollars after expenses plus a defense fund of at least two hundred thousand, which Gompers raised through donations, by selling buttons and stamps, and through the proceeds from the distribution of a pretrial film about the McNamaras, *A Martyr to His Cause*.[75] Telling Masters of his plans went as expected. The dour partner harrumphed and went back to his poetry. Ruby was disappointed but understood and began making plans to mothball their lives in Chicago yet again. Darrow, energized by the challenge, also felt a strange feeling of foreboding. Writing to his friend and former protégé Brand Whitlock, he said: "I feel like one going away on a long and dangerous voyage."[76] Little did he know that he would be marooned in L.A. for nearly two years and return home penniless and nearly friendless. Darrow overestimated his abilities and underestimated Burns and the prosecution. This was not the roughshod justice of Idaho. In Los Angeles, the district attorney had an airtight case.

Darrow's approach was the same as it had been in Boise. The first order of business was to gain control of the story and reshape the public's view of his clients. From the bombing and through the arrests, the prosecution, backed by General Otis's antilabor news machine, had dominated the headlines. On May 1, 1911, Samuel Gompers led the nation in what he called McNamara Day. Marches were held in most major cities. In Los Angeles alone, twenty thousand workers paraded to show their support.[77] That the conservative Gompers celebrated International Labor Day, which commemorated the Haymarket Massacre, was impressive enough, but his willingness to stand shoulder to shoulder with radicals was jaw-dropping. Speaking from Indianapolis, the home of the IABSIW, he declared "the whole thing a deep-seated frame-up" and pledged to get to the bottom of the kidnappings of the McNamara brothers. About McManigal, Gompers was coy, refusing to speak out against the one man who could send his union brothers to the gallows. "I cannot turn my back upon anyone unless I have more evidence that that man has turned his back upon us." In other words, Gompers held out hope, as Darrow did, that McManigal would act more like Steve Adams and less like Harry Orchard. In a rare moment of solidarity, the Socialist Labor Party, led by Daniel De Leon (1852–1914), and the Socialist Party of

America, led by Eugene Debs, joined the AFL in issuing statements in support of the McNamara brothers. Big Bill Haywood took a further step and called for a national strike, which no one heeded.[78] Labor leaders across the political spectrum maintained this united front throughout 1911.[79]

Slowly, citizens in Los Angeles, who constituted the potential jury pool, began to read a different narrative. Even former President Theodore Roosevelt seemed to change his tune. The man who had prematurely condemned Haywood, Moyer, and Pettibone as well as their supporters as "undesirable citizens" begged for caution and called on citizens to avoid any rush to judgment. In an article titled "Murder Is Murder" for the popular *Outlook* magazine, TR maintained that the accused deserved "an absolutely fair trial" and that both the honest, law-abiding laboring man and his business counterpart had the identical view when it came to "morality and good citizenship."[80] After all, perhaps the men were not guilty. Maybe Eugene Debs was right and "union-haters blew up the *Times* as part of their anti-union activity."[81] After May Day, Debs, Gompers, and Darrow continued to push their message into the nation's newspapers. Darrow picked apart the prosecution's case, highlighting its illegal methods and suggesting less sinister explanations for the explosion, such as a gas leak. Deb maintained his conspiracy theory, and Gompers went after Billy Burns in a very public fight, accusing the great detective of manufacturing evidence and acting without scruples.

On May 22, 1911, the Darrows arrived in California. They were warmly greeted in San Francisco by the crusading journalist and newspaper editor Fremont Older (1856–1935), who was a kindred spirit. The next day Older handed Clarence over to the boisterous, barrel-chested Anton Johannsen of the Building Trades union. Together they went to see the McNamaras and then to visit with Job Harriman (1861–1925), the city's leading socialist politician who had set up an office for the defense team. Darrow was happy to have Harriman on board, not so much for his legal skills, which were negligible, as for his political connections. For his part, Harriman, who was running for mayor on the Socialist ticket, calculated that if things went well, freeing the McNamara brothers would propel him into office. Darrow also tapped the well-connected corporate lawyer Joseph Scott (1867–1958), the former pro-labor Indiana judge Cyrus McNutt (1837–1912), and the topnotch criminal lawyer (and good friend of the district attorney John D. Fredericks

[1865–1945]) LeCompte Davis (1864–1957). Finally, he hired two detectives: John Harrington, a Chicago private eye he had brought with him, and Bert Franklin, a local investigator.

Darrow trusted his team with everything. Actually Darrow's blind faith in others was one of his fatal flaws. It had gotten him in trouble before. As his former law partner Cyrus S. Simon said in a cruder way: Darrow was "the world's worst sucker."[82] His selection of Harrington and Franklin almost became his undoing.[83]

Darrow approached the McNamara case as he had the Haywood-Moyer-Pettibone case. He tried to get to the government's star witness to switch sides. In this instance, he needed McManigal to turn coat. He arranged to have his wife, Emma, travel from Chicago to L.A. for a jail cell visit. It is not known if Darrow offered her any compensation or any promise of aid, but it probably mattered little. Emma wanted her husband and the father of their two children back home. "I only have fifteen minutes to stay with you," she said with tears streaming down her cheeks. "I want you to sign a note from Clarence Darrow," she pleaded, and "place yourself in the hands of the union's attorneys."[84] Ortie slumped further and agreed, but the deal did not stick. The lead government prosecutor, the wiry, tall, and well-connected John D. Fredericks, was far craftier than William Borah had been. He dragged Mrs. McManigal before a grand jury to find out what she knew about the McNamaras. That pressure kept McManigal aligned with the state. In vain, Darrow then employed McManigal's favorite uncle, George Behm, to pressure the accused bomber, but to no avail.

Darrow was despondent. He knew that the prosecution had a far stronger case than in the Steunenberg murder trial. Fredericks had more than enough corroborating evidence. So another defense strategy was hatched. It had two parts. First, he had to convince the jury that an alterative explanation for the explosion was just as likely as the prosecution's explanation. To do this, Darrow hired James H. Levering, a civil engineer, to build a model of the *Times* building to demonstrate that the explosion could have been caused by a gas leak. Second, the defense team, including Darrow's brother-in-law Bert Hammerstrom, began to pressure witnesses not to testify and prospective jurors to be sympathetic to the defendants. Indeed, a few prosecution witnesses went missing. Both Kurt Diekelman, a Los Angeles hotel clerk who identified J.B., and John Lofthouse, a friend of J.B.'s from San

Francisco, disappeared. Burns's detectives found Diekelman in Chicago and brought him back to L.A., but Lofthouse's whereabouts remained a mystery.[85] Once the final list of jurors for the voir dire was released, Darrow's key lieutenant, Bert Franklin, approached an old acquaintance, Robert Bain, and offered a deal: four thousand dollars (eighty-six thousand in today's dollars) for a vote for acquittal. It sickened Bain, a Civil War veteran, to agree, but he needed the money. Soon afterward Franklin met the other person on the list whom he thought he could trust, drinking buddy George Lockwood, and made the same offer. Lockwood seemed as hooked as Bain.

Did Darrow know about Franklin's attempted bribery? It seems hard to believe that he didn't, though he evidently never directly or explicitly ordered the deeds. Plausible deniability was maintained. If we assume Darrow orchestrated these dirty tricks, was this an aberration? Geoffrey Cowan's history of the case is convincing: Darrow's conduct during the trial was not above reproach, and many of his closest friends predicted that he would indeed have approved the bribes. Certainly such rumors had swirled around Darrow before, especially in the Steve Adams case. Additionally, Darrow never quite explained how he had obtained the General Managers' Association minute books in the Debs case. According to the preeminent jurist Alan M. Dershowitz (b. 1938), this means only one thing: Darrow "does not deserve the mantle of honor he has proudly borne over most of [the twentieth century]."[86]

Darrow would have shrugged off the rebuke and chided Dershowitz for not getting it. First, the courtroom was not a level playing field. The state's representatives—investigators, jailers, bailiffs, attorneys, and judges—colluded to get arrests, indictments, and convictions. They used the tools of the state's legal system, including harassment, grand juries, and plea agreements, to secure their victories. Sometimes, and more often than Americans realize, the accused were beaten into confessions. Softer methods were used, but wasn't a plea agreement a kind of legalized bribe? Or at least a quid pro quo? To let the opponent, in this case the state prosecutor, dictate the conditions on the battlefield was to surrender before the fight. Moreover, in this winner-take-all death match between capital and labor, what was fair? What was necessary? Further, and perhaps more important, Darrow's legal career was not an end unto itself. He did not seek the approbation of his

ABOVE: In the 1890s, Clarence Darrow was on the verge of becoming the official lawyer for the labor movement. (Darrow Family Scrapbooks, Newberry Library); BELOW: In 1902, Darrow ran for Illinois State Assembly on the Public Ownership League ticket. He won but did not develop a taste for electoral politics. It was the last time he ran for public office. Darrow preferred to influence politics in other ways, such as winning cases in court, helping elect his favored candidates, publishing his fiction and nonfiction, and lecturing. (Courtesy of the Library of Congress)

Pledged to the Following :
The Initative and Referendum.
Public Ownership of Public Utilities.
Nomination by Direct Vote of the People.
Home Rule for Municipalities.

VOTE FOR

☒ CLARENCE S. DARROW

THREE VOTES

PUBLIC OWNERSHIP

CANDIDATE FOR

Representative, 17th Senatorial District.

Comprising of Precincts 1, 2, 3, 4, 5, 6 and 7 of
WARD 9, and Precincts 1, 2, 3, 4, 5, 6, 7, 8, 9 and 10
of WARD 10, and all of WARD 19.

OVER

THINGS ARE COMING HARRISON'S WAY

Democrats Who Formerly Supported Him Are Throwing a Few Missiles Into His Back Yard

LEFT: This political cartoon, circa 1902, shows Darrow (in the back with a brick in his hand) and a few other Chicago politicos attacking Mayor Carter Harrison II. By the turn of the twentieth century, Darrow was heavily involved in city, state, and national politics, representing the interests of working people. (Darrow Family Scrapbooks, Newberry Library); BELOW: In front of the Arbitration Commission, Darrow was brilliant, besting his opponent, George Baer, with more emotion and keener arguments. (Courtesy of the Library of Congress)

PHILADELPHIA, SATURDAY, FEBRUARY 14, 1903

CHARACTERISTIC ATTITUDES OF MR. DARROW WHILE MAKING HIS FINAL PLEA FOR THE MINERS' CAUSE

ABOVE: Darrow (seated, wearing a bow tie and with a hand on his chin) defends William Haywood (sitting to his left), who is accused of murdering former governor Frank Steunenberg. Harry Orchard is testifying in the 1907 murder trial. Darrow is now the undisputed lawyer for the labor movement. (Idaho State Historical Society); BELOW: In 1911, Darrow participated in his last big labor case. Here he sits with J. B. McNamara (on his right), on trial for bombing the Los Angeles Times Building. (Cleveland Public Library Photograph Collection)

FACING PAGE: On trial for allegedly bribing jurors in 1912, Darrow defends himself, appealing to the jurors as a man ensnared in a trap sprung by the prosecution and their capitalist supporters who wanted to end the political career, not to mention the legal career, of the labor movement's lawyer. (Los Angeles Public Library); RIGHT: In 1917, Clarence Darrow was no longer labor's lawyer. After his trials in Los Angeles, he reinvented himself. During the Great War, he was a superpatriot supporting President Woodrow Wilson and the Allies. After the war, he became one of the greatest civil liberties and civil rights lawyers. (Wisconsin Historical Society); BELOW: By the 1920s, Darrow had winnowed his causes considerably, taking cases that centered on the core elements of his political philosophy about individual rights, freedom, and liberty. Starting in the 1880s, Darrow actively opposed the death penalty. He defended Richard Loeb (sitting to Darrow's immediate right) and Nathan Leopold (sitting to Loeb's right) because he believed that the state did not have sanction to kill. (*Chicago Daily News*, Chicago History Museum)

ABOVE: On July 20, 1925, Darrow (standing) and William Jennings Bryan (sitting) squared off in front of the Dayton, Tennessee, courthouse. By defending John Scopes, Darrow fought against the state law prohibiting the teaching of evolution. He wanted individuals to always have the liberty to decide for themselves what was the truth and what was bunk. (Smithsonian Institution Archives); BELOW: In 1926, Darrow defended Ossian and Gladys Sweet, who were accused of murder while defending their home from an angry white mob. Darrow, far right, stands with (from left to right) Henry Sweet, Julian Perry, and Thomas Chawke. Darrow had always been a stalwart friend of African Americans. He became more active in the defense and promotion of civil rights after his turn away from the labor movement. (Walter P. Reuther Library, Wayne State University)

TOP LEFT: In need of money in the midst of the Great Depression, Darrow agreed to defend Grace Fortescue, Thomas Massie, Edward J. Lord, and Albert "Deacon" Jones for the 1932 murder of Joseph Kahahawai. Along with his co-counsel, George S. Leisure (standing to Darrow's left), Darrow sought without much success to shuck the racial issues in the case. Although he was able to arrange for his clients to go free, the case damaged his reputation. (Elmer Gertz Papers, Northwestern University Special Collections); TOP RIGHT: A lifelong Democrat, Darrow backed Franklin D. Roosevelt's 1932 campaign, though he thought that the party had stronger candidates. Darrow remained politically active well into his seventies. (Elmer Gertz Papers, Northwestern University Special Collections); ABOVE: In 1934, President Roosevelt tapped Darrow to head a review board for the National Recovery Administration. Pictured here with Fred P. Mann (front left), Samuel C. Henry (front right), William O. Thompson (rear left), W. W. Neal (rear center), and John F. Sinclair (rear right), Darrow saw the board's work as a defense of the little guy against the monopolists and their allies in the New Deal. (Elmer Gertz Papers, Northwestern University Special Collections)

ABOVE: In 1934, after completing his work for the NRA review board, Darrow agreed to a request from Arthur Garfield Hays (center) to head the American Inquiry Commission's public investigation of the conditions in Nazi Germany. Darrow was aghast at the wholesale destruction of civil liberties and the persecution of Jews and others under Hitler's regime. (Elmer Gertz Papers, Northwestern University Special Collections); BELOW: For most of his adult life, Darrow was an avowed pessimist and often harbored dark moods. Certainly one can see this aspect of Darrow's character in his seventy-ninth birthday portrait. Yet he hoped that his battles to expand freedom, liberty, and equality would make a difference in the lives of average Americans. (University of Chicago Library, Special Collections Research Center)

legal peers. He was a lawyer so that he could fight for the poor, the weak, and the oppressed. He engaged courtrooms not to advance the law or uphold constitutional doctrines; he did so to advance justice, freedom, liberty, and democracy. Darrow was always an iconoclast and a politico first and a lawyer second. That other lawyers held him in low regard, as they both did then and do now, made little difference. He had work to do, and indeed, sometimes his hands got dirty.

Darrow believed that in the cause of fairness, freedom, and liberty the ends justify the means. In other words, his actions were not out of character or counter to his general philosophical outlook. Despite his reputation, in certain circumstances he believed that in the service of the public good, ethical codes sometimes had to be bent or broken. He had learned this from his mentor, John Altgeld. As Darrow told Agnes Wright Dennis, an oral historian with the Illinois Historical Survey, in 1918, Altgeld "was perfectly unscrupulous in getting ends, but absolutely honest in those ends."[87] Darrow may also have been talking about himself.

His first day of battling for the McNamaras in court came on October 11, 1911. It was the first time that Angelenos were able to get a good look at the accused. Under the protection of heavily armed guards, they entered Department Nine of the Superior Court, Judge Walter Bordwell (1835–1929) presiding. The courtroom was filled with spectators and journalists, about sixty of the latter reporting for national and international newspapers. Mary Field was there, reporting for *The American Magazine*, though Darrow had asked her not to come; there was no need to start another battle on the home front. She had ignored him. Who could turn down such an assignment? Not only was the story compelling, but where else could one rub elbows and match wits with journalists like Earl Harding (1879?–1965) of the *New York World* and the muckraking journalist Lincoln Steffens, who represented the *New York Globe* and half a dozen other newspapers. Many noted the stark contrast between the two defendants. John J. was as billed: handsome and charismatic with a manly, winning exuberance. James B. was at best an imperfect rendering of his attractive brother, with a "curiously shaped" head, big ears, a large nose, and beady eyes. He exuded not confidence but diffidence, almost self-loathing. After their shuffle into the courtroom, they sat near their lawyers. Darrow was in a smart, recently pressed gray suit. But it was early in the day, and he had barely begun to work.[88]

After the typical introductions and prefaces, Judge Bordwell got down to the first order of business, selecting a jury. Asking each prospective juror what he thought of labor unions, Darrow weeded prejudiced citizens out of the jury box. On October 17, two made it through. John W. Roberts, a real estate agent, was asked if he had any feelings against unions and claimed he did not. Darrow asked if he would have any trouble trying the brothers. Roberts answered that their guilt would have to be proved beyond a reasonable doubt. Robert F. Bain also appeared in court that day. Darrow put only one question to him: "Unless you were satisfied in your own mind that he was guilty, you wouldn't convict him and wouldn't care anything about what anyone else on the jury thought?" Bain replied yes. The prosecution did not mind an independent-minded juror either.[89]

As jury selection dragged on, Darrow worried about his case. His doubts gnawed at his self-assurance. His spies in the district attorney's office told him that McManigal's testimony had no loopholes. Finding an alternative theory of the crime was now all the more important. Although publicly Darrow maintained the theory of a gas leak, the model experiment had not worked. No gas leak could have caused the catastrophic damage.[90] If he were going to mount a positive defense, another theory would have to be found, but Darrow had run out of ideas. Worse, the prosecution had regrouped and was winning the public relations battle. Two days after the voir dire began Fredericks released the gist of the interviews with McManigal, Burns, and the other main investigator, local attorney Earl Rogers (1869–1922). Fredericks and his cocounsel, Joseph Ford, also cleverly brought several witnesses into the courtroom to make identifications, which were well publicized. The parade of twenty-eight witnesses, who functioned as what one observer called "the silent third degree," had its intended effects. The defendants began to look more culpable, and the public began to question the brothers' assertions of innocence. Behind the scenes, after the federal government initiated a grand jury investigation and seized all records and materials from the ironworkers' headquarters in Indianapolis in late October, there seemed little doubt that the McNamaras would hang. After learning about the contents of the files, Darrow visited the brothers, yelling at them: "My God, you've left a trail a mile wide behind you!"[91]

Darrow's mood soured. Mary and her sister, Sara, tried desperately to cheer him up, as did Ruby. It was pointless. One late October night, Mary hosted a dinner party in his honor (Ruby was not invited). As Sara reported on the evening, Darrow "was so horrid . . . I couldn't stand him."[92] Other friends tried to prop him up, with little to show for it. Anton Johannsen came down from San Francisco to take his friend out to dinner. According to the radical writer Hutchins Hapgood (1869–1944), Johannsen embodied the spirit of labor: gregarious, jovial, powerful, and progressive. Nothing the jocular Johannsen did improved Darrow's demeanor. He was a glum companion that night. As Johannsen later recalled, Darrow had succumbed to "one of his moods of pessimism and discouragement." Walking along the shores of the Pacific Ocean before dinner, Darrow asked rhetorically: "Joe, what is it all about? Why do we make this fight? Labor doesn't understand; it hasn't sufficient imagination. It probably doesn't want us to make this fight." Johannsen poked Darrow in the ribs and said, "Why don't you read one of your own books and try to believe it?" Darrow replied, "It is much easier to write than it is to live."[93] These were dark days; even darker ones were to follow.

The selection of a jury dragged on for weeks. Neither side seemed to be in a hurry, and Darrow was probably stalling to see if the Los Angeles mayoral elections brought, as he hoped, a change of climate. Or perhaps the foot-dragging was to give the defense team time to construct a different defense. It did not; things looked bleak. But at the defense's moment of despair, in mid-November, Darrow's old friend the progressive journalist Lincoln Steffens helped him find a new path. Steffens had approached Darrow to see if he could visit with the brothers, indicating that he was working on an article about the boys and the bombing. Darrow agreed to the request. In truth, Steffens was not writing an article on the brothers, but he wanted to see if the McNamaras would support a defense of "justifiable dynamiting."[94] They agreed. Steffens went back to Darrow to see if he was willing to entertain this radical change in strategy. He was not; no jury would buy that line of thought. "I wish," he said to Steffens, that "we could get a settlement out of court."[95] Steffens then volunteered to arrange a deal: the McNamara brothers would plead guilty, and in return for their confessions their lives would be spared. Desperate for any means to save the lives of his clients, Darrow thought this might be the only way forward.

The next day, Darrow and Steffens swung into action. Steffens went to his contacts among the rich Angelenos and quickly got their approval for the guilty plea. Many likely saw the plan as politically advantageous. It might be the thing to defeat Job Harriman and protect City Hall from anyone who might want to shift political and economic power toward the working class. Within just a few days, Steffens was in contact with DA Fredericks, who was more than happy to listen. Darrow huddled with the defense team and its union benefactors, all except Job Harriman. Darrow knew that the deal to save the McNamaras would likely ruin Harriman's mayoral campaign, if not his political career. Harriman would also have tried his damnedest to veto the idea, and Darrow did not need yet another argument. The only wild card was Gompers. A few days before Thanksgiving 1911 Darrow wired the AFL president, demanding that he or a representative meet with him immediately. Busy leading his troops at the annual AFL convention in Atlanta, Gompers sent Darrow's friend Ed Nockels of the Chicago Federation of Labor, who met with Darrow, agreed to the terms of the deal, and returned to Atlanta.

In the midst of these negotiations, a curious thing happened that forever overshadowed the trial's endgame and Darrow's life. On Tuesday, November 28, Bert Franklin and "Captain" C. E. White, another defense team operative, traveled separately downtown to meet juror George Lockwood at 9:00 a.m. to give him the rest of his payment. They all met at the designated spot: the intersection of Los Angeles and Third streets. Little did Franklin and White know that Lockwood was collaborating with the prosecution and that half a dozen detectives were waiting to pounce. Franklin, an experienced detective himself, felt that something was wrong; Lockwood did not look right. Sensing the trap, he and White quickly scanned for a way out. That was when they saw a man running at them waving his hat. It was Darrow! Before he could reach Franklin, the police moved in, arresting the men for attempted bribery. Darrow quickly made bail and continued to work on the plea deal. The pressure to finish the negotiations was extreme. It now looked as though the defense, not just the clients, would soon be on trial.

On Thanksgiving Day, November 30, 1911, all parties met at Fredericks's mansion, made the final arrangements, and went their separate ways. Darrow went to the jail and convinced his clients to take the deal. There was little resistance from James. The parade of witnesses that the prosecution had brought into court had softened up J.B. considerably.[96] He was willing to plead guilty to the bombing if J.J.'s life was spared. John took more convincing, but after several days he finally conceded. He also agreed to plead guilty to another bombing in the city. The next morning, December 1, was a warm, bright day. Inside the courtroom, reporters noted that Darrow and his clients all looked ill, as if they had either imbibed too much during Thanksgiving dinner or feasted on a rancid bird. The truth surprised them—as well as Harriman. Before the voir dire resumed, counselor Davis asked Judge Bordwell to allow the clients to change their plea of not guilty to guilty. The defendants then told the judge their wishes. For a moment, there was dead silence. Then a baby in the room let out a cry. Pandemonium ensued as reporters and spectators rushed outside to tell the world the news.

Darrow trailed them out, walking into a sea of humanity waiting for him outside the Hall of Records. They wanted answers. In a low voice he told them, "I did the best I could. If I'd have seen any way out of it we would not have pleaded guilty."[97] He rebuffed any attempt by some reporters to link the guilty pleas to the arrest of Bert Franklin. That had nothing to do with it, he charged back. Giving only half the truth, he explained that it "was [the] evidence gathered by the State of California that brought about this plea."[98] The other half was indeed the pressure from Franklin's arrest.

J.B. received life for his actions. He always maintained that he had never intended to hurt anyone. That may have been true, but he was a former printer and perhaps knew what would happen if dynamite were placed next to ink. J.J. was sentenced to fifteen years. All in all, this was a reasonable settlement. Darrow's employers should have approved. After all, Darrow did save their lives. But unionists, their leaders, and their politicians were not happy. Harriman's reaction was understandable; he lost the election. Gompers was furious.[99] Nearly in tears after hearing the news, he claimed that he was "utterly dumfounded" and taken by complete surprise.[100] "Labor was grossly deceived," he told a reporter from *The Washington Star*.[101] Darrow maintained that he had kept the AFL informed of the case's developments and had reported to Gompers through Nockels. The bickering served no purpose. The fragile alliance among the AFL, the IWW, and socialists was rent asunder. The only thing that nearly all labor leaders could agree on was that while the McNamaras had won their lives, the labor movement had essentially lost the case and Darrow was to blame.

❄· 7 ·❄

Darrow Defends Darrow

As much as he would have liked to go home, Clarence Darrow remained in Los Angeles pending the resolution of the arrest of Bert Franklin for attempted bribery. Naively, Darrow believed that he would escape prosecution and that only Franklin and perhaps a few of his other lieutenants would be caught up in the imbroglio. Sure, he might find some trouble, especially with James Levering threatening to have him disbarred for failing to pay in full on the construction of the model of the *Times* building.[1] But DA John Fredericks had given him every impression that if the McNamara brothers pleaded guilty, Fredericks would, in Darrow's words, "not be vicious about the prosecution" and "let it slide along."[2] Darrow showed how gullible he could be as both a jurist and a politico; he clearly did not see the legal and political jeopardy that he was in. Once again he misjudged his opponent. The card-carrying pessimist paid dearly for this uncharacteristic moment of optimism. The McNamara brothers and Steffens were right all along. They had predicted Darrow was to be "the real goat" in all of this.[3] Despite all his tilting at windmills, he never quite learned what the radical journalist C. P. Connolly (1863–1935), who had covered Darrow's defense of Haywood as well as of the McNamara brothers, always knew: "Capital is not a generous foe."[4] The forces that had been pledged to smashing labor in Los Angeles, California, and in fact across the nation and to hanging the McNamara brothers had their sights set on labor's champion. They were out to get Darrow not merely because he had defended the McNamara brothers and got caught in some unseemly ethical problem but because they wanted to destroy that righteous defender of liberty and freedom and of unionists and workers. They sought to pluck that thorn from their side once and for all and, in so doing, to eliminate a political foe—not merely a legal one—and with luck bring down his deep-pocketed backers like Sam Gompers of the American Federation of Labor.[5]

The district attorney's office kept its plans to get Darrow a secret for nearly a month. When a *New York Times* reporter asked Darrow what he made of Franklin's mentioning his name during a hearing of a grand jury, Darrow replied that it was in no way "incriminating."[6] But within a few weeks he learned that Fredericks's target was not Franklin and that the grand jury was just a means to gather evidence on Darrow himself. By mid-January 1912, Fredericks had enough evidence to bring an indictment. On January 27, Darrow retained counsel, hiring Earl Rogers, the dapper, charismatic, smart, effective, and well-connected L.A. lawyer. The handsome ladies' man, who was always marvelously dressed and never without his lorgnette, had as an investigator been closely associated with the prosecution of J. J. and J. B. McNamara. Once again, Darrow wanted someone with inside knowledge of the other team. Moreover, he needed a bulldog, and Rogers fitted the bill. He had a well-deserved reputation for doing anything it took to get his clients off the hook. For good or for ill, Darrow had a similar reputation, with one difference: as historian Geoffrey Cowan has nicely explained, Rogers was not "the attorney of the damned. He was the attorney for the guilty."[7]

Everyone assumed that Rogers's celebrated client was guilty. Darrow maintained his innocence to his final day. But his friends had their doubts. Molly's sister, Sara, thought he had done it, as did Darrow's own defense cocounsel, Jerry Giesler (1886–1962).[8] It was bad enough that his friends thought the worst of him, but soon it became apparent that most of them had abandoned him in his time of need. At the urging of Rogers, Darrow wrote to all his comrades in the labor movement, asking for money for his defense. For the most part, his pleas fell on deaf ears. His former literary protégé Brand Whitlock refused to acknowledge his letters. Gompers did respond, but only to say that he would not raise money for him.[9] Debs penned a long letter explaining in great detail why there was "a strong feeling against you among Socialists." "You may think it very cruel on the part of your former staunch friends and admirers that they are now lacking in sympathy when you most need it," he wrote, "but perhaps you are not entirely blameless and they are not wholly at fault." Revealing his surprise at the hiring of the "notorious corporation corruptionist and all around capitalist retainer" Rogers, Debs chided Darrow for his bad decisions and for loving "money too well." Still, he offered some encouraging words and promised to support him in the press. Money, however, was not forthcoming.[10]

This betrayal caused Darrow to reconsider his political commitment to and alliance with the labor movement. This was the moment when he began to sever his ties with organized labor. It had been coming for some time. After repeatedly taking it on the chin from his friends, not just his enemies, in Chicago and national politics, he realized in his darkest moment of need, isolation, and despair that he could not rely upon the mass movement for which he had always stood up regardless of the case or cause. His pessimism was confirmed yet again; Darrow was alone, abandoned by his friends and colleagues, left to his own wits for survival. This drove Ruby into a rage and her husband into the depths of his worst depression. He looked as bad as he felt. As one reporter noted, "Darrow had the uncertain air of a man whose burden is too heavy and who may collapse at any time under the strain of his load." In the moment of his utter despondency, that day before the indictment was to come, the strain had become almost too much to bear; it almost killed him.[11]

It had already started to rain hard by the time Darrow arrived home from the law office on January 28, 1911. He was later than usual, but Ruby had kept his dinner. He threw his overcoat close to the door and went to the bathroom. He did not want dinner, and Ruby knew better than to push. Coming out of the bathroom, he went into his office for a moment and marched back to the front door. Ruby saw him put a few things into his pockets. One looked like his flask, and the other seemed to be a flashlight. He said goodbye and shut the door. Ruby figured he was off to the bar to talk to Olaf Tvietmoe or Anton Johannsen about the bribery case. Perhaps deep down, she also knew that he might end up at Molly's apartment. If she had known he had grabbed the gun that he had purchased in Boise and had brought with him to L.A. and stuffed it into his trench coat pocket, she would never have let him leave.

Darrow made one stop before Molly's. At a liquor store he uncharacteristically purchased a bottle of whiskey; he was drinking much more than usual these days. Molly opened her door as soon as Darrow knocked. It was a bitter cold, inky, rainy night. She guessed what he wanted: solace, understanding, sympathy, and love. He was depressed. Slumped in a wooden chair at the kitchen table, he put the bottle on the table, asked for two glasses, and poured the drinks. "Mary, I'm going to kill myself," he told her, pulling the gun out and setting it on the table. "They're going to indict me for bribery. . . . I can't stand the disgrace." At that he started to cry. Somehow Mary talked him out of it and convinced him to go home.[12]

A few days later, likely at the instigation of Molly and Ruby, Anton Johannsen and Olaf Tvietmoe came to Los Angeles to show their support, to give a little money, and to raise Darrow's spirits. They still did not forgive him, but they surmised quite correctly that his conviction or perhaps a plea deal might spell doom to the entire California labor movement, if not result in their own incarcerations. Indeed, Darrow had been talking with the district attorney as well as his private benefactors, the officials of the National Erectors' Association, about a plea deal, which the DA ultimately rejected. The unionists needed Darrow free and back in Chicago. But it wasn't these halfhearted friends who got Darrow back into the game. Rather, according to his autobiography, his soul was rejuvenated by a most unlikely encounter with a poor working-class man unconnected to the Los Angeles trials. In his memoir, Darrow conveniently forgot to mention his union buddies and their self-serving attempts to buoy their lawyer. At that moment he knew his reliable friends were individuals outside organized labor.

Not long after his cheering-up party, Darrow sat pensively in his rented office, feet up on the desk, staring blankly out the window, watching the sun set on Los Angeles, the rabidly antiunion town that he had called home for twelve months. He had never planned to stay so long. As the orange light gave a surreal hue to his surroundings, he contemplated all that had come to pass, all that had conspired to keep him there. For a decade and a half he had been a general in the "uncivil" class war that had engulfed the United States.[13] As Darrow explained, the rich and well connected and the mass of common people were "divided into hostile camps" and locked in "mortal combat," each side bent on the destruction of the other.[14] He had battled for organized labor in various courtrooms and at public podiums across the western United States for so long that he scarcely remembered the dreamy confines of his office in Chicago. Sitting in this puny, smelly box made his blood pressure rise. After years of moving from office building to office building, his cavernous lair in Chicago was finally perfect. It was dark and cluttered to the untrained eye. Books, pamphlets, briefs, motions, and newspapers were strewn everywhere but always in exact order and the important ones within arm's reach. His gorgeous, mammoth black flattop desk held all his ideas and secrets, his high-back leather chair was the definition of comfort, and on his walls his heroes—Altgeld, Tolstoy, Whitman, and Carlyle—framed in black beamed down on him in approval.[15] His rented office in L.A. was small and all he could afford now that he had spent all his money defending pawns on the union side and defending himself. He was so deeply wallowing in self-loathing and self-pity he did not hear the knock at the door. All he could think about was his law practice, which was in shambles; his marriage, which teetered on the brink of ruin; his fortune, which was spent; and his health, which was deteriorating He was depressed. "It was one of a long series of days," Darrow remembered, "when I was very sad and when my friends looked good."[16] To put it simply, he felt he could die. Only as the knocking turned to sharp banging did his thousand-mile gaze break. He turned, stood up, and went to see what was the matter. Annoyingly, he grasped the knob and swung the door open. His clerk announced the last person in the world he had expected, George Bissett.

Bissett was like so many Chicago men who hounded him for legal assistance, mostly for free, since his defense of Gene Prendergast in 1894. By notoriety and by reputation, Darrow was the attorney for the down-and-out. Bissett fitted the bill. They had first met in late 1910. Without an appointment, Bissett's mother went to see Darrow. Bissett had just been convicted of murdering a police officer and given life in the state penitentiary. She thought her son, who she knew was no Boy Scout, had not been given a fair trial, and she asked Darrow to take up his appeal. As Darrow recounted in his autobiography, "I said I did not see how I could possibly undertake the case, as the chances were that nothing could be done in the Supreme Court, no matter who handled it." Plus, such legal challenges were expensive, and "I could not afford to go into it, and I told her so." Mrs. Bissett suggested that she could sell her house and give him the money. He flatly refused the offer. She left, and he closed for the day. That night Darrow could not sleep, as

Mrs. Bissett and her story "haunted him" so that he came "to regret that [he] had not taken the case."[17] The next morning she was waiting for him at the office. What could he do but take the case pro bono?

Darrow went to the Chicago jail to visit with his new client. He found a man roughly his son Paul's age who had never had a break in his life. Through the accident of birth, George Bissett had grown up in a poor family, had worked at dead-end common laboring jobs, and had managed to acquire virtually no education. Also, this was not his first run-in with the law. He had been arrested, convicted, and served time for attempted burglary. His new lawyer asked why he had tried to rob a house. He announced that he was a socialist, and he needed the money to start a new newspaper that would proclaim the truth to the masses. So how had the next Charles Kerr, the famous Chicago socialist publisher, landed in prison again? The conviction related to a bar fight gone too far. No stranger to the corner saloon, Bissett had gone for a drink and found several plainclothes policemen there. Knowing Bissett's past, they started in on him. All the men drew their guns, and shots were fired. One of the officers was struck in the heart and died instantaneously. Bissett was hit three times in the belly but incredibly survived to face trial and sentencing. Darrow was able to convince the appeals court that Bissett had acted in self-defense, and the poor man went back to his life of petty crime in the cause of socialism.

Darrow had not heard from or seen Bissett since his release. The man standing in front of him in L.A. was slightly older and looked like hell, "like a tramp," Darrow recalled. "George, you are a long way from home; what are you doing here?" His former client explained that he had heard that his old lawyer was in some sort of jam in Los Angeles and, as soon as he could pack a sack, he had jumped on the nearest freight train bound for the West. Hopping on trains and staying in flophouses, Bissett had hoboed the two thousand miles. But, George, "what did you think you could possibly do?" Darrow asked. "Well," the hulk of a man answered, "I have been here about a week and have been getting a line on Franklin," the Los Angeles detective Darrow had hired who had then turned state's evidence against him. Curious, Darrow asked what Bissett had found. He had learned where Franklin lived and his routine. Bissett planned to kill the man. Darrow was slackjawed but recovered quick enough "to show my appreciation of this most astounding proffer. 'But, George, you have no idea what you are about to do . . .

You must be crazy to think that you could do it without being hanged.'" Bissett replied: "Yes, I've thought of all that, but I owe my life to you, and I'm here to take the chance."[18] Refusing to give his friend license to kill, Darrow gave him enough money for a night in a hotel room with a bath, for a good meal, and for train fare back to Chicago. This ghoulish encounter added to Darrow's surreal L.A. experience but strangely cheered him. At least, after his defense of the labor movement's radical dynamiters and in the midst of a trial for his own freedom, he had friends among those who mattered most. He drew inspiration from those who had not abandoned him: the down-and-out, the lowly, the ne'er-do-wells like George Bissett. They needed him, they backed him, and they wanted him to fight and win. As Darrow was fond of saying, "Greater love hath no man than this, that he who would give his life for his friend."[19] Closing his door again, Darrow collapsed back down into his chair. In his autobiography, he marked this moment as the point at which he began to feel better, ready to battle his enemies not only for his own freedom but also so that he could continue to defend people like Bissett, *individuals*— and importantly not larger political movements—trapped in political, economic, and cultural systems that were frequently unfair, stifling, and cruel. His bribery trial in Los Angeles was a crucial pivot in his life.

Darrow was also reassured that he was not completely alone in his legal battle. Another friend who made a significant difference was Lincoln Steffens. He could have gone back to New York City after the McNamaras had been sentenced, but he stayed to help Darrow not because he thought he was innocent. He had spent much of his career investigating graft. Nothing surprised him anymore. But it did not matter. As the muckraker explained to his sister, "[w]hat do I care if he is guilty as hell?" This was yet another chance to put the Golden Rule into practice. "Sometimes all we humans have is a friend, somebody to represent God in the world."[20] Steffens was Darrow's "constant companion" during those difficult days. Bissett may have administered the much-needed shot in the arm, but Steffens nursed Darrow's confidence back to health. Steffens was convinced that the forces arrayed against Darrow could be challenged and beaten in open court. Darrow came to agree with his friend. Steffens also became one of the most important witnesses for the defense and helped unhinge the case against Darrow.[21]

The district attorney made every effort to convince Darrow that they had him dead to rights, but it was a well-orchestrated bluff to induce a plea deal.

In reality, the prosecution had a major problem, common to all these cases: corroboration. Although Franklin had given his statement, all the dots did not connect back to Darrow. Moreover, the story did not quite make sense. What was Darrow doing on that street corner? The detectives had been there in force not only to nab Franklin but also to arrest Darrow. Only Darrow was not supposed to be there. Lockwood had reported to Fredericks that Franklin had arranged for the "Big One" to be present at the payoff. Both Lockwood and Fredericks thought Franklin meant Darrow. Franklin really meant Captain White, whose nickname was Big One. In any case, Darrow must have caught wind that the operation had been compromised and rushed down to stop it. Allegedly, when Darrow met Franklin, he whispered to him, "Bert, they are on to you."[22] Moments later Franklin was in custody. Even if this account was true, it did not demonstrate Darrow's probable role in the scheme.

To coax Darrow's confession, the prosecution resorted to dirty tricks. Fredericks used the newspapers to announce that he had roped in another one of Darrow's confidants, John E. Harrington. He knew that Darrow would fume and try to make Harrington explain himself. The meeting between the two former friends occurred at a local hotel. To capture the damning discussion for the prosecution, Robert Foster, an agent of the National Erectors' Association—the organization that had waged a national war against the McNamaras' union—bugged the room with a new "telephonic device" (otherwise known as a Dictograph). Darrow never admitted to bribing any juror, in either the hotel room or Rogers's office, which also had been compromised.[23] Fredericks's and the NEA's failures at espionage did not prevent the district attorney from leaking to the press that he had secretly recorded Darrow and that the evidence "would bring about Darrow's conviction."[24] Without any corroborating evidence, Fredericks settled on the only strategy left: he had to impugn Darrow's character and convince the jury that the defendant was capable of the crime for which he was charged. Given these parameters, Darrow and Rogers had only to do three things: offer a reasonable explanation for Darrow's presence on the street corner that morning; demonstrate Darrow's high moral character; and discredit the prosecution.

The trial began on May 15, 1912. Setting aside their rivalry for its duration, Ruby and Molly were there for support. Ruby, however, had the seat immediately behind her husband. Darrow did not look like Darrow. His face, which was drained of all color, was long and drawn and sickly puffy. Betraying his stress and exhaustion, his cheeks twitched involuntarily. As the prosecution introduced its case, Darrow seemed to sink lower in his chair. This drove Rogers nuts. He leaned over and told his client to stop looking so guilty. Ruby had a softer touch and whispered something funny in his ear. Darrow brightened for a second and steeled himself for a long trial. The key to the trial was Bert Franklin, whose testimony was potentially quite damaging. He fingered Darrow as the mastermind behind the plot to bribe George Lockwood as well as Robert Bain. Whatever harm Franklin had done was more than mitigated by Rogers's brilliant cross-examination, which revealed the former detective to be a liar and perhaps a party to a NEA conspiracy to entrap Darrow. Indeed, it was not entirely out of the question that this whole battle had been a frame-up, led by the likes of Harrison Otis, William Burns, and Walter Drew (1873–1961) of the National Erectors' Association. Was it so farfetched that Darrow had become ensnared in a trap like the one laid for the ironworkers?[25]

The defense team scored more points when it was its turn to present Darrow's case. It offered an explanation for Darrow's actions on the day Franklin was arrested. Coincidentally, that morning he had received a call from someone at the Socialist Party headquarters in downtown Los Angeles, located near the corner where Franklin was caught. Darrow was at the right place at the wrong time. It was weak but effective. The bulk of the defense centered on illustrating Darrow's character. The defense offered dozens of shining testimonials collected by Darrow's soon-to-be ex-partner Edgar Lee Masters, who had beaten the bushes in Chicago to gather dozens of letters of support as well as money. Masters hated the job, which he found disgraceful, embarrassing, and damaging to his own legal and literary career. He believed Darrow was guilty and as such would never practice law again. Once done with his dirty task, Masters vowed to leave the partnership, which had in fact long gone to seed. These depositions had the intended effect, but it was Lincoln Steffens who was the defense's most influential commentator on Darrow. The prosecution welcomed Steffens's intrusion into the courtroom. Fredericks disliked the man, he called Stinken Leffens, whom he perceived as an intellectual lightweight and a troublemaker. Fredericks relished the chance to embarrass and discredit him in court. But Steffens was amazing, not only parrying Fredericks's attacks but also dismissing any idea that Darrow had negotiated the McNamara plea deal to save his own skin from the bribery prosecution.

After shooting holes in the prosecution's arguments, Rogers began to get under his opponents' skin, needling them beyond the breaking point. Several times the irritating Rogers got Fredericks and then his assistant Joseph Ford to lose their cool. On two occasions, the yelling turned into fighting. In a rage, Fredericks picked up an inkwell and threw it at Horace Appel, a member of the defense team. A few days later, Ford heaved a heavy ink bottle at Rogers. If that was not enough to make jurors question the integrity and motives of the prosecution and cost them credibility, an incident with John Harrington was. While on the stand, Harrington refused to look Darrow in the eye. When Rogers demanded that Harrington gaze at the man he was accusing of bribery, Fredericks objected on the grounds that Darrow was trying to hypnotize the witness! The courtroom erupted into laughter.

Rogers's trial strategy set the scene for Darrow's closing statement, which even Fredericks admitted after the fact was "one of the greatest ever heard in a court-room."[26] Dressed in a fine-fitting gray suit with his characteristic floppy black bow tie, Darrow looked somewhat rested and raring to go when the court resumed session on August 15. The structure of Darrow's statement was very like that of the Haywood case. He even opened in a similar way. "I am a stranger in a strange land," he told the jurors, "2,000 miles away from home and friends." What followed also mirrored his previous big case. He mercilessly picked on one member of the prosecution—in this case Joe Ford—while tearing apart the DA's case. He made it clear that in his opinion, Ford was "cowardly, sneaky and brutal." At the outset, he stated that this was not a bribery trial. "Will you tell me, gentlemen of the jury," Darrow asked rhetorically, "why the Erectors' Association and the Steel Trust [the organizations that had given aid and comfort to the prosecution] are interested in a case way out here in Los Angeles?" The answer was clear: the plutogogues, as Steffens called them, and their hired hounds, like Fredericks and Ford, had "concocted all sorts of schemes" to silence Darrow inside the dim walls of San Quentin because, according to him, "I have been a lover of the poor, a friend of the oppressed, because I have stood by Labor for all these years, and have brought down upon my head the wrath of the criminal interests in this country." This was payback for the defense of Haywood and the defense of the McNamaras, whose cases "came like a thunderclap upon the world." They hated him for standing in the way of their bloodlust and in the way of their plans to subvert democracy and eliminate liberty and freedom. Darrow tried to explain that the McNamaras were wrong, although they did not mean to kill anyone. Moreover, it was not murder but a social crime in the war between "two great forces—the rich and the poor." Even with the aid of spies, the district attorney had not produced "conclusive evidence" of Darrow's guilt. As a result, the prosecution, especially Ford, "willfully, maliciously, feloniously, criminally, cruelly, distorted evidence" for the sole purpose of making the jurors "have a bad opinion of [him]" and thus vote for conviction. Darrow admitted that he had "done good and evil" in his life, just like any human. But he had not committed this crime. "I am as fitted for jury bribing," he told the jury in jest, "as a Methodist preacher for tending bar." In any case, why bribe jurors if a plea deal was in the works? And if he was to bribe jurors, why would he "have run down there on the street [himself]"? "Lord!" he exclaimed. He had witnesses to his alibi like Frank Wolfe (1860?–1948), the filmmaker and journalist. Others who supported Darrow's explanation of his actions that day included the well-respected Job Harriman, Fremont Older, and LeCompte Davis. If Franklin was to be believed, then all these men were liars. How could they all be "crooks"? Darrow promised the jury that if Judge McNutt had not died after the McNamaras' trial, he too would have testified on his behalf. If only the angel of death had asked Darrow advice on that score, "I would have probably told him, 'Take Ford and spare McNutt.'"

Darrow's direct manner and pointed humor at least swung the jurors' attention, if not their sympathy, to the defense. However, his final words to the jury were a masterstroke that left no dry eye in the courtroom. Darrow was in tears as he delivered his ultimate plea for freedom. By the time he gave those words on the second day of his closing statement, his suit was disheveled and his handkerchief had become a sodden ball, which he finally threw on the floor as he beseeched those who sat in judgment to find him not guilty:

> I have tried to live my life and to live it as I see it, regarding neither praise
> nor blame, both of which are unjust. No man is judged rightly by his fellow-
> men . . . [H]ere I am today in the hands of you twelve men who will one day

say to your children, and they will say to their children, that you passed on my fate . . .

Gentlemen, I came to this city a stranger. Misfortune has beset me, but I never saw a place in my life with greater warmth and kindness and love than Los Angeles . . . I know my life, I know what I have done. My life has not been perfect; it has been human, too human. I have felt the heart beats of every man who lived. I have tried to be the friend of every man who lived. I have tried to help in the world. I have not had malice in my heart. I have had love for my fellowman. I have done it the best I could . . .

There are people who would destroy me. There are people who would lift up their hands to crush me down. I have enemies powerful and strong. There are honest men who misunderstand me and doubt me; and still I have lived a long time on earth, and I have friends—I have friends in my old home who have gathered around to tell you as best they could of the life I have lived. I have friends who have come to me here to help me in my sore distress. I have friends throughout the length and breadth of the land, and these are the poor and the weak and the helpless, to whose cause I have given voice. If you should convict me, there will be people to applaud the act. But if in your judgment and your wisdom and your humanity, you believe me innocent, and return a verdict of not guilty in this case, I know that from thousands and tens of thousands and yea, perhaps millions of the weak and the poor and the helpless throughout the world will come thanks to this jury for saving my liberty and my name.[27]

It is true that Darrow's closing statement was self-serving. But it was also heartfelt and perhaps as accurate a portrait of him—the good and the bad—and the significance of the trial as any painted either then or now. Darrow's main point was right: this scheme to silence him was designed to remove a major political force that defended the weak and stood in the way of the machinations of the elite. Notice, however, here at the end of his statement he seemed to refer more to people like George Bissett than to organized labor. Darrow and his defense of freedom, liberty, and equality were on trial, and its outcome had broader implications for working people everywhere, not just the labor movement. The millions who toiled at the bottom of luck's ladder stood to lose as much as Darrow. To put it another way, those struggling to enjoy liberty's blessing stood to gain by his continued freedom.

Fredericks and Ford tried to turn the momentum, but it was too late. Nothing in their closing statements, which attacked the idea of "social crimes" and attempted to reconnect the criminal acts back to Darrow, convinced the jurors of Darrow's guilt. Ford claimed that Darrow was no friend of labor. "History," he told the jury, "is filled with examples of men whose minds are brilliant, whose sentiments are noble, but whose practices are ignoble."[28] On August 17, 1912, the jury took Judge George H. Hutton's instructions and went to deliberate. It needed only thirty minutes to return its unanimous verdict: not guilty! The celebrations that followed were like rain in the desert of despair. Darrow must have been relieved that Ruby and Molly seemed genuinely appreciative of each other and got along well at the victory luncheon. The only thing that tempered the euphoric pandemonium that followed was the realization that Fredericks intended to pursue the other charge of bribery involving Robert Bain separately. That trial began in November and lasted until March 1913. It was essentially the first trial redux with some notable exceptions.[29] Rogers did not participate; he had checked into a hospital to fight his demons and addictions to alcohol and drugs. This time the hung jury returned a mixed verdict: eight to four for conviction. Plans for a third trial fizzled in late 1913, and in December Darrow finally went home. The champion's homecoming party at the plush Crystal Room of the Sherman House was terrific. As one partyer remembered, "the whole evening was a testimonial of the love and esteem we all had for Darrow. . . . When he finally got up to speak," the man recalled, "it was the first time I saw Darrow affected so emotionally."[30] He stood mute for a few moments, wiped away the tears, and told his remaining friends how much he appreciated them. He needed them now more than ever. The fifty-six-year-old lawyer had arrived home a wounded and abandoned veteran of the undeclared industrial war. He was a victor, yet he was also vanquished. His life and career were in shambles. He was unhealthy emotionally and physically. He was broke, and his marriage was on the rocks. After the last of the booze was gone, Ruby took him home. Both wondered if he had the courage and stamina to begin again.

He would, but his experiences in Los Angeles had changed him. Almost three decades earlier, he had come to Chicago a wide-eyed freethinker, ready to take on urban politics and working-class reforms. His entrance into politics had been easier than his halting path to become a crusading lawyer, especially for unionists in trouble. Nonetheless, he had become organized labor's champion. Yet while he gave all his strength, prowess, and energy to labor's battles with capital, doubts began to grow. His efforts cost him a marriage and were so taxing that he dreamed of leaving the law for literature. But those labor cases kept coming, often rescuing him from the certain destitution that his meager literary career promised. In politics, he grew pessimistic as working-class voters frequently abandoned, if not betrayed, him and those of his ilk and voted against what Darrow saw as their interests. By the time of the Los Angeles cases, Darrow knew very well and firsthand the fickle nature of the labor movement. Its cold disavowal of him when he needed its support convinced Darrow that he should shift his focus. To the end, Darrow remained a stalwart defender of liberty, freedom, and equality. But after Los Angeles, he initially tried to avoid battling for those principles in court and for the labor movement, or really any mass movement. In the years after the McNamara and bribery trials, Darrow discovered that he had to return to the law to make his living and to champion his philosophy. By the time of the Great War, however, Darrow was indeed a changed man, less involved in movement protest politics but nonetheless devoted to defending the powerless against the powerful. Increasingly his future cases, some of which were his most celebrated and most consequential, focused on the rights of individuals to think, act, and live without the hamstringing influences of the state, social customs, and social environments. Significantly, Darrow's shifting away from the labor movement and other movements like the women's movement did not translate into a move away from politics. Quite the opposite. If anything, Darrow became even more political. This old politico crusading for justice and equality had learned one final lesson from Los Angeles: Darrow had to look out for Darrow—politically, legally, and financially. His now-entrenched pessimism fueled a skepticism in others. To the best of his ability, this grumpy pessimist would endeavor to protect and guard himself from others' political, monetary, moral, and legal weaknesses and failings. Thus, the bribery trials were a fulcrum in Darrow's life and career. He emerged tempered by those fires, but ever dedicated to the distilled core of his political commitments and to the promise of American freedom.

· 8 ·

War and Regret

As the Darrows resumed their lives in Chicago, Ruby unpacked and cleaned while Clarence, never much help in keeping the house or his office tidy, nursed a black mood and contemplated the future. There were only two rational, reasonable options. Either he could somehow rebuild his law career, or he could, as he desired, become a lecturer, debater, and renowned author. In the spring of 1913, the latter seemed much more attractive. Technically, he still had a law firm. Though his association with Edgar Lee Masters and Francis Wilson had essentially dissolved before he had left for Los Angeles, not wanting to lose his standing in the state, he had quickly formed a paper firm with Jacob L. Bailey, an office staffer. But it was a practice without clients or income. Reestablishing a partnership with Masters, who was on the verge of poetic greatness, was out of the question. He despised Darrow with an artist's passion.

Writing about Darrow was a way for Masters to vent his frustrations with the man he claimed still owed him several thousand dollars. In "On a Bust," Masters lampooned his old partner, imagining the day someone would make a bronze cast of Darrow's head. It ran, in part: "Your speeches seemed to answer for the nonce—/ They do not justify your head in bronze!" Masters made fun of his nose, the shape of his head, and his "sensual chin." In a quip that made sense one hundred years ago, he proclaimed: "You are a Packard engine in a Ford." More cutting yet, and perhaps in reference to his debacle in Los Angeles, Masters wrote, "A giant as we hoped, in truth, a dwarf."[1]

Darrow rarely held grudges, but he did get even, representing Masters's estranged wife, Helen, during their divorce in 1920.[2] By the mid-twenties the animosity had eased, at least publicly, and from time to time the two former partners shared letters and gifts.[3] Aside from that no doubt personally satisfying divorce case, Darrow did not look for trouble. He turned the page and accepted the fact that as a result of his L.A. trials he had lost friends and made some new enemies. At the same time, he still had influential acquaintances who could help him easily start his career as a lecturer. For Darrow, the courtroom had always been a means to political ends. After the beating he had taken in Los Angeles, the podium looked far more appealing than the defense table. It was a safer place for him to talk about, and earn a living from, the problems of liberty and freedom in America. Further, Darrow sought to distance himself from his legal career. He no longer wanted to be the national labor movement's lawyer. He was as committed to improving the lives of average Americans as ever. But he was winnowing his causes. At this moment, he was more interested in telling workers about those giants of the past whose ideas and actions had elevated minds, souls, and bodies and led to more freedoms and liberties.

Even before he left California, he had delivered several speeches, either talking about his heroes or presenting his analysis of the difficulties of the working class. In December 1912, having just escaped a kind of martyrdom himself, he spoke before the San Francisco Radical Club about his boyhood idol, radical abolitionist and insurrectionist John Brown (1800–1859), who in his 1859 assault on Harpers Ferry, Virginia, had sought "to kindle a flame that should burn the decaying institutions and ancient wrongs in the fierce crucible of a world's awakening wrath."[4] Immediately following the verdict in this second trial, he addressed a mass rally of the Single Tax League of Los Angeles. Six months later, he gave much the same lecture in Chicago at the Single Tax Club dinner. Darrow pleased the listeners with such sentiments as "We can go down thru the ages and find a few great prophets—I won't mention them all—Moses, Jesus, Goethe, Henry George."[5] These biographical pieces became canned lectures that Darrow brought out of his mind's pantry when the occasion or price was right. They were not bad, but not terribly original.

There were three basic problems with Darrow's road show. First, it was nowhere near as remunerative as his law practice had been. He earned about one hundred dollars a lecture (two thousand in today's dollars). At that rate of compensation, he would need to give roughly two lectures a week to maintain his lifestyle. The heavy schedule led to another problem: away from home, he became despondent.[6] Perhaps this explained why at times he could be so ornery onstage. In September 1914, he gave the San Francisco Labor Day address following a parade. Darrow began his oration by announcing that "this is the first time in my life that I have ever participated in a parade." Before the crowd could clap, he added that "I never cared much for them. It makes me tired to walk in the dust." The smattering of polite chuckles stopped after Darrow threw on an even wetter blanket, saying that "the great question between capital and labor cannot be solved by marching." Darrow then went on to criticize progressives and their ameliorative legislation. Only the collective action of workers and their unions could improve life and end poverty. The audience must have liked Darrow's best line—"[T]he best proof of the usefulness of the union is that the employers don't want it"—but they were rightly confused at his utopian concluding remark: "[W]hen all men are capitalists and all men workers, industrial wars will cease."[7]

His labor talks seemed inspired as much by the possibilities of the proletariat as by his great disappointment in those who toiled for the rich.[8] Generally, his working-class audiences listened patiently to labor's great lawyer, but they refused to change their provincial ways. This then was the third realization. After a few years of lecturing, Darrow conceded that it did not have the social or political impact that he sought. However, he never gave it up and remained to the end of his life a sought-after speaker, about which he was immensely proud.

By early 1914, Darrow was ready to go back to the law. He had to. It was the only thing he ever did that made sufficient money. Serendipitously, an opportunity to reenter Chicago's legal world appeared suddenly. A former legal assistant, Peter Sissman, whom Darrow had taken under his wing in 1894, had learned his old mentor was back in town. Mustering up some pluck, he met Darrow for coffee and proposed that they form a partnership. Darrow feigned uninterest, but soon the two were working together, taking cases from all kinds of clients: rich and poor, guilty and innocent, clean and dirty. Everyone was welcome, but not everyone came. A dark cloud had followed Darrow from Los Angeles and hung over the law firm's shingle. Darrow took that in stride. "If people wanted to see me," he once wrote, "my door was open; if they did not care to come I never knew it."[9]

At first, most of the clients were those who needed a good defense but were least able to pay for it. One day, as Darrow sat in his office, waiting for clients, the telephone rang. It was George Bissett! His ne'er-do-well friend, in trouble yet again, was reaching out to the man who had saved his life once before. This time Bissett had been caught with five hundred thousand dollars that he and an accomplice had stolen from a government warehouse. His partner turned state's evidence, and the best that Darrow could do was have Bissett plead guilty. The judge sentenced him to two and a half years in the penitentiary. Another pro bono case involved Isaac "Ike" Bond, a working-class black man accused of murdering a white female nurse, who was last seen answering an emergency call and walking down a dark rural road with a tall African American man. Her half-naked, badly mutilated body had been discovered in a ditch the next day. Police combed Chicago's South Side and arrested Bond, a janitor at a bar in Gary, Indiana, who had previously been convicted of killing a white man in southern Missouri. No one in the black community in Chicago or Gary thought him guilty, and a group of local leaders hired Darrow to defend Bond, who swore his innocence. Given the case's racial issues, Darrow had a terrible time finding witnesses willing to testify. No one had forgotten the 1905 teamsters' strike, with its racially motivated violence, and the horrific race riot in Springfield, Illinois, was only five years past. Darrow and Sissman did their best, but their best was not good enough to counter the prosecution's witnesses and a gullible jury. Bond was convicted and sentenced to life. Darrow tried repeatedly to get the parole board to set him free, but he failed. After serving ten years, Bond contracted tuberculosis and died.

Although Darrow was compelled to take cases like Bond's and Bissett's, he admitted that "it is hell to be the Genl Counsel to the poor."[10] He rarely saw a dime, and the cases took a toll in terms of time and emotion. For much of his career, about a third of his cases and about half his office time was spent defending the poor without compensation. Darrow estimated that three-fourths of all his labor cases were also pro bono.[11] Different clients paid his salary. Although doing so sometimes drew public criticism, Darrow was not above defending grafters, politicians, philanderers, murderers, and the infamously famous and wealthy, all of whom paid handsomely for his services. Darrow had to provide for himself and his family. For instance, he represented alleged murderers, such as Lois Van Keuren, who had shot and killed her businessman husband, John. Darrow convinced the jury that Mrs. Van Keuren had mistaken Mr. Van Keuren for a burglar, and he thus foiled the prosecution's plan to demonstrate that she and her alleged lover, George Penrose, a local jeweler, had planned to murder him.[12]

Darrow also regularly reached out to potential clients who could put his name in every newspaper in the nation. In 1915 he offered to represent Margaret Sanger (1879–1966), the birth control advocate, who was facing federal prosecution for having used the mail to advance her cause. She politely turned him down, jumped bail, and fled to England for a short time. He was, however, able to help Frank Lloyd Wright (1867–1959), the brilliant and innovative architect, escape a Mann Act prosecution—taking an underage woman who was not his wife across state lines—without a trial. Unable to sustain himself on a diet of pro bono work and only a few celebrated cases with deep-pocketed clients, Darrow had to do something he did not want: he reluctantly decided to represent a labor union in a case of national significance. Once again miners were on strike and in need of a lawyer, and Darrow went to defend unionists and liberty and freedom and to make some money. But this would be his last big labor case.

In his encyclopedic biography, Kevin Tierney maintains that after the McNamara trial and the subsequent bribery trials, Darrow no longer expected or wanted cases from the labor movement.[13] Not quite true. While in time Darrow relinquished this part of his practice, from 1914 through the early 1920s unionists and left-wing radicals continued to rely on Darrow. Moreover, his association with the labor movement was no secret. In 1913, Darrow's friend the journalist and filmmaker Frank Wolfe, who had supplied him with an alibi in Los Angeles, released *From Dusk to Dawn*. Loosely based on the events surrounding the *Los Angles Times* bombing trial, it was a major picture. Darrow starred as the lawyer for the protagonist Dan Grayson, an iron molder, a union organizer, and later the governor of a sunny western state, who had been arrested on phony conspiracy charges. In his big scene, Darrow gave a closing statement in Grayson's trial very similar to that of his own trial. Of course, Dan was exonerated. The five-reel docudrama was wildly popular and set attendance records.[14] When unionists found themselves in similar straits to that of Dan Grayson, they called upon Darrow, who gladly helped, especially if it helped pay the rent.

Nor did labor's leaders shun Darrow. Sam Gompers eventually forgave him, at least publicly. They shared the same platform at various gatherings of workers. Darrow was always in high demand as a labor speaker and remained closely associated with several important union leaders, such as Sidney Hillman (1887–1946), of the United Garment Workers and later president of the Amalgamated Clothing Workers of America. Hillman never forgot the role Darrow played in settling the massive garment strike in Chicago in 1910. Unionists remained an important clientele for his law firm. To some, his misadventures in Los Angeles were a decided advantage. For instance, in February 1914 he helped Manfred Peterson and Charles Anderson of Redgranite, Wisconsin, avoid an indictment for dynamiting the derricks of the Wisconsin Granite Company.[15] Darrow was still unafraid of representing all factions within the labor movement, from conservative to radical. But Darrow's relationship with organized labor had changed. He was always willing to defend a union on a local matter or individual unionists or individual radicals. But, after Los Angeles, he focused more on these cases as individual instances of freedom and liberty in jeopardy and less as battles in a larger war against big business and its desire to dominate the American economy and politics and snuff out all dissent. This was true, but there was one exception: in 1914, the Western Federation of Miners (WFM) hired him to help it win an important strike in Michigan. In desperate need of clients, Darrow took the case. He did not make it into a cause célèbre, as he had in Pennsylvania or in Idaho. This was a different Darrow, a lawyer who wanted his side to win but was less devoted to the movement it represented.

Although the Michigan copper strike of 1913–1914 is largely forgotten today, it was one of a handful of extraordinarily violent and consequential battles in the undeclared civil war between capitalists and organized labor that continued unabated from the *L.A. Times* bombing to the late 1930s. On July 23, 1913, thousands of Michigan miners in the Keweenaw Peninsula's copper range, from Victoria to Copper Harbor, went on strike for higher wages, shorter work hours, and safer mines. Resentment had been simmering for years, but after the introduction of the one-man drills, which increased productivity and profitability at the expense of workers' well-being, the miners were ready to take action. In the summer of 1913, the WFM organized many locals in the Upper Peninsula, and union president Charles H. Moyer personally led the strike.

The WFM locals sought not only to shut down the copper mines but also to force a general strike in the peninsula. Initially, the strikers succeeded. But a settlement was far beyond reach. The operators appealed to Michigan's Democratic governor Woodbridge N. Ferris (1853–1928), who promptly sent in a column of the state's National Guard. The soldiers took up positions around the collieries, especially the massive Hecla Calumet Mine, and the governor then called for mediation. To represent the union, Moyer called on his old friend Clarence Darrow. In two meetings with Governor Ferris, in early September 1913, Darrow tried to arrange a settlement akin to that of the Pennsylvania anthracite coal deal, agreeing to some of the bread-and-butter demands of the workers while not recognizing the union. Significantly, Darrow did not seize the moment and utilize the national press to put pressure on the governor or the mine operators to negotiate in good faith. He did not follow the playbook that had worked so well in Pennsylvania, in Idaho, and to some degree in Los Angeles. Rather, he treated the strike as a local issue, confined to the politics of Michigan alone. Although he never stated it publicly, his advocacy for the miners was not aimed at some larger victory for the labor movement, but rather at a fair resolution of the matter at hand for the workers involved. He was no less a steadfast jurist, but the political cause was quite distilled. The results were less than spectacular. Neither side relented, and Governor Ferris was unable to make any headway in resolving the strike.

As the blustery, dreary Upper Peninsula winter settled in, the spirits of striking workers and their families began to sag. To buoy them, Ana "Big Annie" Clemenc (1888–1956), the famous strike leader, who roamed the copper range rallying the troops, arranged a Christmas Eve party in Red Jacket at the town's Italian Hall.[16] More than 500 children and 175 parents attended. Just as the children began to dance on the upstairs stage, someone yelled, "Fire." Chaos ensued as people rushed for the exits. Seventy-three people, many of them children, were trampled to death. Police investigations led to no arrests, but many suspected that the mine operators' goons had somehow caused the carnage. Shortly afterward WFM president Moyer was savagely beaten and shot. As the recuperating Moyer boarded one train for Chicago, Darrow got on another, headed toward the front lines. Once again, he implored Governor Ferris to form a mediation board before the situation worsened. "The people of the upper peninsula," he charged, "were sitting on a keg of powder that was liable to explode at any time."[17] Given the events in Red Jacket, Governor Ferris no doubt agreed, but all efforts to establish some sort of mediation or arbitration committee went for naught. Michigan was not to be Pennsylvania or Idaho. The WFM suffered an expensive defeat, and Darrow a blow to his ego, if not to his reputation too—that is, if people noticed. His handling of this WFM crisis differed greatly from the one in 1906. Then Darrow, who had aligned his career so closely with the labor movement, had taken control of the press and used it brilliantly to his advantage, not only publicizing the conditions of western miners and generating sympathy for his clients but also hammering his political opponents and the plutocrats who put them in office. This time Darrow was more subdued. Although many knew of the strike, he did not rally the labor press, much less the national daily press, behind the Michigan unionists. Neither did he seem to fight for the unionists as he had in Chicago, Oshkosh, Pennsylvania, Idaho, or Los Angeles. Afterward Darrow defended unionists occasionally. He still believed in the cause of the underdog in liberty's great battles. He was no longer, however, the labor movement's champion lawyer.

Back in Chicago, by late summer the fifty-seven-year-old Darrow was ready for a vacation. He decided to visit his son, Paul, whom he had not seen in years, his trials in Los Angeles having kept him away. Much more like his practical, conservative, and private mother, Paul, after earning his business degree, had taken a job managing the Greeley Gas & Fuel Company in Estes Park, Colorado. He and his wife, Lillian, one of his father's former office secretaries, had built a comfortable life and in short order had had three daughters. So their smitten grandfather told Sissman in late summer 1914 to mind the fort while Darrow traveled the thousand miles straight west to Estes Park. Ruby, with whom Paul had little connection and likely a strained relationship, stayed in Chicago.[18]

While Darrow was relaxing with his son and his family, the news came that war had broken out in Europe. Darrow had watched with concern as the nations of the Triple Alliance and those of the Triple Entente jockeyed for a diplomatic solution following the murders of Archduke Franz Ferdinand

and his wife in June 1914. But he was caught off guard when Germany invaded Belgium in the first week of August. Somewhere deep within him, anger welled. "I had exactly the same reaction that I would experience if a big dog should attack a little one," he wrote two decades later in his autobiography.[19] Reducing this conflagration into a fight between two individuals is an important window into Darrow's thinking. He viewed the European conflict as he did so many other instances of injustice. It was a tragic example of the powerful attacking the weak. In this case, Prussian militarism had inflicted unwarranted punishment upon a relatively defenseless foe, depriving Belgians of their freedom and liberty. The murdering of civilians was as callous an act as any state-sanctioned violence that he had witnessed in any of the labor conflicts in Chicago, or Pennsylvania, or Idaho, or Michigan. He squarely and publicly came down on the side of the Allies, the only military power strong enough to restore the political status quo ante in Europe and give freedom and liberty a chance to return. Darrow knew that his reaction was out of sync with the opinions of most of his colleagues and friends on the political left and with many in various political movements from the peace movement to the labor movement, to both of which he previously had had strong ties. In an attempt to justify his support for the Allies as well as to draw the support of American socialists, in late summer 1914 he published a curious short essay in the *International Socialist Review*, asserting (rather fatuously) that there was a silver lining in all those dark war clouds over Europe, Asia, and Africa. While the sorrows of war were numerous, not among them was the destruction of property, he asserted. As in all hellish calamities such as the Chicago fire and the San Francisco earthquake, the rebuilding would spark prosperity and higher wages. In this way, "the destruction of property, together with its re-creation, means only a re-distribution in which the poor get a greater share."[20] Desperately, Darrow was trying to convince his peers that European workers would ultimately profit from the war. What American socialists made of Darrow's article and its spurious argument is unclear, but he had made his choice of war over peace abundantly clear. Darrow was also choosing nationalism over international socialism. He was hardly alone. Indeed, nearly all European socialists made the same choice. Socialists in Germany, Britain, and France all joined their national armies. As historian Theodore Draper wrote, "the Bosnian student who fired the bullet into the neck of the Archduke

Franz Ferdinand also fired into the heart of the international Socialist movement."[21]

A few months later, on October 8, 1914, in Chicago Darrow gave a major address on the war. Still motivated by sympathies for Britain, France, and Russia, he nevertheless toned down any notion that something good could come from the conflict. That argument appealed to no one. Further, Darrow had been dismayed by the butcher's bill for the first three months of fighting. More than five hundred thousand soldiers on all sides had been killed or wounded, and no nation had a clear advantage. Europe's workers were killing one another by the tens of thousands. Talk of a heady postwar economy was not only premature but also heartless. Rather, the war was drifting toward a bloody stalemate. In that context, nothing he said made his friends or his detractors happy. He snubbed both progressives, who believed there was a chance to use the war to advance reform, and socialists, who thought that the war was ushering in the end of capitalism. Darrow had become cynically pessimistic about the war and the possibilities for social and political change. There was no reason to believe the war could lead to any major social progress. "The reason there are so many optimists," he stated, "is because there are so many idiots in the world." Religion, capitalism, socialism, and trade unionism "had been swept away by war." All that remained was killing, and perhaps, Darrow darkly mused, the quick death that bullets and bombs brought was better than the slow "annoying" death of the average worker. "After all it is better to be killed by a lion than nibbled to pieces by mosquitoes." Perhaps the war and the collapse of modern civilization might mean that the meek could inherit a new distribution of property, but only when love replaced hatred, fear, and vengeance would all wars end. Yet the war that Austria had begun needed a resolution. As for this, Darrow was clear: the Allies had to win if freedom and liberty were to have any future in Europe.[22]

To many of Darrow's friends, his support of the Allies and the war was bewildering. Darrow had been on record time and again supporting Tolstoyan, non-Marxist pacifist and socialist beliefs. Wasn't this the same Darrow who had for years lectured and published on the virtues of nonviolence and nonresistance and the evils of militarism? Hadn't he always put the brotherhood of man above war? For nearly twenty years, Darrow had not only maintained but also expounded on his criticisms of state-sanctioned murder and oppression as well as the state's demand for absolute loyalty, fidelity, and patriotism. In his popular book *Resist Not Evil*, he had castigated the "apologists who have seen the horror in the thought of vengeance and still believe in violence and force when exercised by the state." He had been equally hard on the apologists for "wholesale butchery," who in the "pulpit, press, and the school united in teaching patriotism and in proclaiming the glory and beneficence of war."[23] Darrow had counseled cooperation over war and had gone on record opposing the unquestioning patriotism that undergirded America's imperial desires.

After the first weeks of war, Darrow seemingly abandoned all his stances on pacifism, patriotism, and violence. There were those who just did not understand. In April 1915, he wrote to his old girlfriend Mary Field Parton, trying to explain why he supported Britain, France, and Russia. "There can be no peace," he asserted, "while Prussian militarism lives, and I want to see it destroyed." Mary and her sister, Sara, were aghast at the change in their friend. Sara, who had seen him that spring, fought bitterly with him to no avail.[24] He had made up his mind. Many of his friends and political colleagues were greatly disappointed. Eugene Debs never forgave him.

But the switch in Darrow's position was *not* as radical a departure as it appeared. There had always been serious inconsistencies in his thinking about violence and pacifism. Although he had authored a significant pacifist tract, *Resist Not Evil*, many of his cherished idols, such as John Brown and Thomas Jefferson, were not nonviolent. Moreover, his involvement in the class war in America indicated that he understood that while nonresistance to evil and an allegiance to Tolstoy's vision of peaceful cooperation were wonderful ideals, they did not mean much in the battles between unions and employers. By 1915, he had come to see the European conflict in much the same way. Speaking before a federal industrial relations commission, set up in the wake of the 1914 Ludlow Massacre, in which Colorado National Guard troops had killed twenty strikers and family members, Darrow made the analogy between the two. Strikes were wars by another name, and as in Europe, the combatants were often justified in taking action. Moreover, sometimes both sides could be cruel. For Darrow, it was indeed better if one side defeated the other. It was precisely in the service of helping the side he supported win that the labor movement's lawyer had cemented his reputation.[25]

So why abandon pacifism in 1914? Why give up his role as a dissenter and critic of warmongering and violence? Certainly one can add charges of hypocrisy and betrayal to the list of his personal and professional shortcomings. During the Great War, many of his friends would have gladly appeared for the prosecution in the court of public opinion. But their anger at him was as much about his relinquishing nonviolent principles as it was for his support of a war that critics believed was merely a fight among capitalists. In other words, the problem was not the fight but the side he chose. While Darrow never offered a satisfying answer to why he so adamantly supported the war or why he had shifted his views on war and patriotism, his wartime positions and activities reveal a crucial aspect of the man: over time he discarded beliefs and commitments that were not central to his core political philosophy about the expansion and defense of liberty and freedom. He had done this before when he had shucked his feminist beliefs. The distancing of his political and legal career from the labor movement also reveals this intellectual sifting and shifting of causes. In this case, he readily dropped pacifism in order to back the Allies in the hope that they would defeat a berserk government that threatened to snuff out freedom and liberty in Europe and perhaps in America too. Darrow was also repulsed and disgusted at the pain and destruction that Germany with its superior military had inflicted on its neighbors. Stopping the abuse of power to strip the weak and defenseless of their rights was at the center of his political views. According to Darrow, it took only a "twinkling of an eye" to recover from his pacifism.[26] Dropping his belief in nonviolence was logical and necessary in order to save those in front of the Germans' cannons and to check the German imperialist, antidemocratic threat.

From late 1914 through 1917, Darrow gladly championed the war in Europe and longed for Germany's defeat. Initially and significantly, that did not mean he wished for U.S. intervention. A month after he gave his war speech in Chicago, the editors of Indiana's *Fort Wayne Sentinel* asked Darrow and a dozen other public luminaries to answer the question "[S]hall we have a bigger Army and Navy?" He wrote back: "No! All the right thinking people in the world are doing all they can to get rid of armies and navies."[27] He still clung to some of his pacifist notions, but in the spring of 1917, when President Wilson asked Congress for a declaration of war, Darrow became totally devoted to the war effort. He used his considerable gifts as an orator and as a writer and his unique social and political position to advance the cause for war and victory.

At first, President Wilson and his secretary of state, William Jennings Bryan, who, like Darrow, had been a Tolstoyan pacifist, had remained aloof from the European conflict, urging restraint, maintaining trade and diplomatic relations with all sides, and pursuing every peace initiative. For almost a year, Bryan had the president's ear. But the deteriorating relations with the Germans in the spring of 1915, capped by the torpedoing of the RMS *Lusitania* off the coast of Ireland on May 7, 1915, led to a parting of the ways. On June 7, 1915, Bryan resigned, and Wilson began a careful political dance, skillfully weaving between those favoring preparedness and those wishing to stay out of the conflict. In 1916, he ran for reelection on the pledge of keeping the United States out of the war and promising a new world order once peace was obtained. At the same time, he issued public warnings against those who were disloyal to the government, opposed war preparations, or, worse, supported the Germans. His appeals to peace and preparedness drew the broad support of unionists, many progressives, and socialists such as John Reed (1887–1920), Jack London (1876–1916), Helen Keller (1880–1968), and Upton Sinclair (1878–1968), and he won a second term. Peace without victory—Wilson's lofty goal for the Great War—was not to be. On April 6, 1917, the United States joined the fight.[28]

The decision to go to war split the American people. The rift within the Socialist Party was emblematic of the nation as a whole. One day after President Wilson and Congress brought America into the war, the Socialist Party met in St. Louis and ratified an antiwar resolution. A minority that opposed the referendum, including John Spargo (1876–1966), William English Walling, Algie M. Simons, Charles Edward Russell (1860–1941), and Upton Sinclair, bolted from the party, pledging its loyalty to Wilson and the war effort.[29] Fearing that his opponents might erode the public's support for the war, President Wilson established a new propaganda agency, the Committee on Public Information (CPI), and appointed progressive journalist George Creel (1876–1953) its head to sell the war. Creel did a masterful job. The key to his success was enlisting America's leading public figures, including statesman Elihu Root (1845–1937) and Samuel Gompers, who established the American Alliance for Labor and Democracy. It was likely

Gompers who drafted Darrow as well as the pro-war socialists such as Spargo, Walling, and Russell into the service of the CPI.

By August 1917, Darrow was traveling widely in the Midwest, giving speeches in support of the Allies. Often sharing the stage with Gompers and other public figures such as former President William H. Taft (1857–1930) and progressive lawyer Frank P. Walsh, he denounced Germany and American dissenters in the same breath. For instance, in Minneapolis, Darrow scorned the "flannel-mouthed traitors who are scattering German propaganda" while pleading for support in destroying "Prussian militarism."[30] Who were the "flannel-mouthed traitors" Darrow spoke of? At a mass meeting of the American Alliance for Labor and Democracy in New York City's Madison Square Garden on September 15, he made himself clear. Pacifists were the traitors. "Why is it necessary to use two words, 'pacifists' and 'pro-Germans,'" he asked the crowd, "when the latter would suffice?"[31] He had seemingly rejected all his old positions and sentiments. Peace was wrong; war was right. Dissent and legitimate opposition were treason. To the common charge that the capitalists who ran Wall Street were behind America's decision to go to war "for the sake of gold," Darrow replied, "No person who respects fact or logic can say that this is a Wall Street war."[32]

Many of Darrow's old friends and admirers were astonished at these aspersions. Renouncing his own nonviolent convictions was one thing, but attacking pacifists and free speech was something else; it was so very out of character. It was another example of Darrow's willingness to sacrifice his principles, including civil liberties, for a larger goal. Some challenged him. Daniel Kiefer of Cincinnati and Perceval Gerson of Los Angeles separately wrote long letters demanding that Darrow explain himself. Gerson, a doctor who had treated Darrow while he was in Los Angeles, wept at the change in his friend and was wounded by his blanket condemnation of pacifists. Members of the peace movement attended Darrow's speeches and often tried to shout him down. During a speech in Chicago, an old woman in the front row heckled him as he said: "[T]here's only one thing worthwhile talking about and that's crushing the Kaiser's Prussian military machine." She yelled: "But, Mr. Darrow, what would Jesus do?!" At the third such interruption, he turned to the woman and cried out, "I don't know or care what Jesus would do. I don't give a damn. I'm telling you what I think and will do and what I think we all should do!"[33] Darrow tried to respond to his growing throng of new critics in an open response to Kiefer's letter. Largely he repeated the arguments in his stump speech. Pacifists were German sympathizers, this was a war to make the world safe for democracy and not a capitalist-inspired war, and Germany had to be defeated and punished for its crimes. He did, however, admit that he was wrong about nonresistance. He stood by *Resist Not Evil* and said that he still hated war, but he no longer believed that pacifism was "a general rule of life that would cover every case."[34]

Darrow's unstinting allegiance to the war effort was rewarded late in 1917, when he became one of President Wilson's Four Minute Men, whose job it was to roam around the country—or, in Darrow's case, the Midwest—giving brief pro-war, pro-draft, and pro–Liberty Loan pitches. Creel's CPI coordinated the program, eventually hiring seventy-five thousand Four Minute Men, who gave more than 750,000 speeches. Among the most famous were Hollywood stars Charlie Chaplin (1889–1977), Douglas Fairbanks (1883–1939), Mary Pickford (1892–1979), and Lillian Russell (1861–1922). Creel's men also defended Darrow, publishing pro-Darrow editorials in newspapers, lauding his support for the war and disparaging the socialist and pacifist People's Council as the "dregs of the radical current."[35] For the first time in his life, Darrow began receiving universal praise in the press. His apothegms were found everywhere: "The war will regenerate labor." "Pacifists Are Enemies of the Republic!" "If I wanted to serve the Kaiser, I would move to Germany to be near my boss."[36] Darrow's popularity seemingly was at an all-time high, and in June 1918, Creel sent his all-star pitchman to the European front lines on a goodwill tour designed to gather more fodder for his speeches.

A *New York Times* reporter caught Darrow as he embarked for England. "What will you tell them over there?" he asked. "I shall tell the people over there that while America was very slow in getting into the war there were a great many people here, outside of those who were hereditary friends of the Central Powers or enemies of England, who had always been with the Allies, and who were impatient to get into the war earlier." After that jab at German Americans and Irish Americans, Darrow, displaying temporary amnesia or a total disregard for his position of three years previous, announced that he believed "we should have gone in when Belgium was invaded."[37] As with any of his causes, Darrow had internalized the fight as if his life had depended upon the outcome, and once again the ends justified the means.

For three months, Darrow traveled around England and France, visiting the front lines and meeting with such dignitaries as the British minister of information, Sir William Maxwell Aitken (1879–1964) as well as kindred spirits including H. G. Wells (1866–1946) and Sidney (1859–1947) and Beatrice Webb (1858–1943). The trip seemed to go as planned. Shortly after his arrival, the American Alliance for Labor and Democracy released a statement under Darrow's signature arguing against any mercy. "Peace? . . . The earth is not big enough for peace and Prussian militarism at once."[38] Other roseate dispatches from the front followed.[39] However, upon his arrival back in the United States in October, he was no longer so bully on the war. Perhaps it was witnessing all that death and destruction that turned his stomach and his sentiments. While Darrow had found out that those hideous tales of German atrocities were fabrications, as he had thought, he had also learned that an entire generation of men had died or been maimed fighting for mere miles of territory. By 1918, Austria, essentially defeated, had suffered 2 million casualties. By the time Darrow visited Europe, 1 out of every 5 French soldiers had been killed. Germany had more than 1 million battle deaths. Both the British and the Americans had taken enormous losses as well. In the first day of the Battle of the Somme in July 1916 Britain had suffered 20,000 deaths and 40,000 wounded. In about twelve months, the American Expeditionary Force had lost nearly 120,000 soldiers. Learning about the carnage must have taken its toll on Darrow. Additionally, no doubt while talking with Wells and the Webbs, the subject of the government-sponsored repression of dissenters and radicals must have come up. What did Darrow know? What was he doing for his friends on the left, especially Eugene Debs, who had been arrested the day before Darrow had sailed?

What could he say? He had spent the war as a cog in the propaganda machine. He had helped manufacture consent, not criticism or concern. On the way out the door in Chicago, Darrow had sent Debs a telegram offering assistance if he wanted it. Fuming at the thought of aid from a traitor to the cause, Debs refused to respond. Alone with his thoughts on the chilly Atlantic in October, Darrow began to feel a creeping regret. In his rush to support the Allies against the Central Powers, he had given up too much intellectual ground. Conceding pacifism was not difficult, but the more he thought about President Wilson's suspension of civil liberties during the war and his administration's persecution of dissenters like Debs, the more remorseful he became. When he arrived home at Union Station in Chicago, he was no longer a professional patriot. At first, his rebellion was private and small. In late October 1918, he rebuffed the call for the Fourth Liberty Loan, something unheard of among the class of CPI-sponsored propagandists. When asked to explain himself, he declared, "I could not see the need of asking men who needed their money [since] the war would be over by Christmas." A few of Darrow's war buddies upbraided him for the sentiment.[40] Soon, however, he was to break with his pro-war colleagues in a far more public way over the issue of civil liberties. Upon his return, he never again allowed his passions to override his commitment to civil liberties. Rather, he became a champion of individual rights to speak, think, and join. Darrow made his stand on free speech, a notion at the very core of his and America's political philosophy.

Although John Adams (1735–1826) and Abraham Lincoln (1809–1865) had hemmed in civil liberties during war, Wilson far surpassed them by systematically and thoroughly utilizing the tools of government to repress dissenters and stifle dissent. Two months after Congress had fulfilled President Wilson's wish and declared war on the Central Powers, it delivered to him an espionage bill designed to outlaw spies and subversive activities by foreigners. Although several Republican lawmakers, including Darrow's erstwhile nemesis William Borah, attempted to restrain the bill's reach, the final version signed by Wilson provided unprecedented powers to punish not only foreign agents but also citizens. Not satisfied with the law, in 1918, Congress heeded the president's advice and strengthened it with a sedition bill to further attack perceived domestic enemy propagandists and an alien bill to deport pro-German foreign nationals.

During the war and afterward, various administration officials, such as Attorney General Thomas W. Gregory (1861–1933), his successor, A. Mitchell Palmer (1872–1936), and Postmaster General Albert S. Burleson (1863–1937), spent much of their time carrying out a draconian crackdown on Americans. Their relentless pursuit of radicals and critics resulted in the arrest and detention of thousands, the imprisonment of more than a thousand, and the deportation of hundreds. Caught in the government's dragnet were the well-known, such as Eugene Debs, Kate Richards O'Hare (1877–1948), Rose Pastor Stokes (1879–1933), and Emma Goldman (1869–1940), and the unknown, like Alexander Bukowetsky, a Russian émigré who was arrested while attending a concert given by the Union of Russian Workers in Detroit and jailed for almost a year without charges.[41] Postmaster Burleson put nearly two dozen publications out of business during the war, including Max Eastman's (1883–1969) *The Masses*, Victor L. Berger's *The Milwaukee Leader*, and the *International Socialist Review*, run by Darrow's friend Algie M. Simons. Furthermore, government officials at all levels tolerated and sometimes endorsed extralegal attacks upon those suspected as disloyal. The American Protective League (APL) was by far the largest and most zealous, claiming more than one hundred thousand members in six hundred cities. Vigilante groups were responsible for countless acts of harassment and several murders. For example, in September 1917, APL deputies conducted a massive raid all around New York City that garnered more than twenty thousand "slackers"—that is, men who had not yet signed up for the draft. Such lawless activities often turned violent or worse. Shortly after sundown on April 5, 1918, a Collinsville, Illinois, mob with official sanction from the mayor and police abducted and lynched Robert Prager, a German American coal miner, in the belief that he was a spy. In various places, especially the Southwest and Northeast, where the Industrial Workers of the World were active, private and public enforcers attacked, arrested, and in some cases killed those who did not toe the line.

Clarence Darrow should have been apoplectic at the wholesale disregard for constitutional rights, but he was not. As he explained later, "believing as I did in this war, [the violations were] just and necessary." It was all part of the nation's defense. Again, it was in Darrow's makeup to give up one cherished view to protect a different one.[42] Thus, this was a significant reversal of thought. In 1901, for instance, Darrow had sharply criticized the federal and state governments that in the wake of the assassination of President McKinley passed antianarchist laws. Darrow's wartime position, however, was not absolute. Quietly, he helped friends and acquaintances in Chicago who were in trouble with the Justice Department. He also went to Washington, D.C., as part of a delegation to speak with Postmaster General Burleson about his censorship of socialist magazines and newspapers.[43] The junket was fruitless. Aside from these minor exceptions, from the declaration of war in 1917 to the fall of 1918 Darrow avoided any public engagement in the controversies surrounding wartime civil liberties. To him, backing President Wilson's prosecution of the war meant holding in abeyance his revulsion at the overreaching power of the wartime state as well as at vigilante groups that attacked those who dared criticize or organize against the war.

When Tom Mooney (1882–1942) and Warren Billings (1893–1972) were framed for bombing the San Francisco Preparedness Day parade in 1916, Darrow was conspicuously absent from the case. The arrest and death sentence for the Wobblies' bard Joe Hill (1879?–1915) did not move him. While he did agree to help Emma Goldman with her appeal to the U.S. Supreme Court challenging her conviction for interfering with the draft, he asked her attorney, Harry Weinberger (1885–1944), to keep his name off the brief.[44] Incredible mass mistreatment of unionists such as the Bisbee deportations of July 1917—when an army of sheriff's deputies and vigilantes forcibly deported more than one thousand striking miners from Bisbee, Arizona, and deposited them in bullpens in New Mexico—drew no response from Darrow. Significantly, he was not a member of the heralded twelve lawyers whose open letter to the American people contributed to the end of the legal and extralegal repression of Americans.[45]

Once the Great War was over, Clarence Darrow returned to form. Quite publicly he charged that the continued persecution of radicals and dissenters was illegitimate, as these "high-minded, conscientious people had committed no real wrong" and had not received fair trials. Now that the United States was no longer at war, what was to be done? Darrow forcefully argued in defense of civil liberties and free speech, and he boldly claimed that "the prison doors should now be opened!"[46] Also, the Espionage Act, which he deemed unconstitutional, should be repealed. Given that neither happened, Darrow did what he knew: he went back to work as America's foremost lawyer for freedom and liberty. His first order of business was to join the legal defense of the 106 Wobblies arrested in Chicago, charged with violating the Espionage and Sedition acts.

Since its inception in 1905, the Industrial Workers of the World (IWW, or Wobblies) had been subjected to vigilante attacks and government repression, but during the war these assaults had increased in number and intensity. For instance, in addition to Joe Hill's 1915 state murder, on August 1,

1917, Wobbly organizer Frank H. Little (1879–1917) was abducted in the middle of the night and hanged from a Milwaukee Road railroad trestle. President Wilson and nearly all wartime patriots viewed the IWW as a treasonous organization with tremendous potential to disrupt the war effort. To them, IWW stood for "Imperial Wilhelm's Warriors" and the organization was funded with "German gold."[47] They did all they could to eradicate it. After a summer of harassing Wobblies in the West and Southwest, on September 29, 1917, U.S. Department of Justice agents conducted a nationwide raid that resulted in the arrest of more than 160 Wobblies, including Big Bill Haywood, Elizabeth Gurley Flynn (1890–1964), Joseph J. Ettor (1886–1948), Carlo Tresca (1879–1943), and Vincent St. John (1876–1929), for conspiracy and violating the Espionage and Selective Service acts. Immediately, Haywood sent for Darrow. Publicly, Darrow turned them down, citing his war work.[48] However, he offered George F. Vanderveer (1875–1942), the Wobblies' own "counsel for the damned," the use of his top-notch investigative staff.[49] Then, behind the scenes, Darrow and Roger N. Baldwin (1884–1981), of the newly formed National Civil Liberties Union (eventually renamed the American Civil Liberties Union), worked for their release. According to historian Philip Taft, Darrow had George Creel make an intercession with President Wilson, who offered a deal: all charges would be dropped if the IWW would accept the deal without public outcry.[50] Haywood and the other Wobbly leaders turned the offer down. As Vanderveer put it, these "publicity opportunities . . . may never return."[51]

The show trials went on without Darrow. In Chicago, the federal government tried more than a hundred IWW members. Prosecutors produced the flimsiest evidence: letters, editorials, and minute books to show that the entire organization was disloyal and engaged in sabotage. Vanderveer was able to demonstrate that the Wobblies had not been responsible for the 1917 strike wave. Only 3 of the 521 work stoppages between April and September had involved IWW locals. Moreover, several employers and government officials, such as Mayor Wallace M. Short (1866–1953) of Sioux City, Iowa, testified that Wobblies had been exceptional workers in the factories, fields, and docks. It did not matter. After five months of testimony, the jury returned guilty verdicts for all in less than one hour. The defendants were given sentences ranging from five to twenty years in prison. Haywood received the maximum. In late 1919, a rejuvenated Darrow, who had rededicated himself to civil liberties but not the labor movement, joined Vanderveer for the appeal and helped arrange the $274,000 bail ($3.5 million in today's dollars) for thirty-six other Wobbly leaders.[52] Haywood's bail alone was $15,000 ($185,000 in today's dollars). Darrow put up $1,000 of his own money.[53] In 1920, the U.S. circuit court of appeals upheld the convictions. Not wanting to serve his twenty years at Leavenworth Penitentiary, Haywood fled the United States and ended up in the Soviet Union, where he spent his remaining days.

It was clear to those who were watching that Darrow was no longer an uncritical supporter of the Wilson administration. Rather, he had come to see it as yet another example of the strong brutalizing the weak and of the powerful preying on the freedoms of the average individual. Both the Bureau of Investigation (forerunner to the Federal Bureau of Investigation), run by William J. Flynn (1867–1928), and the Military Intelligence Division took note of Darrow's activities on behalf of the IWW. As one field operative noted in a letter to Flynn's redoubtable assistant J. Edgar Hoover (1895–1972), Darrow was no longer friendly to the bureau, but rather a "Radical Socialist" bent on securing the release of dangerous agitators.[54] Although the government informer got Darrow's politics wrong, he did grasp his plan. Darrow indeed wanted all the war prisoners released. No American, no matter his or her station in life, should ever be imprisoned for his or her thoughts or words or political associations.

It is unclear if Darrow knew or cared that he had fallen out of favor with the Justice Department. Regardless, he spent much of 1920 working for the release of jailed Communists. His defense centered on civil liberties. His first case was that of Benjamin Gitlow (1891–1965). The American-born son of Russian-Jewish immigrants, Gitlow joined the Socialist Party at eighteen. Always a radical, he was enamored with and inspired by the November 1917 Russian Revolution. In June 1919, he joined other revolutionary socialists, such as Louis Fraina (1892–1953), William Bross Lloyd (1875–1946), and John Reed, at a convention of the Left Wing Section of the Socialist Party, which generated what became a touchstone document for the Communist movement in the United States: *Manifesto and Program of the Left Wing Section Socialist Party, Local Greater New York*, later published in Reed's and Gitlow's newspaper *The Revolutionary Age*. The leadership of the Socialist Party was not impressed, and in late summer 1919 Reed and

Gitlow abandoned their plans to take over the party. Instead, in Chicago in September 1919, they helped launch the Communist Labor Party (CLP), one of two main American Communist parties.

Back in New York City in November, Gitlow and the other CLP members organized citywide celebrations for the second anniversary of the Russian Revolution. Fearing that the radicals were orchestrating the beginnings of an American Communist revolution, local, state, and federal police arrested thousands, including Gitlow, for violating the state's criminal anarchy law, thus putting to a quick end any political moment Gitlow and his comrades sought. New York's 1902 Criminal Anarchy Act was an outdated statute until State Senator Clayton R. Lusk (1872–1959), head of the Joint Committee to Investigate Seditious Activities (aka the Lusk Committee), dusted it off to persecute Communists.

Gitlow was the first to come to trial. His alleged violation was the publication of the *Left Wing Manifesto* in his newspaper. His lawyers, Charles Recht (1887–1965) and Walter Nelles (1883–1937), tried to get the case dismissed, arguing that Gitlow was not an anarchist, the *Left Wing Manifesto* did not advocate violent overthrow of government, and in any case there was no proof that Gitlow advocated that position. Judge William McAdoo (1853–1930) quashed the motion and set bail at $15,000 ($190,000 in today's dollars) in cash or Liberty bonds. By the time Gitlow stood for trial on January 20, 1920, Darrow had joined the legal team at the request of Nelles. The trial was expeditious. Assistant District Attorney Alexander I. Rorke (1877–1967) sought to convince the jurors of Gitlow's guilt by walking them through the *Left Wing Manifesto*, and Darrow called no witnesses. Rather, at the request of Gitlow, he arranged for his client to address the jury directly. Gitlow wanted to defend himself on the "right of revolution."[55] Darrow had argued against the strategy but in the end acceded to his client's wishes. "Well," he quipped, "I suppose a revolutionist must have his say in court even if it kills him."[56]

Though Judge Bartow S. Weeks (1861–1922) continually interrupted Gitlow's statement, the message came across. In what became known as the Red Ruby address, Gitlow explained that capitalism was on the verge of destruction and that it would be replaced by a new dictatorship of the proletariat based on the principles of revolutionary socialism. "I would be false to myself if I tried to evade that which I support," he told the jury.

"Regardless of your verdict, I maintain that the principles of the Left Wing Manifesto and Program on the whole are correct, that capitalism is in a state of collapse, that capitalism has brought untold misery and hardship to the working man, and that thousands of men in this democratic republic are in jails today on account of their views, suffering tortures and abuses." He asked only that the jury read the manifesto and decide for itself. After Gitlow's hour-long oration, Darrow presented his closing statement. Revolution, he said, was as American as apple pie. "For a man to be afraid of revolution in America would be to be ashamed of your own mother." Sure, the new nation that Gitlow described would come with "birth pains," but Darrow explained all such movements did, from those inspired by Christ to the abolitionist movement of John Brown. Instead of casting their lot with a small band of tyrants, like Attorney General Palmer and "his night-riders," Darrow called on the jury to side with Washington, Jefferson, and Lincoln, who upheld the revolutionary tradition. Then he reminded the jurors that there was such a thing as freedom of speech and the press in America. He was confident that "this jury shall not drive a spike" into those freedoms, which had been "the bulwark of our liberties."[57]

The jury disregarded Darrow, ignored Gitlow, and drove that spike into civil liberties. The defeat stung, especially after the U.S. Supreme Court upheld the conviction in 1925. Justices Oliver Wendell Holmes, Jr. (1841–1935), and Louis Brandeis (1856–1941) provided a dissent that eventually helped establish a doctrine that the Bill of Rights and the Fourteenth Amendment apply equally in all states. That, however, did not help Darrow in the defense of his next two Communist cases.[58]

Like Gitlow, Arthur Person had been arrested in the antiradical dragnets of late 1919. Born in Sweden around 1885, he immigrated to the United States in 1900 and had worked in Rockford, Illinois, in various factories. He and his wife had been socialists and moved into the Rockford branch of the Communist Labor Party in late 1919. Police had raided his home when he was arrested, gathering evidence that he had violated Illinois's antianarchist law. Darrow jumped at the chance to defend the man and employed the defense strategy he had originally planned for Gitlow. In the previous case, Darrow had wanted to hush "the implications of the subversive things" Gitlow had said but was not allowed to.[59] In the Person case, he did just this. Once again, the centerpiece of the prosecution was the *Left Wing Manifesto*.

Darrow stripped the document of its radicalness. Revolution? Conquest? Mass action? Capture? Proletariat? Dictatorship? The collapse of civilization? These were not words to fear. They implied change and not necessarily violence. "The word 'revolution' is used in connection with everything," he explained. A serious change in religious thought, for example. So, if the flimsy evidence, which also included the Rockford CLP's meeting minutes book, did not indicate any crime, what were the prosecutors doing? They were the henchmen of the rich in a plot to "strangle free thought and free speech and the right of man to live." Why? So that they could pursue without criticism their quest to be "profiteers and get their gold."[60]

Person was not a dangerous person. He had no formal education and had followed the family doctor into the CLP as one might take the advice of a dentist or lawyer. Furthermore, Darrow implored the jury to think past its prejudices and recognize that America was a mixture of religious and political creeds. As he told the jury, he would always side with the dreamers because some of those dreams, such as the single tax or railroad regulation, were meaningful and significant, even if initially they were seen as radical. Voting to convict Person for "the crime of idealism" would destroy not only the dream and the dreamer and his civil liberties but also a chance to "liberate the human race." Should they do that, Darrow concluded, "you should hang this court house in crepe and drape your city hall with black and wear sackcloth and ashes until his term expires."[61] This time Darrow's instincts were golden; the jury voted to acquit Person.

His final Communist trial ended in disappointment. For the last two weeks in July 1920, Darrow helped defend twenty men, including William Bross Lloyd, the son of his deceased friend Henry Demarest Lloyd. The younger Lloyd, universally known as the "millionaire socialist," was close to nearly all important figures in the American radical movements, from John Reed and Big Bill Haywood to the up-and-coming Annie Clemenc, and funded their activities and often paid for their legal expenses. His mansion was a refuge, where they went to recuperate and plot revolution. Lloyd, the sergeant-at-arms of the new Communist Labor Party, was proudly arrested in November 1919 for violating the Illinois antianarchist law. The trial was notable in that Lloyd had nineteen codefendants. Other than that, it was a repeat of Gitlow and Person.

Again, the *Left Wing Manifesto* and related CLP documents played a central role. As in the Gitlow case, Darrow downplayed the evidence. As in his defense of Person, he stressed the ominous forces behind these trials, that "gang of profiteers who would strangle freedom that they might get rich, who would traffic in the blood of men, [and] who have determined that in this country no voice of criticism should be raised against them."[62] He called on the jury to give these political dissenters their chance to promote positions and decide the case on facts, not fear. Darrow's defense was an amalgam of the two previous cases, except on one point. During the trial, Marvin E. Barnhardt, the state's assistant prosecuting attorney, asked how could it be that Darrow, the wartime superpatriot, now defended these men who had opposed the war and called for the end of the democratic republic. Goaded into defending himself, in his closing statement Darrow tried his best to explain. He had taken the case firstly because "I have never turned my back upon any defendant no matter what the charge, for when the cry is the loudest the defendant needs the lawyer the worst; I can not only be his lawyer, but his friend, and I have done that." Then, surprisingly, he added, had he known that "here in America a gang of unpatriotic money grubbers would pass in twenty states a statute like this," which threatened to silence every human voice while "fettering the American people, if I had believed that that would flow from this war, perhaps I would not have believed we should have gone into it." Finally, he warned the jury that if it voted for conviction that it would destroy civil liberties and essentially "make us a nation of slaves, and I shall love it no more."[63] There it was: regret and disillusionment about what he had done (and not done) and about the direction of the nation. During the war he had joined the wrong side and through his actions added to its power. He had done it for just cause, according to him. The defeat of German imperialism was more important than his previously held beliefs in pacifism and nonresistance as well as in civil liberties. But he had gone too far for war, as the Wilson administration had. His frustrating efforts to bring back civil liberties made him glum. And Darrow was indeed all the more forlorn when the jury in the case against Lloyd and his comrades returned guilty verdicts on all counts.

Truthfully, Darrow's spirits had been sagging for some time. Before he had left for Europe in 1918, 140 of his friends had thrown him a sixty-first birthday party. A newspaper reporter recorded the highlights, such as the Reverend Walter MacPherson's telling the crowd that he would rather go to hell with Clarence Darrow than heaven with the Reverend Billy Sunday (1862–1935). And Dr. G. Frank Lydston roasted Darrow a bit, recounting a story of a witness whom Darrow pressed to describe the size of a rock he had got hit with. The witness replied it was "as long as your head but not as thick." The laughter died away as Darrow began his birthday greetings. As the reporter explained, Darrow's speech about life at sixty-one seemed to provide "many good arguments for suicide." He wrote: "In a low keyed musical voice, Mr. Darrow dwelt on the melancholy of existence, its cruelty, boredom and banality." At the end of the First World War, he was firmly convinced that life was not worth living. Moreover, Darrow was tired of the "life of war" that he had lived.[64] The combat he had seen had shaped him. In the pivotal years of the 1910s, through the battlefields of Los Angeles and of France, he had been wounded, but those experiences compelled him to distill his political beliefs from a wide-ranging and often contradictory set of convictions and commitments to a handful of dearly held political causes. In some ways, Darrow had never changed; he always backed the underdog snared in the traps laid by the privileged. After the war, however, he concentrated on aiding these unfortunate individuals, not movements, and using these cases to make larger political statements in the cause of advancing American democracy by expanding rights, liberties, and freedoms.

❊ 9 ❊

The Old Lion Still Hunts

On the first Thursday of March 1921, Clarence Darrow read the news he had been dreading for five months. The morning papers heralded the inauguration of Warren Gamaliel Harding (1865–1923) as the twenty-ninth president of the United States. Anger, then disgust welled within him. The conservative swing in national politics made him dyspeptic. He had thrown his weight squarely behind the Democratic candidate, James B. Cox (1870–1957). On the campaign trail, Darrow had called Harding a tool of capitalists and an enemy of workers. He offered strong praise for Woodrow Wilson, especially his postwar proposals for a lasting peace and a League of Nations, and commended Cox for taking up his mantle.[1] None of it had mattered. Afterward, much to the chagrin of his political friends and allies, Darrow did not join the challenges to the new administration. Rather, in still another change in political direction, Darrow turned away from left-wing activism and toward the defense of civil liberties and civil rights.

The break with the progressives was most decisive, as he came to disagree with much of their postwar agenda as antithetical or at least not central to the promotion of peace, liberty, and freedom. After the 1920 election, Darrow became an opponent of the League of Nations, joining a chorus of naysayers, some of whom he could not even stand, such as Republican Senator William Borah. Darrow believed that the League's Covenant was too weak to foster peace and understanding in the world.[2] He was equally skeptical of the League's Permanent Court of International Justice (aka the World Court), urging the United States to steer clear of that entangling tribunal, which he viewed as not a court at all, but rather as a potential source of future wars.[3]

He also parted ways with the reformers over several other key controversies of the day. It surprised no one that Darrow was a "wet." He had been speaking against prohibition for decades, often to hostile crowds.[4] A temperate drinker himself, he nevertheless hated the Eighteenth Amendment (1919) and its concomitant Volstead Act (1921).[5] The laws were "foolish and brutal."[6] "I am opposed to it," he wrote in 1928, "because I am opposed to interference of people with individual conduct. . . . Freedom is a hard thing to preserve." So he was fighting against prohibition in order to "preserve liberty" and stand in opposition to those who always were "trying to more and more control the conduct of [their] fellows."[7] Their efforts constituted an outrageous attack on civil liberties that soaked up valuable political energy, which could have been applied to social reforms that might have made a difference and created more freedom and happiness. Darrow declared that prohibitionists were nothing more than the intellectual descendants of those fanatics who had led the Spanish Inquisition and later burned witches in New England. Any ideas toward enforcement were "folly." Prohibition was "a tragedy and a hoax" that hurt civilization more than helped it.[8]

Darrow's revulsion at the Eighteenth Amendment was only slightly more public than his criticisms of the amendment that followed. In the 1880s and 1890s Darrow had been a vocal advocate of women's suffrage as well as equality between the sexes. He had also backed free love and easy divorces. But by the time of the passage of the Nineteenth Amendment (1920), which removed major gender handicaps in politics, he had reconsidered. Why did Darrow reverse course? Was it that he was growing into a grumpy old man? Certainly, he was a curmudgeon. And certainly, he was aging with ill grace and worse health. Poor hygiene habits had led to brittle teeth and bad gums. Rheumatism, neuralgia, and breathing problems from decades of smoking made daily activities a chore, if not painful. Further, his bouts of depression had become longer and deeper, at times so bad, he said, as to "raise the dead within me."[9] On top of that, he no longer seemed to like women, particularly feminists. Mary Field blamed Ruby for that. "Against the collective woman he rages as he would like to against the little pissant wife whose pettiness and jealousies have galled him for years," she once quipped.[10] Darrow's own words suggest that he disliked the intrusion of women into arenas formerly dominated by men, such as politics and the law, as well as into manly hangouts, such as barbershops, bars, and polling stations. He even claimed to believe that women did not belong on juries or even should not be lawyers and said so publicly.[11] Yet despite his now well-deserved reputation as a stodgy old man, he maintained his support for liberal divorce laws and procedures, continually mocked the Christian fundamentalist view of women (and snakes), and was often quite charitable to individual women who sought out his aid.[12]

Old age, bad health, and misogyny thus discounted, what then accounts for Darrow's disapproval of the Nineteenth Amendment? It was his pessimism about political movements that pushed him away from this democratic reform. He doubted that widening the polity would have any effect on politics for average Americans. In this, his view was similar to that of many anarchists, who saw voting as a sop for discontent.[13] Voters had let him down too many times. Providing women with suffrage rights did nothing to change what he saw as a fundamental truth about the working-class electorate: it often voted against its own interests. Adding more traffic at the polls did little to nothing, as the election of Harding proved. Furthermore, the electorate often acted in ways that were detrimental to civil rights and civil liberties. The Eighteenth Amendment, for instance, was put into the U.S. Constitution because voters and lobbying groups such as the Women's Christian Temperance Union pressured politicians, who acquiesced, some readily and some not.

It was that same pessimistic realization about political movements that encouraged Darrow also to back away from his support of the labor movement. For decades, when mentioning his name, newspaper reporters always included "noted labor lawyer" as an appositive. But after the three Communist trials, he shied away from the label that had followed him since the Pullman strike in 1894. As he wrote to his friend H. L. Mencken (1880–1956), he no longer wanted to be known as a "labor lawyer" but as just "a lawyer."[14] He still had sympathies for the working class and its leaders, such as Sidney Hillman.[15] When the occasion arose, he spoke on their behalf and continued to take various cases from unions. In Chicago, for example, he represented the union-run Master Cleaners' Association in its bloody battle with nonunion dry cleaners. Moreover, he lobbied Presidents Wilson and Harding for the release of Eugene Debs (who was quite appreciative of it),[16] and he spoke publicly about the moral imperative to free all wartime political prisoners.[17] But he took on no more big labor cases; he did not take up their cause. In his view, they were not consequential in the promotion of freedom and liberty. Darrow tried to remain friends with Debs and others like Allan L. Benson (1871–1940), who had run for president on the Socialist ticket in 1916.[18] Yet his politics became more mainstream. Darrow voted for the Democratic presidential candidates throughout the 1920s, brushing aside the appeal of such politicians as Wisconsin Senator Robert M. La Follette (1855–1925), whom Darrow personally liked. But when La Follette ran for president on the Progressive ticket in 1924, Darrow cast his ballot for conservative Democrat John W. Davis (1873–1955). Debs chastised Darrow for supporting that "tool of Wall Street" and declared his former friend "unworthy to ever again be trusted by the people."[19]

Darrow was no Wall Street stooge. He was an avowed pessimist, especially about politics and various social movements. Yet he still held on to his longtime goals of expanding and defending liberty and freedom, both of which he continued to believe were at risk.[20] "America seems to have an epidemic of intolerance," he wrote in an article about "our growing tyranny" for *Vanity Fair*.[21] Darrow was still called to fight for Americans even though he maintained that they were morally weak and often refused to stand up for what was right and to oppose what was wrong.[22] Significantly, now in the 1920s, the grouchy old lawyer sought a change of venue. He was still dedicated to smashing those structures, forces, and individuals that tried to oppress and condemn the weak and poor, but his particular causes had changed. The Old Lion, as he came to be known, still hunted, but his prey were now the enemies of civil liberties and civil rights: the blind advocates of capital punishment, religious zealots, and race bigots. Darrow was no longer organized labor's champion. Rather, he was more interested in helping not social movements but individuals who were being trampled on by larger, more powerful social and political forces that sought to control their minds, to dictate where and how they lived and if they lived at all. Just as Darrow had regarded the robber barons of an earlier age, so he saw these three groups as foes to his cherished, distilled beliefs about civil rights and civil liberties and worthy opponents that he wished to vanquish.[23] His three biggest cases of the 1920s rested squarely on these issues.

Early Sunday morning, June 1, 1924, the Darrows were comfortably resting in bed. Clarence was sleeping soundly. The weather had finally improved. After a few gray, cold midwestern May days, small evening showers were the harbingers of clearer, drier, and warmer days ahead. All that boded well; the changed weather meant he would be breathing and moving more easily. The morning peace was broken by the din of the doorbell. Clarence did not move; he never did at the sound of the door. Ruby waited for a second bell before getting up to answer it. At the door she was surprised to see not one but four well-dressed men. She recognized the first, who pushed by her, demanding to see her husband. It was Jacob Loeb, the former school board president. She guessed the men behind him were relatives and lawyers, perhaps both. Always protective of Clarence, Ruby asked that they come back later. Loeb said that there was no time to waste; he had to speak with Darrow immediately. Before Ruby could argue, the old attorney shuffled into the foyer, hair a mess, robe haphazardly draped.

Although still groggy from sleep, Darrow quickly pieced together what was happening in his apartment. Like everyone else in the world, Darrow had followed the story of young Robert Franks, a neighbor boy in Darrow's Hyde Park suburb, who had been kidnapped and sadistically murdered ten days earlier. He knew that Richard, the son of Jacob Loeb's brother, Albert—a vice president at Sears, Roebuck, and Company—had been questioned by the police, along with his friend Nathan Leopold. Having Richard's uncle standing in front of him, Darrow surmised only one thing: the district attorney had filed charges. Loeb explained that the situation was worse than that. Both boys had confessed and were likely to hang. Darrow glanced at Ruby. He wasn't asking for her permission. Despite feeling "weary," they both knew he'd take the case.[24] He had opposed the death penalty on principle and in particular since the 1880s. It was the cruelest, most torturous instance of the state's depriving someone of his or her freedom and liberty. He was compelled to take the case. Also, they needed the money. Their debts ran into the tens of thousands of dollars, and these were paying clients with lots of money. They would also not have to travel. He consented, and the men left quickly.

The next day Darrow went downtown to see the boys. It seemed incredible that these two darlings of Chicago's upper crust could have committed what newspaper reporters were calling yet another "Crime of the Century."[25] As he walked the half mile directly north of his law office to the Cook County Jail, he became lost in thought. He wanted to do right by these boys, not so much because of who they were but because they faced the worst fate, state-sanctioned killing. In his forty-seven years as a lawyer, he had defended 102 clients who faced execution. He had failed to save only one, Gene Prendergast, his first case. His revulsion against capital punishment stemmed from his devotion to civil liberties and was a cornerstone for his call for a new way of understanding crime and criminals. In 1922, Darrow had published *Crime: Its Cause and Treatment*, which contained all his thoughts on the subject. The book was quite reminiscent of Altgeld's *Our Penal Machinery*. Darrow emphasized that the nation's legal and penal systems amplified suffering and did not reduce it. Instead of dividing society into law abiders and lawbreakers, he wanted the legal system to recognize that individuals had no free will. Either because they inherited a damaged brain or endocrine system or, much more likely, because they were raised and lived in an impoverished environment, they were compelled to carry out "antisocial" acts. Rather than hurt or kill them, Darrow called for psychological and medical treatments and the economic advancement of the working class. This hopeful pessimist wrote that only with "intelligence, kindliness, tolerance and a large degree of sympathy and understanding" could society advance. Yet he was not holding his breath either that society in general was decent and generous. Thus, until that utopian day such civil liberties as the prohibition of cruel and unusual punishments had to be defended.[26]

As he arrived at the jail, he realized that this case posed a challenge to some of his theories of criminology. For years, he had maintained that the disease of "crime" was largely an epidemic among the poor, not the rich. Embarrassingly, on several occasions and in print, he also had asserted that kidnapping for ransom "was not a crime" but a "profession."[27] After meeting with his clients, he knew that neither of these rules applied. The boys' economic environment seemingly had little to do with the murder of Bobby Franks. Darrow had to take his own advice and call in expert psychologists (alienists in the lingo of the day) to figure out what had motivated Dickie Loeb and Babe Leopold to kill.

Fortunately for the defense, money was not a problem. If Darrow and Benjamin and Walter Bachrach—the other members of the defense team—needed experts, they could be brought in. Karl Bowman, chief medical officer at the Boston Psychopathic Hospital; William Alanson White, superintendent of St. Elizabeths Hospital for the Insane in Washington, D.C.; and Harold Hulbert, a private neuropsychiatrist, were among the dozen behavioral scientists who interviewed Loeb and Leopold for the defense. They were able to elicit not only what had happened but likely why.

Nathan Leopold and Richard Loeb were born six months apart. At the time of the murder they were nineteen and eighteen respectively. They had spent their lives in the lap of luxury. Their families were among the wealthiest in Chicago, if not the nation. Nathan's father, Nathan, Sr., had made his first fortune in the shipping business and a second as a box manufacturer. Richard's father had also made millions in the business of shuttling goods around the country. After a career as a Chicago lawyer, Albert Loeb had risen quickly at Sears and essentially ran the company as Julius Rosenwald (1862–1932) had pulled back to focus more time on his philanthropic endeavors. While their parents worried about profits, parties, and politics, both boys grew up under the care of governesses. This was where the problems started. Emily Struthers, who looked after Dickie, never physically abused him but was a tyrant. Believing Dickie was destined to be a brilliant man, she pushed him mercilessly. While other neighborhood children played games, Struthers kept Richard confined to his room studying. She prodded him through the Harvard School for Boys. He did well enough to enter the University of Chicago at fourteen. Later he transferred to the University of Michigan, becoming the school's youngest student to attain a baccalaureate degree. He had achieved much, though he displayed little passion. At Michigan, he was only a mediocre student. He learned to hate his books, to hate Struthers, and to hate life. Slowly his animosity searched for an outlet. Beginning with lying about his schoolwork and his grades, Dickie graduated to stealing and hiding secret sins, which at first were venial, not cardinal, such as reading detective stories. Soon, however, his acts of rebellion took on a far darker character.

Nathan had a similar but in many ways more pathological story. Unbeknownst to his parents, his governess, Mathilda "Sweetie" Wantz, was a sexual predator who had abused him since he was twelve. Sadly, Nathan was not the only young Leopold whom she attacked. Nathan took refuge in his books. He was extraordinarily bright, especially gifted in languages and ornithology. Unsurprisingly, it was hard for him to make friends his age. He was short, diffident, and melancholy. Like Richard, he had gone to the Harvard School for Boys and done very well; he later became the youngest graduate of the University of Chicago.

The two misfits met after their first year at college. They became fast friends, lovers, and partners in crime, forging an obsessive relationship based on lies, deception, and destruction. They were codependent, caught up in each other's twisted inner lives. Inspired by the pulp fiction he read, Dickie loved to imagine himself a jailed master criminal who was continually whipped, beaten, and abused by guards. Nathan had similar sadomasochistic dreams. Influenced by Friedrich Nietzsche's (1844–1900) concept of the superman, Nathan reveled in the delusion of being a powerful, loyal slave who did the bidding of a benevolent king. Together the boys acted out their fantasies by plotting and perpetrating various crimes, including a spate of arsons, incidents of vandalism, and petty thefts. After committing a robbery in November 1923 on the University of Michigan campus, the two changed their modus operandi.

Dickie had become preoccupied with the idea of the perfect crime. On the way home from Ann Arbor, the two discussed what that might be. They quickly agreed that it had to involve kidnapping, ransom, and murder, as all the great crime stories did. The murder, they reasoned, was necessary; how else could they escape without being identified? The next question was, who? Dickie suggested, apparently in jest, his brother Tommy. Too great a likelihood of getting caught. Maybe Hamlin Buchman, who had spread rumors of their homosexual relationship? The problem was that Buchman was strong. They needed a weaker victim who could be easily overpowered. Eventually they set aside whom to kill to work out other logistical issues. By spring 1924 they were ready. On May 21, Nathan, posing as an out-of-town businessman, Morton Ballard, rented a fancy automobile and picked up Richard. In the afternoon, they trolled their Hyde Park neighborhood for the perfect victim. They first found Johnny Levinson, a student at the Harvard preparatory school, but he refused to get into the car, and there were too many people around to snatch him. Another boy came into view: Armand Deutsch. Richard put the kibosh on the idea: he was the grandson of Julius

Rosenwald. His father could lose his job! Driving for a few hours more, they finally swept down Ellis Avenue and came upon Bobby Franks. He fitted the bill. He was small and scrawny. His father was a rich businessman. Jacob Franks had made his money in the pawn business as well as local Democratic politics. Nathan pulled over, and Dickie, who was Bobby's cousin, beckoned him in. At first, the boy begged them off. He was only two blocks to his house. But finally he agreed. Dickie lived just across the street anyway. What harm could there be?

Bobby got in the front passenger seat of the green Willys-Knight. Moments later Dickie grabbed the chisel he had brought for the purpose and beat Bobby over the head. He then dragged the stunned, moaning boy over the front seat into the back. After stuffing his mouth with a cloth and taping it shut, Dickie watched as the life left his body. Slowly they drove to where they planned to dump the body, even stopping for dinner. Once refreshed, they drove to a remote field on the Illinois-Indiana border where Nathan often went bird-watching. They stripped the body, poured acid on the face and genitals, and stuffed Bobby in a drainage culvert. They then made their way back home, called the Frankses, and announced that they had Bobby alive and well. Bobby's parents were told to await further instructions about the ransom. But by the time they contacted the Frankses again, Bobby's body had been found, and their plans quickly unraveled.

The police were initially baffled. There had been so many kidnappings, killings, and mutilations already that year. As Darrow predicted, prohibition had given rise to gangs and relentless violence. Chicago in the 1920s was, in the words of one historian, "the slaughterhouse of America."[28] The Franks abduction and execution were just one more to investigate. Making matters difficult was the lack of eyewitnesses and evidence, except for a pair of eyeglasses found at the crime scene. The police initially assumed they were Bobby's, but diligent detective work traced those tortoiseshell spectacles back to Nathan Leopold, Jr., who had dropped them while disposing of the body. This evidence along with the boys' shoddy alibis raised the suspicions of Robert E. Crowe (1879–1958), the formidable and dashing state's attorney for Cook County. Within a few days he had their confessions and what he termed a "hanging case."[29] All Crowe needed was to solidify the links between the boys and the evidence and gather his own psychological assessments showing that they were immoral but sane. The case seemed airtight, and already Crowe could feel the glow of an approving public that would reward him with higher office.

Once Darrow had the whole story courtesy of his alienists and realized Crowe's plans, he devised a bold legal strategy to save the boys' lives. "Fighting Bob" Crowe was no fool. Darrow and the dogged prosecutor had clashed before. In 1923, they had battled during the corruption trial of Fred Lundin (1868–1947), a Republican party boss and one of Crowe's political rivals. Darrow's defense had been masterful; he had trounced Crowe, who now in 1924 savored the opportunity to return the favor. But Darrow was already two steps ahead of him.

With Judge John R. Caverly (1861–1939) presiding, the trial was set to begin on July 21. The morning was set aside for motions, and Darrow indeed had some business. "We know, your honor," Darrow conceded, "the facts in this case are substantially as they have been published in the newspapers and what purports to be their confession, and we can see we have no duty to the defendants, or their families, or society, except to see that they are safely and permanently excluded from the public." Crowe perked up, fearing Darrow's next words. "After long reflection and thorough discussion . . . we have determined to make a motion in this court for each of the defendants in each of the cases to withdraw our plea of not guilty and enter a plea of guilty [to kidnapping and murder]."[30] Crowe bolted straight up, yelling his objection, but to no avail. The Old Lion had outflanked him. Taking a play out of the McNamaras' defense, Darrow had reset the chessboard. Crowe's strongest position came only if he had a jury to convince that the lives of Loeb and Leopold had been forfeited the moment that they had captured Bobby Franks. With the entering of new pleas, Crowe and Darrow were on a more level ground, fighting only to win the sympathy of one judge, not twelve jurors. Darrow knew that Illinois law provided a mitigation hearing in a death penalty case. And if the defense demonstrated that Loeb and Leopold were mentally ill, Judge Caverly could choose life in prison rather than execution.

On July 23, the Loeb and Leopold mitigation hearing began. Lasting a month, the hearing drew thousands to the courthouse. The lucky muscled their ways to the seats inside the sweltering and stuffy courtroom. Although no longer spry, Darrow held up just fine, though he perspired mightily. Crowe boiled too, but often more at the defense. Loeb's and Leopold's lawyers seemed to have the upper hand with Judge Caverly. Crowe essentially pursued his pretrial plan: connect the murderers to the murder and use scientific testimony to demonstrate their sanity. Fighting Bob called eighty-two witnesses. Darrow left most, like Bobby's mother and father, untouched. Tackling the alienists' testimony was another matter. For weeks Judge Caverly presided over dueling psychiatric interpretations of the homicidal duo. Both sides seemed to struggle to demonstrate their points. Darrow's scientists were not able to show conclusively that a malfunctioning endocrine system in either boy had compelled them to commit the killing. But Crowe's experts, who maintained that the two suffered no mental illness, were far less polished, and Darrow scored points by revealing the superficial nature of their examinations. Darrow worked feverishly, and with Crowe gaining back the ground he had lost in the pretrial motions, Darrow knew that the lives of the defendants came down to his closing statement.

The afternoon heat had yet to break when Darrow began before a packed courtroom on August 22. Following the normal opening pleasantries, he launched into an attack on the prosecution and its "cry for blood," which amounted to a slap "in the face of all the better and more humane thought of the age."[31] Crowe and his colleagues were without mercy and compassion. Their blind lust for revenge had driven them to compass the deaths of Dickie Loeb and Babe Leopold, two minors who were "diseased of mind . . . and tender of age."[32] No experts were needed to demonstrate the children's mental illness, Darrow maintained, carefully avoiding a recitation of the conflicting and confusing scientific testimony. What other than mental disease could have explained this "senseless act of immature boys"?[33] Why had they done it? "Not for money; not for spite; not for hate. They killed him as they might kill a spider or fly, for the experience."[34] Or as they themselves had said, for the thrill of it.

Darrow was at a loss to explain their cruelty. It must have been some combination of heredity, environment, education, and wealth. Regardless, he begged the judge not to sentence his clients to death. Doing so would violate "every precedent of the past" as well as state policy "to take care of the young."[35] It was against civil liberties. In defending Loeb and Leopold, Darrow insisted that he was "pleading for life, understanding, charity, kindness, and the infinite mercy that considers all." He was pleading for all children and for the future of our individual rights. If Judge Caverly sentenced them to death, he would be turning to face the barbarous past. Instead, Darrow urged the judge to join him in rejecting capital punishment and rendering a decision that demonstrated that "all life is worth saving."[36]

Crowe knew he was in trouble. On the twenty-fifth, Darrow had left everyone in the courtroom in tears. But the state's attorney had a few surprises up his sleeve. First, he attacked the Old Lion. Echoing the reviews of *Crime: Its Cause and Treatment*, he denounced Darrow's theories of criminology as dangerous.[37] Then he began to poke holes in the defense's reasoning. Both men—not boys—had motive for both crimes. The kidnapping was their way of raising money, and the murder was premeditated and part of their plan to elude justice. Crowe offered an alternative theory to bolster the motive. He claimed that Leopold knew Loeb had committed at least four other heinous crimes, including a castration and another murder, and that Leopold was blackmailing Loeb for sex. This revelation led to the next. Crowe asserted that Bobby Franks had been sexually assaulted, quite likely after he died. Darrow and his cocounsel strenuously objected, but it remained to be seen if Crowe's antics had affected Judge Caverly.

On September 10, 1924, Judge John Caverly handed down the sentences. Darrow knew that the odds were on his side. Since 1840, 90 murderers in the state had been hanged, and only 4 of them had pleaded guilty. And in the previous ten years, out of the 450 killers who confessed to their crimes before sentencing, only 1 had been executed. But the judge's first words about "a crime of singular atrocity" and meeting the court's "responsibilities" made his stomach sink.[38] Citing the defendants' ages, Judge Caverly surprised everyone by handing down life sentences. Darrow had done it; he had saved their lives.

Over the next few weeks it must have been difficult for America's best-known pessimist not to dream optimistically what the Leopold and Loeb fee might mean. He had asked the families for $200,000 ($2.5 million in today's dollars). Finally, he and Ruby could pay off their debts and he could retire from the courtroom. He might even take up writing, lecturing, and debating full-time. The problem was that the money did not appear. After a few bashful inquiries, Darrow was told that the defense would receive no more than $100,000. He was shocked to find out that the Loebs had deducted his retainer ($10,000) and split the check three ways so that each lawyer— Darrow and the Bachrach brothers—would each receive $30,000 ($375,000 in today's dollars). Money be damned, he tried to retire from the law anyway.[39]

He discovered that his notoriety paid handsomely in several ways. He was now able to publish his essays in significant mainstream magazines, such as *Vanity Fair* and, more important, Mencken's *American Mercury*, the most popular and influential periodical of its day.[40] Darrow also drew thousands to his lectures and debates. He particularly loved touring the Midwest and the East Coast, sometimes with Ruby, sometimes without. He relished those solo trips to New York City. They were a chance to visit Mary Field Parton. The two had rekindled their relationship at the start of the Loeb and Leopold trial, when Mary had suddenly appeared in Chicago to cover the case, but she left early after Darrow refused to give her the inside scoop. Nonetheless, they remained friends. Away from Chicago, Mary and Clarence enjoyed unchaperoned nights after his public lectures. A life of leisure suited Darrow just fine. He was a hit everywhere he went. He had finally become a public intellectual, an opinion maker and at times a cynic, who loved to engage and enrage the American public while singling out the foes of liberty and freedom for ridicule and advocating tolerance as well as those ideas that might advance civilization. Nothing riled his audiences and readers more than the great bugaboo of the 1920s: evolution.

As a concept for describing the natural history of the earth, evolution is rooted in the scientific discoveries of the eighteenth century. The growing collections of fossils as well as the development of a chronology for subterranean strata pointed European naturalists to incontrovertible conclusions: the earth was far older than they thought, and it had hosted a wide variety of species, some of which were extinct, some of which endured unaltered, and some of which had changed their form. In other words, the central story of the earth's natural history was change and transmutation. By the 1850s it was increasingly hard to deny the evidence demonstrating evolution, and many intellectuals, even Christians of various kinds, embraced it. In itself, evolution did not reject Christian theology or cosmology. Rather, for many naturalists, theologians, ministers, and interested parishioners God was the agent behind biological change.

Charles Darwin and his two magnum opuses—*On the Origin of Species* (1859) and *The Descent of Man* (1871)—revolutionized the understanding of evolution. He provided a novel and seemingly simple explanation for the succession of species: the extinction of some and the rise of others. The keys were heredity and environment. In any given climate, the animals that survive, procreate, and thrive were the ones that inherited useful and effective characteristics as well as modified variations that gave them an edge to survive. Over time, these biological modifications led to new species. Conversely, animals that failed to adapt disappeared. Natural selection, Darwin concluded, was the mechanism for change. This ignited fierce controversies. Detractors charged that Darwin's claims had no proof, while others added that he had at best made God superfluous and at worse eliminated him altogether.

There were those who readily embraced Darwin. Freethinkers, Marxist socialists, feminists, and other radicals saw evolution and natural selection as means to undermine the privileged elite and their ideologies, whether sacred or secular. Others saw in Darwin's postulates a means to improve human society. Social Darwinists such as Herbert Spencer and eugenicists like Charles B. Davenport (1866–1944) believed that humans were in competition with one another for survival. Whereas the former tended to think that the fittest would rise to the top, the latter argued for selective breeding and sterilization to achieve human perfection. Darwinism's most strident critics came primarily but not exclusively from Roman Catholics and evangelical Protestants. In particular, a new kind of conservative Protestant, fundamentalists, railed against Darwin. Among their heavy hitters was Darrow's erstwhile friend William Jennings Bryan, who was by the 1920s not only advancing the cause of a literal interpretation of the Bible but also leading a crusade against the teaching of Darwin and evolution.

After an ignominious exit from politics at the eve of the Great War, Bryan had found a new life in Miami, Florida, making a fortune in the real estate boom and embracing a rejuvenated evangelical Christianity. He became, as one historian has written, "the most effective spokesman" for creationism and the elimination of the teaching of evolution.[41] In so doing, he also became Clarence Darrow's greatest nemesis. The two had long before broken off their friendship, and they agreed on virtually nothing. Darrow was a wet; Bryan was a dry. Darrow supported civil rights for African Americans; Bryan acquiesced to the Ku Klux Klan's influence on the Democratic Party.[42] To Darrow, Bryan was a threat to modern life. Indeed, Bryan wanted to stamp out modern secularism and its ideological commitments. Subjected to modern scientific ideas, American students, Bryan was convinced, were turning away from Christianity and thus becoming easier prey to a Bolshevik plot to

take over the United States.[43] Further, he blamed Darwin's theory for starting the Great War. Hadn't Germany's leaders acted on the belief that they
were in a struggle for their very existence? Bryan's fame only grew as he crisscrossed the country, expounding the virtues of evangelical Christianity.

Darrow thought Bryan and the entire antievolution movement pernicious
poppycock that had the potential of stifling freedom of inquiry for students,
teachers, and scholars. The Great Commoner had transformed himself into
a pious general in the "war on modern science" that aimed to replace inquiry
with dogma and to crush academic and even religious freedoms.[44] Darrow
endorsed Darwin's theory of evolution. While the first to admit that he was
not an "expert" on the subject, Darrow had read widely on natural history.
Further, by the 1920s he had established himself as the nation's infidel.[45]
Publicly, he claimed that agnosticism was the only honorable position. Did
God exist? Was there an afterlife? There was no proof, and as such, the agnostic "refuses to accept what [he] regards as blind faith."[46] Or, as he said
more frequently, "I am an agnostic . . . because I do not pretend to know
where many ignorant men are sure."[47] Christianity had become "a sop to
keep people satisfied and almost nothing else."[48] Evolution explained the
rise and fall of species, and scientific insights into heredity and environment helped raise questions about fate and the future of human civilization.
Importantly, like William Jennings Bryan, Darrow ascribed to neither Social Darwinism nor eugenics. In fact, he was an outspoken critic of the latter. "Amongst the schemes for remolding society," he wrote, "this is the most
senseless and impudent that has ever been put forward by irresponsible fanatics to plague a long-suffering [human] race."[49]

Despite his faith in the eventual victory of scientific reasoning over religious canon, Darrow worried that Bryan and his minions might succeed in
the short run. As a result, he resolved to challenge Bryan and the antievolutionists every chance he could. When, in late June 1923, Bryan published
an attack on modernists in Darrow's hometown newspaper, the *Chicago
Tribune*, Darrow responded with a front-page salvo of his own. He demanded
that Bryan answer fifty-five questions, such as: How did Noah gather all the
animals on all the continents and acquire enough food and water to preserve them for forty days? If the earth was created less than six thousand
years ago, how could one explain civilizations that flourished more than ten
thousand years ago? If God stopped the sun for Joshua, wouldn't all life on

earth have perished?[50] Bryan refused to dignify Darrow with a response. But within two years the two were screaming at each other in what Bryan saw as an epic contest between evolution and Christianity, "a duel to the death."[51]

Since the early 1920s, fundamentalist organizations, with Bryan in the lead, had been trying to induce state legislatures to pass laws prohibiting the teaching of evolution in public schools. Their first victory came in Tennessee in March 1925, when state representative John W. Butler (1875–1952) authored a bill to prohibit the teaching of "any theory that denies the story of the Divine creation of man as taught in the Bible, and to teach instead that man has descended from a lower order of animals."[52] Almost immediately, the American Civil Liberties Union (ACLU) published advertisements in Tennessee newspapers offering to defend anyone accused of breaking the new law. A group of civic boosters in Dayton, a small town of a few thousand about eighty miles southwest of Knoxville, responded. This was their chance to put their crumbling mill town back on the map. All they needed was a willing sacrifice, a patsy, a teacher willing to take the rap. They found their man in John T. Scopes (1900–1970), a popular local high school teacher and football coach who had just taken over the biology class. The shy, well-liked, "clean-cut" twenty-five-year-old was a more than willing participant.[53] Within weeks, the local cabal had enlisted high-powered lawyers for the show trial: Bryan for the prosecution and Darrow for the defense. For eight days in July 1925, Dayton was the center of the world's attention.

Bryan was the first to arrive. Thousands of fans met the pith-helmeted sixty-five-year-old at the train station. One would have never known that Rhea County was a Republican enclave, and even Bryan was flabbergasted when a torchlight parade carried him into a town transformed into an evangelical bazaar. As one close observer wrote, "Dayton took on the character of a revivalist-circus. Thither swarmed ballyhoo artists, hot dog vendors, lemonade merchants, preachers, professional atheists, college students, Greenwich Village radicals, out-of-work coal miners, I.W.W.'s, Single Taxers, 'libertarians,' revivalists of all shades and sects, hinterland 'soothsayers,' Holy Rollers, an army of newspaper men, scientists, editors and lawyers."[54] Banners were strung across the main street and on buildings welcoming the Great Commoner and espousing the faith: "Read your BIBLE," "God Is Love," and "Where Will You Spend Eternity?"[55]

Darrow's reception was much more somber. No parade, just a handful of the curious and the admiring. The venue, the Bible Belt, as Mencken called that swath of America, was this lawyer's nightmare. These were not his people; they were Bryan's. Darrow had arrived alone, "a lion in a Den of Daniels," as a friend of his put it.[56] George Rappleyea (1894–1966), the manager of the local coal mine and the instigator of the trial, drove Darrow to the town's only mansion, a long-abandoned yellow Victorian, rumored haunted, where the defense team had its headquarters. Joining Darrow were Scopes, to whom Darrow took an instant liking, and his close friends the preeminent civil liberties attorneys Arthur Garfield Hays (1881–1954) and Dudley Field Malone (1882–1950), as well as John R. Neal (1876–1959), a former law professor at the University of Tennessee who had been dismissed for advocating evolution. The ACLU-sponsored team was more than a match for the crowded prosecution, which featured Bryan, his son William, Jr. (1889–1978), local Attorney General Tom Stewart (1892–1972), and a handful of local legal notables: J. Gordon McKenzie, Wallace Haggard, and Herbert E. and Sue K. Hicks (the latter was the famous subject of a Johnny Cash song about a boy named Sue).[57]

The prosecution's plan was simple. As Stewart explained in his two-sentence opening statement, his side intended to show Scopes violated the law by teaching a theory that denied the divine creation of man. The defense strategy was far more nuanced, with the ultimate goal being to generate a case for the U.S. Supreme Court. To set the groundwork for that, they needed to demonstrate that the law violated civil liberties in the U.S. Constitution, especially the establishment clause; to show that the law was as unreasonable as codifying that the earth was flat; and, finally, to demonstrate that the law was based on the false assumption that evolution and Christianity were incompatible.[58] For Darrow and his colleagues, their case rested on their ability to enter expert testimony about the Bible and evolution into the record. Without that, the case was essentially open-and-shut.

Yet another "trial of the century" began early on Friday, July 10, 1925, in the vain hope of beating the heat. Dayton and particularly the courthouse, which was stuffed with onlookers, were hellishly hot and humid. The only cool thing in town was Clarence and Ruby's relationship. Arriving a few days after her husband, Ruby set about creating more comfortable accommodations and keeping an eye out for Mary. Since Ruby had discovered

Darrow's renewed affair with Mary, the marriage had publicly soured, with Darrow's indifference toward Ruby plain enough to draw comment. No matter. Soon enough, he was consumed by the case.

Judge John T. Raulston (1868–1956) strode into the courtroom, carrying two books: the state's legal code and the King James Bible. "I wondered why he thought he would need the statutes," Darrow quipped in his autobiography.[59] In all his cases, he might not have had a more unfriendly magistrate. As he revealed after the trial, Raulston revered Bryan and loathed Darrow.[60] After a carefully worded but certainly antievolution benediction that made Darrow wince, jury selection began; it lasted only two hours, probably a record for Darrow in a big case. Court then adjourned for the weekend, leaving Monday open for pretrial motions. Here the defense laid out its constitutional challenge to the Butler Law, calling on Judge Raulston to quash the indictment against Scopes. Neal, Hays, and Darrow made memorable speeches, but it was Darrow's that made the greatest impression. It was an all-gun salvo against "this foolish, mischievous, and wicked act."[61] Darrow pleaded for tolerance and understanding. "Unless there is left enough of the spirit of freedom in the state of Tennessee, and in the United States, there is not a single line of any constitution that can withstand bigotry and intolerance when it seeks to destroy the rights of the individual; and bigotry and intolerance are ever active." Speaking directly to Judge Raulston, he said, "[Y]our life and my life and the life of every American citizen depends after all upon the tolerance and forbearance of his fellow man." Finally, Darrow urged the judge to rule against the law to stop the march "backward to the glorious ages of the sixteenth century, when bigots lighted fagots to burn the men who dared to bring any intelligence and enlightenment and culture to the human mind."[62] The next day Judge Raulston ruled against the motion to quash; the trial would continue.

The jury made its first appearance on Wednesday, July 15, but only for a short while. In fact, the jurors witnessed only a few hours of the eight-day trial. After the opening statements and witnesses for the prosecution, the defense brought in its first expert, zoologist Maynard M. Metcalf, who planned to testify on the compatibility of evolution and Christianity. Stewart immediately objected. Raulston sent the jury out, and both sides argued about the admissibility of Metcalf's testimony and that of all the defense's experts. The judge ruled two days later. The jury would not hear any expert evidence.

Darrow finally had had enough. "I do not understand why every request of the state and every suggestion of the prosecution should meet with an endless waste of time, and a bare suggestion of anything on our part should be immediately over-ruled," he shouted. "I hope you do not mean to reflect upon the court?" Judge Raulston said slowly, eyes narrowed at Darrow. "Well," Darrow replied calmly, "your honor has the right to *hope*."[63] Only an apology the following Monday saved Darrow from a contempt citation and fine.

Monday, July 20, proved to be unforgettable. Over the weekend, perhaps at the suggestion of H. L. Mencken, Darrow had hatched an ingenious plan, a last-ditch effort to attack the prosecution, the Butler Law, and Bryan and his acolytes.[64] He would put Bryan on the stand. If Raulston prevented Darrow from illustrating that Christianity and evolution could fit together—so-called theistic evolution—then Darrow would attack from the other direction, demonstrating that the literal interpretation of the Bible was unreasonable and that therefore, any law demanding its public teaching was an undue legal burden. When Hays called Bryan to the stand, Stewart strenuously objected, but Bryan was content to be seated. He wanted to face Darrow's examination. This was the moment he had been waiting for. Back in June, when Bryan learned of Darrow's involvement in the case, he cheered. He relished the chance to stick it to the "Darrowites."[65]

The famous exchange between Darrow and Bryan—perhaps the most famous courtroom scene in American history—occurred outside. In addition to the unrelenting heat, Raulston feared that the building's floor was collapsing from the weight of the audience. Thus, the courtroom met the carnival. Three thousand spectators were on hand as Darrow began poking holes in Bryan's beliefs. Drawing inspiration from such skeptics as Thomas Paine and even his own father, Darrow started simply: "Do you claim that everything in the Bible should be literally interpreted?" Bryan replied: "I believe everything in the Bible should be accepted as it is given there." A whale swallowed Jonah? "I believe in a God who can make a whale and can make a man and make both do what He pleases." God stopped the sun for Joshua? "Now, Mr. Bryan, have you ever pondered what would have happened to the earth if it had stood still? . . . Don't you know it would have been converted into a molten mass of matter?" Bryan retorted: "I have been too busy on things that I thought were of more importance than that." More questions about the age of the earth, the length of days, and various biblical inconsistencies prompted increasingly heated banter. Darrow landed punches, and sometimes Bryan made self-inflicted wounds. When asked if he had made his own calculations about the age of the earth, Bryan said that he hadn't thought about it. "Do you think about things you do think about?" asked Darrow. "Well, sometimes," responded Bryan. The courtroom broke out into raucous laughter. At the end of the afternoon Bryan had lost his patience and charged that Darrow's only purpose was "to slur at the Bible." The Old Lion shot back. "I object to your statement," he yelled. "I am examining you on your fool ideas that no intelligent Christian on earth believes!"[66] With that Judge Raulston adjourned the court. It was clear to most that Darrow had achieved exactly what he wanted to, making Bryan look like an intolerant antediluvian ignoramus.[67]

The next day Judge Raulston began the session by striking Bryan's testimony. There was nothing for the defense to do but concede the fight. Darrow urged the jurors to find Scopes guilty so that they could then appeal the case. The jurors obliged. Raulston then fined Scopes one hundred dollars. The Monkey Trial was over. That evening Dayton's high school students threw a party in honor of Darrow, who danced and smoked with them. He and Ruby left the next day. Bryan stayed on to work on a new stump speech. Five days later, however, he died from complications related to his diabetes. A few malicious reporters blamed his death on Darrow's examination. Mencken joked that God had aimed at Darrow and missed. Darrow was respectful: Bryan was "a man of very extraordinary powers . . . I sincerely regret his death, and extend my sympathy to his grief-stricken family."[68] On appeal, the Tennessee Supreme Court overturned the conviction on a technicality but ruled the Butler Law constitutional. Effectively, the justices had turned back the clock on the evolution fight before the Scopes case. Darrow pressed onward against the antievolutionists, but the ACLU never seriously tried to find another test case. The law remained on the books until 1967.[69]

Darrow barely had any time to rest after the Scopes trial. His lecturing schedule kept him roaming from the Midwest to the South to the East Coast. While in New York City, speaking on crime and evolution—and, of course, visiting with Mary—he received a telegram from his friends at the National Association for the Advancement of Colored People (NAACP). They urgently needed to meet with him. Ossian Sweet (1894–1960) and ten co-defendants were charged with committing murder while defending Sweet's new home in Detroit from an angry white mob. That the association's top brass—Arthur Spingarn (1878–1971), Charles Studin (ca. 1875–1950), James Weldon Johnson (1871–1938), and Walter White (1893–1955)—showed up at Arthur Garfield Hays's Greenwich Village apartment instantly indicated the gravity of the situation. Spingarn spoke for the group; Darrow nodded. What followed was testimony to the absurdities of race in America. Fixing his gaze on Spingarn, Darrow said, "I understand. I know the suffering your people have endured." There was a pregnant pause. Spingarn, who had a dark complexion, explained that he was Jewish. Chuckling out of embarrassment, Darrow turned to the "swarthy-skin" Studin and said, "[T]hen, you understand." Studin told Darrow he was also white. Slack-jawed, Darrow turned to White. "Well, with your blue eyes and blond hair I could never make the mistake of thinking you colored." White kindly informed Darrow that he was indeed an African American. More amused than sheepish, Darrow put his legal retirement on hold yet again to take the case in the name of liberty and the freedom of two African Americans to choose to live where they wanted.[70]

For nearly three decades, Darrow had been an outspoken supporter of African American civil rights.[71] It was fundamental to his outlook. No other Americans suffered as blacks had. No others had so consistently and concertedly been denied basic freedoms and liberties. Time and again Darrow had come to the aid of famous black Americans, such as Chicago city councilman, and future pioneering congressman. Oscar DePriest (1871–1951), as well as ordinary citizens.[72] Well in advance of most of his peers, he argued that race was a social construct that meant "nothing," serving only to separate people.[73] This social cleavage allowed one group, which called itself "whites," to take economic advantage of another group, labeled "blacks." Thus, to Darrow, the race problem in America was essentially a class problem. The effects were debilitating. With opportunities foreclosed to them, blacks were often in trouble with the law, disproportionately populating the nation's prisons. They were too often the victims of the hangman's noose and the mob's anger. When Darrow spoke against capital punishment, he always made reference to black Americans who were killed by state-sanctioned violence, often for crimes that they did not commit or for the atrocious reason of maintaining the "purity of the white blood."[74]

Darrow's analysis of the problem was astute, but he had unconventional views on the solution. While many agreed with him that "this race question can never be finally settled excepting upon one principle, and that is, that all people are equal,"[75] more than a few looked askance at his call for "race amalgamation."[76] He had also called on blacks to abandon the Republican Party and become politically independent; and to give up their obsequious ways and refuse to work for tips; to stop wasting their time, talent, and money supporting black churches. However, he had refused to condemn lynching and racial violence in absolute terms, falling silent after various antiblack pogroms in Chicago and elsewhere.[77] He also had advocated "emigration on the part of those who love freedom" to countries that offered more opportunity to African Americans.[78] Infamously, in 1910, having been invited to speak with a group of civil rights leaders at Cooper Union in New York City, Darrow had offered an overly nuanced discussion of lynching and a harsh rebuke of black voters, churchgoers, and workers. The event's host, the Reverend Percy Stickney Grant (1860–1927), got up halfway through Darrow's talk, whispered harsh words into Darrow's ear, and pulled him offstage.[79] All of which Spingarn, Johnson, Studin, and White knew when they arranged to bring Darrow into the Detroit case. They also knew that they were getting the best criminal and civil liberties lawyer in America and the iconic defender of the oppressed.

Ossian Sweet's quest for the American dream had turned into a nightmare. Born in 1894, Sweet had grown up in Bartow, Florida, a postReconstruction phosphate mining boomtown forty miles east of Tampa. He was only too glad to escape. Not only did a life of backbreaking mining or farming not appeal to him, but he also sought a refuge from the omnipresent terror of the New South. As a young boy he had witnessed the immolation of an African American man, Fred Rochelle. A mob had accused, judged, and executed him for murdering a white woman. It was Sweet's hope that his education—first at Wilberforce University in Xenia, Ohio, and then at Howard University in Washington, D.C.—and his medical degree would enable him to live a comfortable life in the black middle class. A family, a home, and his profession were all he wanted. And for a moment they seemed within his grasp. In 1921 he moved to Detroit and started a thriving practice. The next year he and Gladys Mitchell (1901–1928), a fetching debutante from Pittsburgh, married, and in 1924 they had a baby girl, Ivy. In the spring of 1925, the Sweets set out to buy a house. That was when the trouble began.

The Sweets wanted to live somewhere other than the Black Bottom, the crowded, decrepit section of Detroit reserved for blacks. They found a bungalow on Garland Avenue on the overwhelmingly white east side of town. They took precautions as they moved in on September 8, 1925. Already that year white mobs, organized by the Ku Klux Klan, had attacked several residential race pioneers. City police, infested with KKK members, had provided little protection. Sweet nonetheless had arranged a police escort for their first day. An ominous crowd gathered after sundown but dissipated with the darkness. The following night a larger mob, perhaps in the thousands, returned. Ossian was ready, bringing reinforcements and weapons. Along with Gladys, his brothers Otis and Henry were there, as was the Sweets' chauffeur, Joe Mack, and a group of friends: William Davis, John Latting, Leonard Morse, Norris Murray, Charles Washington, and Hewitt Watson. About eight-thirty, stones and bricks began to pelt the house, smashing windows. Racial slurs rose from the chanting crowd: "Get the damn niggers!"[80] Ossian had seen this before, when he was a boy. Another window broke upstairs. Ossian was downstairs with Gladys arguing about what to do when all of a sudden they heard the unmistakable sound of gunfire. For moments that seemed like hours, pandemonium ruled as shots were fired outside and inside. The ensuing silence was followed by a banging on the front door. Police officers came in, swearing. Two members of the crowd had been hit, one of them, Leon Breiner, fatally. All eleven were arrested, crammed into a police van, and taken downtown, where they were charged with conspiracy and murder.

The local defense team was a who's who of Detroit's black legal talent: Charles Mahoney, Julian Perry, and Cecil Rowlette, all of whom were retained by the local NAACP branch. The association's national leadership had concerns, however. Walter White did not think that the Sweets' lawyers had the experience to handle the case. Moreover, the lack of a white attorney potentially harmed their case. Putting Darrow, Arthur Hays, and Herbert Friedman, a colleague from Chicago, and Darrow's friend in Detroit, Walter Nelson, on the defense solved that problem and importantly elevated the case's profile, making it a national concern, exactly what the NAACP wanted.[81]

The bloated legal team got to work in late October 1925. Unlike jury selection in the Scopes case, the voir dire in Detroit was critical. Darrow had to weed out the bigots the best he could. In his folksy, nonconfrontational way, he was remarkably successful. Unbeknownst to the prosecution, led by District Attorney Robert Toms (1886–1960), the defense was even able to seed a friend of Rowlette's onto the jury.[82] The prosecution's case hinged on Michigan's legal definition of "mob," a group of menacing people, twelve or more with weapons or thirty without. Toms sought to show that there had been no crowd outside the Sweets' home and that what the defendants had done was premeditated murder. To a person, albeit with some muffed lines, all of Toms's sixty-nine witnesses testified that September 9 had been a regular late-summer night; there had been no carousing, no mob, no molesting the new neighbors, and no violence until the gunmen in the Sweet home opened fire. Darrow's cross-examination was brilliant, the greatest "I've ever heard in my life," Rowlette commented years later.[83] He tripped up several witnesses on the size of the crowd that night and made others reveal their deep-seated animosity toward African Americans. Much to the distress of the prosecution, the police officers who testified, and who likely coached the witnesses, couldn't even keep their stories straight.

Halfway through the trial, prospects for the Sweets were improving. The defense team lightened up a bit, and Darrow occasionally managed to escape Ruby's watchful eyes even as he prepared his own witnesses and crafted his closing statement. The centerpiece of the defense was Ossian Sweet, who was unflappable and convincing, describing how that Garland Street crowd reminded him of that lynch mob he had witnessed as a child. A "human sea" had flooded the street that night, threatening his home, his wife, and his friends.[84] If there was any conspiracy, Darrow showed it had been perpetrated by the Waterworks Improvement Association, the Klan-inspired organization that had rallied the Sweets' neighbors against them. Even under a nasty cross-examination by lawyers who considered him "quasi-intelligent," Sweet, who had studied with Marie Curie (1867–1934) and attended the lectures of pioneering neurosurgeon Anton von Eiselsberg, held his ground.[85]

Although finishing his seventh decade, Darrow showed no signs of fatigue during his closing, which began on Monday, November 23. He explained that the trial was not about murder but about race hatred, which had denied a decent man and woman with their newborn a place to live and a chance to better themselves. Worse, Ivy's parents were on trial for a killing that the police and prosecution had failed to demonstrate was their fault. In fact,

Toms could not point to one of the eleven defendants with any certainty. The shots may have come from a member of the crowd or the police. In an era when ballistics was more inference than science, Darrow was right: the evidence was inconclusive. The only irrefutable fact was that the Sweets' neighbors were racists, "Noble Nordics," Darrow said sarcastically, bent on mobbing. What would one expect the Sweets to do? Given the long history of racism and discrimination that began with slavery and continued through the violent purges and lynchings of the twentieth century, it was logical that they would defend themselves. After all, it was in man's nature, and significantly in Michigan's legal code, that one's home was one's castle. Darrow pleaded for tolerance and asked the jurors to blaze a path to a better, more peaceful future. "I ask you more than everything else, I ask you in behalf of justice, often maligned and down-trodden, hard to protect and hard to maintain, I ask you in behalf of yourselves, in behalf of our race, to see that no harm comes to them." Now crying along with the judge and several jurors, Darrow begged the jurors to release his clients "in the name of the future, the future which will one day solve these sore problems, and the future which is theirs as well as ours, I ask you in the name of the future to do Justice in this case."[86]

Despite Darrow's heroics, the jury was hopelessly deadlocked. Liberal Judge Frank Murphy (1890–1949) had no choice and declared a mistrial. The second trial was a replay of the first, except that only Henry Sweet, who had confessed to police that he had fired that night, was the sole defendant. This time the Darrow magic worked perfectly. Henry was acquitted, and Toms dropped the charges against the ten others.

As the 1920s drew to a close, Darrow was on top of the world. He had distanced himself from left-wing politics and progressives and had moved away from the women's movement and the labor movement. But his commitment to liberty, freedom, and justice for the oppressed and for those caught in the terrible snares of the state justice system remained as strong as ever. Further, the decade's three big cases had generated enough income for him to build that retirement nest egg he so desired. Fortune seemed to follow him at every turn. In 1928 his son, Paul, sold his and his father's interests in the Greeley Gas & Fuel Company for fabulous profits, which were reinvested in the bullish stock market. Better yet, Paul, taking a job as a banker, moved his family—with those adoring granddaughters—to Chicago.[87] Darrow could not have been more popular on the lecture circuit, selling out everywhere from New York City to Philadelphia to Charleston, West Virginia. At every stop, he challenged his audience over issues of civil rights and civil liberties. His messages about evolution or skepticism or crime and punishment always divided listeners. Darrow would not have had it any other way. Controversy was good for business. When on the day after Christmas in 1926 he harangued an all-black audience at New York City's Salem Methodist Episcopal Church about African Americans' being "too blooming pious,"[88] black ministers had had enough. In 1928, the National Interdenominational Ministerial Alliance, a consortium of African American clergymen, banned Darrow from their churches.[89] Darrow was unrepentant and with his criticism an equal opportunist. On March 11, 1927, speaking in Mobile, Alabama, he denounced lynching and racial discrimination. As he finished, word came to the podium that the local Ku Klux Klan was preparing to tar and feather him. Quickly and unceremoniously, Clarence and Ruby were shuttled safely out of the state.[90]

In May 1928, Darrow announced his retirement from the law, returning to Ashtabula, Ohio, for one last case. Hundreds of cheering admirers showed up for Darrow's appeal for a local man, James Munsene, convicted on a bribery charge. Ominously, the trial ended in a hung jury. Was the world really going to let Darrow retire from the law? If so, what was he going to do? Lecture and write his autobiography, he answered.[91] Life was good. Back in Chicago, a young lawyer met him in the office hallway. "Mr. Darrow, how are you?" "Disappointed," crowed the old pessimist. "Why?" probed the man. "Because, things turned out better than I expected."[92] Darrow, however, spoke too soon.

⚜ 10 ⚜

No Rest, No Retirement, No Retreat

Clarence Darrow's seventieth birthday party on April 18, 1927, was national news. A committee of 115 of his friends and admirers organized the no-holds-barred, buttoned-down gala affair. In the ritzy Palmer House hotel in downtown Chicago, 1,200 well-wishers, including his first wife, Jessie, his son, Paul, and John T. Scopes, enjoyed a three-course meal of Darrow's favorite dishes and a full program of speeches and frivolity. Comedian Will Rogers (1879–1935), who couldn't make it out of Beverly Hills, telegrammed in: "Darrow is the only freethinker America has ever allowed to reach 70."[1] The one person not seeming to enjoy himself, however, was Darrow.[2] He sank further and further in his chair as Chicago labor lawyer and rising political star Donald Richberg (1881–1960) spoke of Darrow's legal accomplishments, as philosopher Shirley J. Case (1872–1947) talked about Darrow's religious beliefs, as Walter White lauded Darrow's work on behalf of African Americans, as author and politico Zona Gale (1874–1938) talked about Darrow's literary efforts, and finally, as Unitarian minister and social activist John Haynes Holmes (1879–1964) detailed Darrow's humanitarian achievements. Only after the evening's highlight—the unveiling of a bust of Darrow made by British artist Kathleen Wheeler (1884–1977)—did Darrow pull himself out of his chair to address the crowd.

It was not inspirational. "As one grows older, I think more and more, one comes to realize the futility of life," he declared. But one still had to fight, as he had, "for liberty . . . for freedom." His wish for the future was both simple and, as his life's efforts had proved, utopian: to "establish tolerance in this world [so that] everybody else might have their pet theories of making men good or moral or intelligent or whatever they please as long as they left the individual free."[3]

Retirement from the courtroom was blissful. He and Ruby had reconciled, happily traveling to various places—from tourists' traps close to home, like Fish Creek, Wisconsin, an artists' village north of Green Bay, to a whirlwind excursion to the Middle East. He also devoted time to the three social and political problems he most wanted to see solved before his death. Maintaining his commitment to liberty and freedom meant advocating publicly for the abolition of capital punishment, the end of prohibition, and civil rights for African Americans.[4] After nearly fifty years of spectacular political and legal successes and failures, Darrow had distilled his causes down to these three civil liberties and civil rights issues. His crusade against the death penalty was perhaps his oldest public stance, and the latter two issues were nearly equally as dear to him. At the root of all three were overreaching and overbearing systems of oppression and intolerance that inflicted undue punishments and unwarranted limitations on individuals. He traveled frequently, lecturing and debating these topics at times and places of his choosing. Retirement from the law meant that he no longer felt the need to take on engagements merely for the money. Retirement also meant that Darrow had time for volunteering. He helped establish and later led the American League to Abolish Capital Punishment, under the auspices of which he spoke at prisons and lobbied politicians for penal code reform. His message had not wavered for decades: execution was prompted not by justice but by hate. Juries and judges were no better than the so-called criminals.[5] Darrow's abhorrence of capital punishment even caused him to take a handful of cases following his retirement in order to defend those facing the hangman's noose or the electric chair.[6] He did, however, far prefer public speaking to the courtroom.

Darrow's rhetorical flare showed no signs of slowing. Neither did his commitment to the Democratic Party. Darrow was as political and partisan as ever, and he went all out for 1928 Democratic presidential candidate Alfred E. Smith (1873–1944). When he wasn't lauding Smith, he was excoriating the Republican Herbert C. Hoover (1874–1964). That Hoover was not quite cut from the same cloth as Warren Harding or Calvin Coolidge (1872–1933) made no difference to Darrow. Hoover was an enemy of liberty and freedom who by supporting Prohibition refused to "respect the feelings of a free people."[7] As the election neared, Darrow became more shrill.[8] Sounding like Henry Lloyd, Darrow proclaimed that Hoover believed in socialism for the rich, but not for the poor. He told thousands of voters to ignore the Republicans' call to vote for their candidate. "It's like asking the ox to vote for the butcher," he thundered.[9]

Darrow could not have been shocked; he'd seen it so many times before. The prey did indeed vote for the predator, and Hoover won handily. Darrow was wrong on one thing, though. Hoover did not so much lead the sheep to the slaughterhouse as govern meekly while the entire flock was wiped out. Although the connections between the great stock market crash of October 1929 and the ensuing Great Depression were complex, the results of the economic catastrophe were not: under Hoover's watch, the United States— its economy, its politics, and its very social fabric—was ripped apart. As rarefied and clinical as they are, the numbers do tell a tale. In one horrible month, from October to November 1929, the New York Stock Exchange lost $26 billion. In the first three years of the Hoover era, manufacturing production fell by nearly 50 percent. Private construction fell from $7.5 billion in 1929 to $1.5 billion in 1932. In 1930 and 1931, more than thirty-six hundred banks failed, taking with them $2.5 billion in deposits. In those same years, nearly fifty-five thousand businesses shut their doors for good. In 1932 unemployment averaged 25 percent, and in some places it was much higher.[10]

Quantitatively, things were bad; qualitatively, things were worse. All Darrow had to do was look outside his apartment's beautiful bay windows. The unemployed were everywhere, digging in Jackson Park trash cans, hoping for a discarded meal. At the city dump, the hungry nearly outnumbered the seagulls. Darrow did not escape the ruin. The stock market crash destroyed his savings, which he estimated to be about $300,000 ($3.9 million in today's dollars).[11] He had seen the crash coming as early as January 1929, when he wrote to his son, Paul, his financial adviser, that stocks were far too high. Perhaps more of an optimist, Paul had held on to his and his father's stocks too long. Both Clarence and Ruby blamed Paul for the ruin.[12] They were overwrought with despair at the loss of their fortune, but they were not destitute. They had money for the essentials—their apartment and food—but little else.

Darrow's plan was to survive the economic collapse, which the nation hoped would be temporary, by lecturing, debating, and writing more than he originally planned in 1928. He also sold off parts of his amazing book collection.[13] Darrow's home now looked much like his father's, with books filling every conceivable nook and cranny; he could afford to downsize. He avoided going back to the law. He had neither the desire nor the energy to resume a full-time practice. Thus, despite the need for money, he turned down the opportunity to defend Lila Jimerson, in the notorious "witch murder" in which Jimerson, a Seneca Indian woman, had bludgeoned Clothide Marchand, wife of the artist Henri Marchand.[14] That had been his kind of case, but no longer. Instead, he hoped to turn his cultivated reputation as skeptic and critic into large speaking fees. He refused to retreat from any of his cherished ideals or habits, but given the circumstances, the onus was on him to make those beliefs pay.[15]

For two years, working with George G. Whitehead, a well-seasoned advance man who had previously organized national Chautauqua circuits, Darrow kept himself quite busy with his debate and lecturing schedule. He remained as good, smart, and entertaining as ever. He pulled no punches and liked to fight people just above his weight class. He focused on what he knew best: prohibition, the death penalty, and skepticism. Occasionally he ranged beyond these to debate censorship or the merits of socialism. In 1931, he participated in a radio show titled *Famous Trials of History* hosted by Roscoe Pound (1870–1964), defending Revolutionary War general Benedict Arnold against charges of treason. These were the exceptions.[16] Of his three regular topics, Darrow spent most of his time by far talking about religion. The other two subjects had lost some of their charge. In the early 1930s, the end of prohibition was in sight. The normally pessimistic Darrow even predicted with glee that the ban on alcohol was "moribund."[17] Continuing to give his "Crime: Its Cause and Treatment" address, he was also making inroads into the abolition of capital punishment. The League to Abolish Capital Punishment successfully introduced legislation in California, Colorado, New Jersey, Vermont, and Kansas, the latter passing its ban in 1931.[18] Thus poking holes in cherished religious beliefs became his stock-in-trade.

Darrow's skepticism was unstinting and yet another aspect of his core philosophy about letting individual liberties and freedoms flourish. Organized religion tied people down to a set of nonsensical principles that often did more harm than good. A lifetime of reading and research had given him no cause to reverse course and declare allegiance to some deity. Rather, he had witnessed all sorts of tragedies, big and small, that convinced him otherwise. He saw no divine providence at work in 1928, when the son of his friend Winston Curtis contracted polio at college. Similarly, if there were a god, Darrow wondered, why did he detest African Americans? What sort of god would make an entire people suffer for the color of their skin? Further, he adamantly refused to believe in an afterlife and the persistence of personal consciousness after death. There simply was no evidence, and taking all this on faith was a kind of collective insanity.[19] As Darrow once wrote, "I still believe that two and two is four, and that a dead man is *DEAD*."[20] He drew strength from these views. "I am satisfied," Darrow wrote in a *New York Times* symposium on personal immortality, "that as I had a beginning I shall have an end and the end is death."[21]

Where Darrow found comfort, others found consternation, which also proved great for business. His debates and lectures on religion were sellouts, with audiences of as many as three thousand.[22] The popularity of Darrow's so-called religious forums raised the ire of many in the religious community. He had particularly angered black ministers. Characterizing their work as "self-hypnotism" and their theology as a "narcotic," Darrow called on the black faithful to invest in education and industry and not in churches.[23] In a rare display of solidarity, after the Catholic Church in New York banned Darrow, several black Protestant churches followed suit, asserting Darrow's "claim to atheism [was] merely a publicity stunt."[24] Darrow was used to it, having already found himself (rather proudly) on the Daughters of the American Revolution's "blacklist."[25] Nonetheless, he may have indeed winced from the unrelenting flak from African American ministers. Banning him from their churches was one thing, but calling him the "Negro's worst enemy" was something else.[26]

A more immediate concern was the fact that even with controversy trailing him, Darrow never made enough money from lecturing to keep his and Ruby's finances far above water. Each event garnered about four thousand dollars.[27] But after rental fees, George Whitehead's promotional charges, and travel costs, there was not that much left when the profit was split two or sometimes three or four ways with the other event speakers. Two years into the Great Depression, Darrow sought other ways to make ends meet.

At first, he tried everything but the law. In 1931, he agreed to narrate Samuel Cummins's Universal Pictures educational film *The Mystery of Life*, a rather facile survey of the evolution of life on earth. Before the picture's release, there was a stormy censorship controversy as James Wingate of the New York State Board of Censors cut out everything he deemed indecent, from copulating snails to naked babies on their mothers' breasts. Protests from Darrow and his buddy at the ACLU Arthur Garfield Hays got some of the objectionable material back in; the bare-bosomed prehistoric woman was restored but not the randy snails. The brouhaha drew people to the theaters, and there was talk of another Darrow movie, this one about the penal system, which never materialized.[28] In any case, Darrow had devised a better moneymaking idea: he would write his autobiography.

Several public celebrities, such as Lincoln Steffens and Helen Keller, were cashing in on their fame by writing their own stories. Darrow aimed to do the same with his own, *The Story of My Life*. After securing a contract from Charles Scribner's Sons Publishers, he wrote most of it while on a European tour with Ruby. In spring 1931, he returned to find out that the accomplished writer Charles Yale Harrison (1898–1954) was just finishing a biography of Darrow. In vain, Darrow tried to convince Harrison to delay publication of the biography so that the autobiography would have a chance to sell without a competitor. Harrison's publisher, Harrison Smith, was unobliging, and both books were released simultaneously. By far, Darrow's did better, staying on the bestseller lists for most of the spring of 1932. Generally, the reviews were positive, and some, like future U.S. attorney general Thurman Arnold's (1891–1969), were glowing. Particularly satisfying was R. L. Duffus's joint review of Darrow's and Harrison's books in *The New York Times*, finding the former superior to the latter. Though some reviewers carped—*The Nation*'s labor reporter, Benjamin Stolberg, declared that it "read as though it had been carelessly dictated to a stenographer"—Darrow's last book was his most successful. Sadly, it was not enough. As the Great Depression dragged on, Darrow returned to the one thing that had always given him sustenance, the law.

Despite his well-earned reputation of defending anyone caught in the crosshairs of justice, Darrow had always had limits. He had refused, for example, to represent mobsters, once supposedly telling Al Capone in no uncertain terms he'd never "have anything to do with him."[29] Nearly a year after the stock market crash of 1929, Darrow, however, had changed his mind. Here it was again: Darrow was taking care of Darrow. As he had learned from his L.A. experiences, he knew that no one else would. In this case, he needed the money. Darrow came out of legal retirement to defend George "Red" Barker, the notorious business agent for the Chicago teamsters who had ties with Capone and who used strong-arm tactics to control and expand the union. On September 29, 1930, Barker had been one of the first of Chicago's so-called public enemies to be arrested on the trumped-up charge of vagrancy. It was a ploy to detain Barker and his colleague William "Three Fingered Jack" White while prosecutors made the case for extortion. Capone's men reached out to Darrow, who agreed to represent Barker but not White. Disingenuously—Darrow knew full well that if he sprang Barker, White would be close behind—Darrow explained to reporters that his historic ties to Chicago's labor movement in general and the teamsters in particular had compelled him to take the case, which he claimed was not about organized crime but rather about civil liberties and using the city's vagrancy ordinance to ensnare people the police did not like. "If the authorities wish to harass the lawless they should indict them and try them on charges of which they are guilty."[30] Barker escaped prosecution, but his criminal life finally caught up with him in June 1932, when an assassin shot him dead. Darrow never made further mention of the Barker case, and he refused to take another like it.[31] Fortunately, a few cases more his style landed in his lap.

On March 25, 1931, nine African American young men—Olen Montgomery, Clarence Norris, Haywood Patterson, Ozie Powell, Willie Roberson, Charlie Weems, Eugene Williams, and Andrew and Leroy Wright—were arrested for allegedly raping two white women, Victoria Price and Ruby Bates, while all eleven were bumming a ride on a freight train traveling from Chattanooga to Memphis, Tennessee. They were taken into custody in Scottsboro, Alabama, thus becoming the Scottsboro Nine. Despite the lack of conclusive evidence, their first lawyer, Stephen R. Roddy, failed to win them an acquittal. All nine were then sentenced to death. Two groups— the International Labor Defense, a Communist-front organization, and the NAACP—fought for the right to appeal the young men's cases. Unlike its actions in the Sweet cases, the NAACP was sluggish and lost valuable time. As a last-ditch effort to get the Scottsboro Nine on its side, the NAACP's Walter White called Clarence Darrow in early May 1931. Given his politics and his track record on civil rights and civil liberties, Darrow was the perfect choice and White's best chance at taking control of the case. It was not, however, meant to be. The ILD refused to back off. When Darrow suggested all the lawyers forsake their affiliations and join forces, the ILD countered by offering Darrow a seat at its defense table. Darrow refused to betray the NAACP. Aside from their work together in Detroit, the association had hosted several of his appearances at various venues, including Howard University, where he gave a week's worth of lectures to its law students in early 1931.[32] With a heavy heart, Darrow withdrew from the Scottsboro appeals.[33]

The Christmas of 1931 marked the lowest point for the Darrows. Their finances were stretched so thin Ruby took the unusual step of sending handmade holiday cards in lieu of the typical store-bought ones.[34] But in their moment of despair, during that bitter Chicago winter, a telegram arrived with the promise of work, money, and warmer weather. The dispatch came from Julian Ripley, the brother-in-law of Grace Fortescue, who, along with her son-in-law and two other men, was in need of legal help. Darrow probably looked twice at the note's origins: Honolulu, Hawaii. Immediately, he knew exactly what this was about.

Something had gone terribly wrong on the evening of September 12, 1931, a Saturday night—Navy Night—when officers and sailors left their confines to roam the island, looking for a good time. That night a young officer, Lieutenant Thomas "Tommie" Massie (1905–1987), and his twenty-year-old wife, Thalia (1911–1963), attended a party at the Ala Wai Inn. The two had a strained relationship made worse by liquor and rumors of Thalia's dalliances. That night the Massies had arrived together but became separated; Tommie danced with others while Thalia went to the private rooms upstairs. There was an altercation, with Thalia arguing with some of Tommie's colleagues and their wives. She left the party to walk home in the balmy night. According to various statements, including Thalia's original one to the police, she left about 11:30 p.m. About half an hour later, she was spotted by George Goeas and his wife. They noticed her walking slowly down John Ena Road, followed by a white man, a haole, as they were called.

Then she disappeared for another hour. At approximately 1:00 a.m. Sunday, Eustace Bellinger and his wife were driving home along Ala Moana Road when suddenly a woman appeared in the middle of the road. It was Thalia. The car stopped, and Thalia looked in. She was clearly injured, her face badly bruised. "Are you white people?" she asked desperately. They took her home immediately. At 1:30, Tommie called. He was worried; he had been looking for her. "Please come home. Something awful has happened" was all she said.[35] Fifteen minutes later Tommie called the police to report that his wife had been raped by a group of four or five Hawaiian men.

The so-called Ala Moana case was in the newspapers for months, and like everyone else, Darrow kept track of it. Although attacks on native Hawaiians were sadly all too common, a rape of a haole, a white foreigner, was novel and shocking. It was not long before the Honolulu police arrested five men: Ben Ahakuelo, Henry Chang, Horace Ida, Joe Kahahawai, and David Takai. A grand jury quickly returned indictments. The trial began on November 16, 1931. The accused had an excellent defense team, led by William Heen. To the ethnically diverse jury he demonstrated that there were significant problems in the prosecution's case. In addition to shoddy police work, Thalia's story proved too weak to garner any convictions. The timeline of the assault—and there indeed had been an assault, though likely not a rape—left too many questions. Eyewitness accounts put the men elsewhere at the time of the alleged crime. Furthermore, Thalia's identification of the men and their car was tenuous at best. Her performance on the witness stand left lingering doubts. The jury spent ninety-seven hours in deliberations without result. In the middle of December 1931, Judge Alva Steadman had no recourse other than to declare a mistrial and release the men, who nonetheless had to remain in the area and report twice a week to William Dickson, the local probation officer.

Following the trial, tensions on the island were at an all-time high.[36] Haoles tended to believe that the nonwhite jurors had deprived Thalia Massie of the justice she deserved. Some, particularly those stationed at the Pearl Harbor naval base, took it upon themselves to defend her honor by going out at night and beating up native Hawaiians and those of Japanese and Chinese descent. One night a group of marauding sailors abducted Horace Ida with the intent of forcing a confession. They savagely beat him, and as reporters explained the next day, the bruises on his face and body negated any statement by the defendant. That, however, gave Grace Fortescue, Thalia's mother, a horrible idea.

Before the Ala Moana trial, Fortescue had come from the mainland to give her daughter moral support and help nurse her back to health. She was convinced, likely correctly, that only new evidence or a confession from one of the defendants would result in a conviction. But she had to avoid the mistake of those overzealous sailors. Instead of beating out a corroborating statement, she planned to scare one out of Joe Kahahawai. On the morning of January 8, 1932, Fortescue along with her son-in-law and two sailors, Edward J. Lord and Albert "Deacon" Jones, kidnapped Kahahawai while he was checking in with his parole officer. They brought him back to Fortescue's bungalow, tied him up, and pointed guns in his face, demanding he admit that he had raped Thalia and broken her jaw. Neighbors heard a loud bang—a slamming door, they thought—later that morning. Kahahawai had been shot in the chest and died about twenty minutes later. Police caught the culprits as they tried to dispose of the body by throwing it into the ocean. Not long after the four were arrested and indicted—surprisingly for kidnapping and only second-degree murder—Ripley reached out to Clarence Darrow.

The family was willing to pay any price, and Darrow quoted them the hefty sum of forty thousand dollars plus expenses (six hundred thousand in today's dollars). But he harbored nagging doubts. The racial elements of the case bothered him greatly. The killing of Kahahawai represented everything he detested about American life: intolerance, privilege, and cruelty. Despite having tentatively agreed to go to Hawaii, in early March 1932 he tried to back out, sending Ripley, who was handling all legal arrangements, a letter along with a copy of his closing argument in the Sweet trial. He could not, he explained, be compelled to take a position against his former statements about liberty, freedom, and equality. Ripley quickly dispatched a response, stating that his clients shared his sentiments and that he would not have to relinquish his "position on the race question."[37] Darrow agreed to take the case. He knew that race played a central factor in Kahahawai's death and that he was on the wrong side of the argument. But the temptation was too strong; he needed that fee. Before departing for Hawaii, he desperately tried to convince his friends and political colleagues that racial issues were not central. There was even a chance, Darrow wrote his old friend Lincoln

Steffens, that his work might "do much to allay the race feeling" that had gripped the island.[38] That was feeble rationalization more than anything else. Darrow was defending his own reputation as the champion of civil rights and civil liberties. As in the case of "Red" Barker, Capone's lieutenant, Darrow chose a fee over principles. In this case, his reputation as well as his clients' freedom was on the line. The only way to redeem both would be if somehow he could make the issues of white supremacy and racial privilege go away. On the slow boat to that tropical paradise, he thought hard about how he could winnow away the racial issues from the case.[39]

After just over a week of travel, on March 24, 1932, Clarence and Ruby Darrow, along with George S. Leisure, a young New York lawyer and unabashed, starry-eyed admirer who had agreed to work for free, arrived in Honolulu.[40] After chatting briefly with reporters and learning that his autobiography was selling briskly at local bookstores, Darrow went to the hotel to relax and plot. The case, *Territory of Hawaii v. Fortescue et al.*, presented the series of problems that nearly all of Darrow's cases did: a hostile local jury pool, unhelpful newspaper reporters, and long odds to defeat the prosecution's goals. Adding to his deficit was the issue that nearly all the facts were already in evidence. Basically, he had two options: he could plead guilty to the charges and then fight for mitigation before the judge, as he had in the Leopold and Loeb case, or he could plead his case before a jury and take his chances, as he had in the Sweet cases. He chose the latter.

Darrow's opposition was John C. Kelley, one of the territory's best lawyers, who styled himself the "Clarence Darrow of Honolulu."[41] Kelley had the easier job as he had plenty of evidence from the abduction: the murder weapon, the shell casings, the bullet from the kill shot; Kahahawai's body and clothes; the blood from the crime scene; and the damning statements taken after the defendants were caught red-handed trying to dispose of the body. Thus, Darrow had to come up with a defense strategy that turned the state's case on its head. He had done so many times before, most notably in the Leopold and Loeb case, which provided a kind of blueprint. As in the defense of those murderers, Darrow planned to use alienists to provide an alternative rationale for the crime. Additionally, he decided to circumvent the rule of law by appealing to an "unwritten law," that of honor slaying, which by custom allows a man to kill another for the rape of his wife. Also, Darrow had two aces up his sleeve.

The trial began on April 4, 1932, in Judge Charles S. Davis's courtroom, two weeks short of Darrow's seventy-fifth birthday and a month after the Lindbergh baby had been kidnapped.[42] Under the weather, Darrow had tried to delay it a few days. Pulitzer Prize–winning journalist Russell Owen, who had come to cover the trial for *The New York Times*, noted that Darrow looked enfeebled, his eyes sunken under his brow.[43] Initially, the trial did not go well for the defense. Darrow failed to get the all-haole jury he wanted. Instead, five jurors were mainland Americans of European descent; three had been born in China; another three were from Europe; and the final juror was of Irish, Hawaiian, Scottish, French, and Tahitian ancestry. After the jurors were impaneled, Darrow leaned over to Leisure and dryly stated that they might as well concede defeat.[44] After Kelley's masterful opening, Darrow whispered to his cocounsel, "[W]ouldn't you know, it would be just my damn luck to lose the only case I ever had in my life in which the United States public was all on my side!"[45]

Not long into the trial, Darrow played his first ace. He secretly brought to Honolulu two experienced alienists from San Francisco: Edward Huntington Williams and Thomas Orbison. Darrow's psychological defense rested on the notion of temporary insanity and took advantage of the one missing fact from the trial: the prosecution could not prove who had fired the shot that killed Kahahawai. Everyone knew that Jones's gun had been used, but Darrow alleged quite craftily that "the evidence will show that the defendant Massie . . . held the gun in his hand from which the fatal shot was fired in this case."[46] The circumlocutory statement allowed Darrow the crease to lead his expert witnesses through the argument that at the moment that the bound and terrified Kahahawai allegedly confessed to his kidnappers, Massie snapped, grabbed Jones's gun, and involuntarily fired it. Massie maintained that he had no memory of the episode at all. Both psychiatrists testified that the murder was the result of, as Orbison put it, a "mental bomb" or, as Williams stated, a "somnambulistic ambulatory automatism."[47] Not to be outdone, Kelley, who had studied Darrow's cases, had predicted this line of defense, and his own alienists testified that Massie, if he was the shooter, was sane.

Darrow's last ace was Thalia Massie, who took the witness stand on April 20. Darrow walked through her well-known statement in the hope of making jurors realize why Tommie had shot Kahahawai. Thalia was riveting on direct examination. There was nary a dry eye in the courtroom. Kelley's cross-examination did not focus on the fabrications, lies, and misleading comments. He refused to retry the Ala Moana case. Rather, he went after her character, seeking to demonstrate that she was not stable and thus an unreliable witness. Kelley had an ace of his own. In 1931, Thalia had sought psychological counseling from E. Lowell Kelly (1905–1986), who was then at the University of Hawaii. Now, Kelley wanted Thalia, on the witness stand a year later, to identify Dr. Kelly's psychological evaluation. Thalia's jaw dropped when Kelley handed her the document. "Where did you get this?" she demanded. "I'm asking the questions, not answering them," Kelley responded curtly. Thalia exclaimed that the document was private and proceeded to rip it into pieces. The lawyers and Judge Davis were stunned. Spectators in the courtroom cheered approvingly, but Kelley had proved his point. As Thalia walked off the stand, he retorted, "Thank you, Mrs. Massie. At last you've shown yourself in your true colors."[48] Darrow immediately objected, but it was too late.

Closing statements began on Tuesday, April 26. The courtroom was packed. Without judicial sanction, seats were going for twenty-five dollars apiece. As one reporter wrote, they were there to "hear the old lion, Clarence Darrow, roar."[49] He began by lamenting the "terrible story" of Thalia's assault and the "grief, sorrow, trouble" that plagued Tommie for weeks and months, driving him to this point.[50] Thalia clearly was hurt physically and emotionally, and justice so far had been denied. "Gentlemen"—he appealed to the jurors with his foot up on the jury box foot railing—"I wonder what Fate has against this family anyhow?"[51] Tommie, his fellow sailors, and his mother-in-law had not intended to kill Kahahawai. "When Kahahawai said, 'Yes, I done it,'" Darrow explained, accepting Tommie's testimony as fact, "everything was blotted out," and the gun was fired.[52] "If you put yourself in Tommie Massie's place, what would you have done?" Finally, Darrow asked the jurors "to heal, not to destroy," and to help him complete his mission of bringing "peace and justice to an Island wracked and worn by strife."[53]

It was good, but not Darrow's best. In his summary, reporter Russell Owen saw flashes of the old, vigorous Darrow with his "sweeping gestures and flashing eyes."[54] But the four-and-a-half-hour closing, brief by Darrow standards, was interrupted by a few breaks when Darrow had to sit and catch his breath. By comparison, Kelley was cool and effective. He reminded the jurors that their duty was to decide on the basis of established, written law and to punish those who had violated it. He told them to ignore "the great Darrow." In any case, the facts were plain. The abduction was premeditated and carried out in a conspiracy, which happened months after the alleged rape. Kelley doubted that Kahahawai confessed to Tommie Massie, who all too conveniently remembered only that supposed statement and nothing else. Further, if they had not planned to kill Kahahawai, why did they all have guns? Why had they not sought medical help after he was shot? Why had they tried to dispose of the body?

The National Guard in Honolulu was on high alert as the jury deliberated for days. Well-substantiated rumors held that the jurors were split ten to two for an acquittal.[55] Darrow was happy with that, but he did not trust it. While the jury was out, he secretly met with Admiral Yates Stirling, Jr. (1872–1948), and Governor Lawrence M. Judd (1887–1968) to see what could be done in the event of a guilty verdict. It turned out that Darrow's pessimism was well placed. The jurors were indeed split ten to two, not for acquittal but for conviction. All four defendants were eventually found guilty of manslaughter with a request for leniency. Shocked, Darrow "slid down on a chair, and his chin fell toward his chest."[56] "I can't understand it," he told reporters. "The verdict is a travesty on justice and on human nature."[57] Of the jurors, he wondered "how anybody could be so cruel."[58] Jurors saw themselves quite differently. It was the skilled prosecution that had led to the convictions. As one juror said after the trial, Darrow "talked to us like a lot of farmers. That stuff may go over big in the Middle West but not here."[59] Still, Darrow had one more trump card.

The weekend before the sentencing, Ruby and Clarence had gone tent camping to relax. Indeed, reporters noted that Darrow looked refreshed on Monday, May 4, when everyone assembled in Judge Davis's courtroom to hear how long those convicted would be imprisoned. They all were given the maximum ten years at hard labor. Then, suddenly, Judge Davis ordered the courtroom cleared. Sheriff Gordon Ross appeared and took his new prisoners to the governor's office. Ten minutes later, Governor Judd commuted all sentences from ten years to one hour. Massie, Fortescue, Jones, and Lord were free by lunch. Darrow had outfoxed a prosecutor yet again.

The Darrows set sail back to the mainland on Sunday, May 5. Clarence, seasick again, spent much of the trip in his stateroom. His Hawaii getaway had not been much of a vacation. Despite diversions—he did go swimming and even surfed with Olympic swimmer Duke Kahanamoku (1890–1968)—work and illness defined his trip. The solitary confinement on the SS *Malolo* did, however, give him a chance to write his version of the Massie trial, which was first published in *Scribner's Magazine* and later placed as an addendum in the second edition of his autobiography. It did little to dampen the firestorm of criticism Darrow's defense of Massie and the governor's commutation had created. Critics found it "difficult to see in it any victory for law and order or for justice."[60] African American leaders were particularly upset. Darrow's defense of Massie, Fortescue, Lord, and Jones threw his withdrawal from the Scottsboro case under a different light. Was he a champion of civil rights? Even if he was, what could they say about a man who took cases for money over cause? Longtime allies such as U.S. Representative Oscar DePriest rapped Darrow for defending lynchers. Some even wondered if it was a sign of "senility."[61] African American priests and ministers, his old foes in the black community, relished this chance to attack Darrow anew.[62] He tried to repair the damage by granting an interview with African American journalist E. W. Wilkins from the *Kansas City Call*. Wilkins's article, which was reprinted in black newspapers across the country, was fair, but Darrow was unrepentant. He never wavered from his argument that racial harmony had always been his goal.[63] Publicly, he endeavored to make the Massie case yet another example of his core philosophy, of civil liberties and civil rights and of ending animosity among different races. Few saw the connections or believed his words. It didn't matter. The Massie trial irrevocably harmed Darrow's standing among minority groups, those, of course, in Hawaii as well as African Americans.

Following his Hawaiian expedition, Darrow capitalized on his fame and relentlessly pursued his public life. He continued speaking, though his message darkened, if that was even possible. A reporter who had attended an early 1934 Darrow debate with John Haynes Holmes on the question "Can civilization be saved?" noted that Darrow was as "blackly pessimistic" as ever. The world was doomed to "pestilence, mobs, and a resurgence of dark medieval passions."[64] Darrow laid the blame squarely on the shoulders of capitalists. They had brought nothing but "economic slavery." Holmes countered that New Dealers, armed with social scientific theories and statistics, could indeed save civilization and called on Darrow to join in the battle to put the nation back together. He refused, saying dryly: "[Y]ou can't count on me. I'm too old."[65]

Darrow did not want to be part of the Roosevelt revolution, which aimed to save capitalism from the capitalists, sought to boost the political and economic power of the average American, tried to foster a caring and more equitable society, and attempted to save the United States and in fact the entire world from the nightmares of totalitarianism. It was not that Darrow did not sympathize with Franklin Roosevelt, whom he had known for many years, or his agenda.[66] Rather, he was uncertain if FDR was the man for the job and was skeptical that the New Deal was the right medicine to cure America of its ills. To him, the New Deal experiment was too big, too controlling, and too intrusive. It was an affront to civil liberties and American freedoms. Darrow had supported Governor Roosevelt in the 1932 presidential election, though with hesitation, as Roosevelt was never quite clear about his intentions. Darrow took that to mean that FDR did not know what he was doing. Before the 1932 Democratic National Convention, which was held in Chicago, Darrow lent his lukewarm endorsement to Roosevelt but maintained that "there are others who probably are better men."[67]

Roosevelt's first months in office had done little to gain Darrow's praise and approval. The New Dealers had focused their attention on repairing the banking and financial systems, creating work relief, and restarting the agricultural and industrial sectors of the economy. Although Roosevelt's alphabet soup administration did much to stabilize the economy and bring about a measured recovery, Darrow was unimpressed. He saw the Agricultural Adjustment Administration's plan to create scarcity in farm commodities by destroying crops, killing livestock, and paying farmers not to farm as ludicrous. In a nation that was admittedly ill clad and ill nourished, it made no sense to destroy cotton or food. He was even more disappointed with the National Recovery Administration (NRA), which oversaw industrial recovery.

Under the leadership of the irascible retired general Hugh S. Johnson (1882–1942), the NRA had two jobs: it was in charge of work relief, and it brought regulation to industrial production. The New Dealers believed that industry had failed because of its incessant pursuit of undercutting the competition, which meant using more inexpensive materials and slashing wages. Eventually this myopic quest for low prices flooded markets with inferior goods, fostered monopoly, eliminated consumer purchasing power, and nearly destroyed capitalism itself. The NRA sought to eliminate this downward spiral through the creation of codes of fair competition so that all actors in the industrial sector had to abide by similar wage, hour, and raw materials rules. During the summer of 1933, a consortium of businessmen and government officials hammered out hundreds of industrial codes, more than seven hundred in all. Although the NRA's staffers dictated some terms, industrialists largely had a free hand in formulating the codes, most of which sanctioned that telltale sign of monopoly: price-fixing. Darrow found this repulsive and a direct challenge to American freedom and liberty.

Darrow was by no means the only one to criticize the NRA. The halting nature of the recovery, industrial strife, and stubbornly high unemployment led some to label the NRA the "National Run Around" or "No Recovery Allowed." The loudest complaints came from the small manufacturers—the so-called little man—who by January 1934 had sent more than nine thousand letters to various government officials decrying price-fixing and cartelization of various industries.[68] This ruckus reached fever pitch in the winter of 1933. Two Republican senators, William Borah and Gerald Nye (1892–1971), put considerable pressure on the Roosevelt administration to take action. In January 1934, FDR approved the creation of a review board for the NRA that would investigate complaints. Several names to lead the board were bandied about. Senators Borah and Nye quickly removed themselves from the list. When crusading politician-judge Samuel Seabury (1873–1958), who had just wrapped up his successful corruption investigation of New York City mayor James "Jimmy" Walker (1881–1946), turned Hugh Johnson down, the NRA's chief counsel, Donald Richberg, suggested his friend and hometown colleague Clarence Darrow, who agreed at the rate of twenty-five dollars per day (four hundred per day in today's dollars) plus expenses.[69]

Publicly, as Richberg explained, the NRA wanted a "well-known antimonopolist" to lead the board, reveal the codes' shortcomings, show how to improve them, and honestly demonstrate to the nation that the New Deal had only the best intentions, the best minds, and the best plan. Johnson shared some of Richberg's idealism but also hoped the board would act like a sop to soak up the public's and Congress's discontent. Initially, Johnson considered the choice of Darrow a masterstroke. The old man exuded political legitimacy. Only later did Johnson come to regret the appointment, calling it in his memoir "a moment of total aberration."[70] And for good reason. Darrow had little to no experience presiding over government hearings. He remained a defense lawyer. He was neither impartial nor dispassionate. Further, regardless of the Massie case, Darrow had never given up his advocacy of freedom and liberty. Darrow was squarely and immovably on the side of the little man, that small manufacturer, and saw his plight against the NRA as a civil liberties issue. Worse for the NRA's leaders, by 1934 he was less a fan of FDR and the New Deal than ever.[71] For Johnson and President Roosevelt, signing on Darrow was signing on to a world of trouble.

Perhaps they should have known better. For years, Darrow had been on record as opposing a strong central government. As he had written a friend in 1930, "I have all my life been a believer in state's rights and think it is most important for the preservation of any sort of individual liberty."[72] Darrow was particularly upset that the federal government had "interfered in giving suffrage to women, which was not its affair" and grossly intervened in society with prohibition.[73] Likely, neither FDR nor Johnson had followed Darrow's career carefully enough to know this or the sifting and distilling of his political philosophy. Nonetheless, they had some warning that Darrow was not an apparatchik. In May 1934, Darrow's old law partner and sometime nemesis Edgar Lee Masters wrote Raymond Moley (1886–1975), a member of FDR's brain trust, a letter stating that the Darrow appointment was a huge mistake. Citing Darrow's "dubious reputation," which included the fiasco over municipal ownership of Chicago's street railways and the indictment for jury bribing, Masters unfairly labeled Darrow a faithless "political infidel" bent on fame and fortune. Worse, Masters mischaracterized Darrow's board as the vanguard of a "socialist or communist state." Whatever Darrow's interest in this job, he was not to be trusted. Writing prophetically, Masters urged Moley to preempt an impending disaster. "Having fanged the administration," he predicted, Darrow "may be content to crawl away."[74] Although the letter reached President Roosevelt's desk, Darrow was not relieved and was allowed to assemble his team, which indeed fanged the NRA, poisoning it fatally.

The fully assembled review board—which included New York City lawyer John F. Sinclair; William W. Neal, a small-business man from North Carolina; Fred P. Mann, a retail merchant from North Dakota; and four of Darrow's friends: Chicago druggist Samuel C. Henry, erstwhile socialist

Charles Edward Russell, former law partner and left-wing radical William O. Thompson, and Chicago lawyer Lowell Mason, who, like Darrow, had had his life's savings erased by the stock market crash—began its work in March and stayed in the capital for more than three months, receiving more than three thousand complaints, holding nearly sixty hearings, and investigating thirty-four NRA codes. Its three main reports constituted a major blow to the Roosevelt administration, highlighting the "evils," "unfair practices," and "monopolistic conditions" either created by or ratified by various codes.[75] The first report was released to the public in late May 1934 and created an uproar that even Darrow did not expect. Much to the chagrin of President Roosevelt and General Johnson, it condemned the codes for iron and steel, coal, rubber, and several other industries.[76] A supplementary report, written by Thompson and additionally signed by Darrow, condemned the Federal Trade Commission for abdicating its responsibilities and the NRA for giving sanction to monopolies. Thompson argued that there was no hope for the small-business man under the current setup and that only "a planned economy, which demands socialized ownership and control," could bring about a full economic recovery.[77]

Stricken but not stunned, General Johnson and Richberg lashed out in an effort to save the NRA and their political lives. Both penned long responses to the review board's first report.[78] In the transmittal letter to President Roosevelt, Johnson cried foul, calling it "superficial, intemperate and inaccurate." "At the public expense," he continued, the board had used "unfair methods" to "promote private purposes." He recommended that the board be abolished forthwith. In his own cover letter, Richberg echoed his boss, asserting that Darrow's "haphazard, one sided investigation" had produced a nonsensical report that only "philosophic anarchists who apparently oppose any government control of anybody, including criminals," could be proud of. In Richberg's estimation, Darrow and his colleagues had "shamefully" abused the public trust and furnished "ammunition for the malicious sniping of political partisans, for the covert scheming of monopolists and for the mean attacks of chiselers who seek private profit."[79]

Richberg predicted correctly. Darrow's reports and the supplementary statement were fodder for the cannons that opponents leveled at the New Deal. On the one hand, critics cast President Roosevelt as the tool of monopolists, and on the other, he was a dupe or worse for allowing radicals like

Darrow inside the administration. Republicans in the House of Representatives began inquiries into the NRA's alleged promotion of monopolies and the charge that alleged socialists, such as Darrow and Rexford Guy Tugwell (1891–1979), had infiltrated FDR's brain trust.[80] Johnson and Richberg vehemently defended the brain trust and the NRA in the press, and in general the national magazines and newspapers backed them over Darrow. *The New York Times* saw Darrow's work as a blundering attempt to stir up controversy; *Business Week* attacked him for failing to make an "impeccably judicial study" of the NRA; and *The Nation*'s Paul Y. Anderson, a onetime Darrow admirer, was shocked by the Darrow reports' "ludicrous inconsistencies" and "glaring inaccuracies" and joined Johnson's call for the board's abolition.[81]

All the sound and fury finally got to Darrow. In late May, he was ready to make peace. He contacted General Johnson, who suggested that they go for a drive. Both men were coy with reporters upon their return to Darrow's hotel, the famous Willard Hotel. On the side, Johnson suggested that the two had struck a deal whereby the Darrow board of review might "leave the field with some dignity."[82] The Darrow board continued to work for almost another month, and Johnson instituted a few new rules about price-fixing and revised a couple of codes. Significantly, the public sniping between the NRA and the review board ended. Darrow had grown sick of all the fighting at the hearings, many of which devolved into "a long interminably dreary bickering."[83] He had grown tired of the internecine battles among his own staff. Even before the final report was issued John Sinclair and William Thompson jumped ship, both in very public and damaging ways.[84] Finally, he no longer desired to box with Johnson. On June 28, Darrow sent President Roosevelt the board's third and final report along with his resignation. Confident he had saved his agency, Johnson, however, underestimated the effect of Darrow's work. Within a year the NRA had been dissolved as the Supreme Court ruled it and its codes unconstitutional. It was the coup de grâce following Darrow's fatal bite.

Everyone expected that the National Recovery Review Board would be Darrow's last job. The seventy-seven-year-old had grown tired and ill while working long hours at the hearings and compiling, editing, and composing the board's reports. That nagging cough had grown worse. Ruby pushed him to give up cigarettes, but Clarence refused.[85] However, the speculators and reporters were wrong: Darrow was headed back to Chicago, not to retire again but to get back to work. On June 24, 1934, as Ruby packed their things, there was a knock at their Willard Hotel door. It was Arthur Garfield Hays, Darrow's old friend and fellow champion of civil liberties not only in the United States but in Europe too. By the look on his face, they could tell that this was no casual friendly visit.

Hays had become concerned about the growing threats posed by Adolf Hitler's regime in Germany and had even gone there to defend Georgi Dimitrov (1882–1949), a member of the Bulgarian Communist Party who had been prosecuted in Germany for setting fire to the Reichstag, which housed Germany's parliament. The Nazis used this arson attack to expand their assault on civil liberties and critics of the state. Upon his return to the United States, Hays had established the American Inquiry Commission, an unofficial organization the goal of which was to expose Nazi atrocities against Jews, unionists, radicals, and anyone opposed to Nazi terrorism. Hays wanted Darrow, the world-renowned lawyer for fairness, equality, justice, freedom, and liberty, to chair the commission's two days of public hearings, set for July 3 and 4 in New York City. With Darrow out front, Hays knew America, if not the world, would pay attention. Darrow needed no time to think. He was in. Darrow hated fascism, detesting everything it stood for, which was the antithesis of his distilled creed about individual rights, liberties, and freedoms. In the 1920s, he had defended several antifascist Italians, including Calogero Greco, Donato Carillo, and Armando Borghi.[86] Darrow also spoke out against the Nazis, sounding the alarm about their war on Jews. At a 1933 symposium on the topic, he expressed his horror at the destruction of morality in Germany and his fears about Hitler's plans. "I am glad that here in Chicago, a city as free and as liberal and as independent as any city I know of in the world," he told an appreciative audience, "men and women are raising their voices and taking their stand against the despotism in Germany, which is aimed now against the Jewish race, and the Jewish religion, but tomorrow may be well raised against any other race and any other religion!"[87] Darrow, long a staunch ally of Jewish Americans, had protested anti-Semitism for decades. In Chicago, Darrow supported the work of the Protective League, which aimed to eliminate violence against Jewish merchants, workers, and peddlers. He had also spoken out against other outrages, like the persecution of Leo Frank (1884–1915), the Jewish businessman who was falsely convicted of the murder of Mary Phagan (1899–1913) and who was later lynched. Darrow was a frequent friendly debater with prominent Jewish intellectuals, including Rabbi Stephen S. Wise (1874–1949) and Rabbi Eugene Mannheimer (1880–1952).[88] So respected was he among American Jews that he was offered honorary membership in Rabbi Joseph Jasin's Miami Beach Temple Israel. The lifelong agnostic accepted without hesitation.[89] Now, in their time of desperate need, Darrow was more than willing to lend his name, his credibility, and his respectability to help them.

The American Inquiry Commission made headlines. As Americans celebrated their independence, their democratic institutions, their freedoms and liberties, they learned what life in Nazi Germany had become. It was, as Communist leader Ernest Torgler explained, "nothing more than a condition of arbitrary lawlessness."[90] The German court system had been transformed into a means to facilitate "legalized murder" in the face of a "credulous world." It was a "return to barbarism," Torgler told the horrified commissioners, who also listened to testimony from a widow whose husband had been murdered by German storm troopers, a man who had been incarcerated in a concentration camp, and a seven-year-old boy who had witnessed firsthand the new Nazi educational curriculum.[91] Darrow was visibly moved, saddened, shaken, and angered, rather uncharacteristically telling reporters that he wished Hitler dead. "If there are any more murders tomorrow I hope it will end in the killing of Hitler," he proclaimed. There was no room for tolerance, patience, or forgiveness; Germany's leader was "a very dangerous man and ought to be destroyed."[92]

Soon after the hearings, the Darrows returned to Chicago. In the winter of 1934 Darrow was not well. He emerged in the spring of 1935, testifying before the U.S. Senate Finance Committee, which was debating the future of the National Recovery Administration. Darrow urged its "annihilation," much to the displeasure of his old friend Sidney Hillman, who argued just the opposite.[93] Despite illnesses and age, however, Darrow remained exceedingly political to the bitter end, supporting those people and causes that he thought would advance freedom and liberty. In 1936, he joined the Non-Partisan Committee for the Re-election of Vito Marcantonio (1902–1954), the charismatic far-left-winger congressman from New York City who ardently supported, among other issues, civil rights. Darrow also maintained his ties to the NAACP, remaining on its board of directors as the association renewed its drive for a federal law banning lynching. He continued to campaign against the death penalty and at seventy-eight was reelected the president of the American League to Abolish Capital Punishment. From that perch, he lobbied for clemency for Bruno R. Hauptmann (1899–1936), the man convicted and sentenced to death for murdering the Lindbergh baby. Darrow did not merely speak out on celebrated cases. He also pleaded on behalf of the lowly. When John Haefner, the son of the Kinsman, Ohio, shoemaker whom Darrow had known as a child, was imprisoned for killing his wife, Darrow conferred with prison officials, prosecutors, and the Ohio parole board to secure his release. His efforts for Hauptmann and Haefner were unsuccessful.[94] The law is a "horrible business," Darrow told a reporter in April 1936. "This is no such thing as justice—in or out of court."[95]

The next year Darrow celebrated his eightieth birthday with a small party hosted by the Progressive Lawyers Club at Henrici's restaurant, arguably Chicago's finest. It was a quiet affair. No speeches, no pomp and circumstance.[96] That spring Darrow did consent to two newspaper interviews: one from Russell Owen of *The New York Times* and the other from Victor Hackler of the Associated Press. Darrow sat with Owen in his apartment, chatting in front of his large bay windows overlooking his beloved Jackson Park. "Do you think I look 80 years old?" Darrow asked his companion. "Mr. Darrow," joked Owen, "you have always looked 80 years old." For the next few hours the two reviewed Darrow's long legal and political career. He was unrepentant about his deeds, words, and thoughts. He remained, as he put it himself, "a pessimist with hope." The world was violent, cruel, and inhumane, Darrow explained, but there was always a slim chance it might improve. But it would do so only through the expansion of tolerance, liberty, and freedom. Darrow told Hackler much the same, adding that his "efforts in behalf of unfortunates has [sic] brought me the greatest and most lasting gratification" in life. It was his hope that young lawyers would follow his example and devote their careers to the "more genuine, humane ambition to benefit the poor . . . rather than mainly themselves."[97]

These apparently were Darrow's last public words. The man whose name had appeared in *The New York Times* more than eight hundred times in his lifetime now disappeared from its pages. Shortly after his birthday, his health took a serious turn for the worse.[98] His heart began to fail. After enduring another sickly winter, on Sunday, March 13, 1938, a month short of his eighty-first birthday, Clarence Darrow died. He had been confined to his apartment for the last six months of his life with only a few visitors.[99] He slipped into a coma his last week. The afternoon that he died Ruby, Paul, and his sister Jennie Darrow Moore were at his side. He inhaled one last deep breath, as one might do when sleeping, and then released it and drew no more.[100] Every newspaper in the country carried the sad news, including African American newspapers, whose reporters focused on his significant contributions rather than on his one perceived lapse.[101] Ruby was destroyed by her husband's death, and George Whitehead stepped forward to handle the funeral. On March 14, hundreds filed by Darrow's body in an un-adorned coffin at the Skeeles-Biddle Funeral Parlor. The following day the coffin and bier were moved again. The funeral began inside Bond Chapel on the University of Chicago campus, where federal judge and former law part-ner William H. Holly delivered the only eulogy.[102] "Though we lay you in the grave and hide you from the sight of man," his friend said, "your brave words will speak for the poor, the oppressed, the captive and the weak; and your devoted life will inspire countless souls to do and dare in the holy cause for which you lived and died."[103]

Clarence Darrow was cremated. On March 15, Paul Darrow and George Whitehead took his ashes and walked to Jackson Park and on the bridge, now the Clarence Darrow Memorial Bridge, scattered them over the lagoon. It had been Darrow's favorite spot on earth, and although he had suggested that his ashes might be taken back to Kinsman, Ruby decided to leave him where he had been happiest.[104] Ruby, who lived for another twenty years, had a difficult time adjusting. "Without him," she wrote to a friend three years later, "nothing seems of any worth!"[105] She moved out of their apart-ment to a nearby hotel and began the painful task of sorting through her husband's papers. Eventually she sold most of them to Irving Stone (1903–1989), who wrote a biography that she did not care for.[106] Darrow had not left her much money, and she regretfully sold many of their possessions even as she labored to preserve her late husband's memory.[107] As he had foreseen, religious fanatics used his death to advance their ideologies. Shortly after his death, rumors appeared that he had recanted "all pagan ideas" on his deathbed and that a psychic had contacted Darrow, who "now knows that *we do* survive death with our personality, memory and mind in-tact."[108] Ruby did her best to ignore the nuts, but on the first anniversary of

Clarence's death, a Detroit spiritualist, Claude P. Noble, appeared on the Jackson Park bridge, recited the Lord's Prayer, and called out: "Clarence Darrow, I am here in fulfillment of our pact and if you can manifest yourself, please do it now." Nothing happened, but that did not stop Noble from coming back every year for most of a decade.[109]

As an agnostic, Darrow was never certain what the future held. Ruby once said that he never worried whether he was headed to heaven or hell because "he had so many good friends in either place."[110] He was also fairly certain that one could not come back. In any case, he did not want a medium to contact him. "God help the man who dared to restore me to life!" he quipped to a close friend.[111] He knew he was to suffer the same fate as Voltaire, Paine, Ingersoll, and other skeptics who allegedly found religious faith in their final moments. Darrow never put stock in deathbed confessions or in spirits from the beyond. So either Darrow's ghost is lazy, enjoying his rest and unwilling to be bothered, or as he would have said himself, dead is dead.[112]

Afterword

Clarence Darrow's death has not stopped us from invoking his ghost in all sorts of legal, social, and political situations. What would he say about the legalization of marijuana? What would he say and do about the prison at Guantánamo Bay, Cuba? How would he react to the social, political, and economic dominance of Wal-Mart and its mimetic competitors who run roughshod over everyone and everything in pursuit of profits and lower prices? What would he say about gay marriage, immigrant rights, and the Second Amendment? WWCDD: What would Clarence Darrow do? The answers are hard to pose for two reasons. First, as he famously said himself, Darrow never quite understood or explained why he did anything. In other words, who knows? Second, I add that it all depends on which Darrow you mean. Over the course of his life and career, Darrow sifted, winnowed, and shifted his causes and battles. As a young man he became the labor movement's lawyer and champion, seeing organized labor as *the* political force that would push and realize greater freedoms and liberties for average Americans. Nearly all his efforts went toward this cause, and he willingly gave up other parts of his life and philosophy and career for the success of the union movement. His trials in Los Angeles represented the apogee of that period of his life. After his bribery trials, a different Darrow emerged, one less devoted to the labor and similar mass movements and one more committed to fighting for civil rights and civil liberties.

So back to the point, my training as a historian makes me uneasy at these conjectures. I would say that we could draw from Darrow's story what we wish. Clarence Darrow the labor lawyer would see fighting corporate greed as paramount while Darrow the cultural radical would be interested in gay marriage (to the extent that he was interested in marriage at all). And Darrow the champion of civil rights and civil liberties would be concerned about the overreaching of the federal government in the post–September 11 era as well as the attacks on individual rights of citizens and aliens. Darrow and his commitments were malleable. Yet there is something irreducible about him too. For five decades, an amazingly long time in American politics, he fought to expand liberties, rights, and freedoms so that average people could have a fair chance of living the American dream. To those institutions, systems, and privileged elite that stood in the way of this, he was an iconoclast. Today, to the extent that we still live in a nation where the accident of birth has an overwhelming influence on one's future, Darrow would be at the forefront of the political and legal efforts to expand civil rights and civil liberties and to enhance the abilities of average Americans to get ahead. Do today's controversial issues meet Darrow's distilled philosophical standards? One can't be certain, but quite possibly he would have a lot of work to do.

NOTES

BIBLIOGRAPHIC ESSAY

ACKNOWLEDGMENTS

INDEX

Notes

Preface

1. Clarence S. Darrow, *Industrial Conspiracies: Lecture Delivered in Heilig Theatre, Port-land, Oregon, September 10, 1912* (Portland, Ore.: Otto Newman Publishing, 1912), 7.
2. Clarence Darrow, *Farmington* (Chicago: A. C. McClurg and Company, 1904; reprint, New York: Charles Scribner's Sons, 1932), 7.
3. Henry Adams, *The Education of Henry Adams: An Autobiography* (Boston: Houghton Mifflin, 1917), 36.
4. Letter, John R. Gregg to Colin Miller, March 5, 1942, John R. Gregg Papers, Box 4, Manuscripts and Archives Division, New York Public Library, Astor, Lenox and Tilden Foundations.

1: A Midwestern Childhood

1. Clarence S. Darrow, *The Story of My Life* (New York: Charles Scribner's Sons, 1932; reprint, New York: Da Capo Press, 1996), 1.
2. Ibid., 21.
3. Ibid., 6.
4. Ibid., 1.
5. Ibid.
6. Ibid., 4.
7. Ibid., 2; and Charles Yale Harrison, *Clarence Darrow* (New York: Jonathan Cape & Harrison Smith, 1931), 7.

8. Darrow, *The Story of My Life*, 2.

9. Ibid., 4.

10. Ibid., 3.

11. Colonel Ralph Plumb, "Reminiscences; Old Times in Trumbull County," *19th Century Voices of Trumbull County, Ohio*, comp. Grace Calvin Allison (Warren County, Ohio: Trumbull County Chapter OGS, 1993), 58.

12. Darrow, *The Story of My Life*, 8, 9.

13. Ibid., 8.

14. Susan Jacoby, *Freethinkers: A History of American Secularism* (New York: Henry Holt, 2004), 4.

15. Jacoby, *Freethinkers*, 4–5.

16. WPA, *The Ohio Guide* (New York: Oxford University Press, 1940), 433.

17. *History of Trumbull and Mahoning Counties with Illustrations and Biographical Sketches* (Cleveland: H. Z. Williams and Brothers, 1882), 288.

18. Darrow, *The Story of My Life*, 13.

19. Clarence Darrow, *Farmington* (Chicago: A. C. McClurg and Company, 1904; reprint, New York: Charles Scribner's Sons, 1932), 19.

20. Ibid., 32.

21. Ibid.

22. Ibid., 35.

23. Ibid., 33.

24. Ibid.

25. Darrow, *The Story of My Life*, 16–17.

26. Ibid., 20.

27. Ibid.

28. Darrow, *Farmington*, 34.

29. Darrow, *The Story of My Life*, 27.

30. Ibid.

31. Harrison, *Clarence Darrow*, 40.

32. Darrow, *Farmington*, 142.

33. Ibid., 29; and Darrow, *The Story of My Life*, 15, 13.

34. Darrow, *The Story of My Life*, 13.

35. Ibid., 14.

36. Darrow, *Farmington*, 39.

37. Ibid., 38.

38. Ibid., 43–44.

39. Ibid., 41; and Whittlesey Adams, "Trumbull County Spelling Match of Fifty Years Ago," *19th Century Voices of Trumbull County, Ohio*, comp. Allison, 88.

40. Darrow, *Farmington*, 41.

41. Ibid., 238.

42. Ibid., 239.

43. John Booth, "Tells of Underground Railroad of Old Slavery Days," *19th Century Voices of Trumbull County, Ohio*, comp. Allison, 432–34.

44. Irving Stone, *Clarence Darrow for the Defense* (New York: Doubleday, Doran, 1941), 470.

45. Darrow, *The Story of My Life*, 11.

46. Orson S. Fowler, *The Octagon House: A Home for All. With a New Introduction by Madeline B. Stern* (reprint, New York: Dover Publishing, 1973; 1853 original), 4, 3. Emphasis in the 1853 original.

47. Darrow, *The Story of My Life*, 15.

48. George E. MacDonald, *Fifty Years of Freethought* (reprint, New York: Arno Press, 1972; 1929 original), 289.

49. MacDonald, *Fifty Years of Freethought*, 289.

50. Darrow, *The Story of My Life*, 24.

51. Ibid., 17.

52. Darrow, *Farmington*, 52.

53. Ibid.

54. Darrow, *The Story of My Life*, 18.

55. Ibid., 19.

56. Darrow, *Farmington*, 78.

57. Ibid.

58. Ibid., 47.

59. Ibid., 50.

60. *History of Trumbull and Mahoning Counties*, 295.

61. Darrow, *The Story of My Life*, 22.

62. Ibid.

63. Ibid., 23.

64. Ibid., 26.

65. Ibid., 22.

66. Ibid., 27.

67. Ibid., 26.

68. Ibid., 27.

69. Ibid., 28.

70. Ibid.

71. Ibid.

72. Darrow, *Farmington*, 15.

73. Darrow, *The Story of My Life*, 28.

74. Darrow, *Farmington*, 182.

75. Ibid.

76. Ibid., 183.

77. Ibid., 184.

78. Ibid.

79. Ibid., 185–86.

80. Ibid., 186.
81. Ibid., 187.
82. Ibid., 190.
83. Ibid.
84. Ibid., 191.
85. Ibid.
86. Ibid., 192.
87. Ibid., 193.
88. Darrow, *The Story of My Life*, 29.
89. Stone, *Clarence Darrow for the Defense*, 17.
90. Darrow, *The Story of My Life*, 381.
91. Ibid., 19.
92. Ibid., 29.
93. Ibid.
94. Ibid., 30.

2: A Bum Profession

1. Clarence S. Darrow, *The Story of My Life* (New York: Charles Scribner's Sons, 1932; reprint, New York: Da Capo Press, 1996), 30, 31.
2. Letter, C. S. Darrow to the editor, *Truth Seeker*, March 20, 1880.
3. Darrow's original letterhead can be found in the Orrmel H. and Edward H. Fitch Papers, MSS 392, Box 1, Ohio Historical Society.
4. Clarence Darrow, *Response of Clarence Darrow to Birthday Greetings, April 18, 1918* (Chicago: Walden Book Shop, 1918), 8.
5. See, for example, letter, C. S. Darrow to Northway and Fitch, July 25, 1883, Fitch Papers, Box 1; and letter, Darrow to Northway and Fitch, August 3, 1883, Fitch Papers, Box 1.
6. Darrow, *The Story of My Life*, 34.
7. Kevin Tierney, *Darrow: A Biography* (New York: Thomas Y. Crowell, 1979), 26; and see "Wayne Harvest Home Picnic," *Jefferson Gazette*, September 2, 1881.
8. Darrow, *The Story of My Life*, 37.
9. Ibid., 32.
10. See *Brockway v. Jewell*, 52 Ohio St. 187 (1894).
11. Darrow, *The Story of My Life*, 35. See also *Brockway v. Jewell*, 52 Ohio St. 187 (1894); and Frank Siedel, *Out of the Midwest: More Chapters in the Ohio Story* (Cleveland: World Publishing, 1953), 21–30.
12. Darrow, *The Story of My Life*, 32.
13. See *History of Ashtabula County, Ohio with Illustrations and Biographical Sketches of Its Pioneers and Most Prominent Men* (Philadelphia: Williams Brothers, 1878), 1–49.
14. Clarence Darrow, "Frank Lowden, the Farmer's Friend," *Scribner's Magazine* 83 (April 1928): 396.

15. Clarence Darrow, "Political Issues," *Democratic Standard* (Ashtabula, Ohio), March 12, 1885.

16. Darrow, *The Story of My Life*, 39.

17. Ibid.

18. See, for example, Tierney, *Darrow*, 35.

19. Darrow, *The Story of My Life*, 41.

20. Ibid.

21. Ibid., 13.

22. Henry George, *Progress and Poverty: An Inquiry into the Cause of Industrial Depressions and of Increase of Want with Increase of Wealth* (reprint, New York: Modern Library, 1938; 1879 original), 10.

23. Ibid., 559.

24. Ibid., 299–328.

25. Ibid., 543, 552.

26. Richard Schneirov, *Labor and Urban Politics: Class Conflict and the Origins of Modern Liberalism in Chicago, 1864–97* (Urbana: University of Illinois Press, 1998), 119–23.

27. Darrow, *The Story of My Life*, 41.

28. Ibid.

29. John P. Altgeld, *Our Penal Machinery and Its Victims*, new rev. ed. (Chicago: A. C. McClung and Co., 1886), 8.

30. Ibid., 11.

31. As quoted ibid., 25.

32. Ibid., 74.

33. See Edgar Lee Masters, *The Tale of Chicago* (New York: G. P. Putnam's Sons, 1933). Masters and Darrow did not get along well, and Masters makes no mention of Darrow in his history of Chicago.

34. See Betty J. Irwin, "But Never Onionville: Chicago's Nicknames," in *Place Names in the Midwestern United States*, ed. Edward Callary (Lewiston, N.Y.: Edwin Mellon Press, 2000), 147–62.

35. Donald L. Miller, *City of the Century: The Epic of Chicago and the Making of America* (New York: Simon & Schuster, 1996), 178.

36. Marianne Weber, *Max Weber: Ein Lebensbild* (Tübingen: J.C.B. Mohr, 1926), 299.

37. Miller, *City of the Century*, 457.

38. See Vice Commission of Chicago, *The Social Evil in Chicago: A Study of Existing Conditions with Recommendations by the Vice Commission of Chicago* (Chicago: Gunthrop-Warren Printing Co., 1911), 71–113.

39. William T. Stead, *If Christ Came to Chicago: A Plea for the Union of All Who Love in the Service of All Who Suffer* (Chicago: Laird & Lee Publishers, 1894), 129.

40. Erik Larson, *The Devil in the White City: Murder, Magic, and Madness at the Fair That Changed America* (New York: Vintage, 2003), 12, 62.

41. Thomas E. Hill, "The Great 8-Hour Speech," *Eight-Hour Day* (Chicago, Illinois),

May 1, 1886, George A. Schilling Scrapbook 1, George A. Schilling Papers, Abraham Lincoln Presidential Library and Museum.

42. Schneirov, *Labor and Urban Politics*, 168–73.

43. Ray Ginger, *Altgeld's America: The Lincoln Ideal Versus Changing Realities* (Chicago: Quadrangle Books, 1958), 35–36.

44. See James Green, *Death in the Haymarket: A Story of Chicago, the First Labor Movement, and the Bombing That Divided the Gilded Age America* (New York: Pantheon, 2006).

45. Carl Sandburg, quoted in Richard C. Lindberg, *Quotable Chicago* (Chicago: Wild Onion Books, 1996), 81.

46. Darrow, *The Story of My Life*, 42.

47. Letter, Clarence Darrow to William Kent, December 19, 1914, quoted in Tierney, *Darrow*, 38.

48. Darrow, *The Story of My Life*, 45.

49. Ibid., 42.

50. Ibid., 43.

51. "The Convention Which Begins at Chicago To-Day," *New York Times*, February 19, 1889.

52. Darrow, *The Story of My Life*, 46.

53. Ibid.; and "Take Him for All in All: Reminiscences of Clarence Darrow," Microfilmed Papers of Elmer Gertz, Reel 1, Northwestern University Library Special Collections.

54. Clarence Darrow, "The Workingmen and the Tariff," *Chicago Herald*, February 21, 1889.

55. Darrow, *The Story of My Life*, 47.

56. Ibid., 48.

57. *The Sunset Club: The Meetings of 1893–94 and a List of the Members to January, 1895* (Chicago: The Club, 1895), 37.

58. Darrow, *Realism in Literature and Art* (Chicago: C. H. Kerr & Company, 1899), 56.

59. Ibid., 60.

60. Ibid., 61.

61. Ibid., 62.

62. Sunset Club of Chicago, *Echoes of the Sunset Club* (Chicago: Howard, Bartels & Co, 1891), 4.

63. Ibid., 5.

64. Schneirov, *Labor and Urban Politics*, 263–70.

65. "Only a Space of Time," *Chicago Evening Post*, November 7, 1891.

66. Letter, C. S. Darrow to Henry D. Lloyd, January 4, 1888, Microfilmed Papers of Henry D. Lloyd, Reel 2, Wisconsin Historical Society.

67. Schneirov, *Labor and Urban Politics*, 280–81, 305.

68. Darrow, *The Story of My Life*, 49.

69. Ibid., 96.

70. Unidentified clipping, May 2, 1895, *Chicago Daily News* [?], Darrow Family Scrapbooks, Scrapbook No. 1, Newberry Library.

71. Karen Abbott, *Sin in the Second City: Madams, Ministers, Playboys, and the Battle for America's Soul* (New York: Random House, 2007), 51; and Tierney, *Darrow*, 55.

72. Alan Hynd, *Defenders of the Damned* (New York: A. S. Barnes and Co., 1960), 99.

73. See, for example, "Victory for the City: Taxpayers' Interests Protected," *Chicago Herald*, December 25, 1889.

74. Henry D. Lloyd, *A Strike of Millionaires Against Miners or the Story of Spring Valley: An Open Letter to the Millionaires*, 2nd ed., rev. enl. (Chicago: Belford-Clark Co., 1890), 19.

75. Destler, *Henry Demarest Lloyd and the Empire of Reform* (Philadelphia: University of Pennsylvania Press, 1963), 225.

76. Ibid., 226.

77. Lloyd, *A Strike of Millionaires*, 121. Despite its notoriety in the Gilded Age, there has not been much scholarly attention paid to the Spring Valley lockout. The aftermath of the strike led to one of the nastiest race riots in Illinois's history. See Felix L. Armfield, "Fire on the Prairies: The 1895 Spring Valley Race Riot," *Journal of Illinois History* 3 (Autumn 2000): 185–200.

78. Larson, *Devil in the White City*, 119.

79. In his biography of Harrison, Claudius O. Johnson repeats the suggestion that error in counting votes—either intentional or unintentional—resulted in the loss of several thousand votes for Harrison. The final count for the top three vote getters was Washburne (Republican), 46,957; Cregier (Democrat), 46,588; and Harrison (independent), 42,931. No love was lost between Cregier and Harrison after the election of 1891. See Claudius O. Johnson, *Carter Henry Harrison*, vol. I: *Political Leader* (Chicago: University of Chicago Press, 1928), 74, 288–89.

80. Unidentified clipping, May 2, 1895, *Chicago Daily News*[?], Darrow Family Scrapbooks, Scrapbook No. 1, Newberry Library.

81. Letter, Clarence Darrow to Robert Gros, Robert Gros Papers, Box 1, Folder 4, Stanford University Library, Special Collections Department.

3: Becoming the "Attorney for the Damned"

1. Clarence Darrow, *The Story of My Life* (New York: Charles Scribner's Sons, 1932; reprint, New York: Da Capo Press, 1996), 57.

2. For more information on Goudy's life, see *Album of Genealogy and Biography, Cook County, Illinois with Portraits* (Chicago: Calumet Book & Engraving Co., 1895), 119–22; and "William Charles Goudy," *Dictionary of American Biography*, vol. 4 (New York: American Council of Learned Societies, 1931), 443–44.

3. See, for example, *Decatur Daily Republican*, October 24, 1892; *Decatur Daily Review*, October 26, 1892; and *Decatur Herald-Dispatch*, October 29, 1892.

4. Letter to the editor, *Democratic Standard* (Ashtabula, Ohio), September 2, 1887, Darrow Family Scrapbooks, Scrapbook No. 1, Newberry Library.

5. Ibid.

6. Letter, Clarence Darrow to George Schilling, October 15, 1887, Microfilmed Papers of Elmer Gertz, Reel 1, Northwestern University Special Collections; and Harvey J. Kaye, *Thomas Paine and the Promise of America* (New York: Farrar, Straus, and Giroux, 2005), 178, 189–90.

7. See Ray Ginger, *Altgeld's America: The Lincoln Ideal Versus Changing Realities* (Chicago: Quadrangle Books, 1958), 72–73; Harry Barnard, *Eagle Forgotten: The Life of John Peter Altgeld* (Secaucus, N.J.: Lyle Stuart, 1938), 156–57; and *Chicago Tribune*, April 28, 1892.

8. James Green, *Death in the Haymarket: A Story of Chicago, the First Labor Movement and the Bombing That Divided Gilded Age America* (New York: Pantheon Books, 2006), 282.

9. Darrow, *The Story of My Life*, 100–11.

10. "Altgeld Hanged in Effigy," *New York Times*, June 30, 1893.

11. Quoted in Green, *Death in the Haymarket*, 254.

12. Darrow, *The Story of My Life*, 102.

13. Ibid.

14. Richard Schneirov, *Labor and Urban Politics: Class Conflict and the Origins of Modern Liberalism in Chicago, 1864–1897* (Urbana: University of Illinois Press, 1998), 157.

15. "Clarence S. Darrow Resigns," *Daily Inter Ocean* (Chicago), September 13, 1893.

16. *Chicago Evening Post*, September 13, 1893; and *Chicago Daily News*, May 2, 1895. Both are in the Darrow Family Scrapbooks, vol. 1, Newberry Library.

17. Darrow, *The Story of My Life*, 57.

18. Mark Aldrich, *Death Rode the Rails: American Railroad Accidents and Safety, 1828–1965* (Baltimore: Johns Hopkins University Press, 2006), 2–3.

19. Darrow, *The Story of My Life*, 57. Emphasis added.

20. There have been several valiant attempts, however. Readers should consult Erik Larson's brilliant *The Devil in the White City: Murder, Magic, and Madness at the Fair That Changed America* (New York: Vintage, 2003); and the world's fair chapter in Donald L. Miller's *City of the Century: The Epic of Chicago and the Making of America* (New York: Simon & Schuster, 1996), 488–516.

21. See Norman Bolotin and Christine Laing, *The World's Columbian Exposition: The Chicago World's Fair of 1893* (Urbana: University of Illinois Press, 2002).

22. "Harrison's Murder Avenged," *New York Times*, July 14, 1893.

23. "His Last Address," *Chicago Tribune*, October 29, 1893.

24. "Is He Legally Dead?," March 25, 1894, no newspaper identified, Darrow Family Scrapbooks, Scrapbook No. 1, Newberry Library.

25. Claudius O. Johnson, *Carter Henry Harrison*, vol. 1: *Political Leader* (Chicago: University of Chicago Press, 1928), 126–28.

26. "Harrison Is Killed," *Chicago Tribune*, October 29, 1893.

27. "As Told by a Neighbor," *New York Times*, October 30, 1893.

28. "Prendergast Is Now Secluded in an Outlying Station," *Chicago Tribune*, October 29, 1893.

29. "Assassinated," *New York Times*, October 29, 1893.

30. Ibid.; "Prendergast Safe in Jail," "The Coroner's Inquest," "As to Prendergast's Sanity," and "A Great City in Mourning," *New York Times*, October 30, 1893; "Prendergast Was a Silver Crank," *New York Times*, October 31, 1893; Larson, *The Devil in the White City*, 58; and Richard Lindberg, *Return to the Scene of the Crime: A Guide to Infamous Places in Chicago* (Nashville, Tenn.: Cumberland House, 1999), 296–300.

31. "Assassinated," *New York Times*, October 29, 1893.

32. Ibid.; "Threats Made on Thursday," *New York Times*, October 29, 1893.

33. Harrison's cabinet selections were not merely local news. The story was covered by *The New York Times*. See "Mr. Harrison's Inauguration: The Cabinet of the World's Fair Mayor of Chicago," *New York Times*, April 18, 1893.

34. "Harrison's Murder Avenged," *New York Times*, July 14, 1893.

35. "Altgeld Could Be Impeached," *Chicago Tribune*, October 30, 1893.

36. See Christopher Slobogin, "Insanity Defense," in *The Oxford Companion to the Supreme Court of the United States*, ed. Kermit L. Hall, James W. Ely, Jr., Joel B. Grossman, and William M. Wiecek (New York: Oxford University Press, 1992), 433.

37. "As to Prendergast's Sanity," *New York Times*, October 30, 1893; "The Assassin Promptly Indicted," *New York Times*, October 31, 1893; and "Jury Prompt to Act," *Chicago Tribune*, October 31, 1893.

38. Irving Stone, *Clarence Darrow for the Defense* (Garden City, N.Y.: Doubleday, Doran, 1941), 70.

39. "Denounced in Jail," *Chicago Tribune*, November 1, 1893; and "The Assassin in His Prison," *New York Times*, November 1, 1893.

40. "Prendergast's Trial Begun," *New York Times*, December 7, 1893.

41. "Henry George Will Be Called by the Defense This Week," *New York Times*, December 17, 1893.

42. "The Prendergast Murder Trial," *New York Times*, December 19, 1893.

43. "Bad Day for Assassin Prendergast," *New York Times*, December 20, 1893; "The Prendergast Murder Trial," *New York Times*, December 21, 1893; "Don't Believe Prendergast Insane," *New York Times*, December 24, 1893.

44. "Murderer Prendergast Excited," *New York Times*, December 29, 1893.

45. "Prendergast Found Guilty," *New York Times*, December 30, 1893.

46. "To Save Prendergast's Neck," *New York Times*, December 31, 1893.

47. Ibid.

48. "Prendergast May Gain a Week," *New York Times*, February 27, 1894.

49. "He Kissed Mr. Darrow," *Chicago Record*, June 30, 1894.

50. "A Respite for Prendergast," *New York Times*, March 23, 1894.

51. *In re Prendergast*, James Todd's Closing Statement, Part II, p. 9, University of Minnesota Law Library, Special Collections. The page numbering in this legal document restarted at every change of stenographer. I have labeled each start a part. Hence "Part II" refers to the place where the second stenographer began.

52. *In re Prendergast*, James Todd's Closing Statement, Part II, 44.

53. Ibid., 45.

54. Ibid., Part III, 1.

55. Ibid., Part III, 8.

56. Ibid., Part III, 11.

57. Ibid., Part III, 14.

58. Ibid., Part III, 15.

59. Ibid., Part V, 11b.

60. "Errands of Mercy That Failed," *Literary Digest* (March 8, 1913): 547–50.

61. See Henry D. Lloyd, *A Strike of Millionaires Against Miners or the Story of Spring Valley*, 2nd ed., rev. and enl. (Chicago: Belford-Clark Co., 1890), 298; and letter, Henry D. Lloyd to Clarence Darrow, November 23, 1894, Microfilmed Papers of Henry D. Lloyd, Reel 5, Wisconsin Historical Society.

62. Shelton Stromquist, *A Generation of Boomers: The Pattern of Railroad Labor Conflict in 19th Century America* (Urbana: University of Illinois Press, 1987), 25–26, 45–46.

63. Pullman strikes always garnered national coverage. See "A Strike of Pullman Employees," *Rocky Mountain News* (Denver), February 15, 1882; "The Chinese Club," *St. Louis Daily Globe-Democrat*, March 7, 1883; and "Wood Carvers at Pullman on Strike," *Milwaukee Sentinel*, January 7, 1888.

64. Quoted in Liston Edgington Leyendecker, *Palace Car Prince: A Biography of George Mortimer Pullman* (Niwot: University Press of Colorado, 1992), 216.

65. On the Burlington strike, see Nick Salvatore, *Eugene V. Debs: Citizen and Socialist* (Urbana: University of Illinois Press, 1982), 74–82. For another discussion of the fights among unions at the end of the nineteenth century, see Robert E. Weir, "Dress Rehearsal for Pullman: The Knights of Labor and the 1890 New York Central Strike," in *The Pullman Strike and the Crisis of the 1890s: Essays on Labor and Politics*, ed. Richard Schneirov, Shelton Stromquist, and Nick Salvatore (Urbana: University of Illinois Press, 1999), 21–42.

66. William H. Carwardine, *The Pullman Strike* (Chicago: Charles H. Kerr and Co., 1894), 77–78.

67. Barnard, *Eagle Forgotten*, 281.

68. United States Strike Commission, *Report on the Chicago Strike, June–July 1894* (Washington, D.C.: GPO, 1894), xxii.

69. "Pullman Shops Idle," *Milwaukee Sentinel*, May 12, 1894.

70. "The Pullman Strike," *Galveston Daily News*, May 14, 1894.

71. See Daniel Ray Papke, *The Pullman Case: The Clash of Labor and Capital in Industrial America* (Lawrence: University Press of Kansas, 1999), 18–19. See also "The

Pullman Strike," *Penny Press* (Minneapolis), May 14, 1894; "GN," *Penny Press* (Minneapolis), May 15, 1894; and Nick Salvatore, *Eugene V. Debs: Citizen and Socialist* (Urbana: University of Illinois Press, 1982), 128–29.

72. Almont Lindsey, *The Pullman Strike: The Story of a Unique Experiment and of a Great Labor Upheaval* (Chicago: University of Chicago Press, 1942), 129; "Inconclusive Arbitration," *Milwaukee Sentinel*, May 15, 1894; and "Pullman Strike," *Penny Press* (Minneapolis), June 3, 1894.

73. "After Lyman Gage," *Milwaukee Journal*, June 15, 1894.

74. "The Pullman Strike," *Galveston Daily News*, June 17, 1894; and "A.R.U.," *Penny Press* (Minneapolis), June 21, 1894.

75. "Boycott Begins To-Day," *Milwaukee Sentinel*, June 26, 1894.

76. "Embracing More Railroads," *New York Times*, June 29, 1894.

77. Papke, *Pullman Case*, 130.

78. "A Proclamation by the President of the United States of America," *A Compilation of the Messages and Papers of the Presidents, 1789–1897*, ed. James D. Richardson, vol. 10 (Washington, D.C.: GPO, 1899), 499–500. See also Troy Rondinone, "Guarding the Switch: Cultivating Nationalism During the Pullman Strike," *Journal of the Gilded Age and Progressive Era* 8 (January 2009): 83–109.

79. Darrow, *The Story of My Life*, 58.

80. Ibid., 60.

81. Ibid., 61.

82. Ibid., 63.

83. Ibid., 61.

84. "A Heavy Blow at Industry," *New York Times*, July 16, 1894.

85. Letter, Clarence Darrow to Henry D. Lloyd, November 22, 1894, Reel 5, Wisconsin Historical Society.

86. Arthur Weinberg, *Attorney for the Damned: Clarence Darrow in His Own Words* (New York: Simon & Schuster, 1957), xv.

4: Fighting for the People in and out of Court

1. "Debs in the Law's Grasp," *New York Times*, July 11, 1894.

2. "Debs Behind Prison Bars," *New York Times*, July 18, 1894.

3. "Plan of the Strikers' Defense," *New York Times*, July 23, 1894.

4. "Debs Behind Prison Bars," *New York Times*, July 18, 1894.

5. "Labor's Rights and Wrongs," *New York Times*, September 28, 1894.

6. "Conspiracy Trial Closed," *New York Times*, September 29, 1894.

7. Ibid.

8. "Debs Gets Six Months," *New York Times*, December 15, 1894.

9. David Ray Papke, *The Pullman Case: The Clash of Labor and Capital in Industrial America* (Lawrence: University Press of Kansas, 1999), 54.

10. "The Testimony Against Debs," *New York Times*, January 29, 1895.

11. Ibid.

12. "The Debs Trial May Be Discontinued," *New York Times*, February 12, 1895; and "The Debs Case Is Continued Until May," *New York Times*, February 13, 1895.

13. Letter, C. S. Darrow to Lyman Trumbull, October 9, 1894, Lyman Trumbull Family Papers, vol. 4, Abraham Lincoln Presidential Library and Museum.

14. It has been more than fifty years since a biographer has investigated the life and career of Justice Fuller. See Willard L. King, *Melville Weston Fuller* (New York: Macmillan, 1950). A reprint of this book has just been issued.

15. "The Debs Habeas Corpus Case," *New York Times*, January 15, 1895; and C. S. Darrow, S. S. Gregory, and Lyman Trumbull, *Ex Parte: In the Matter of Eugene V. Debs, et al.: Petition for a Writ of Habeas Corpus, No. 11, Original, In the Supreme Court of the United States, October Term 1894* (Washington, D.C.: GPO, 1894).

16. "Debs's Prayer for Release," *New York Times*, January 17, 1895; "No Writ of Error for Debs," *New York Times*, January 18, 1895; and "Eugene V. Debbs [*sic*] Is Admitted to Bail," *New York Times*, January 22, 1895.

17. Henry James, *Richard Olney and His Public Service, with Documents Including Unpublished Diplomatic Correspondence* (Boston: Houghton Mifflin, 1923), 12.

18. "The Government's Right," *New York Times*, March 27, 1895.

19. Darrow et al., *Ex Parte, Eugene V. Debs, et al., Habeas Corpus: Brief and Argument for Petitioners*, 15.

20. Ibid., 43, 49.

21. Ibid., 73–74.

22. Ibid., 94–97.

23. Unidentified clipping [1895], Darrow Family Scrapbooks, Scrapbook No. 2, Newberry Library.

24. "Debs to Serve His Term," *New York Times*, May 28, 1895.

25. *In re Debs*, 158 U.S. 564 (1895).

26. Clarence Darrow, *The Story of My Life* (New York: Charles Scribner's Sons, 1932; reprint, New York: Da Capo Press, Inc., 1996), 67.

27. See Gerald G. Eggert, *Richard Olney: Evolution of a Statesman* (University Park: Pennsylvania State University Press, 1974), 152–64; and Papke, *The Pullman Case*, 90–91.

28. Grover Cleveland, "The Government in the Chicago Strike of 1894," *McClure's Magazine* 33 (July 1894): 227–40.

29. George Brown Tindall, ed., *A Populist Reader: Selections from the Works of American Populist Leaders* (New York: Harper & Row, 1966), 75–79.

30. Quoted in Chester McArthur Destler, *Henry Demarest Lloyd and the Empire of Reform* (Philadelphia: University of Pennsylvania Press, 1963), 263.

31. Ibid., 265.

32. Platform of People's Party Convention, Springfield, Illinois, July 4, 1894, Microfilmed Papers of Henry D. Lloyd, Reel 52, Wisconsin Historical Society.

33. See also letter, C. S. Darrow to C. L. Withington, November 9, 1905, Microfilmed Papers of Henry D. Lloyd, Reel 15, Wisconsin Historical Society. In the letter, Darrow claimed that thirty thousand people had marched and that the crowd had been so wild no one heard any speeches. Certainly that might have been the case for many.

34. "Crowd the Auditorium: Greatest American Audience, Room Is Packed to Limit," *Searchlight* (October 25, 1894), Darrow Family Scrapbooks, Scrapbook No. 1, Newberry Library.

35. Destler, *Henry Demarest Lloyd*, 283.

36. Letter, Clarence S. Darrow to Henry D. Lloyd, November 22, 1894, Microfilmed Papers of Henry D. Lloyd, Reel 5, Wisconsin Historical Society.

37. Letter, Henry Lloyd to Clarence Darrow, November 23, 1894, Microfilmed Papers of Henry D. Lloyd, Reel 5, Wisconsin Historical Society.

38. Letter, Clarence Darrow to Henry Lloyd, November 24, 1894, Microfilmed Papers of Henry D. Lloyd, Reel 5, Wisconsin Historical Society.

39. Harry Barnard, *Eagle Forgotten: The Life of John Peter Altgeld* (Secaucus, N.J.: Lyle Stuart, 1938), 348.

40. "Men to Run the Race," *Chicago Herald*, February 18, 1895.

41. Ibid.

42. "CS Darrow for Congress," no date, no newspaper indicated, Darrow Family Scrapbooks, Scrapbook No. 1, Newberry Library

43. "Free Silver and Debt," *Chicago Record*, May 4, 1895, Darrow Family Scrapbooks, Scrapbook No. 1, Newberry Library.

44. J.M.H. Frederick, *National Party Platforms of the United States, Presidential Candidates, Electoral and Popular Votes* (Akron: J.M.H. Frederick, 1896), 88.

45. See Michael Kazin, *A Godly Hero: The Life of William Jennings Bryan* (New York: Alfred A. Knopf, 2006).

46. William Jennings Bryan, "Cross of Gold Speech," in *A Populist Reader*, ed. Tindall, 203.

47. Ibid., 211.

48. Kazin, *A Godly Hero*, 61.

49. Ibid.

50. "The Fourth Ballot: A Stampede to Bryan—The Convention in Continuous Uproar," *New York Times*, July 10, 1896.

51. Darrow, *The Story of My Life*, 92.

52. "Illinois for McKinley: His Plurality Will Probably Be Nearly 100,000," *New York Times*, November 4, 1896.

53. Darrow, *The Story of My Life*, 92–93.

54. Ibid., 93.

55. Clarence Darrow, "The Divorce Problem," *Vanity Fair* (August 1927): 31.

56. Clipping, "Is Still Grinding Alone," October 27, 1898, Thomas I. Kidd Scrapbook, Wisconsin Historical Society.

57. "Considering a Strike," *Oshkosh Enterprise*, May 15, 1898 [?],Thomas I. Kidd Scrapbook, Wisconsin Historical Society; and "1,500 Men Are Out," *Milwaukee Sentinel*, May 17, 1898.

58. Quoted in Virginia Glenn Crane, *The Oshkosh Woodworkers' Strike of 1898: A Wisconsin Community in Crisis* (Madison: Wisconsin Sesquicentennial Commission, 1998), 121.

59. Quoted ibid., 102.

60. "Conference Agreed To," *Milwaukee Sentinel*, May 27, 1898.

61. "Recognition of Union," *Milwaukee Sentinel*, June 6, 1898; and "Recognition of Union," *Milwaukee Sentinel*, June 20, 1898.

62. "Recognition of Union," *Milwaukee Sentinel*, June 20, 1898.

63. "Good Feeling in Oshkosh," *Milwaukee Sentinel*, August 22, 1898.

64. "Unruly Wisconsin Strikers," *New York Times*, June 24, 1898; "What It Cost Oshkosh," *Milwaukee Sentinel*, July 3, 1898; "Oshkosh Riots Resumed," *New York Times*, August 6, 1898; "The Riots at Oshkosh," *New York Times*, August 7, 1898; "Oshkosh Strike at an End," *Milwaukee Sentinel*, August 5, 1898; "Furniture Factories Combine," *New York Times*, October 11, 1898; "Wisconsin Labor Men Aroused over Infamy at Oshkosh," *Chicago Dispatch*, August 15, 1898, Thomas I. Kidd Scrapbook, Wisconsin Historical Society; "Wisconsin's Disgrace," *Toledo Union*, July 20, 1898, Thomas I. Kidd Scrapbook, Wisconsin Historical Society; newspaper clipping, "Pledge T. I. Kidd Support," Thomas I. Kidd Scrapbook, Wisconsin Historical Society; "Labor Riots at Oshkosh," *Chicago Tribune*, June 23, 1898, Thomas I. Kidd Scrapbook, Wisconsin Historical Society; "Millionaires of Oshkosh Adopt Tactics of the Spaniards," *Chicago Dispatch*, August 16, 1898, Thomas I. Kidd Scrapbook, Wisconsin Historical Society; and Virginia Glenn Crane, "The Very Pictures of Anarchy: Women in the Oshkosh Woodworkers' Strike of 1898," *Wisconsin Magazine of History* 84 (2001): 44–59.

65. See "Labor Men on Trial," *Chicago Record*, October 15, 1898; and "Strikers at the Bar," *Chicago Record*, October 17, 1898.

66. Crane, *The Oshkosh Woodworkers' Strike of 1898*, 439–46.

67. "Kidd Case at Oshkosh," *Milwaukee Journal*, October 14, 1898; and "Strikers at the Bar," *Chicago Record*, October 17, 1898.

68. "Labor Men on Trial," *Chicago Record*, October 15, 1898.

69. "Testimony in Kidd Case," *Milwaukee Sentinel*, October 21, 1898.

70. "Say Strikers Beat Them," *Milwaukee Journal*, October 24, 1898.

71. Clipping, "Is Still Grinding Along," October 27, 1898, Thomas I. Kidd Scrapbook, Wisconsin Historical Society.

72. "Thomas I. Kidd Testifies," *Chicago Record*, October 25, 1898; and "Thomas Kidd on the Stand," *Milwaukee Journal*, October 23, 1898.

73. Clarence S. Darrow, *The Woodworkers' Conspiracy Case*, 2nd ed. (Chicago: Campbell Printers, 1900), 5, 38, 45, 54, 72.

74. Ibid., 5, 7, 8, 9, 15, 16, 17, 19, 22, 28, 31, 39, 42, 54. See also "Strikers on Trial," *Chicago Record*, August 16, 1898.

75. Darrow, *The Woodworkers' Conspiracy Case*, 17.

76. Ibid. 16, 18, 30, 33–35.

77. Ibid., 79–80.

78. Clipping, "They Are Not Guilty," November 3, 1898, Thomas I. Kidd Scrapbook, Wisconsin Historical Society.

79. "Labor's Defense: Eloquent and Masterly Speech of Hon. Clarence S. Darrow," *Labor Advocate* (Birmingham, Ala.), July 1, 1899.

80. "Oshkosh Woodworkers Will Decide To-Day," *Milwaukee Sentinel*, April 23, 1899; and "No Strike This Week," *Milwaukee Sentinel*, April 24, 1899.

5: Labor's Lyrical Lawyer

1. Kevin Tierney, *Clarence Darrow: A Biography* (New York: Thomas Y. Crowell Publishers, 1979), 139.

2. Timothy B. Spears, *Chicago Dreaming: Midwesterners and the City, 1871–1919* (Chicago: University of Chicago Press, 2005), 205–33. See also Christine Stansell, *American Moderns: Bohemian New York and the Creation of the New Century* (New York: Henry Holt, 2000), 44, 50–54, 204–6.

3. Clarence S. Darrow, "Woman," *Belford's Magazine* 5 (July 1890): 254.

4. Ibid., 260–61.

5. Gertrude Barnum, "The Immorality of Clarence Darrow," quoted by Irving Stone, *Clarence Darrow for the Defense* (New York: Doubleday, Doran, 1941), 115, 525n114.

6. George E. MacDonald, *Fifty Years of Freethought*, vol. 2 (New York: Truth Seeker Co., 1929–1931), 234.

7. Stansell, *American Moderns*, 147–77.

8. Here Darrow was partially following in Robert Ingersoll's footsteps. See Ingersoll's homage to Whitman and to Burns: Robert G. Ingersoll, "What Is Poetry?: Testimonial to Walt Whitman" and "Robert Burns," in *The Works of Robert G. Ingersoll*, vol. 3 (New York: Dresden Publishing Co., 1901), 77–119, 277–304.

9. Clarence S. Darrow, "Literary Style," *Tomorrow* 1 (January 1905): 29.

10. Clarence S. Darrow, "Tolstoi," *Rubric* 1 (January 1902): 27.

11. Ibid., 38.

12. Clarence Darrow, "Some Paragraphs Addressed to Socialists," in *Realism in Literature and Art: Little Blue Book No. 934* (Girard, Kan.: Haldeman-Julius Co., 1925), 60.

13. Kevin Tierney discusses the brief meeting with Kropotkin in *Darrow: A Biography* (New York: Thomas Y. Crowell, 1979), 173.

14. Clarence S. Darrow, *Resist Not Evil* (Port Townsend, Wash.: Breakout Productions, 1994; 1902 original), 10.

15. Ibid., 11.

16. Clarence Darrow, *Farmington* (New York: Charles Scribner's Sons, 1904; reprint, 1932), 194.

17. Ibid., 195.

18. Ibid., v.

19. "The Heart of a Boy," *New York Times*, October 8, 1904; Sara Andrew Shafer, "Through the Eyes of a Boy," *Dial* 37 (October 1, 1904): 237; "Farmington," *Independent* 55 (December 22, 1904): 1455; and "Farmington," *Critic* 46 (January 1905): 93.

20. Francis Hackett, "An American Boy," *New Republic* 22 (March 3, 1920): 36; and "Farmington," *New York Times*, December 11, 1932.

21. See "Kinsman Ignores Famed Son, Clarence Darrow," *Cleveland Press* (July 24, 1962); and Nils P. Johnson, Jr., "Kinsman and Mr. Darrow: The Defense Rests—Finally," *Ohio Magazine* (November 1989): 24–61.

22. Clarence Darrow, *An Eye for an Eye* (New York: Fox, Duffield & Co., 1905), 3.

23. Ibid., 7.

24. Grace Isabel Colbron, "Mr. Darrow's 'An Eye for an Eye,'" *Bookman* 22 (February 1906): 629. See also "Review of *An Eye for an Eye*," *Independent* 59 (November 2, 1902): 1052.

25. Anna Alex, "Review of *An Eye for an Eye*," *Everyman* 7 (May 1908): 157.

26. R. Baird Shuman, "Clarence Darrow's Contributions to Literary Naturalism: *An Eye for an Eye*," *Revue des langues vivantes* 34 (1970): 390–400. See also letter, Theodore Dreiser to Clarence Darrow, February 1, 1926, Clarence Darrow Collection, http://darrow.law.umn.edu/letters.php?pid=374&skey=1926, accessed July 7, 2010.

27. Abe C. Ravitz, *Clarence Darrow and the American Literary Tradition* (Cleveland: Press of Western Reserve University, 1962), 94; and Oscar Cargill, *Intellectual America: Ideas on the March* (New York: Cooper Square Publishers, 1941), 113.

28. "Errands of Mercy That Failed," *Literary Digest* 46 (March 8, 1913): 547–50; and Ravitz, *Clarence Darrow and the American Literary Tradition*, 25–26, 35–42, 100, 102, 147.

29. See Stansell, *American Moderns*, 45.

30. John R. Commons, quoted in Georg Leidenberger, *Chicago's Progressive Alliance: Labor and the Bid for Public Streetcars* (De Kalb: Northern Illinois University Press, 2006), 58–59.

31. Ibid., 62–63.

32. John Franch, *Robber Baron: The Life of Charles Tyson Yerkes* (Urbana: University of Illinois Press, 2006), 13.

33. Clarence S. Darrow, "The Chicago Traction Question," *International Quarterly* 12 (October 1905): 13–14. See also George C. Sikes, "Traction Problems: Chicago and Cincinnati Compared," George Schilling Papers, Scrapbook 2, Abraham Lincoln Presidential Library and Museum.

34. Darrow, "The Chicago Traction Question," 16–18.

35. Franch, *Robber Baron*, 135.

36. Ibid., 131–44.

37. Leidenberger, *Chicago's Progressive Alliance*, 75–77; and see Darrow, "The Chicago Traction Question," 21.

38. Clarence S. Darrow, *The Story of My Life* (New York: Charles Scribner's Sons, 1932; reprint, New York: Da Capo Press, 1996), 109; and Kevin Tierney, *Darrow: A Biography* (New York: Thomas Y. Crowell, 1979), 161–62.

39. "Chicago City Election," *New York Times*, April 5, 1899.

40. "Mayor Harrison Talks: Harrison and Bryan to Meet Soon at Monticello Club—Altgeld's Influence Gone," *New York Times*, April 6, 1899.

41. See George Schilling's eulogy for John Altgeld, George Schilling Papers, Box 2, Abraham Lincoln Presidential Library and Museum.

42. Mary Darrow Olson obituary, March 17, 1902, unidentified clipping, Darrow Family Scrapbooks, Scrapbook No. 1, Newberry Library.

43. Darrow, *The Story of My Life*, 112.

44. "Public Ownership League," George Schilling Papers, Box 2, Abraham Lincoln Presidential Library and Museum.

45. Leidenberger, *Chicago's Progressive Alliance*, 78–98; and "Here Is the Lawyer Whose Long Record Is the Best Proof of His Strong Love for the People," *Hearst's Chicago American*, October 25, 1902.

46. Chester McArthur Destler, "On the Eve of the Anthracite Coal Strike Arbitration: Henry D. Lloyd at United Mine Workers Headquarters, October–November 1902," *Labor History* 13 (March 1972): 284; and telegram, Henry D. Lloyd to John Mitchell, October 27, 1902, Microfilmed Papers of Henry D. Lloyd, Reel 15, Wisconsin Historical Society.

47. Arthur Weinberg, ed., *Attorney for the Damned* (New York: Simon & Schuster, 1957), 285–86; and Tierney, *Darrow*, 184.

48. Robert H. Wiebe, "The Anthracite Strike of 1902: A Record of Confusion," *Mississippi Valley Historical Review* 48 (September 1961): 230; and Perry K. Blatz, *Democratic Miners: Work and Labor Relations in the Anthracite Coal Industry, 1875–1925* (Albany: State University Press of New York, 1994), 4.

49. See Priscilla Murolo and A. B. Chitty, *From the Folks Who Brought You the Weekend: A Short, Illustrated History of Labor in the United States* (New York: New Press, 2001), 43.

50. Destler, "On the Eve of the Anthracite Coal Strike Arbitration," 282. Emphasis in original.

51. Quoted in Robert J. Cornell, *The Anthracite Coal Strike of 1902* (Washington, D.C.: Catholic University Press, 1957), 170; and Joseph Dorfman, *Thorstein Veblen and His America* (New York: August M. Kelley, 1934; reprint, 1966), 208.

52. Anthracite Coal Strike Commission, *Report to the President on the Anthracite Coal Strike of May–October, 1902* (Washington, D.C.: GPO, 1903), 39–41.

53. Chester McArthur Destler, *Henry Demarest Lloyd and the Empire of Reform* (Philadelphia: University of Pennsylvania Press, 1963), 474.

54. "Cleveland on Coal Strike," *New York Times*, August 8, 1908.

55. Excellent summaries of President Theodore Roosevelt's role can be found: Robert H. Wiebe, "The Anthracite Strike of 1902: A Record of Confusion," *Mississippi Valley Historical Review* 48 (September 1961): 229–251; Lewis L. Gould, *The Presidency of*

Theodore Roosevelt (Lawrence: University Press of Kansas, 1991), 65–71; and Stacy A. Cordery, *Theodore Roosevelt in the Vanguard of the Modern* (Belmont, Calif.: Wadsworth/Thomson Learning, 2003), 86–91.

56. Destler, "On the Eve of the Anthracite Coal Strike Arbitration," 293–94. See also Thomas I. Kidd, "What Is the Best Way to Settle the Miners' Strike?" *Inter Ocean*, October 5, 1902, George Schilling Papers, Scrapbook 2, Abraham Lincoln Presidential Library and Museum.

57. Darrow, *The Story of My Life*, 116.

58. Ibid., 115.

59. "Baer and Darrow Make Last Charges," *North American* (Philadelphia, PA), February 13, 1903.

60. Ibid.

61. Ibid.

62. "Coal Strike Commission Will Lose No Time in Deciding Case and May Summon Mitchell," *North American*, February 16, 1903.

63. Anthracite Coal Strike Commission, *Report to the President on the Anthracite Coal Strike*, 80–87.

64. "Victory, Says Mr. Mitchell," *New York Times*, March 22, 1903; and "Arbitrators Award," *United Mine Workers Journal* (March 26, 1903): 1.

65. "Mr. Baer Is Reticent," *New York Times*, March 22, 1903.

66. Letter, Clarence Darrow to Henry D. Lloyd, April 2, 1903, Microfilmed Papers of Henry D. Lloyd, Reel 14, Wisconsin Historical Society.

67. Darrow, *The Story of My Life*, 117.

68. Mary Harris Jones, *Autobiography of Mother Jones* (Chicago: Clark H. Kerr & Co., 1925; reprint, 2004 Dover ed.), 33; and Craig Phelan, *Divided Loyalties: The Public and Private Life of Labor Leader John Mitchell* (Albany: State University of New York Press, 1995), 196, 199–200.

69. Darrow, *The Story of My Life*, 117.

70. "Darrow's Friends Hopeful," *Chicago Record*, January 20, 1903; and "Labor Men for Darrow," *Chicago Record*, January 21, 1903.

71. Henry Demarest Lloyd, "Speech at the Mitchell, Darrow, and Lloyd Reception, 1903," *Men, the Workers* (New York: Doubleday, Page & Co., 1909), 253–54.

72. "Tribute to Miners' Great Leader, John Mitchell, Auditorium Is Thronged: Darrow and Others Also Greeted by Admiring Thousands—Some Strong Speeches Made," *United Mine Workers Journal* (February 19, 1903): 1; and Arthur and Lila Weinberg, *Clarence Darrow: A Sentimental Rebel* (New York: G. P. Putnam's Sons, 1980), 106.

73. Weinberg and Weinberg, *Clarence Darrow*, 106.

74. "Darrow Is Sworn In," *Daily News* (Chicago), February 18, 1903.

75. Letter, Samuel Gompers to Clarence Darrow, March 5, 1903, in Stuart B. Kaufman, Peter J. Albert, and Grace Palladino, eds. *The Samuel Gompers Papers*, vol. 6, *The American Federation of Labor and the Rise of Progressivism, 1902–06* (Urbana: Uni-

versity of Illinois Press, 1997), 113; and letter, Brand Whitlock to Clarence S. Darrow, February 11, 1903, Clarence Darrow Collection, http://darrow.law.umn.edu/letters .php?pid=394&skey=1903, accessed July 7, 2010. See also David Nasaw, *The Chief: The Life of William Randolph Hearst* (Boston: Houghton Mifflin, 2000), 168–85.

76. Ray Ginger, *Altgeld's America: The Lincoln Ideal Versus Changing Realities* (New York: Funk & Wagnalls, 1958), 268.

77. "Darrow's Big Change of Front" and "Darrow Stirs Anger: Unionists Regard His Action as Treachery," unidentified newspaper clippings, Darrow Family Scrapbooks, Scrapbook No. 3, Newberry Library.

78. "To the Friends of Municipal Ownership and the Referendum!," George Schilling Scrapbooks, Scrapbook 2, Abraham Lincoln Presidential Library and Museum. There are two copies of this, one in English and one in German.

79. "Labor Men Call Darrow 'Traitor,'" unidentified newspaper clipping, Darrow Family Scrapbooks, Scrapbook No. 3, Newberry Library.

80. "Darrow Tells Why He Deserted Cruice," ibid.

81. "Darrow Is Here for the Fray," ibid.

82. "Cruice Denounces Darrow," ibid.

83. "Darrow Makes Reply to Attack in Letter," ibid.

84. "Harrison Is Mayor: His Plurality over Graeme Stewart, Republican, 6,948," *New York Times*, April 8, 1903.

85. Darrow, *The Story of My Life*, 120.

86. *Journal of the House of Representatives of the 43D General Assembly of the State of Illinois* (Springfield: Phillips Bros., 1903), 1364, 1372.

87. "Votes Against Bill for Relief of Mrs. John P. Altgeld," unidentified newspaper clipping, Darrow Family Scrapbooks, Scrapbook No. 3, Newberry Library.

88. Letter, Clarence Darrow to Henry Lloyd, March 19, 1903, Microfilmed Papers of Henry D. Lloyd, Reel 14, Wisconsin Historical Society; and see letter, Darrow to Lloyd, April 2, 1903, Microfilmed Papers of Henry D. Lloyd, Reel 14, Wisconsin Historical Society.

89. Edgar Lee Masters, *Across Spoon River: An Autobiography* (New York: Farrar & Rinehart, 1936), 270.

90. Ibid., 270–71.

91. Ibid., 271.

92. By the 1920s Darrow was often at odds with feminists. See, for example, his letter to Alice Beal Parsons, March 13, 1926, Alice Beal Parsons Papers, Special Collections Research Center, Syracuse University.

93. Letter, Clarence Darrow to Mrs. Lloyd, October 19, 1903, Microfilmed Papers of Henry D. Lloyd, Reel 15, Wisconsin Historical Society.

94. "Amirus Darrow," *Chicago Chronicle*, April 25, 1904.

95. Ginger, *Altgeld's America*, 275.

96. "Better Wages for Car Men," *New York Times*, October 4, 1902.

97. Nasaw, *The Chief*, 173.

98. Tierney, *Darrow*, 196.
99. "Insane and Unsafe," *New York Times*, July 9, 1904.
100. "Campaign Ad for Mayoral Candidate John Maynard Harlan, 1905," *Encyclopedia of Chicago*, http://www.encyclopedia.chicagohistory.org/pages/3634.html, accessed July 24, 2009.
101. "Municipal Ownership Wins in Chicago," *New York Times*, April 5, 1905.
102. "Dunne's Traction Plans: City Ownership in Chicago May Still Have Hard Row to Hoe," and "Dunne to Speak Here," *New York Times,* April 6, 1905.
103. *Chicago Record-Herald*, November 8, 1905, quoted in Richard Morton Allen, *Justice and Humanity: Edward F. Dunne, Illinois Progressive* (Carbondale: Southern Illinois University Press, 1997), 23. Although publicly both men stated that there were no hard feelings, Darrow and Dunne did not mention this episode in their autobiographies. Dunne's most recent biographer, Richard Morton Allen, is critical of Darrow, who he said "abandoned Dunne and the fight for municipal ownership at the first major setback." Allen, *Justice and Humanity*, 129.
104. Letter, Clarence Darrow to Mayor Edward F. Dunne, June 19, 1905, Clarence S. Darrow Papers, Box 1, Library of Congress.
105. "Chicago's Special Counsel Resigns," *New York Times*, November 8, 1905; and Leidenberger, *Chicago's Progressive Alliance*, 99–134.

6: In Defense of Dynamiters

1. Clarence S. Darrow, *Industrial Conspiracies* (Portland, Ore.: Turner, Newman, and Knispel Printers, 1912), 16, 19.
2. Ibid., 29.
3. Ibid., 14, 32.
4. Debs, quoted in Louis Adamic, *Dynamite: The Story of Class Violence in America* (New York: Chelsea House, 1958; 1931 original), 20.
5. J. Anthony Lukas, *Big Trouble: A Murder in a Small Western Town Sets Off a Struggle for the Soul of America* (New York: Simon & Schuster, 1997), 100–101.
6. Adamic, *Dynamite*, 126, 147.
7. Lukas, *Big Trouble*, 108.
8. Ibid., 154.
9. Ibid., 218.
10. Peter Carlson, *Roughneck: The Life and Times of Big Bill Haywood* (New York: W. W. Norton, 1983), 16.
11. "Ex-Governor Killed by Dynamite Bomb," *New York Times*, December 31, 1905.
12. Ibid.
13. Abe C. Ravitz and James N. Primm, eds., *The Haywood Case: Materials for Analysis* (San Francisco: Chandler Publishing Co., 1960), 24.
14. Joseph Wanhope, *The Haywood-Moyer Outrage: The Story of Their Illegal Arrest and*

Deportation from Colorado to Idaho (New York: Wilshire Book Co., 1906), 5; and B. T. Cowart, "James McParland and the Haywood Case," *Idaho Yesterdays* 16 (1972): 24–29.

15. James McParland, "Pinkerton Reports," in Ravitz and Primm, eds., *The Haywood Case*, 70.

16. See Albert E. Horsley, *The Confessions and Autobiography of Harry Orchard* (New York: McClure's, 1907); Wanhope, *The Haywood-Moyer Outrage*, 18; "The Murder Charge at a Labor Union's Door," *Harper's Weekly* 51 (May 25, 1907): 764–65.

17. "Prisoners in Special Train," *New York Times*, February 19, 1906; Ravitz and Primm, eds., *The Haywood Case*, 94–96; and Adamic, *Dynamite*, 147.

18. James H. Hawley, "Steve Adams's Confession and the State's Case Against Bill Haywood," *Idaho Yesterdays* 7 (1963–1964): 16–27.

19. "Plotted to Murder Many State Officials," *New York Times*, February 20, 1906.

20. Letter, Clarence Darrow to John Mitchell, March 13, 1906, Microfilmed Papers of John Mitchell, Reel 11, Catholic University of America.

21. William D. Haywood, *Bill Haywood's Book: The Autobiography of William D. Haywood* (New York: International Publishers, 1929), 135.

22. "To Aid Steunenberg Murder Suspects," *New York Times*, February 24, 1906.

23. *U.S. Reports* 192 (1906); and see also 203 *U.S. Reports* 221 (1906).

24. Clarence Darrow, *The Story of My Life* (New York: Charles Scribner's Sons, 1932; reprint, New York: Da Capo Press, 1996), 134.

25. Lukas, *Big Trouble*, 332.

26. David H. Grover, "Borah and the Haywood Trial," *Pacific Historical Quarterly* 32 (1963): 69.

27. Wanhope, *The Haywood-Moyer Outrage*, 3.

28. "Assert Roosevelt Seeks Their Death," *New York Times*, May 2, 1907. See also Lukas, *Big Trouble*, 387–406; "President Roosevelt and the Moyer-Haywood Trial," *Outlook* 86 (May 4, 1907): 1–2; and Stephen Scheinberg, "The Haywood Trial: Theodore Roosevelt's 'Undesirable Citizens,'" *Idaho Yesterdays* 4 (Fall 1960): 10–15.

29. See "President Gives the Lie," *New York Times*, April 3, 1907; "The President and Labor," *New York Times*, April 20, 1907; "Going to Quiz Roosevelt" and "Denounce the President," *New York Times*, April 22, 1907; "Roosevelt Replies to Labor Attacks" and "Undesirable Citizen," *New York Times*, April 24, 1907; "Chicago Men Angry," "Undesirable Citizens," and "What Local Leaders Say," *New York Times*, April 25, 1907; "Approve the President," *New York Times*, April 30, 1907; "Jaxon Answers Roosevelt," "Socialists Assail President," and "Assert Roosevelt Seeks Their Death," *New York Times*, May 2, 1907; "20,000 Parade for Accused Miners," *New York Times*, May 5, 1907; "Thinks Haywood Jury Hard to Get," *New York Times*, May 7, 1907.

30. "Haywood Trial to Begin To-Day," *New York Times*, May 9, 1907; "No Haywood Juror Out of the Panel," *New York Times*, May 10, 1907; "Haywood Venire May Be Exhausted," *New York Times*, May 19, 1907; "Talesman [*sic*] Approves Roosevelt Letter," *New York Times*, May 25, 1907; and Lukas, *Big Trouble*, 447–55.

31. Haywood, *Bill Haywood's Book*, 209.

32. Darrow, *The Story of My Life*, 151.

33. Haywood, *Bill Haywood's Book*, 210.

34. Oscar King Davis, "Haywood Defense Shrewdly Laid Out," *New York Times*, June 25, 1907.

35. Morris Friedman, *The Pinkerton Labor Spy* (New York: Wilshire Book Co., 1907), 196–97; and "Ex-Pinkerton Man Talks for Haywood," *New York Times*, June 30, 1907.

36. Haywood, *Bill Haywood's Book*, 216.

37. Clarence Darrow, *Darrow's Speech in the Haywood Case* (Girard, Kan.: Wayland, 1907), 7.

38. Ibid., 8.

39. Ibid., 10.

40. Ibid., 24.

41. Ibid., 29.

42. Ibid., 109–10.

43. W. E. Borah, *Haywood Trial: Closing Argument of W. E. Borah* (Boise: Statesman Shop, 1907), 3. See also David H. Grover, "Borah and the Haywood Trial," *Pacific Historical Quarterly* 32 (1963).

44. Borah, *Haywood Trial*, 5.

45. Ibid., 9.

46. Ibid., 36.

47. Ibid., 29.

48. Ibid., 41.

49. Ibid., 129.

50. Lukas, *Big Trouble*, 737.

51. Ibid., 725.

52. Herbert K. Russell, *Edgar Lee Masters: A Biography* (Urbana: University of Illinois Press, 2001), 50–51, 149, 163, 192.

53. Darrow, *The Story of My Life*, 164.

54. Ibid., 170.

55. Irving Stone, *Clarence Darrow for the Defense* (Garden City: Doubleday, Doran & Co., 1941), 247.

56. Kevin Tierney, *Darrow: A Biography* (New York: Thomas Y. Crowell, 1979), 232.

57. "Banker Let His Cook Get $25,000 on Notes," *New York Times*, February 16, 1906; and untitled article, *New York Times*, February 18, 1906.

58. Letter, Clarence Darrow to Victor Berger, August 6, 1909, Microfilmed Papers of Victor Berger, Reel 14, Wisconsin Historical Society.

59. Remembrance of Margaret Parton, n.d., Mary Field Parton Papers, Newberry Library.

60. Mary Harris Jones, *Autobiography of Mother Jones* (Chicago: Charles H. Kerr & Co., 1925), vi.

61. Letter, Clarence Darrow to Mary Field, March 15, 1910, Microfilmed Papers of Mary Field Parton, Reel 1, Newberry Library.

62. "Fire Kills 19," *New York Times*, October 2, 1910. See also "Los Angeles Ruins Yield Five Bodies," ibid.

63. Eugene Debs, "The Los Angeles Times—Who Committed That Crime?" *Appeal to Reason* (October 15, 1910): 1.

64. "Gompers Regrets Explosion," *New York Times*, October 2, 1910.

65. Peter J. Albert and Grace Palladino, eds., *The Samuel Gompers Papers*, vol. 8, *Progress and Reaction in the Age of Reform, 1909–13* (Urbana: University of Illinois Press, 2001), 129.

66. *The Forty-Year War for a Free City: A History of the Open Shop in Los Angeles* (Los Angeles: The Times, 1929), 1; and Sidney Fine, *Without Blare of Trumpets: Walter Drew, the National Erectors' Association, and the Open Shop Movement, 1903–57* (Ann Arbor: University of Michigan Press, 1995), 97.

67. "Fire Kills 19," *New York Times*, October 2, 1910.

68. William J. Burns, *The Masked War: The Story of a Peril That Threatened the United States by the Man Who Uncovered the Dynamite Conspiracy and Sent Them to Jail* (New York: George H. Doran Co., 1913), 12, 31. See also *The William J. Burns International Detective Agency, Inc.* (Chicago: s.n., 1924).

69. Geoffrey Cowan, *The People v. Clarence Darrow: The Bribery Trial of America's Greatest Lawyer* (New York: Times Books, 1993), 121.

70. See Andrew Wender Cohen, *The Racketeer's Progress: Chicago and the Struggle for the Modern American Economy* (Cambridge, U.K.: Cambridge University Press, 2004), esp. 91–98.

71. See Fine, *Without Blare of Trumpets*, 83. See also Lukas, *Big Trouble*, 306.

72. Albert and Palladino, eds., *The Samuel Gompers Papers*, vol. 8, 214.

73. Darrow, *The Story of My Life*, 175.

74. Many noticed this similarity between the two cases. See C. P. Connolly, "Protest by Dynamite: Similarities and Contrasts Between the McNamara Affair in Los Angeles and the Moyer-Haywood-Pettibone Trial in Boise," *Collier's* 48 (January 13, 1912): 9–10, 23–24.

75. "Report of the McNamara Ways and Means Committee," *American Federationist* 19 (March 1912): 230–31. See also Samuel Gompers, *The McNamara Case* (Washington, D.C.: American Federation of Labor, 1911).

76. Cowan, *The People v. Clarence Darrow*, 124.

77. Herbert Shapiro, "The McNamara Case: A Crisis of the Progressive Era," *Southern California Quarterly* 59 (Fall 1977): 274.

78. "Quiet Day for Prisoners," *New York Times*, May 1, 1911. See also William W. Robinson, *Bombs and Bribery: The Story of the McNamara and Darrow Trials Following the Dynamiting in 1910 of the Los Angeles Times Building* (Los Angeles: Dawson's Book Shop, 1969), 9.

79. Albert and Palladino, eds., *The Samuel Gompers Papers*, vol. 8, 291.

80. Theodore Roosevelt, "Murder Is Murder," *Outlook* 98 (May 6, 1911): 12–13. Roosevelt's article made Gompers and Otis angry. He penned a response the next month. See Theodore Roosevelt, "Mr. Gompers, General Otis, and the Dynamite Charges," *Outlook* 98 (June 17, 1911): 330–32.

81. Robinson, *Bombs and Bribery*, 9. The California State Federation of Labor agreed with Debs. See Philip Taft, *Labor Politics American Style: The California State Federation of Labor* (Cambridge, Mass.: Harvard University Press, 1968), 49.

82. Moses Koenigsberg, *King News: An Autobiography* (Philadelphia: F. A. Stokes Co., 1941), 312.

83. "Wife Accuses Edward Lord," *New York Times*, August 23, 1908.

84. As quoted in Cowan, *The People v. Clarence Darrow*, 151.

85. "McNamara Witness Missing," *New York Times*, October 30, 1911.

86. Alan M. Dershowitz, "Introduction," Darrow, *The Story of My Life*, vi.

87. Clarence S. Darrow, interview by Agnes Wright Dennis, November 9, 1918, Illinois Historical Survey, Illinois History and Lincoln Collections, University of Illinois at Urbana-Champaign.

88. "James B. M'Namara Murder Trial Begins," *New York Times*, October 12, 1911.

89. "Too Much Biased Against M'Namara," *New York Times*, October 17, 1911.

90. The McNamaras' grand jury delivered its final report on January 5, 1911. It dismissed completely the notion that the explosion had anything to do with a gas leak. See "Final Report of the Los Angeles County Grand Jury, 5 January 11," Walter Bordwell Papers, Box 7, Folder 4, Special Collections Department, Stanford University.

91. Sara Bard Field, interview by Dorothy Erskine, Regional Oral History Office, Bancroft Library, University of California at Berkeley, 262.

92. As quoted in Cowan, *The People v. Clarence Darrow*, 194.

93. Remembrance of Anton Johannsen, Clarence S. Darrow Papers, Box 2, Folder 16, University of Chicago Special Collections.

94. Lincoln Steffens, *The Autobiography of Lincoln Steffens* (New York: Harcourt, Brace & World, 1931), 663.

95. Ibid., 668.

96. "Silent Third Degree Crushed M'Namara," *New York Times*, December 6, 1911.

97. Quoted in Cowan, *The People v. Clarence Darrow*, 255.

98. "Both M'Namaras Plead Guilty to Los Angeles Dynamiting," *New York Times*, December 2, 1911.

99. Samuel Gompers, *Seventy Years of Life and Labor: An Autobiography* (New York: E. P. Dutton & Co., 1957; 1925 original), 240–42.

100. "Both M'Namaras Plead Guilty to Los Angeles Dynamiting," *New York Times*, December 2, 1911.

101. Albert and Palladino, eds. *The Samuel Gompers Papers*, vol. 8, 299.

7: Darrow Defends Darrow

1. "Would Disbar Darrow," *New York Times*, December 6, 1911.

2. *The People of the State of California v. Clarence Darrow, No. 7374, in the Superior Court of the State of California in and for the County of Los Angeles*, March 3, 1913, 3657–3658, Microfilmed Papers of Walter Drew, Bentley Historical Library.

3. Lincoln Steffens, *The Autobiography of Lincoln Steffens* (New York: Harcourt, Brace & World, 1931), 681.

4. C. P. Connolly, "The Saving of Clarence Darrow: Factors and Motives That Led to the Dramatic Close of the McNamara Case," *Collier's* (December 23, 1911): 9.

5. See letter, Ruby Darrow to Paul Darrow, August 23, 1912, Clarence Darrow Collection, http://darrow.law.umn.edu/letters.php?pid=498&skey=1912, accessed July 8, 2010; and letter, Ruby Darrow to Paul Darrow, January 14, 1913, http://darrow.law .umn.edu/letters.php?pid=500&skey=1913, accessed July 8, 2010. See also Geoffrey Cowan, *The People v. Clarence Darrow: The Bribery Trial of America's Greatest Lawyer* (New York: Times Books, 1993), 297, 298–99.

6. "Now Names Darrow in Bribery Tale," *New York Times*, December 12, 1911.

7. Cowan, *The People v. Clarence Darrow*, 289.

8. Sara Bard Field, interview by Dorothy Erskine, Regional Oral History Office, Bancroft Library, University of California at Berkeley, 264; William W. Robinson, *Bombs and Bribery: The Story of the McNamara and Darrow Trials Following the Dynamiting in 1910 of the Los Angeles Times Building* (Los Angeles: Dawson's Book Shop, 1969), 46; and Cowan, *The People v. Clarence Darrow*, 280.

9. Cowan, *The People v. Clarence Darrow*, 283; and Peter J. Albert and Grace Palladino, eds., *The Samuel Gompers Papers*, vol. 8, *Progress and Reaction in the Age of Reform, 1909–13* (Urbana: University of Illinois Press, 2001), 358–59.

10. Letter, Clarence Darrow to Eugene V. Debbs [*sic*], February 12, 1912, Debs Collection, Cunningham Memorial Library, Indiana State University; and letter, Eugene V. Debs to Clarence S. Darrow, February 19, 1912, in J. Robert Constantine, ed., *Gentle Rebel: Letters of Eugene V. Debs* (Urbana: University of Illinois Press, 1995), 71–73.

11. Connolly, "The Saving of Clarence Darrow," 9.

12. Margaret Parton, "Sketch of the Life of Mary Field Parton," n.d., typescript, Mary Field Parton Papers, Newberry Library.

13. J. Anthony Lukas, *Big Trouble: A Murder in a Small Western Town Sets Off a Struggle for the Soul of America* (New York: Simon & Schuster, 1997), 749.

14. Clarence S. Darrow, *The Story of My Life* (New York: Charles Scribner's Sons, 1932; reprint, New York: Da Capo Press, 1996), 152.

15. Abram E. Adelman, "Take Him for All in All: Reminiscences of Clarence Darrow" [typescript], Microfilmed Papers of Elmer Gertz, Reel 1, Northwestern University Special Collections.

16. Darrow, *The Story of My Life*, 196.

17. Ibid., 192–93.

18. Ibid., 197–98.

19. Ibid., 198; and see Clarence S. Darrow, *Industrial Conspiracies* (Portland, Ore.: Turner, Newman & Knispel, 1912), 30.

20. Letter, Lincoln Steffens to Laura Steffens, June 25, 1912, in Ella Winter and Granville Hicks, eds., *The Letters of Lincoln Steffens*, vol. 1, *1889–1919* (New York: Harcourt, Brace, 1938), 300.

21. Connolly, "The Saving of Clarence Darrow," 9.

22. Quoted in Cowan, *The People v. Clarence Darrow*, 319.

23. "Darrow's Trial Near," *New York Times*, May 6, 1912; "Link Darrow's Name in Bribery Charge," *New York Times*, May 28, 1912; and Cowan, *The People v. Clarence Darrow*, 298.

24. "Link Darrow's Name in Bribery Charge," *New York Times*, May 28, 1912.

25. Herbert Shapiro, "The McNamara Case: A Crisis of the Progressive Era," *Historical Society of Southern California Quarterly* 59 (Fall 1977): 272.

26. "The Darrow Acquittal," *Literary Digest* 45 (August 31, 1912): 323.

27. Luke North, ed., *Plea of Clarence Darrow in His Own Defense to the Jury That Exonerated Him of the Charge of Bribery at Los Angeles, 1912* (Los Angeles: Golden Press, 1912), 3, 4, 5, 6, 10, 11, 14, 15, 18, 28, 51, 52, 53, 54, 55, 56; Lincoln Steffens, *The Autobiography of Lincoln Steffens* (New York: Harcourt, Brace and Co., 1931), 477; "Darrow Closes in Tears," *New York Times*, August 16, 1912; and Alfred Cohn and Joe Chisholm, *Take the Witness!* (New York: Frederick A. Stokes Co., 1934), 223.

28. Robinson, *Bombs and Bribery*, 40–41; and Cowan, *The People v. Clarence Darrow*, 410.

29. See "Second Plea of Clarence Darrow," *Everyman* (May 1913): 3–24.

30. Letter, Henry A. Rabe to Elmer Gertz, March 18, 1957, Microfilmed Papers of Elmer Gertz, Northwestern University Special Collections.

8: War and Regret

1. Edgar Lee Masters, "On a Bust," in *Songs and Satire* (New York: Macmillan, 1916), 98–99.

2. Herbert K. Russell, *Edgar Lee Masters: A Biography* (Urbana: University of Illinois Press, 2001), 140–41, 149–51.

3. Letter, Clarence Darrow to Paul Darrow, April 7, 1923, Clarence Darrow Collection, http://darrow.law.umn.edu/letters.php?pid=162&skey=1923, accessed July 2, 2010.

4. "Address of Clarence Darrow on John Brown," *Everyman* 9 (March 1913): 9, 10, 12.

5. Clarence Darrow, "Henry George," *Everyman* 9 (September–October 1913): 20–21.

6. This dislike of traveling and lecturing on his own continued well after this period. See letter, Ruby Darrow to Paul Darrow, November 5, 1929, Clarence Darrow Collection, http://darrow.law.umn.edu/letters.php?pid=508&skey=1929, accessed July 8, 2010.

7. Clarence Darrow, "If Men Had Opportunity," *Everyman* 11 (January–February 1915): 21, 24.

8. See, for example, Clarence S. Darrow, "Straight Talk to the Rails: Extracts from Address Delivered at an Open Meeting of Railroad Men in Chicago, April 30, 1915," *International Socialist Review* 16 (1915–1916): 718–20.

9. Clarence S. Darrow, *The Story of My Life* (New York: Charles Scribner's Sons, 1932; reprint, New York: Da Capo Press, 1996), 204.

10. Letter, Clarence Darrow to Mary Field, April 27, 1915, Mary Field Parton Papers, Newberry Library.

11. U.S. Commission on Industrial Relations, *Final Report and Testimony Submitted to Congress*, vol. 11, Senate document 415 (Washington, D.C.: GPO, 1916), 10796.

12. "Jury Sets Mrs. Van Keuren Free," *Waterloo Times-Tribune* (Iowa), March 15, 1914.

13. Kevin Tierney, *Darrow: A Biography* (New York: Thomas Y. Crowell, 1979), 276.

14. Steven Ross, *Working-Class Hollywood: Silent Film and the Shaping of Class in America* (Princeton, N.J.: Princeton University Press, 1998), 95–98. See advertisements for the film in *Racine Journal-News* (Wisconsin), March 20, 1914; and *Cedar Rapids Evening Gazette* (Iowa), June 26, 1914.

15. "No Evidence; Freed," *La Crosse Tribune* (Wisconsin), February 21, 1914.

16. See Virginia Law Burns, *Tall Annie: A Biography* (Laingsburg, Mich.: Enterprise Press, 1987).

17. "Unions Working for Settlement," *Ogden Standard* (Utah), January 1, 1914.

18. For hints at the strained relationship between Ruby and Paul, see letter, Ruby Darrow to Ruth Gage Thompson, n.d., Elmer Gertz Papers, Box 39, Northwestern University, Special Collections.

19. Darrow, *The Story of My Life*, 211.

20. Clarence Darrow, "The Cost of War," *International Socialist Review* 15 (1914): 361–62.

21. Theodore Draper, *The Roots of American Communism* (Chicago: Ivan R. Dee, 1985; 1957 original), 50.

22. "Clarence Darrow on the War," *Everyman* (October–November 1914): 21–28.

23. Clarence Darrow, *Resist Not Evil* (Chicago: Charles Kerr Publishers, 1902), 11, 57.

24. Letter, Clarence S. Darrow to Mary Field Parton, April 27, 1915, Mary Field Parton Papers, Newberry Library; and interview with Sara Bard Field, conducted by Amelia R. Fry, Suffragists Oral History Project, University of California, Berkeley, 270.

25. See U.S. Commission on Industrial Relations, *Final Report and Testimony*, 10786, 10794, 10801.

26. Darrow, *The Story of My Life*, 210.

27. "Shall We Have a Bigger Army and Navy?," *Fort Wayne Sentinel* (Indiana), November 14, 1914.

28. Michael Kazin, *A Godly Hero: The Life of William Jennings Bryan* (New York: Alfred A. Knopf, 2006), 217–38; and Ernest Freeberg, *Democracy's Prisoner: Eugene V. Debs, the Great War, and the Right to Dissent* (Cambridge, Mass.: Harvard University Press, 2008), 35–39.

29. Draper, *The Roots of American Communism*, 93.

30. "Some Inside Facts," *Agitator*, September 5, 1917; and "Labor Mobilizes to Pledge Support and Warn Disloyalists," *La Crosse Tribune* (Wisconsin), September 4, 1917.

31. "Pacifists Fail to Stop Big Meeting in Madison Square," *Lima Sunday News* (Wisconsin), September 16, 1917.

32. Clarence Darrow, *The War: Patriotism Through Education Series*, No. 26, Under the Auspices of the National Security League, November 1, 1917 (New York: National Security League, 1917), 15.

33. Letter, Henry A. Rabe to Elmer Gertz, March 18, 1957, Elmer Gertz Papers, Box 1, Northwestern University Special Collections.

34. Clarence Darrow, "Brief for the War (a Letter)," in Arthur and Lila Weinberg, *Clarence Darrow: Verdicts Out of Court* (Chicago: Ivan R. Dee, 1963), 337.

35. "Dregs of the Radicals," *Bismarck Daily Tribune* (North Dakota), September 5, 1917. For another, see "Straight Goods," *Fort Wayne Journal-Gazette* (Indiana), December 26, 1917.

36. See *New Castle News* (Delaware), October 10, 1917; "Pacifists Are Enemies of the Republic," *Racine Journal-News* (Wisconsin), November 3, 1917; editorial page, *Evening Tribune* (Albert Lea, Minnesota), September 27, 1917; and "Topic of the Times," *New York Times*, May 18, 1918.

37. "To Tell Our War Ideals," *New York Times*, July 22, 1918.

38. "No Time to Think of Peace," *New York Times*, August 9, 1918.

39. See "Darrow Reaches U.S. Front: Chicago Attorney Impressed by Confidence Among Allied Nations," Darrow Family Scrapbooks, Scrapbook No. 1, Newberry Library.

40. Darrow, *The Story of My Life*, 214.

41. R. G. Brown, Zechariah Chafee, Jr., et al., *To The American People: Report upon the Illegal Practices of the United States Department of Justice* (Washington, D.C.: National Popular Government League, 1920), 24–27.

42. Clarence S. Darrow, *War Prisoners* (Chicago: John F. Higgins, 1920), 6.

43. "Socialist Paper Barred," *New York Times*, July 7, 1917.

44. See *Goldman v. U.S.*, 245 U.S. 474 (1918); and Tierney, *Darrow*, 306.

45. See Kenneth D. Ackerman, *Young J. Edgar: Hoover, the Red Scare, and the Assault on Civil Liberties* (New York: Da Capo Press, 2007), 306–11; and National Popular Government League, *To the American People* (Washington, D.C.: The League, 1920).

46. Darrow, *War Prisoners*, 19.

47. Philip Taft, "The Federal Trials of the IWW," *Labor History* 3 (1962): 60.

48. Ralph Chaplin, *Wobbly: The Rough-and-Tumble Story of an American Radical* (Chicago: University of Chicago Press, 1948), 225.

49. Melvyn Dubofsky, *We Shall Be All: A History of the Industrial Workers of the World* (New York: Quadrangle, 1969), 429; and Tierney, *Darrow*, 301.

50. Taft, "The Federal Trials of the IWW," 62n19.

51. Helen C. Camp, *Iron in Her Soul: Elizabeth Gurley Flynn and the American Left* (Pullman: Washington State University Press, 1995), 82; and "IWW Gaining Here, Senators Are Told," *New York Times*, January 23, 1919.

52. "Bail for 'Big Bill,'" *Daily Northwestern* (Oshkosh, Wisconsin), April 3, 1919.

53. Peter Carlson, *Roughneck: The Life and Times of Big Bill Haywood* (New York: W. W. Norton, 1983), 317.

54. Letter, Edward J. Brennan to Frank Burke, March 6, 1920, Bureau of Investigation Records, RG 65, OG 88457, National Archives; and index card for Clarence Darrow, Military Intelligence Division (MID) Records, RG 165, National Archives.

55. Max Eastman, "Foreword" to *The Whole of Their Lives: Communism in America—A Personal History and Intimate Portrayal of Its Leaders*, by Benjamin Gitlow (New York: Charles Scribner's Sons, 1948), x.

56. Benjamin Gitlow, *I Confess: The Truth About American Communism* (New York: E. P. Dutton & Co., 1939), 70.

57. *The "Red Ruby" Address to the Jury by Benjamin Gitlow, Also Darrow, the Judge, and Giovanitti* (New York: Workers' Defense Conference, 1920), 8, 9, 10, 11, 12; and Akira Sanbonmatsu, "Darrow and Rorke's Use of Burkeian Identification Strategies in *New York vs. Gitlow* (1920)," *Speech Monographs* 38 (1971): 36.

58. See *Gitlow v. People of State of New York*, 268 U.S. 652 (1925); and Paul C. Bartholomew, "The Gitlow Doctrine Down to Date," *American Bar Association Journal* 54 (August 1968): 785–87; and M. B. Carrott, "Expansion of the Fourteenth Amendment to Include Freedom of Expression," *North Dakota Quarterly* (Autumn 1971): 5–20.

59. Eastman, "Foreword," x.

60. Defense Committee of the Communist Labor Party of Illinois, *Address of Clarence Darrow in the Trial of Arthur Person in Rockford, Illinois, April 24th, 1920* (Chicago: Defense Committee of the Communist Labor Party of Illinois, 1920), 3–7, 17, 19, 23, 24, 26.

61. Ibid., 28–30.

62. *The People of the State of Illinois v. William Bross Lloyd, et al., Supreme Court of Illinois, December Term AD 1921, Abstract of Record* (Chicago: Gusthorp Warren Printing Co., 1921), 768, in *People v. Lloyd* Microfilm, Reel 2.

63. Ibid., 770–72.

64. "Darrow Finds Life Cruel," *Racine Journal-News* (Wisconsin), April 20, 1918.

9: The Old Lion Still Hunts

1. "Asserts Harding Enemy of Labor," *Sandusky Star-Journal* (Ohio), October 29, 1920.

2. Victor S. Yarros, *My 11 Years with Clarence Darrow* (Girard, Kan.: Haldeman-Julius Publications, 1950), 15. See also Clarence Darrow, "Woodrow Wilson," *Reedy's Mirror* 29 (April 15, 1920): 311–13. Darrow had harbored anti-League views before 1920 but

put them away for the election. See *The Darrow-Kennedy Debate on "Are Internationalism and the League of Nations Practical and Desirable Schemes for Ending War?"* (Chicago: John F. Higgins, 1918).

3. "Drags Us into Future Wars, Says Darrow," unidentified newspaper clipping, Darrow Family Scrapbooks, Scrapbook No. 4, Newberry Library.

4. See "Clarence Darrow Is Hissed," *Chicago Heights Star*, May 21, 1914; and *The Great Commoner: Speech of Hon. Clarence Darrow of Chicago at the Opera House, Youngstown, Ohio, Sunday, May 2, 1909* (n.p., 1909?).

5. Letter, Clarence Darrow to Upton Sinclair, September 27, 1930, Upton Sinclair Papers, Manuscript Department, Lilly Library, Indiana University–Bloomington.

6. Letter, Clarence Darrow to James W. Beck, June 11, 1930, James M. Beck Papers, Box 2, Princeton University Archives, Department of Rare Books and Special Collections.

7. Letter, Clarence S. Darrow to William C. Ewing, January 23, 1928, Clarence Darrow Collection, http://darrow.law.umn.edu/letters.php?pid=463&skey=1928, accessed July 9, 2010.

8. Clarence S. Darrow, "The Ordeal of Prohibition," *American Mercury* 2 (August 1924): 427. See also Clarence Darrow and Victor S. Yarros, *The Prohibition Mania: A Reply to Professor Irving Fisher and Others* (New York: Boni and Liveright, 1927); Clarence Darrow, *Liberty vs. Prohibition* (New Bedford, Mass.: New England Union Label League, 1909); and Natalie Schretter, "I Remember Clarence Darrow" [typescript], 6, S. A. Haldeman Papers, Manuscripts Department, Lilly Library, Indiana University–Bloomington.

9. Letter, Clarence Darrow to Mary Field Parton, June 10, 1929, Mary Field Parton Papers, Box 1, Newberry Library.

10. As quoted in Donald McRae, *The Last Trials of Clarence Darrow* (New York: William Morrow, 2009), 333.

11. See Clarence Darrow, "Liberty, Equality, Fraternity: Why Rights for Women Have Brought About the Decline of Some Notable Institutions," *Vanity Fair* 7 (December 1926): 31, 110; and Clarence Darrow, "Women and Justice: Are Women Fit to Judge Guilt?," *McCall's* (June 1928); 13, 65–66.

12. Clarence Darrow, "Why Was God So Hard on Women and Snakes?," *Haldeman-Julius Monthly* 8 (September 1928): 122–24; and Clarence Darrow, "The Divorce Problem," *Vanity Fair* 8 (August 1927): 31–32.

13. United States Senate, *Industrial Relations: Final Report and Testimony Submitted to Congress by the Commission on Industrial Relations*, vol. 11 (Washington, D.C.: Government Printing Office, 1916), 10788.

14. Letter, Clarence Darrow to H. L. Mencken, May 11, 1924, Microfilmed Papers of H. L. Mencken, Reel 12, Manuscript and Archives Division, the Astor, Lenox and Tilden Foundations. New York Public Library.

15. Clarence Darrow, "The Ideal of a Labor Union," in *Clarence Darrow: Verdicts Out of Court*, ed. Arthur and Lila Weinberg (Chicago: Ivan R. Dee, 1963), 102–5; and letter,

Clarence Darrow to Sidney Hillman, March 26, 1927, Amalgamated Clothing Workers Union Papers, Box 71, Kheel Center, Cornell University.

16. Letter, Eugene V. Debs to Clarence Darrow, February 1, 1922, Clarence Darrow Collection, http://darrow.law.umn.edu/letters.php?pid=412&skey=1922, accessed July 9, 2010.

17. See Andrew Wender Cohen, *The Racketeer's Progress: Chicago and the Struggle for the Modern American Economy, 1900–1940* (New York: Cambridge University Press, 2004), 228–30; and Ernest Freeberg, *Democracy's Prisoner: Eugene V. Debs, the Great War, and the Right to Dissent* (Cambridge, Mass.: Harvard University Press, 2008), 279–95, 316.

18. Nancy Cox-McCormack, "Reminiscences of Chicago, 1911–1920," 17, Nancy Cox-McCormack Papers, Box 1, Tennessee State Library and Archives.

19. J. Robert Constantine, ed., *Letters of Eugene V. Debs*, vol. 3, *1919–1926* (Urbana: University of Illinois Press, 1990), 526–27; "Beg Pardon," *Capital Times* (Madison, Wisconsin), March 3, 1921; and letter, Clarence Darrow to Joseph Jasin, Februrary 27, [1924?], Joseph Jasin Papers, Jacob Rader Marcus Center of the American Jewish Archives.

20. See *Is the Human Race Permanently Progressing Toward a Better Civilization? Affirmative: Professor John C. Kennedy, Negative: Mr. Clarence S. Darrow* (Chicago, John F. Higgins Printers, 1919); *Pessimism: A Lecture by Clarence Darrow* (Chicago: Rational Education Society, 1920); *Is Civilization a Failure? Affirmative: Clarence S. Darrow, Negative: Professor Frederick Starr* (Chicago: Workers University Society, 1920); and *Wishart-Darrow Debate Concerning a General Purpose in the Universe* (Grand Rapids, Mich.: Extension Club, 1928).

21. Clarence Darrow, "Our Growing Tyranny: A Consideration of the Lamentable Motive Instigating the Latest Crusade by the 'Blue-Noses,'" *Vanity Fair* (February 1928): 104.

22. U.S. Senate, *Industrial Relations*, 10798.

23. Matilda Fenberg, "The Most Unforgettable Character I've Met," *Reader's Digest* (April 1959): 87.

24. Darrow, *The Story of My Life*, 232.

25. Clarence S. Darrow, "Crime and the Alarmists," *Harper's Magazine* 153 (October 1926): 535.

26. Clarence Darrow, *Crime: Its Cause and Treatment* (New York: Thomas Y. Crowell, 1922), 7, 26–27, 143. See also Darrow, "Crime and the Alarmists," 535–44; U.S. Senate, Commission on Industrial Relations, *Final Report and Testimony*, 10795; Clarence Darrow, "Crime and Economic Conditions," *International Socialist Review* 17 (1916): 219–22; Clarence S. Darrow, *Crime and Criminals* (Chicago: Charles H. Kerr and Co., 1907); *Can the Individual Control His Conduct?: A Debate Between Clarence Darrow and Dr. Thomas V. Smith* (Girard, Kan.: Haldeman-Julius Co., 1928); *Environment vs. Heredity: Debate Between Clarence Darrow and Albert Edward Wiggam* (Girard, Kan.: Haldeman-Julius Co., 1931); and James Edward Sayer, *Clarence Darrow: Public Advocate* (Dayton, Ohio: Wright State University, 1978), 22.

27. Darrow, *Crime and Criminals*, 14, 16, 20.

28. Donald McRae, *The Last Trials of Clarence Darrow* (New York: HarperCollins, 2009), 6.

29. Simon Baatz, *For the Thrill of It: Leopold, Loeb, and the Murder That Shocked Chicago* (New York: HarperCollins, 2008), 235.

30. Quoted ibid., 283.

31. Clarence S. Darrow, *Plea of Clarence Darrow in Defense of Richard Loeb and Nathan Leopold, Jr., on Trial for Murder, August 22nd, 23rd, and 25th, 1924* (Chicago: Ralph Fletcher Seymour, 1924), 6.

32. Ibid., 22.

33. Ibid.

34. Ibid., 27, 66; and Baatz, *For the Thrill of It*, 157.

35. Darrow, *Plea of Clarence Darrow in Defense of Richard Loeb and Nathan Leopold*, 112.

36. Ibid., 121.

37. See Donald Richberg, "The Causes of Crime," *New Republic* 32 (November 22, 1922): 339–40; Robert H. Gault, review of *Crime: Its Cause and Treatment* in *Journal of Criminal Law and Criminology* 13 (1922–1923): 621–22; and review of *Crime: Its Cause and Treatment* in *Catholic World* 116 (January 1923): 556–67.

38. Quoted in Baatz, *For the Thrill of It*, 401, 402.

39. "The Hangman Cheers Up," *Independent* (May 23, 1925): 571.

40. Terry Teachout, *The Skeptic: A Life of H. L. Mencken* (New York: HarperCollins, 2002), 187.

41. Paul K. Conkin, *When All the Gods Trembled: Darwinism, Scopes, and American Intellectuals* (Lanham, Md.: Rowman & Littlefield, 1998), 75.

42. Michael Kazin, *A Godly Hero: The Life of William Jennings Bryan* (New York: Alfred A. Knopf, 2006), 263–89.

43. See Jeffrey P. Moran, *The Scopes Trial: A Brief History with Documents* (Boston: Bedford/St. Martin's, 2002), 17; and Susan Jacoby, *Freethinkers: A History of American Secularism* (New York: Metropolitan Books, 2004), 227. See also James Leuba, *The Belief in God and Immortality: A Psychological, Anthropological and Statistical Study* (Boston: Sherman, French & Co., 1916).

44. Clarence Darrow, "The War on Modern Science," *Modern World* I (July 1927): 301–303.

45. Letter, Clarence Darrow to W. C. Curtis, March 6, 1926, Winterton Curtis Papers, Western Historical Manuscript Collection, University of Missouri–Columbia.

46. Clarence Darrow and Wallace Rice, *Infidels and Heretics* (Boston: Stratford Co., 1929), v–vi.

47. John T. Scopes and William Jennings Bryan, *The World's Most Famous Court Trial, Tennessee Evolution Case: A Complete Stenographic Report of the Famous Court Test of the Tennessee Anti-Evolution Act, at Dayton, July 10 to 21, 1925, Including Speeches and Arguments of Attorneys* (Cincinnati: National Book Company, 1925), 99.

48. *Darrow-Case Debate: Has Religion Ceased to Function?* (Chicago: Maclaskey & Maclaskey, 1921), 8.

49. Clarence Darrow, "The Eugenics Cult," *American Mercury* 8 (June 1926): 137. See also Clarence Darrow, "The Edwardses and the Jukeses," *American Mercury* 6 (October 1925): 147–57.

50. "Darrow Asks W. J. Bryan to Answer These," *Chicago Tribune*, July 4, 1923.

51. Edward J. Larson, *Summer for the Gods: The Scopes Trial and America's Continuing Debate over Science and Religion* (New York: Basic Books, 1997), 143.

52. Arthur Garfield Hays, *Let Freedom Ring* (New York: Boni and Liveright, 1928), 25.

53. Ibid., 33.

54. Ibid., 26–27.

55. Marcet Haldeman-Julius, *Clarence Darrow's Two Great Trials: Reports of the Scopes Anti-Evolution Case and the Dr. Sweet Negro Trial* (Girard, Kan.: Haldeman-Julius Co., 1927), 3.

56. "A Lion in a Den of Daniels," *J.U.H. Weekly* (June 13, 1925): 4.

57. "Johnny Cash Indebted to a Judge Named Sue," *New York Times*, July 12, 1970.

58. Arthur Garfield Hays, "The Strategy of the Scopes Defense," *Nation* (August 5, 1925): 157–58.

59. Darrow, *The Story of My Life*, 256.

60. "Monkey Trial, Judge Believes, Accomplished Little of Benefit," unidentified newspaper clipping, Microfilmed Papers of Elmer Gertz, Northwestern University.

61. Scopes and Bryan, *The World's Most Famous Court Trial, Tennessee Evolution Case*, 74.

62. Ibid., 87.

63. Ibid., 212.

64. Teachout, *The Skeptic*, 217.

65. As quoted in Larson, *Summer for the Gods*, 132. See also "We'll Make Apes of 'Em Says Bryan," *Chicago Examiner*, June 12, 1925.

66. Clarence Darrow, *The Famous Examination of Bryan at the Scopes Evolution Trial* (Girard, Kan.: Haldeman-Julius Publications, 1925), 11, 17, 18, 61.

67. Letter, Clarence Darrow to H. L. Mencken, August 5, 1925, Microfilmed Papers of H. L. Mencken, Reel 12, Manuscripts and Archives Division, New York Public Library, Astor, Lenox and Tilden Foundations.

68. "Darrow and Scopes Comment on Death," *Chattanooga Times*, July 28, 1925; Hays, *Let Freedom Ring*, 79; Teachout, *The Skeptic*, 218–19; and Larson, *Summer for the Gods*, 200.

69. Conkin, *When All the Gods Trembled*, 98.

70. Walter White, *A Man Called White: The Autobiography of Walter White* (New York: Viking, 1949), 75–76; and Otis Sweet, interview by Alex Baskin, transcription, 11, August 1, 1960, Bentley Historical Library, University of Michigan.

71. See, for example, letter, Charles Chesnutt to Clarence Darrow, February 8, 1907, Clarence Darrow Collection, http://darrow.law.umn.edu/letters.php?pid=398&skey=1907, accessed July 3, 2010.

72. See, for example, William M. Tuttle, Jr., *Race Riot: Chicago in the Red Summer of 1919* (New York: Atheneum, 1970), 194–96; and Clarence Darrow to Mary Field Parton, April 27, 1915, Microfilmed Papers of Mary Field Parton, Newberry Library.

73. "Darrow Apologizes for Being a Nordic," *Pittsburgh Courier*, April 3, 1926; and Clarence Darrow, "Address Before the 17th Annual Conference of the NAACP, Chicago, 27 June 1926," Clarence S. Darrow Papers, Box 10, Library of Congress.

74. United States House of Representatives, *Capital Punishment: Hearings Before the Subcommittee on the Judiary of the Committee on the District of Columbia* (Washington, DC: GPO 1926), 73. See also Clarence S. Darrow, "The Problem of the Negro," *International Socialist Review* 2 (November 1901): 321–35; Clarence Darrow, "Address to the Prisoners at Joliet," *Everyman* 11 (November 1915): 14; "Darrow Makes Plea Against Crime Rule," *Chicago Defender*, December 27, 1924; and "Clarence Darrow Calls Prejudice Unjustifiable," *Chicago Defender*, April 18, 1925.

75. Darrow, "The Problem of the Negro," 329.

76. "Equality of Privilege," *Baltimore Afro-American*, May 21, 1910.

77. See Darrow, "The Problem of the Negro," 325–26, 332–33; and "Darrow Makes Pleas Against Crime Rule," *Chicago Defender*, December 27, 1924.

78. "No Cases Are Diagnosed and No Prescriptions Given in These Weekly Articles," *Chicago Defender*, September 18, 1920.

79. "Socialist Advises Negroes to Strike," *New York Times*, May 13, 1910.

80. Haldeman-Julius, *Clarence Darrow's Two Great Trials*, 41.

81. Kevin Boyle, *Arc of Justice: A Saga of Race, Civil Rights, and Murder in the Jazz Age* (New York: Henry Holt, 2004), 197–259.

82. Cecil L. Rowlette, interview by Alex Baskin, transcript, August 1, 1960, 8, Bentley Historical Society; and William C. Osby, Sr., interview by Alex Baskin, July 27, 1969, 7, Bentley Historical Society.

83. Cecil L. Rowlette, interview by Alex Baskin, transcript, August 1, 1960, 10, Bentley Historical Society.

84. McRae, *The Last Trials of Clarence Darrow*, 287.

85. Haldeman-Julius, *Clarence Darrow's Two Great Trials*, 49; and McRae, *The Last Trials of Clarence Darrow*, 235, 288.

86. David Lilienthal, "Has the Negro the Right of Self-Defense?," *Nation* 121 (December 23, 1925): 725.

87. Weinbergs, *Clarence Darrow*, 363; and Tierney, *Darrow*, 390.

88. "Crowd of 2,000 Hear Darrow Discuss the Race Question," *Chicago Defender*, December 26, 1925.

89. "Ministers Call on President Coolidge," *New York Amsterdam News*, April 4, 1928. See also Jeffrey P. Moran, "Reading Race into the Scopes Trial: African American

Elites, Science, and Fundamentalism," *Journal of American History* 90 (December 2003): 891–911.

90. "Mob Attacks Darrow in South," *Chicago Defender*, March 12, 1927; "Dixie Whites Drive Darrow from Mobile," *Baltimore Afro-American*, March 12, 1927; and "Darrow Denies That He Was Threatened," *New York Amsterdam News*, March 16, 1927.

91. "Clarence Darrow Returns Home to Try His Last Case," *Chicago Defender*, May 19, 1928; "Darrow Jury Disagrees," *New York Times*, May 13, 1928; and "Clarence Darrow to Write Autobiography," *Chicago Defender*, November 17, 1928.

92. Abram Adelman, "Clarence Darrow—Take Him for All in All," *Age of Reason* 19 (October 1955): 1.

10: No Rest, No Retirement, No Retreat

1. Carroll Binder, "Darrow's Friends Meet to Laud Him," *Chicago Daily News*, April 19, 1927. See also J. G. Bennema, "Clarence Darrow's Birthday Party," *International Engineer* 51 (May 1927): 391–92.

2. John Haynes Holmes, *I Speak for Myself: The Autobiography* (New York: Harper & Brothers, 1958), 260–61; and letter, M. S. Novick to Elmer Gertz, March 11, 1957, Microfilmed Papers of Elmer Gertz, Reel 1.

3. *Verbatim Report of the Speeches, Seventieth Anniversary Dinner to Clarence Darrow, Palmer House, Chicago, Illinois, April 18, 1927*, 75–79, Clarence S. Darrow Papers, Box 25, Library of Congress.

4. Carroll Binder, "Darrow Surveys His World at 70," *Chicago Daily News*, April 16, 1927.

5. "Darrow Lays Crime to Curb on Liberty," *New York Times*, February 18, 1928; "Would Force Jury to View Execution," *New York Times*, February 20, 1928; and "Experts on Crime to Hold Congress," *New York Times*, September 2, 1928.

6. "Darrow Gives Plea to Fulfill Pledge," *New York Times*, January 13, 1928; and "Darrow Keeps Pledge by Saving Man's Life," *New York Times*, March 13, 1929.

7. Clarence Darrow, "Emperor or President," *Nation* 127 (June 5, 1929): 673.

8. George G. Whitehead, *Clarence Darrow—The Big Minority Man* (Girard, Kan.: Haldeman-Julius Publications, 1929), 23–24.

9. "Says Hoover Favors Socialism for Rich," *New York Times*, October 25, 1928.

10. Arthur M. Schlesinger, Jr., *The Age of Roosevelt: The Coming of the New Deal* (Boston: Houghton Mifflin, 1958), 87; Anthony J. Badger, *The New Deal: The Depression Years, 1933–40* (New York: Hill & Wang, 1989), 11–14; and David E. Stannard, *Honor Killing: Race, Rape, and Clarence Darrow's Last Case* (New York: Penguin Books, 2005), 34.

11. Letter, Clarence Darrow to Paul Darrow, October 29, 1929, Clarence Darrow Collection, http://darrow.law.umn.edu/letters.php?pid=265&skey=1929, accessed July 4, 2010.

12. See letter, Ruby Darrow to Paul Darrow, November 5, 1929, Clarence Darrow Collection, http://darrow.law.umn.edu/letters.php?pid=508&skey=1929, accessed July 4,

2010; letter, Clarence Darrow to Paul Darrow, January 18, 1929, Clarence Darrow Collection, http://darrow.law.umn.edu/letters.php?pid=249&skey=1929, accessed July 4, 2010; and letter, Clarence Darrow to Paul Darrow, September 29, 1929, Clarence Darrow Collection, http://darrow.law.umn.edu/letters.php?pid=261&skey=1929, accessed July 4, 2010.

13. Letter, Clarence S. Darrow to Paul Darrow, February 20, [1930?], Clarence Darrow Collection, http://darrow.law.umn.edu/letters.php?pid=149&skey=, accessed July 4, 2010.

14. "Darrow Declines Call," *New York Times*, April 30, 1930; and "National Affairs: Witch Murder," *Time* (April 7, 1930): 14.

15. Letter, Ruby Darrow to Ruth Gage Thompson, August 18, 1930, Elmer Gertz Papers, Box 39, Northwestern University Special Collections.

16. "Plan Censorship Debate," *New York Times*, January 18, 1931; "Four Debate Socialism," *New York Times*, January 31, 1931; "Darrow and Beck to Participate in the 'Famous Trials of History,'" *New York Times*, March 15, 1931; and "The Microphone Will Be Present," *New York Times*, March 22, 1931.

17. "Darrow Sees Dry Era End," *New York Times*, April 3, 1930; and "Darrow Flays Hoover in Dry Debate," *New York Times*, March 29, 1930.

18. "To Fight Death Penalty," *New York Times*, February 4, 1930; "Kansas Still Bans the Death Penalty," *New York Times*, March 21, 1931; "Darrow Predicts Winter Crime Wave," *New York Times*, September 7, 1931; and "Darrow to Speak at Williams," *New York Times*, January 11, 1934.

19. Clarence Darrow, *The Myth of the Soul* (Girard, Kan.: Haldeman-Julius Co., 1929).

20. Letter, Clarence Darrow to Irvin E. Rockwell, May 15, 1933, Rockwell-Darrow Collection, Box 1, Boise State University Special Collections. Emphasis in original.

21. "Personal Immortality: What I Believe," *New York Times*, April 8, 1928.

22. "Inside the Story of Darrow Forums," *Christian Century* (December 2, 1931): 90; and Holmes, *I Speak for Myself*, 261–62.

23. Clarence Darrow, "The Religion of the Negro," *Crisis* 21 (June 1930): 90.

24. "Darrow's Atheism Doubted by Pastors," *Pittsburgh Courier*, January 3, 1931.

25. "Says Bay State D.A.R. Blacklists Liberals," *New York Times*, April 4, 1928; and "Chicago 'Blacklisted' Dine," *New York Times*, November 30, 1930.

26. "Darrow Is Negro's Worst Enemy," *Pittsburgh Courier*, August 1, 1931.

27. "Inside the Story of the Darrow Forums," 90.

28. "Mr. Darrow Presents," *Time* 9 (July 20, 1931): 25–26; "Censorship of Darrow's Film Is Hit," *New York Times*, November 14, 1931; and "Darrow Predicts Winter Crime Wave," *New York Times*, September 7, 1931. See also letter, Clarence Darrow to Paul Darrow, March 24, 1931, Clarence Darrow Collection, http://darrow.law.umn.edu/letters.php?pid=310&skey=1931, accessed July 9, 2010.

29. Alan Hynd, *Defenders of the Damned* (New York: A. S. Barnes and Co., 1960), 116–17.

30. "Darrow Forsakes Retirement to Defend Vagrants," *Zanesville* [Ohio] *Signal*, September 30, 1930; "Darrow Hits Chicago War on Enemies," *Evening Tribune* (Albert Lea, Minnesota), September 30, 1930; John Hutchinson, *The Imperfect Union: A History of Corruption in American Trade Unions* (New York: E. P. Dutton, 1972), 203; and David Witwer, *Shadow of the Racketeer: Scandal in Organized Labor* (Urbana: University of Illinois Press, 2009), 48–50.

31. "Chicago Gangdom Raising $100,000 to Defend Alleged Lingle Slayer; Seek to Retain Darrow," *New York Times*, January 10, 1931.

32. "Darrow Is Lecturing at Howard Law School," *Pittsburgh Courier*, January 10, 1931; and "Clarence Darrow at Howard U.," *Chicago Defender*, January 17, 1931.

33. Clarence Darrow, "Scottsboro," *Crisis* (March 1932): 81; and Dan T. Carter, *Scottsboro: A Tragedy of the American South* (Baton Rouge: Louisiana State University Press, 1969), 51–103.

34. Stannard, *Honor Killing*, 298.

35. Theon Wright, *Rape in Paradise* (New York: Hawthorn Books, 1966), 46–47.

36. "The Incipient Race War in the Hawaiian Islands," *China Weekly Review* 59 (January 23, 1932): 232; "Hoover and Honolulu," *New Statesman and Nation* 3 (January 23, 1932): 84–85; and "Honolulu Uproar," *Literary Digest* 112 (January 30, 1932): 10.

37. Stannard, *Honor Killing*, 304.

38. Letter, Clarence Darrow to Lincoln Steffens, April 8, 1932, Lincoln Steffens Collection, Series II, Box 1, Columbia University Rare Book and Manuscript Library.

39. Clarence Darrow, "The Massie Trial," *Scribner's Magazine* 92 (October 1932): 213–18.

40. Letter, George S. Leisure to Elmer Gertz, April 29, 1957, Elmer Gertz Papers, Box 38, Northwestern University Archives.

41. "Darrow's Health Poor," *New York Times*, April 4, 1932.

42. "Massie Trial Opens Today," *Honolulu Advertiser*, April 4, 1932.

43. Russell Owen, "Delay Is Unlikely in Honolulu Trial," *New York Times*, April 2, 1932; and "Darrow's Health Poor," *New York Times*, April 4, 1932.

44. Peter Van Slingerland, *Something Terrible Has Happened* (New York: Harper & Row, 1966), 233.

45. Letter, George S. Leisure to Elmer Gertz, June 13, 1957, Elmer Gertz Papers, Box 38, Northwestern University Special Collections.

46. Stannard, *Honor Killing*, 342.

47. "Direct Examination of Defense Expert Dr. J. Orbison, Los Angeles Psychiatrist," *The Essential Words and Writings of Clarence Darrow*, ed. Edward J. Larson and Jack Marshall (New York: Modern Library, 2007), 258; and Wright, *Rape in Paradise*, 238. See also Russell Owen, "Massie Takes Blame in Hawaiian Murder: Can't Recall Firing," *New York Times*, April 17, 1932.

48. Russell Owen, "Mrs. Massie in Court Tears Up Evidence of a Domestic Rift," *New York Times*, April 21, 1932.

49. Stannard, *Honor Killing*, 363.

50. "The 'Unwritten Law': The Massie Case, Honolulu 1932," *Attorney for the Damned*, ed. Arthur Weinberg (New York: Simon & Schuster, 1957), 107.

51. Ibid., 110.

52. Ibid., 114.

53. Ibid., 117.

54. Russell Owen, "Massie Jury Is Out; Darrow Asks for Mercy in a 4½ Hour Plea," *New York Times*, April 28, 1932.

55. Russell Owen, "Disagreement Predicted: Prosecutor Rejects Plea for 11-to-1 or 10-to-2 Acquittal Verdict," *New York Times*, April 29, 1932.

56. Russell Owen, "Maximum Term 10 Years," *New York Times*, April 30, 1932.

57. Van Slingerland, *Something Terrible Has Happened*, 281.

58. Owen, "Maximum Term 10 Years."

59. Ibid.

60. Ernest F. Brown, "The Massie Trial," *Current History* 36 (June 1932): 334.

61. "Darrow 'Under Fire' for Activity in Hawaii Case," *Pittsburgh Courier*, April 30, 1932; "Honolulu Murderers Get Off with 1-Hour Sentence," *Philadelphia Tribune*, May 5, 1932; "Berger Flays U.S. Action in Hawaii," *Baltimore Afro-American*, May 14, 1932; "Clarence Darrow Crosses," *Atlanta Daily World*, May 20, 1932 (quote); and "What Do You Say About It?: Do You Think Clarence Darrow Injured His Prestige with Members of Our Race by Defending the Massies in Honolulu?," *Chicago Defender*, May 21, 1932.

62. "Hits Darrow," *Atlanta Daily World*, June 8, 1932; and "Darrow Not So Hot, Thinks This Catholic Editor," *New Journal and Guide*, July 4, 1932.

63. Clarence Darrow, "Conditions in the Hawaiian Islands, Speech Before the Chicago Bar Association, 4 June 1932," Clarence S. Darrow Papers, Box 10, Library of Congress.

64. "4 in Massie Case Reach California," *New York Times*, May 14, 1932; "Darrow Envisages a 'Doomed' World," *New York Times*, January 18, 1934.

65. "Civilization Lost, Darrow Declares," *New York Times*, January 20, 1934.

66. See letter, Franklin D. Roosevelt to Clarence Darrow, February 23, 1931, http://darrow.law.umn.edu/letters.php?pid=376&skey=1931, accessed July 9, 2010.

67. "Darrow Lauds Roosevelt," *New York Times*, May 8, 1932.

68. "NRA Plans Board to Aid 'Little Man,'" *New York Times*, January 25, 1934; "Little Man Board Distinct from NRA," *New York Times*, January 26, 1934; "Board to Review Code Complaints," *New York Times*, February 20, 1934; and "NRA Calls Critics to Sessions Today," *New York Times*, February 27, 1934; "Text of Gen. Hugh S. Johnson's Address at Opening of NRA Meeting in Capital" and "Review Board Ready to Act on Monopoly," *New York Times*, February 28, 1934.

69. Draft of Executive Order 6632, Office File 466-E: National Recovery Review Board, Box 22, folder January–May 1934, Franklin D. Roosevelt Library.

70. Hugh S. Johnson, *The Blue Eagle from Egg to Earth* (New York: Doubleday & Co., 1935), 271.

71. Julian Street Diary, July 11, 1934, Julian Street Papers, Box 21, Princeton University Archives. See also "Mr. Darrow's Views," *New York Times*, April 26, 1930.

72. Letter, Clarence Darrow to James M. Beck, June 11, 1930, James M. Beck Papers, Box 2, Princeton University Archives, Department of Rare Books and Special Collections.

73. Clarence Darrow, "Personal Liberty," in *Freedom in the Modern World*, ed. Horace M. Kallen (New York: Coward-McCann, 1928), 131.

74. Letter, Edgar Lee Masters to Raymond Moley, May 21, 1934, Office File 466-E, National Recovery Review Board, folder June–December 1934, Box 23, Franklin D. Roosevelt Presidential Library.

75. National Recovery Review Board, *First Report to the President of the United States* (typescript final draft), 6, 10, 14, Office File 466-E, Franklin D. Roosevelt Presidential Library.

76. See "The National Recovery Review Board Is Created to Investigate Monopolistic Codes, Executive Order No. 6632, March 7, 1934," *The Public Papers and Addresses of Franklin D. Roosevelt with a Special Introduction and Explanatory Notes by President Roosevelt*, comp. Samuel I. Rosenman (New York: Random House, 1938), 137–38.

77. National Recovery Review Board, *Special and Supplementary Report to the President by Clarence Darrow, Chairman, and William O. Thompson, Member* (typescript final draft), Office File 466-E, folder January–May 1934, Box 22, Franklin D. Roosevelt Presidential Library.

78. "NRA Review Board Splits in 2 Groups," *New York Times*, May 3, 1934; and "In Washington: Belief Is Growing Makeup of Darrow Board Was Blunder," *New York Times*, May 16, 1934.

79. National Recovery Administration, *Reports of the Administrator and General Counsel of the National Recovery Administration in Reply to the Report of National Recovery Review Board* (typescript final draft), 1–2, 3–4, 18, Office File 466-E, Franklin D. Roosevelt Presidential Library.

80. "House to Inquire into 'Brain Trust,'" *New York Times*, March 30, 1934; "Inquiry into NRA Sought in House," *New York Times*, May 23, 1934; "12 in 'Brain Trust' Called Socialists," *New York Times*, May 28, 1934.

81. "In Washington: Belief Is Growing Makeup of Darrow Board Was Blunder," *New York Times*, May 16, 1934; "Darrow Stirs Up New Controversy," *New York Times*, May 27, 1934; "Darrow Rocket": 9 and "Let Us Take Stock," *Business Week* (May 26, 1934): 40; and Paul Y. Anderson, "The Darrow Report," *Nation* (May 30, 1934): 611. See also Paul Y. Anderson, "Courts Are Only Cockpits for Lawyers to Fight In," *St. Louis Post-Dispatch*, May 10, 1925, and "Clarence Darrow, Humanitarian," *St. Louis Post-Dispatch*, July 3, 1928.

82. "Gen. Johnson and Darrow Confer as They Motor," *New York Times*, May 24, 1934; "Darrow to End Work of Board This Week," *New York Times*, May 27, 1934; and Lowell B. Mason, "Darrow v. Johnson," *North American Review* 237 (December 1934): 531.

83. Mason, "Darrow v. Johnson," 526.

84. See "NRA Review Board Splits in 2 Groups," *New York Times*, May 3, 1934; "J. F. Sinclair Quits the Darrow Board," *New York Times*, May 8, 1934; "Thompson Quits the Darrow Board," *New York Times*, June 14, 1934; and William O. Thompson, Mary van Kleeck, and Earl Browder, *NRA from Within: International Pamphlets*, No. 41 (New York: Labor Research Association).

85. "Report on NRA Expected to Be Darrow's Last Job," *New York Times*, May 21, 1934.

86. "Will Protest on Borghi," *New York Times*, February 28, 1928; "Fascist 'Frame-Up' Doubted by Darrow," *New York Times*, February 20, 1928; and "Detective Kills One as Anti-Fascist Mob Beats Him at Rally," *New York Times*, April 7, 1930.

87. Clarence Darrow, "What I Think of Nazi Germany," typescript speech, n.d., Clarence S. Darrow Papers, Box 10, Library of Congress.

88. "Chicago Protective League," *New York Times*, March 25, 1901; "Chicago Plea for Frank," *New York Times*, May 4, 1915; "Petitions for Frank Signed by 15,000," *New York Times*, May 12, 1915; "The Case Against Anti-Semitism: Clarence Darrow, World-Famous Criminal Lawyer, on the Jewish Question," *Jewish Times*, April 24, 1931; "Palestine's Merits and Limits Debated," *New York Times*, April 15, 1931; poster announcing debate between Clarence S. Darrow and Rabbi Eugene Mannheimer, 1928, Eugene Mannheimer Papers, Box 10, American Jewish Archives; and *Is Zionism a Progressive Policy for Israel and America?: Affirmative Dr. Stephen S. Wise, Negative Clarence Darrow, 24 October 1927*, SC-13378, American Jewish Archives.

89. Letter, Clarence Darrow to Rabbi Joseph Jasin, February 23, 1923, SC-5681, American Jewish Archives.

90. "Exile Asks World to End Nazi Terror," *New York Times*, July 3, 1934.

91. "Plea for Red Made by Darrow Board," *New York Times*, July 4, 1934.

92. "Exile Asks World to End Nazi Terror," *New York Times*, July 3, 1934.

93. "Darrow Is Undecided About Trip," *New York Times*, March 10, 1935; "Labor Benefits, Says Hillman," *New York Times*, March 21, 1935.

94. "Darrow Aids Friend's Son," *New York Times*, October 21, 1934; "State's Case Weak, Darrow Says," *New York Times*, November 13, 1934; "Darrow Urges Delay," *New York Times*, April 2, 1934; "Darrow Is Re-Elected," *New York Times*, January 12, 1936; "Back Marcantonio Race," *New York Times*, September 29, 1936; and "Anti-Lynching Law to Be Sought Again," *New York Times*, January 5, 1937.

95. "Law Is 'Horrible' Says Darrow, 79," *New York Times*, April 19, 1936.

96. "Clarence Darrow on 80th Birthday," *New York Times*, April 24, 1937.

97. Letter, Clarence Darrow to Victor Hackler, April 14, 1937, Elmer Gertz Papers, Box 39, Northwestern University Special Collections. See also letter, Clarence Darrow to Robert R. Gros, November 4, 1933, Robert Gros Papers, Box 1, Stanford University Special Collections.

98. Letter, Henry L. Mencken to Ruby Darrow, May 17, 1937, Microfilmed Papers of H. L. Mencken, Reel 12, Manuscripts and Archives Division, New York Public Library, Astor, Lenox and Tilden Foundations.

99. Letter, George Whitehead to H. L. Mencken, March 17, 1938, Microfilmed Papers of H. L. Mencken, Reel 12, Manuscripts and Archives Division, New York Public Library, Astor, Lenox, and Tilden Foundations.

100. "Clarence Darrow Is Dead in Chicago," *New York Times*, March 14, 1938; and letter, Ruby Darrow to Hadrian H. Baker, August 2, 1940, in "Take Him for All in All" (typescript draft with documents) by Abram E. Adelman, Microfilmed Papers of Elmer Gertz, Reel 1, Northwestern University Special Collections.

101. See "Clarence Darrow, Friend of Race, Dies," *Chicago Defender*, March 19, 1938; "Clarence Darrow Was a Friend, Says Harlem," *New York Amsterdam News*, March 19, 1938; and "Darrow Denied Religion, Yet Lived It Best," *Baltimore Afro-American*, March 19, 1938. See also Resolution, Cleveland NAACP, ca. March 13, 1938, Clarence S. Darrow Papers, Box 2, University of Chicago Special Collections.

102. "Hundreds Honor Darrow," *New York Times*, March 15, 1938.

103. Eulogy of Judge William H. Holly, Clarence S. Darrow Papers, Box 2, University of Chicago Special Collections.

104. "Clarence Darrow's Ashes," *Unity* (March 16, 1938): 82; and "Darrow's Ashes Strewn," *New York Times*, March 20, 1938.

105. Letter, Ruby H. Darrow to Charles Mantinband, SC-7729, American Jewish Archives.

106. Letter, Ruby Darrow to Julian Street, July 29, 1942, Microfilmed Papers of Julian Street, Princeton University Archives Department of Rare Books and Special Collections.

107. Letter, Charles W. Olsen to Elmer Gertz, April 4, 1957, Microfilmed Papers of Elmer Gertz, Reel 1, Northwestern University Special Collections.

108. Letter, Hadrian H. Baker to Ruby Darrow, July 31, 1940, in "Take Him for All in All" (typescript draft with documents) by Abram E. Adelman, Microfilmed Papers of Elmer Gertz, Reel 1, Northwestern University Special Collections. Emphasis in original.

109. Letter, Ruby Darrow to Hadrian H. Baker, August 2, 1940, in "Take Him for All in All" (typescript draft with documents) by Abram E. Adelman, Microfilmed Papers of Elmer Gertz, reel 1, Northwestern University Special Collections; and "Darrow's Spirit Fails to Keep Sixth Date," *Baltimore Sun*, March 14, 1944.

110. Irving Stone, *Clarence Darrow for the Defense* (Garden City: Doubleday, Doran & Co., 1941), 518.

111. Letter, Will Durant to Arthur and Lila Weinberg, December 21, 1962, SC-12825, American Jewish Archives.

112. John W. Gunn, "A Day with Clarence Darrow," *Haldeman-Julius Monthly* 2 (July 1925): 175–81; Clarence Darrow, "Why I Have Found Life Worth Living," *Christian Century* (April 19, 1928): 504–5; and letter, Clarence Darrow to Max Otto, February 6, 1935, Max Otto Papers, Box 3, Wisconsin Historical Society.

Bibliographic Essay

My emphasis on Darrow's political career and politics differentiates my biography from others. That said, there are a number of fine accounts of his life. I recommend starting with Darrow's own writings, especially *Farmington* (New York: Charles Scribner's Sons, 1904) and *The Story of My Life* (New York: Charles Scribner's Sons, 1932; reprint, New York: Da Capo Press, 1996). To date, there are four other major in-depth biographies: Charles Yale Harrison's *Clarence Darrow* (New York: Jonathan Cape & Harrison Smith, 1931) is the oldest, thus carries the story only through the 1920s; Irving Stone's beautifully written *Clarence Darrow for the Defense* (Garden City, N.Y.: Doubleday, Doran & Co., 1941) is a great read but not always factually accurate; Kevin Tierney's *Darrow: A Biography* (New York: Thomas Y. Crowell, 1979) is the most comprehensive; and Arthur and Lila Weinberg's *Clarence Darrow: A Sentimental Rebel* (New York: G. P. Putnam's Sons, 1980) is the highly readable and perceptive product of decades of careful research and thought. For those inclined to search the Internet first, go the Clarence Darrow Collection at the University of Minnesota's Law Library (http://darrow.law.umn.edu/index.php). You won't be disappointed! It has an amazing collection of letters, discovered by Randall Tietjen, a Minneapolis lawyer and Darrow historian.

For those who want to read more, I suggest digging into two piles of books. First, there are a number of fine anthologies of Darrow's writings: Arthur Weinberg's *Attorney for the Damned* (New York: Simon & Schuster, 1957); Arthur and Lila Weinberg's *Verdicts Out of Court* (Chicago: Quadrangle Books, 1963); S. T. Joshi's *Clarence Darrow on Religion, Law, and Society* (Athens: Ohio University Press, 2005); and Edward J. Larson and Jack Marshall's *The Essential Words and Writings of Clarence Darrow* (New York: Modern Library, 2007). Second, there are a growing number of books that focus on specific Darrow cases. My favorites are: Geoffrey Cowan, *The People v. Clarence Darrow: The Bribery Trial of America's Greatest Lawyer* (New York: Times Books, 1993); J. Anthony Lukas, *Big Trouble: A Murder in a Small Western Town Sets Off a Struggle for the Soul of America* (New York: Simon & Schuster, 1997); Edward J. Larson, *Summer for the Gods: The Scopes Trial and America's Continuing Debate over Science and Religion* (New York: Basic Books, 1997); Kevin Boyle, *Arc of Justice: A Saga of Race, Civil Rights, and Murder in the Jazz Age* (New York: Henry Holt, 2004); Phyllis Vine, *One Man's Castle: Clarence Darrow in Defense of the American Dream* (New York: Amistad, 2004); David E. Stannard, *Honor Killing: Race, Rape, and Clarence Darrow's Spectacular Last Case* (New York: Viking Penguin, 2005); Simon Baatz, *For the Thrill of It: Leopold, Loeb, and the Murder That Shocked Chicago* (New York: Harper, 2008); Howard Blum, *American Lightning: Terror, Mystery, Movie-Making, and the Crime of the Century* (New York: Crown Publishers, 2008); and Donald McRae, *The Last Trials of Clarence Darrow* (New York: William Morrow, 2009).

Archival collections that contain materials relating to Clarence Darrow are scattered across the country. In addition to the online Clarence Darrow Collection, major collections are located at the Library of Congress, the Newberry Library, the Northwestern University Library Archives, and the University of Chicago Library Archives.

Acknowledgments

I should like to thank the authors that I have listed in my bibliographic essay, most of whom I do not know personally, for their fine, inspiring books. I also need to acknowledge a debt to Willard D. Hunsberger, whose amazing *Clarence Darrow: A Bibliography* (Metuchen, N.J.: Scarecrow Press, 1981) was an indispensable resource. Many friends and colleagues offered encouragement, assistance, and support during the writing of this book. Specifically, I need to express my sincere gratitude to my editor, Thomas Lebien, who has been so kind to me and who has worked so diligently and patiently to make this biography readable, engaging, and argumentative. Everyone should be so fortunate as to have an editor like Thomas. I'd like to thank a few others at Farrar, Straus and Giroux, particularly Daniel Crissman, Jeff Seroy, Meredith Kessler, and Susan Mitchell. Additionally, I'd like to thank my departmental colleagues, especially Andrew Austin, Tim Dale, Harvey Kaye, Craig Lockard, and Kim Nielsen. Others at the University of Wisconsin–Green Bay, especially Dean Scott Furlong, Associate Provost Tim Sewall, Pam Schoen, and Chris Terrien, helped me with grants, my sabbatical, and various essential tasks. Gary Anderson, Eric Arnesen, Tim Dale, Clete Daniel, Roger Daniels, Dave Edmunds, James Green, Marcel La Follette, Gene and Dottie Lewis, Kriste Lindenmeyer, Nina Mjagkij, Jerry Podair, Mick and Irene Schubert, Ed Wehrle, David Witwer, and James Wolfinger provided lots of encouragement, support, and advice. David M. Prouty of UNITE HERE graciously allowed me access to the papers of the Amalgamated Clothing and Textile Workers Union. I owe a debt of gratitude to those who read parts of or the entire manuscript in draft form: Gary Anderson, Tim Dale, Fred Kersten, Nina Mjagkij, Kim Nielsen, Jeff Pickron, Jerry Podair, and James Wolfinger. I owe a special thanks to my spouse, Vickie Kersten, who is my first reader and read chapters before I had a chance to cut them down. Her unflagging enthusiasm for and assistance with this project carried me along when I tired. She got me monologuing about Darrow on our daily walks. Carefully and kindly, she managed to help me move along so that when we arrived home, I could outline the next parts. One could not ask for a better friend!

Ruby Darrow, Clarence's second wife, once said that "biographers are greedy as octopi for things that can be set within quotation marks."* All too true, but I have had some help. I have a long list of people who work in libraries and archives to thank: Cheryl Schnirring, Abraham Lincoln Presidential Library; Jennifer Cole and Camille Servizzi, American Jewish Archives; Lee Anne Kolker, Bancroft Library; William K. Wallach, Karen Jania, and Jennifer Harrold, Bentley Historical Library; Shannon Wilson, Berea College; Debbie Vaughan, Chicago Historical Museum; Anna H. Graves, Colby College; Joan R. McKenzie, College of Physicians Library; Tara C. Craig, Columbia University; Patrizia Sione, Cornell University; Kathy Shoemaker, Emory University; Matthew Hanson, Franklin D. Roosevelt Presidential Library; David Vancil, Indiana State University–Terre Haute; Phyllis Lyons, Idaho State Historical Society; Aaron T. Kornblum, Judah L. Magnes Museum; Jeffrey M. Flannery, Library of Congress; Diana La Femina, Lilly Library; Elaine Grubin, Massachusetts Historical Society Library; Steve Nielsen, Minnesota Historical Society; Mitchell A. Yockelson, National Archives and Records Administration; Maurice Klapwald and Laura Ruttum, New York Public Library; Helen Long, Newberry Library; Jane Davey, Northwest Museum of Arts and Culture; Nick Munagian, Northwestern University; AnnaLee Pauls, Amanda K. Hawk, and Ben Primer, Princeton University; Ellen M. Shea, Schlesinger Library; Randy Bixley, Southern Illinois University–Carbondale; Mary Elizabeth Hinton and Diane L. Cooter, Syracuse University; Donna Christian, Toledo–Lucas County Public Library; Mauricio Hermosillo and Aislinn Catherine Sotelo, UCLA; David Pavelich and Christine Colburn, University of Chicago; Julie R. Monroe, University of Idaho; Linda Stahnke, University of Illinois at Urbana–Champaign; David F. McCartney, University of Iowa; Katherine Hedin, University of Minnesota; Elizabeth Engel, Alla Barabtarlo, and Peter R. McCarthy, University of Missouri–Columbia; Alexandra Shadid, University of Oklahoma; Bruce Tabb and Erin Wolfe, University of Oregon; Rey A. Antonio, University of Virginia; Jeff Brunner, Joan Robb, and Emily Rogers, University of Wisconsin–Green Bay; Debra Anderson and Jean Wentz, University of Wisconsin–Green Bay Area Research Center; Josh Ranger, University of Wisconsin–Oshkosh Area Research Center; and Susan L. Gordon, Tennessee State Library and Archives. My apologies to anyone I've overlooked.

Finally, I'd like to acknowledge of the role of three people in the publication of this book. I owe a great deal to the three women with whom I live. Vickie, Bethany, and Emily have propped me up when I needed help. They have put up with my typical moodiness before I have written a new chapter. And they have worked diligently to make me see the lighter and brighter sides of life by taking me to Disney on Ice, movies, and malls (when I should have been writing) and by seducing me into one more hour on the game system,

*Letter, Ruby Darrow to Ruth Gage Thompson, n.d., Elmer Gertz Papers, Box 39, Northwestern University Archives.

kindly letting me assume my favorite role as Lego Batman (when I should have been writing). They happily endured the "Summer of Darrow," when we drove to Washington, D.C., so that I could work at the Library of Congress, circuitously stopping in Kinsman, Ohio, on the way back to see the Darrow house. In terms of family, I have what Clarence Darrow always longed for, and I know it and appreciate it. And yes, Emily and Bethany, my book about Darence Clarrow is finally done!

Index